AF807786

PHILIP SIMON MILLER BUTCHER, BANKER, AND BENEFACTOR

HIS LIFE AND LEGACY IN DOUGLAS COUNTY, COLORADO

In memory of Mr + Mrs Miller and their generosity to Douglas County and Castle Rock.

BY: DEBBIE BUBOLTZ-BODLE

Debbie Buboltz

Philip Simon Miller
Butcher, Banker, and Benefactor

His Life and Legacy In Douglas County, Colorado

Copyright © 1998 Debbie Buboltz-Bodle

Front cover photo by Robert Oliver

All rights reserved. This book may not be duplicated in any way without the expressed written consent of the publisher, except in the form of brief excerpts or quotations for the purposes of review. The information contained herein may not be duplicated in other books, databases or any other medium without the written consent of the author. Making copies of this book, or any portion for any purpose other than your own, is a violation of United States copyright laws.

Library of Congress Cataloging-in-Publication Data

Buboltz-Bodle, Debbie, 1950-

Phillip Simon Miller: butcher, banker, and benefactor; his life and legacy in Douglas County, Colorado / Debbie Buboltz-Bodle.
p. cm.
Includes bibliographical references and index
ISBN 0-929526-84-8
1. Miller, Phillip Simon, 1895-1995. 2. Bankers—Colorado—Biography. 3. Philanthropists—Colorado—Biography. 4. Douglas County (Colo.)—History. I. Title.
HG2463.M55B83 1998
332. 1'092—dc21
[B] 98-46446
CIP

Production Services By:

Phoenix Publishing Group
4123 N. Longview
Phoenix, AZ 85014
Phone: 602-274-7236
Fax: 602-996-6928

Book Design By:

Running Changes
1307 E. Oregon Avenue
Phoenix, AZ 85014
Phone: 602-285-1834

KAESTLER FAMILY TREE

- **Adam Kaestler (September 15, 1835 - January 26, 1890)**
  & Lina Green (October 16, 1851 - March 5, 1924)
  - **Lena Kaestler (October 21, 1868 - November 12, 1908)**
    & Philip Simon Miller (December 10, 1867 - September 17, 1940)
    m. April 20, 1892
    - **Adam Philip Miller (May 6, 1893 - March 7, 1983)**
      & Dorothy L. Dickson (1905 - May 1, 1984)
      m. June 30, 1931
    - **Philip Simon Miller Jr. (October 11, 1895 - June 7, 1995)**
      & Jessie Ethel Stewart (September 27, 1900 - November 2, 1987)
      m. November 3, 1919
  - **Minnie Kaestler (April 12, 1870 - January 2, 1895)**
  - **Adam Kaestler Jr. (March 6, 1871 - May 6, 1897)**
    & Katherine Mueller (1875 - 1963)
    - **Lena Kaestler (February 13, 1894 - September 13, 1894)**
    - **Gerd Adam Kaestler (April 13, 1895 - December 28, 1953)**
      & Lena M. Lindig (September 26, 1905 - August 15, 1995)
      m. July 5, 1924
      - **Norma Jean Kaestler (July 19, 1925 -)**
        & Beryle Lawrence Gish (May 23, 1923 -)
        m. August 9, 1944
        - **Beryle Lawrence Gish Jr. (July 9, 1945 -)**
          & Cheryl Callahan (August 20, 1947 -)
          m. November 23, 1968
          - **Kendra Gish (December 15, 1969 -)**
        - **Marilyn Gish (October 1, 1948 -)**
          & Joseph Smogorzewski (December 31, 1946 - February 27, 1980)
          m. June 20, 1970
          - **Heather Smogorzewski (September 22, 1979 -)**
      - **Gerd Adam Kaestler Jr. (February 26, 1932 -)**
        & Elizabeth Spitzer (July 5, 1934 -)
        m. February 23, 1957
        - **Larry Michael Kaestler (November 22, 1957 -)**
        - **Donald Lee Kaestler (March 11, 1964 -)**
  - **William (Willie) Kaestler (January 2, 1873 - July 22, 1880)**
  - **Emil Kaestler (August 22, 1879 - August 16, 1880)**
  - **Frank W. Kaestler (September 18, 1881 - August 16, 1948)**
  - **Mary Kaestler (June 1, 1886 - May 10, 1887)**

STEWART AND BENEDICT FAMILY TREE

- **Alexander Stewart (1856 - March 1924)**
  & Lucinda Irene Cummins (February 8, 1860 - March 20, 1948)
  m. 1876
  - **Jessie Ethel Stewart (September 27, 1900 - November 2, 1987)**
    & Philip Simon Miller Jr. (October 11, 1895 - June 7, 1995)
    m. November 3, 1919
  - **Bernice Catherine Stewart (January 18, 1903 - January 27, 1994)**
    & Charles Edwin Benedict (August 16, 1893 - October 5, 1983)
    m. October 7, 1921
    - **James S. Benedict (August 10, 1924 - May 10, 1979)**
      & Shari Ann Nicholls (May 8, 1929 -)
      m. January 11, 1950
      - **James E. Benedict (January 10, 1951 -)**
      - **Charles A. Benedict (December 5, 1953 -)**
        & Claudia Haack (December 8, 1960 -)
        m. September 5, 1987
        - **Connor Benedict (February 25, 1994 -)**
        - **Kendra Benedict (October 25, 1996 -)**
      - **Diane Benedict (July 28, 1955 -)**
        & Richard Gene Fling (October 4, 1955 -)
        m. December 29, 1973
        - **Eric Richard Fling (January 4, 1975 -)**
        - **Steven Scott Fling (July 21, 1977 -)**
      - **Melissa L. Benedict (November 9, 1966 -)**
    - **Shirley Benedict (July 18, 1927 - July 12, 1961)**

MILLER FAMILY TREE

- **John George Miller**
  & Augusta ILch Miller
  - **Philip Simon Miller (December 10, 1867 - September 17, 1940)**
    & Lena Kaestler (October 21, 1868 - November 12, 1908)
    m. April 20, 1892
    - **Adam Philip Miller (May 6, 1893 - March 7, 1983)**
      & Dorothy L. Dickson (1905 - May 1, 1984)
      m. June 30, 1931
    - **Philip Simon Miller Jr. (October 11, 1895 - June 7, 1995)**
      & Jessie Ethel Stewart (September 27, 1900 - November 2, 1987)
      m. November 3, 1919

Family Tree concept and design by
Jimmy Olsen and John Bodle

Kaestler Family

Kaestler Children, 1871, Peoria, Illinois.
left to right: Minnie, Adam, Jr., Lena

Norma Gish and Gerd Adam Kaestler, Jr. Collection.

Lena Kaestler, Mr. Miller's mother, as a teenager at her Lutheran Confirmation or First Communion, Peoria, Illinois.

Norma Gish and Gerd Adam Kaestler, Jr. Collection.

Kaestler Family, 1873, Peoria, Illinois.
left to right: Minnie, Mother Lina, Willie (on lap), Father Adam, Sr., Adam, Jr. (on lap), and Lena.

Norma Gish and Gerd Adam Kaestler, Jr. Collection.

Table Of Contents

PREFACE

This book is the outgrowth of a five-page research paper which I wrote in 1967 as an assignment at Douglas County High School in Castle Rock, Colorado, for Mr. James McKay in an American History class. I entitled it "The History of Banking In Castle Rock." It was really easy because "The Bank of Douglas County," was the only one there at the time!

I interviewed my father, Mr. Willis Buboltz, who was on the Board of Directors and had worked there since 1952. I interviewed Mr. Philip Miller, the President, who had founded the bank in 1939. I interviewed Mr. Josef Winkler, who was one of the original stockholders and Directors of the bank. Finally I talked to Mr. Charles "Bickey" Briscoe, who happened to be a bus driver at our school but used to be in the banking business in Castle Rock in the early years.

I learned that there had been two other banks in Castle Rock, prior to the 1939 opening of The Bank of Douglas County. There had been The First National Bank of Douglas County at Castle Rock from 1903 until 1933. Then there had been The Castle Rock State Bank which opened in 1917 during World War I and closed in 1932. I wrote a small history of each of these banks and explained why they had gone out of business.

Mr. Miller had two very old scrapbooks that one of the early stockholders, Mr. E. G. Breslow, had compiled. These scrapbooks dated from 1917 until 1954. There were fascinating old advertisements and articles from The First National, The Castle Rock State Bank and The Bank of Douglas County including years worth of Statements of Condition, which I really didn't understand. Remember, I was only sixteen!

After my dad explained Statements of Condition, I documented how The Bank of Douglas County had grown in its nearly thirty years in existence and how it continued to grow each year and show a profit. I was very proud of my research paper and I expected to receive a grade of "A."

You can imagine my devastation when Mr. McKay handed it back to me a few days later with a grade of "B minus." He had written on the paper, "This is an excellent report but it needs many more footnotes." After class I argued with him as to how I could have had more footnotes when the foundation of the paper revolved around interviews and scrapbooks! It was months before I ever told anyone my grade! I put the paper in my metal file box, finally got over my devastation and eventually forgot all about it.

In the summer of 1991, I was visiting Mr. Miller in Cherry Creek Care Center in Aurora, Colorado and he was remembering the early days of the bank. He was literally dazzling me with recollections such as the name of the first man who ever deposited money the day the bank opened, as well as the names of stockholders from 1939! But the most amazing thing was that he remembered my research paper, "The History of Banking In Castle Rock!" His memory was better than mine! I hadn't thought about that paper in years! I commented to my dad and Mr. Miller that I ought to update it. They both agreed and this book was born that day! The only problem was I had to finish my Senior year in college and wouldn't be able to start working on the book for another year.

In the meantime, I returned to Phoenix and found the paper in my metal file box right where I had put it twenty-four years ago. The note cards I had written from the interviews were still there, too. My dad miraculously located the two scrapbooks and Mr. Miller gave him permission to mail them to me. That last year of college was the longest year of my life because I just wanted to start working on this book! In the summer of 1992, I graduated and was finally free to begin this project.

I had no idea when I started it, where it would end up. Although I had known Mr. and Mrs. Miller from the time I was a small child, I don't remember the first time I met them. As with grandparents who were always there as a part of our lives, we don't remember the exact moment of introduction. We just know that we have known them, forever. So it was with Mr. and Mrs. Miller. I had known them forever, it seemed. However, I soon discovered that I knew very little about them. In short, I had no idea what this project would entail.

I could have never guessed that the research would take me clear back to the mid-1800's in Germany, then to the late 1800's in Peoria, Illinois, then to the early 1900's in Denver, Colorado and Elizabeth, Colorado and finally to the early 1920's in Castle Rock. I was completely unaware of Mr. Miller's philanthropy and his many years of service to the community starting in those early 1920's. I knew about the Library because my mother had been involved in it, and I knew about the Bank because my dad had worked there since I was two years old. But I didn't know Mr. Miller was originally a butcher and owned meat markets. I also didn't know he had a fuel and feed store, which is still in existence today, or an insurance company, which is part of an existing Castle Rock insurance group. I didn't know he had been involved in the first electric and sewer systems in Castle Rock. I didn't even know the extent of his loyalty to the Douglas County Fair. I knew nothing about his family, his life, or his early years before he married Mrs. Miller.

I did fortunately have a tremendous amount of knowledge of Mrs. Miller's early years and their lives together after their marriage. I had learned these things during many beauty shop conversations with Mrs. Miller as I fixed her hair each week in the mid-70's when I owned The Powder Box Beauty Salon in Castle Rock. I also lived through many of these events and knew the facts from personal experience. However, all the other information in this book has come from years of research, hours of interviews, phone calls, letter writing, newspaper articles, census records, school records, cemetery records, bank records, photos, maps, family information from both Mr. and Mrs. Miller's families, historians from Falcon, Castle Rock, Arvada, Denver and Golden, Colorado, friends from Arkansas to California and anyone else who would talk to me! My parents, Willie and Ellen Buboltz, absolutely went above and beyond the call of duty these past six years and I could have never done this project without their help.

As I finish this book it is summer again, only now it is six years later. Mr. Miller is no longer alive. When he passed away in 1995 he left a Perpetual Charitable Trust in excess of $30 million to eight different beneficiaries. The Bank of Douglas County has been sold but is still thriving as FirstBank of Douglas County. This book has taken many twists and turns and finally it developed a life of its own and I just had to let it lead me! I have interviewed old friends and made new friends. I have been reminded of good times and bad. I have relived Castle Rock in the early days and I have loved every minute of it.

People continue to ask me why I decided to write this book. My answer is always the same. Mr. and Mrs. Philip Miller did so much for the people of Castle Rock and Douglas County that I just couldn't let the story go unwritten. I knew years ago about the Trust because Mrs. Miller told me. And I knew that the Legacy they were leaving behind couldn't go unwritten either. Their benevolence and their philanthropy, their love of children and community had to be documented. Although Mr. Miller was a private and humble man, I wrote this book with his blessing.

A friend of mine once said that writing a story is like writing a song. Writing history is like writing a symphony. I have tried to do both in this book. I hope you enjoy the music. I also hope you understand why there are so many footnotes!!! Thanks, Mr. McKay!

June, 1998—Debbie Buboltz-Bodle

DEDICATION

This book is lovingly and respectfully dedicated to the memory of Philip Simon Miller, the Butcher, the Banker, the Benefactor, and to the memory of his wife Jessie Ethel Miller, "Jerry," the woman who epitomized the adage, "Behind every great man, there is a great woman."

INTRODUCTION

IT IS A TYPICAL DAY!

It is a typical day in mid-1970's at The Bank of Douglas County in Castle Rock, Colorado. Philip Miller, the President, is sitting in a high-backed leather chair at his large kidney shaped desk in the first office on the left upon entering the Bank. He is dressed immaculately, as usual, with a dark suit, probably brown, dress shirt probably white and a stylish tie, probably red. His cowboy boots are shined and his cowboy hat is hanging somewhere within arms reach. By now his hair is a distinguished white, still thick with only a small receding hairline. Although he is in his upper seventies, the few wrinkles around his eyes are smile lines and not age lines for it sort of seems that this man has never really grown old!

He looks across the lobby to the teller windows, which aren't windows anymore but rather counters. Sometimes there are three or four people in line at each one, waiting to make deposits or withdrawals, to cash checks or to make payment on a loan. Although he likes to see customers, he doesn't like for them to have to wait in line. He understands human nature. People are impatient in this stress and strain era.

He marvels at the seemingly modern concept of the "Personal Banker," supposedly created by some large bank in some even larger city. Not such a contemporary idea. In the early days, everyone in Castle Rock had a Personal Banker. He saw to that. It was either himself, Willie Buboltz, Bob Oliver or Dona Sherlock. For many years, each employee knew the name of each customer and probably all the children! He always wanted it to be a friendly, hometown bank, not an impersonal, financial institution. Ever since those early days, he has been trying his best to make sure each and every one of the customers at The Bank of Douglas County had a Personal Banker. His office door is always open and a customer can feel free to walk in and talk to him at anytime. He is, in a word, accessible. If an "old time rancher" happens to walk in the bank, he quickly moves from behind his desk and out to the lobby to speak with this person and invite him in to sit for a spell, while they reminisce about the good old days, when Castle Rock was small and the prices of land and cattle were reasonable.

At the drive-up window and the two remote units there might be two or three cars, their drivers waiting patiently to do business. There are a couple of loan officers whose offices are right next to his.

They are interviewing customers and reviewing loan applications. He thinks back to the time when 90% of their loans were agricultural. Although the loan policy is still conservative and they don't loan money for every little trinket, they have been forced by changing times to loan to the baby boomers and yuppies, a younger generation whose needs and wants are much more eclectic and demanding than in the early days when land, cattle, home, family, mom and pop businesses and savings accounts were the most important aspects of life.

Directly across the lobby from him are maybe two or three customer service representatives who open new accounts and help customers with whatever they need, whenever they need it. In the back and out of sight is the operations crew, the people responsible for all the posting and bookkeeping and recording of the day to day transactions in the bank, the Proof Department. He recalls the days when they posted by hand, and then graduated to the era of the posting machine and he realizes the age of computers is here, which he is still resisting, but won't be able to resist for much longer. (Records show that the last day "By Hand" was December 28, 1979 and the Bank went "On Line" January 1, 1980.) Also in the back are people taking care of the mail and the daily correspondences that occur in the "Bank by Mail" system. All totaled, there are probably about twenty five employees, some who have been there fifteen to twenty years or more. But it wasn't always like this. He thinks back to the early days. And he remembers.

At one time there were only three employees, and although they shared the work load, he did many of these duties himself. He would often open the mail and take care of the replies but, ideally, he let his wife, Jerry, do the correspondence because she was a better writer! He would meet with customers and review applications for loans. Some he would approve, others, would later be considered by the Board of Directors. While attending to all these jobs he was doing the executive work of an Officer.

As the day went on, he would accept deposits and loan payments, cash checks, handle withdrawals and open new accounts. At the end of the business day he would count money and balance the drawer. In this capacity he was acting as a Teller. During spare time, or at the end of the day, he would hand write every transaction in an account ledger or journal. In this capacity he was doing the work of the Bookkeeper. Sometimes customers might require the services of an Officer, a Teller and a Bookkeeper in one visit, in which case he would attempt to be all things to all people!

He fondly remembers the old teller cages, which an early employee called "jail bars" and the white tile floors which he was constantly mopping during the winter months in an attempt to keep them dry and clean so customers wouldn't slip and fall. Those tiles have since been replaced with the more safety conscious wall to wall carpet. Memories of long ago and far away.

No one even remembers that from the day the Bank opened on August 29, 1939 until March 10, 1951, it was open six days a week. But he remembers! Contrary to popular belief that banks were never open on Saturdays until the modern era of the 70's and 80's, The Bank of Douglas County had been open Monday through Saturday for the first twelve years in business. This was to accommodate the farmers and ranchers whose lifestyle and vocation kept them busy all week but who came to town on Saturdays to do their banking and shopping. In 1972, after the remodeling and expansion of the building, he once again resumed Saturday hours because customers were requesting it, and by then, they had the convenience of the new drive-up facilities.

He sits back in his chair and looks out the window at the familiar sights of Main Street, Castle Rock, USA. Diagonally across the street, he can see the famous stone courthouse, built during 1889-1890, (which will be tragically and irreparably burned, in March of 1978.) Directly across the street he looks at the old Keystone Hotel building which housed his first Miller Meat Market in the early 1920's. A few doors north of that, although the building is gone, replaced by a modern office complex, he recalls where he opened the Castle Rock Fuel and Feed Store in the mid-1920's. He stays like this maybe for ten minutes, lights out, thinking back, introspectively. He remembers the dusty dirt streets and the creaky wooden sidewalks. He remembers the beautiful trees which lined the downtown area of Castle Rock. Suddenly, Attorney Jim Folkestad breaks the silence with a knock on the door. "Why are you sitting here with the lights out in the middle of the day?" he wants to know. Mr. Miller smiles that famous smile and without even thinking he says, "I can see the pretty girls on the street better this way!" Funny thing, we all thought it was to save money!

THE EARLY LIFE OF PHILIP SIMON MILLER, HIS FAMILY AND FRIENDS

"There sure were a lot of
Lenas and Adams in this family!"
Second Cousin, Gerd Adam Kaestler, Jr.

Philip Simon Miller, Jr. was born October 11, 1895 in Peoria, Illinois. A farming community located on the Illinois River in the north central part of the state, Peoria was well on its way to becoming one of the most populated towns in Illinois. Many immigrants had settled there, including a large number of Germans. Family records on both sides of his family show his grandparents were part of this group, having all been born in Germany.[1]

Little is known about his paternal grandparents, John George Miller and Augusta Ilch Miller. Unavailable information includes immigration and citizenship records or any details of their marriage.[2] A close friend, Robert Oliver, remembers Mr. Miller telling him that the family had come from Austria and that their name had originally been Mueller.[3] While birth and death certificates reflect the ancestry as German, it is very likely that certain members of the family came from Austria and at one time their name was Mueller. John and Augusta Miller had definitely come to this country by 1867, because when Philip's father, Philip, Sr. was born on December 10th of that year, they lived in Peoria, Illinois.[4]

The heritage is more definitive on the side of his maternal grandparents, Adam and Lina Green Kaestler. Family records show they, too, were born in Germany with supporting evidence such as photos taken in Germany, a German phonebook and Bible, and certain family documents written in German. As late as 1910, in the will of Philip's grandmother, Lina, specific names are still written with the German spelling and usage: Lina for Lena, Fischer for Fisher, Gerd for George.[5]

Adam Kaestler, Sr. was born September 15, 1835. He was sixteen years older than his wife, Lina Green Kaestler, who was born October 16, 1851.[6] As with the Miller family, it is not known how, or when, Adam, Sr. and Lina came to the United States or the details of their marriage. They, too, settled in Peoria, Illinois where all their children were born and where they lived the remainder of their lives.[7]

Their first child, Lena Kaestler, was born October 21, 1868.[8] The oldest of seven children, she would outlive her father, both her sisters, all but one brother, and still die at a very young age. She would also give birth to two sons, one who would change the course of history in Castle Rock, Douglas County, Colorado. That son was Philip Simon Miller, Jr.

When Lena was born in the mid-1800's, large families were very common and the Kaestler family was no exception. According to the family tree, Lena had two sisters and four brothers: Minnie, born in April of 1870; Adam, Jr., born in March of 1871; Willie, born in January of 1873; Emil, born in August of 1879; Frank, born in September of 1881; and Mary, born in June of 1886.[9] Early pictures of Lena taken around 1872 with her brother, Adam, Jr. and sister, Minnie, show her as a cute little girl with long, curly hair and chubby little cheeks!

A teenaged picture reveals a lovely, diminutive young woman, holding a Bible, presumably at her Lutheran Church Confirmation or First Communion. Her hair is elegantly arranged on top of her head and she is wearing a long, beautiful, intricately decorated dress.

Tragically yet typically, during this time in history, children often died young as was the case in the Kaestler family. In July of 1880, Willie died at the age of seven years old. Less than one month later, Emil died at the age of eleven months. In 1887, Mary also died at the age of eleven months. Only four of the Kaestler children lived to adulthood: Lena, Minnie, Adam, Jr., and Frank. On a snowy day in January of 1890, their father, Adam Kaestler, Sr., died at the age of 55.[10] Lena was twenty-one, Minnie and Adam, Jr. were teenagers, and Frank was just nine. The human mind is boggled when wondering how Mrs. Kaestler, Lena's mother, could withstand the deaths of her husband and three children before she, herself, had even reached the age of forty.

Lena, Minnie and Adam, Jr. were the only ones to marry, while Lena and Adam, Jr. were the only ones to have children. Frank never married and was the only one to live a full lifespan.[11] If all the family members had lived, there would have been a huge extended family. Phil and his older brother, Adam, would have known their Grandfather Kaestler, many aunts and uncles and probably a host of cousins and second cousins. As it was, during their childhood years, they only knew Grandmother Lina, Uncle Frank, and cousin

Gerd Adam, Sr. It wasn't until they were grown men, returning to Peoria in 1948 for Uncle Frank's funeral, that Phil and Adam met their two second cousins, Gerd Adam, Jr. and Norma Gish, the son and daughter of Gerd Adam, Sr.[12]

To further add an air of intrigue to the family tree, Lena's mother, Lina Kaestler, remarried after the death of Adam, Sr. and her new husband's name was Adam Fischer. Lena's brother, Adam, Jr. had a daughter, also named Lena, who died in infancy and a son named Gerd Adam, Sr. Years later, he married Lena Lindig and they had a son named Gerd Adam, Jr. who once wrote to me, "There sure were a lot of Lenas and Adams in this family!"[13]

Lena Kaestler and Philip Simon Miller, Sr. (nicknamed Butch) were married on April 20, 1892 at Trinity Evangelical Lutheran Church in Peoria, Illinois when they were both twenty-four years old. Witnesses at the wedding were Lena's sister and brother, Minnie and Adam, Jr., Anna Garrels, who would soon become an in-law of Minnie's, and a friend, Anna Weber.[14]

Butch Miller was a bit of a scrapper! According to the marriage license, his vocation was that of a saloon keeper![15] During prohibition, he would run bootleg whiskey in Colorado, and, in his elderly years he would operate a pool hall! With a larger than life physique, Phil once described his father as a "wonderful, handsome and husky man, with fists bigger than my two arms."[16] When this big, burly man was placed next to dainty, doll-like Lena they must have made quite a pair!

Soon after their marriage, Butch's vocation apparently changed, because Phil always said, "I was born and raised in a meat market. My father was a butcher and his father before him was a butcher."[17] Indeed, by the time Adam and Phil were born in 1893 and 1895, respectively, both their birth certificates indicated that their father's profession was that of a butcher.[18] Family members have speculated John Miller believed meat cutting was a far more acceptable profession than was saloon keeping and forcibly convinced his newly married son to learn the family butchering business. It was a good career move and provided him a profession for, largely, the rest of his life. In light of what the future would bring, it was probably also a God-send.

It has been further speculated that Lena's father, Adam Kaestler, may have been a butcher as well, because a watch fob with miniature butchering tools has been passed down through the Kaestler side of the family.[19] There is also the possibility that the two men were business acquaintances, maybe even working together at one time in a meat market in Peoria and perhaps it was through them that Lena and Philip, Sr. were introduced.

The years after her marriage were alternately happy and sad for Lena Miller as she experienced three births and three deaths in her immediate family within five years. In May of 1893, while living at 521 Hurlburt Street in Peoria, her first son, Adam Philip, was born, and the joy and wonder of new motherhood filled her life.[20] As the first grandchild and the first nephew, he was very much loved and never lacked attention! Unbeknownst to Lena, this bouncing little boy would grow up to become a foster father, giving his love and attention to twenty bouncing little boys!

In February of 1894, her namesake niece, baby Lena Kaestler, was born to Adam, Jr. and his wife, Katherine, but died within seven months of birth, bringing a clouded sadness to the family. The following year, in 1895, the gray Illinois winter was made even more depressing when Minnie passed away on the 2nd day of January at only twenty-five years of age. Given the special closeness that exists between sisters, this death must have left a huge void in Lena's life. At twenty-six years old, she was the only surviving daughter.[21]

Hopefully, her grief was eased somewhat with the anticipation of two births during the coming year. In April of 1895, a healthy baby boy, Gerd Adam, Sr., was born to Adam, Jr. and his wife Katherine,[22] and, by then, Lena knew that she and Butch were expecting another child. Little Adam, now nearly two years old, would not only have a new cousin, but soon he would have a new sibling, as well. Two deaths, two new lives.

On October 11, 1895, while living at 1013 West Jefferson Street in Peoria, her second son, Philip Simon, Jr., was born and named after his father Philip Simon, Sr.[23] Lena could not have known that she had just given birth to a little boy who would grow up to be a great man. He would someday become widely known for his benevolence and philanthropy, as a kind and gentle man who, through his wealth and generosity, would improve the quality of people's lives and alter the course of history in a small town in Colorado, some 2000 miles to the west. All she knew, on this Illinois autumn day in 1895, was that she and her husband had been blessed with yet another son.

Over the years the question was often asked why Philip, who was the second son, had been named "Jr." after his father instead of Adam, who was the first son. In studying the Kaestler Family Tree it becomes obvious that Adam was named in memory of Lena's father, Adam, Sr., who had died three years earlier and also after her brother, Adam, Jr., to whom she was very close. Adam's middle name of Philip was given after his father. Then when the second son was born he was given the honor of being Philip Simon, Jr.

Two years later, in May of 1897, when Lena was twenty-eight, as if this family hadn't suffered enough tragedy, Adam, Jr. died at the age of twenty-six, leaving his young wife, Katherine, and their two year old son, Gerd Adam, Sr. Katherine would eventually remarry, twice, have three more children, and outlive both husbands. It is interesting to note that Katherine's maiden name had been Mueller, but as far as Gerd Adam, Jr. knew, there was no relation or connection whatsoever to the John Miller family.[24]

The deaths of Minnie and Adam, Jr. must have been painful losses for Lena. With only three years difference in their ages, they had grown up together. It is likely that they shared childhood joys, teenage traumas, the excitement of early adulthood and marriage as well as the wonder of childbirth and parenting. Furthermore, with the deaths of their father, two brothers, a sister and Adam's baby daughter, they had together suffered more losses during their young lives than most brothers and sisters do throughout an entire lifetime. These experiences, undoubtedly, created a very strong bond between the three of them. To watch Minnie and Adam die within the span of two years was probably devastating for Lena, as well as for her mother, who now had only two living children. Sixteen year old Frank was suddenly thrust into the position of being the only surviving son. But, the tragedy did not end there. In the early 1900's, Lena Kaestler Miller was diagnosed with tuberculosis.

In those days tuberculosis was known as consumption, or the great white plague. Unlike today, where there are vaccinations and medicine, there was no actual prevention or cure. It was one of the leading causes of death until the 1940's when anti-tuberculous drugs were developed. The course of the disease was elusive and the prognosis was often grim. The recommended prescription at that point in time was to move to a high, dry, moderate climate, the kind they had "out west."

When one hears the saying, "Go west young man," it conjures up visions of the gold rush in the lawless Rockies, where survival was a feast or famine concept depending on how much or how little gold was discovered. However, by the turn of the century, the wild, wild, west had settled down into a new frontier with Denver as the hub of the region, both financially and industrially. The influx of tuberculosis patients, as well as the relocation of doctors and medical personnel, brought an increase in population while Denver became an important medical center as well. The development of hospitals and clinics has been credited with prolonging the lives of many tuberculosis patients during that time, while ultimately improving the quality of medical care and catapulting the Colorado medical profession into the 20th Century.[25]

Therefore, in 1906 or 1907, Butch Miller, with high the hopes of improving his wife's health and building a good life for his two young sons, moved his little family west, away from the harsh winters and the humidified summers of Illinois to the mile high altitude of Denver, Colorado, where the air was dry and clear and the "sun shone almost every day of the year." There are conflicting dates as to when this move actually took place. Butch's obituary indicates they moved to Colorado in 1906, while Adam's obituary reports 1907. The Denver City Directory, which was published annually during the month of June, registers them, for the first time, in 1907.[26]

The Millers moved into a house at 344 St. Paul Street,[27] in a neighborhood which was known as Harmons Subdivision, a residential area directly northeast of the present-day, trendy Cherry Creek Shopping Center. While Lena concentrated on her health and home, Butch worked as a meat cutter for J. W. Young and the boys were enrolled in a local grammar school.[28] The Denver School Census and Cumulative Chronological Attendance Records for Grammar Schools are not available for students born before 1903.[29] Consequently, there are no records for Phil and Adam, who were born in the 1890's. According to the Beeler's Official Map of the City and County of Denver, the school located closest to where they lived, both on St. Paul Street, and at a future location on Tenth Avenue, was the Corona School at 846 Corona Street and was obviously the school they attended. Built in 1889, it is still in existence today, however, the name was changed on September 2, 1929 to Dora Moore Elementary in honor of the woman who was principal there for thirty-five years, including the years Phil and Adam attended.[30]

In researching this school, I learned that in addition to Mr. Miller, several other people who would become well-known and wealthy were alumni of Corona: Two former Denver Mayors, Quigg Newton and William H. McNichols, Actor, Douglas Fairbanks, Sr. and former First Lady, Mamie Doud Eisenhower, wife of President Dwight Eisenhower.[31] On a more personal note, my grandmother on my mother's side of the family, Mrs. P. K. Yonge, attended the Corona School from first though eighth grade, possibly during a few of the same years Mr. Miller did.

In late 1907 or early 1908, Butch left J. W. Young and opened the Philip S. Miller Meat Market at 2805 Third Avenue. In all probability, he chose this building because it was only a few blocks from their home and allowed him to be nearer to Lena.[32] Thus located, the family prepared to face the uncertain future. It is hard to imagine the heartbreak and panic of a happily married couple with two young boys when confronted with the prospect of an incurable disease. However, Colorado had a healing atmosphere and an overall feeling of peacefulness and quietness, helping many tuberculosis patients regain their health in the clean, clear air.

From the front window of her home, Lena could see the towering Rocky Mountains, crowned with snow all year around, looking down protectively on Denver as the four seasons ebbed and flowed. Hopefully, she experienced all the beauty of Colorado during those final years of her life: from the feel of soft summer rains, to the smell of burning autumn leaves, to the jolt of crisp winter snow, to the sight of colorful spring flowers. It is likely that she cherished every moment spent with her husband and her two sons, for she now lived with the very real possibility that if the tuberculosis progressed, she might die.

Despite good medical care and the moderate Colorado climate, the disease, in fact, did progress and by autumn of 1908, Lena was suffering the final stages of tuberculosis. Her last visit from the doctor was November 10, l908 and two days later, on November 12, Lena Kaestler Miller died, at her home on St. Paul Street, less than one month after her 41st birthday.[33] Adam was fifteen, and Phil had just recently turned thirteen.

According to family information, photographs, and cemetery records, her body was then sent back to Illinois where she was buried four days later on November 16, 1908, in the Kaestler family plot, in the North Hill section of Springdale Cemetery in Peoria. The headstone simply reads “Lena Miller.” Next to baby Lena and directly behind sister Minnie, Lena had finally come home. Her mother, Lina Fischer, now had only one surviving son, twenty-seven year old Frank, and three surviving grandsons, Adam, Philip, Jr., and thirteen year old Gerd, Sr., in the Kaestler family lineage.[34]

The years following Lena’s death were sad and lonely for Butch and the boys. The little family, always closely knit, became even closer as their grief drew them together. They continued to live in Denver at the St. Paul address and, presumably, the boys remained in school but it is not quite clear where Butch worked during the next year. The Denver City Directory shows that he was a butcher but gives no employer or work address.[35]

The year 1910 brought big changes for Butch and his sons. They moved to an apartment at 1035 Tenth Avenue, which was just west of Ogden Street in an area known as the South Division of Capitol Hill. It is likely that they moved to this location because it was only two blocks north of the Corona School where Phil, now fifteen years old, would soon complete eighth grade. Butch opened another Philip S. Miller Meat Market on the west side of downtown Denver at 1119 Champa Street. He would operate this business for approximately the next seven years, until 1917. By now, Adam was seventeen years old and out of school. In those days young people very frequently only attended until the eighth grade and then quit to work and help support the family. Apparently not a bit interested in the butchering business, he went to work as a clerk for Lee Young Merchandise Company.[36]

In 1912 the Millers moved again, this time to a house at 88 West Cedar Avenue just west of Broadway, in the Byers area of Denver. Adam went to work as a packer at T. F. Lynch Ccompany. During that same year, at the age of seventeen, Phil began his vocation as a meat cutter, working for his father in the Miller Market on Champa Street, where, he always said, his dad taught him everything he knew about butchering! Despite a few challenges along the way, this would remain his profession for most of the next twenty-five years.[37] In 1913 Adam started work as a warehouseman at W. S. Sanderson and Brothers Coffee Roaster and Props Denver Spice Mills, at 1124 15th Street.[38] A very well respected company in the Denver area, Sanderson was famous for its special blends of coffee and tea and its unique selection of spices. Adam would remain at this job for the next five years.

In 1914 the three Miller men moved to 1019 Champa Street, conveniently located only one block from the Miller Meat Market and just ten blocks from Sanderson. The following year they moved directly next door, to 1017 Champa Street, were they lived for the next two years. The final entry in the Denver City Directory for Butch and Phil or the Miller Meat Market on Champa was in 1916.[39] There was no entry in 1917 because by then, they had moved to Elizabeth, Colorado, a small farming and ranching community approximately forty miles southeast of Denver. However, the Directory definitely records that Adam remained in Denver where he continued to work for Sanderson, and moved into a room at 1635 Court Place, which was a Gentlemen's Residence Quarters.[40]

It is interesting to note that the house where Lena died at 344 St. Paul Street, the apartment at 1035 Tenth Avenue and the house at 88 West Cedar Avenue are still in existence as I write this book. Rooms above the now famous Duffy's Restaurant at 1635 Court Place may very well be part of the original building in which Adam lived. The building at 2805 Third Avenue where the first Miller Meat Market was located is still there, but has been remodeled extensively and is currently part of the The Pendelton Store at Third Avenue and Detroit Street, in the upscale shopping area known as Cherry Creek North.

However, the building and the barn at 1119 Champa, where the second Miller Meat Market was located, as well as the two homes at 1017 and 1019 Champa, are no longer in existence. These were all razed during the development and construction of the Auraria Campus in the 1970's.[41] One of the few landmarks remaining in the immediate vicinity to remind us there was once a thriving community in this west Denver neighborhood is St. Elizabeth's Roman Catholic Church which has been in existence since its dedication in August of 1891.[42] With its beautiful spire, which can be seen pointing skyward from many areas of downtown Denver, it stands one block north of where the Miller Meat Market and the two homes on Champa were located. Sanderson later became known as the American Tea, Coffee and Spice Company, and remained in business for many years. It eventually was razed and is now a parking lot in the middle of downtown Denver.[43]

Although the location of their residences and the nature of their jobs is fairly clear, not much is known about their personal lives during the years after Lena's death. However, the era from 1914-1917 becomes much clearer due to photograph albums belonging to Emil Walz, Jr., of Arvada, Colorado, son of Anna Weishaupl Walz, who was Phil Miller's first girlfriend.[44]

Like Phil Miller, Anna Magdalene Weishaupl had a strong German background. Her father, Alois, had been born in Bavaria, Germany in May of 1856 and it was there, as a young man, that he learned the trade of Brewmaster. Anna's mother, Karolina Spagerer, had also been born in Germany in June of 1860. They met and were married there on November 9, 1884.[45]

Alois and Karolina came to the United States in the mid-1880's and settled in Omaha, Nebraska, which was located, coincidentally, in a county also known as Douglas! During the years in Douglas County, Omaha, Nebraska, Alois continued his trade as a Brewmaster and their first four children were born: William, known as Bill, Caroline, known as Lena, Mary and Anna. When Anna was about a year old, the family moved to Denver and settled on the west side of town. Two more children were born soon after that move: Alois, who died in childhood at the age of five, and Walberta, known as Wallie.[46]

At the time the Millers moved to the Champa Street address in 1914, the Weishaupls lived at 1244 Quivas Street in west Denver, where Alois worked as a Brewmaster at Neef's Brewery, conveniently located directly across the street from the family home. Anna was the same age as Phil, and in all probability, she had attended Central School, which was only a few blocks from where she lived.[47] Like Phil and Adam, she, too, quit school after the eighth grade to help support the family. One of her first jobs was as a chocolate dipper in a candy factory![48] The 1915 Denver City Directory lists Anna as working at the H. H. Tammen Company, a manufacturer of Indian curios, and a dealer in souvenirs, toys and fireworks with offices, sample displays and stock rooms at 17th and Larimer and factories at 26th and Larimer. According to Emil Walz, Jr., his mother worked at both locations over the years, supervising women who did piecework in their homes, sewing moccasins and making Indian dolls.[49]

Although it is not totally clear how the two families met, Emil Walz, Jr. has speculated that because the Miller family and the Weishaupl family lived and worked in the same part of west Denver, it is likely that they became acquainted when the Weishaupls did business at the Miller Meat Market or when either Phil or his father delivered meat to Anna's home. Because the Weishaupl home was within walking distance of the Miller Market this is a very plausible explanation. It is also substantiated by the fact that the very first picture of Phil to appear in Anna's album shows him standing by the Miller Meat Market delivery wagon.[50]

Mr. Walz suggested yet another possibility which could explain the connection between the two families. The area in west Denver in which the Weishaupls and the Millers lived was heavily populated with Germans during these years and many belonged to a very popular and active social and athletic club known as the German Turnverein. Anna's mother, Karolina, as well as Anna and her best friend, Emma Hurley, were very active in this organization and it is possible, that given their German ancestries, the two families may have met during one of the Turnverein activities.[51]

In any event, these albums contain pictures of Phil and Anna and a host of other friends and family. This includes Chester and

Hazel Hance; Adam and Butch and Butch's mother, Grandmother Augusta, and many of Anna's family members such as her sister Mary, her sister Wallie, her brother Bill and his wife Lou. Also located there are photos of Anna's mother Karolina, Anna's sister Lena, and her husband Bill Moerlin, and their twins Albert and Alberta. Many of these pictures were taken by Bill Moerlin and the appearance of the twins is very significant in that it narrows the dates and helps determine the time frame of certain pictures. The twins were born in July of 1915 and were around a year to a year and a half old at some of these family functions.[52]

The albums indicate very clearly that not only were Phil and Anna close, but that the two families were as well. These pictures were taken at family outings and picnics in the mountains around Devil's Head, at various homes in Denver, as well as at Bill Weishaupl's farm in Littleton and at the Miller's home and property in Elizabeth. One picture shows Phil and Anna riding in a little go cart, laughing and enjoying themselves. Another shows them dressed up to go out for an evening. Anna is wearing an elegant, long black dress, Phil is wearing a tie with his hat in hand. The chronology of these pictures verifies that this was not just a casual friendship but, rather, a long term relationship which began when the Millers lived in Denver and continued for possibly two or three years. The pictures reflect that Anna Weishaupl was a beautiful woman with dark hair and eyes and high sculptured cheekbones. Phil was equally handsome and dapper, and together they made a very attractive couple.[53]

As was previously mentioned, sometime during the latter part of 1916 or the early part of 1917, the lure of small-town, country life beckoned to Butch, and along with Phil and Grandmother Augusta, they left Denver and moved to Elizabeth.[54] Butch and Phil raised cattle and pigs, and opened another Miller Meat Market. Pictures in Anna's album indicate that Adam often went to Elizabeth on weekends to help his dad and brother with the animals. Pictures also verify the fact that she and Phil continued seeing each other after he moved to Elizabeth, but apparently not for long. No one seems to know why the relationship ended. It may have been simply the distance to travel between west Denver and Elizabeth made it difficult to carry on a serious relationship. In any event, shortly after the move no more photos of Phil were added to Anna's album.[55]

Former Elizabeth resident, Don McBreen, remembered his mother, Eunice Foster McBreen, telling him that she and Phil attended a country school, known as the Osborn School which was six or seven miles north of Elizabeth. This school is no longer in existence, and consequently, no records could be located. Don McBreen further remembered Eunice telling him that she and Phil dated once or twice. This would have been prior to 1918 when she married Bonnar McBreen. Additionally, she said classmates nicknamed Phil, "Philb". Eventually "Philb" quit school to work full-time for his father in the meat market.[56]

On December 15, 1917, during the early part of World War I, Adam enlisted in the Navy. On his tour of duty he was assigned to a military transport ship, the USS Harrisburg, where, as a Fireman First Class, he made twenty-two trips overseas.[57] Despite the fact that Phil and Anna were not seeing each other, the Miller-Weishaupl family friendship apparently did not end because in May of 1919, Adam sent Anna some pictures of the USS Harrisburg. Those pictures are now in the possession of Emil Walz, Jr. and he kindly allowed me to reprint the picture of the ship for use in this book.

When Adam was discharged on September 28, 1919, he returned to Elizabeth where Butch and Phil were still operating their meat market and continuing to raise cattle and pigs for slaughter. Phil was about to be married and had a small house on a few acres. Adam moved in with Butch and Grandmother Augusta and began farming and helping out with the animals.[58]

Anna Weishaupl continued to work at H. H. Tammen Company where she later met and fell in love with Emil Walz, Sr. a bright, good looking, successful Tammen's salesman. After two years in the Army during World War I, where he was awarded the Victory Metal, he returned to Denver in 1919 and went back to work at H. H. Tammen where he had been employed before enlisting.[59] They probably met around 1923 and were married September 10, 1924, which was also her twenty-ninth birthday! Their son, Emil, Jr., was born November 24, 1929. Because of the new baby, and because Emil, Sr.'s recently widowed mother had moved in with them, Anna could no longer keep her supervisory position at H. H. Tammen. Instead, she became a Tammen's pieceworker in her own home, sewing beads on Indian moccasins and assembling small Indian papooses. The ability to earn money in one's own home was indeed a fortunate opportunity for Anna during the Depression years. When H. H. Tammen closed in the 1950's, she concentrated on her bead work skills. Jewelers from all over Denver would bring beads to her for repair. Some were very expensive, but she had a reputation for honesty and excellence and her skills were much sought after. When she wasn't working, she was also an accomplished pianist, enjoyed cooking and playing cards![60]

Emil, Sr. had a very successful career as a salesman at H. H. Tammen and after it closed in the 1950's he worked for H. R. Meininger and Company, a well known Denver art supply dealer which is still in existence. Also an accomplished musician, he would play the cornet while Anna played the piano. He, too, was an avid card player, and he and Anna spent many snowy Colorado evenings happily shuffling the decks! In the early 1960's he developed a serious illness which forced him to retire around 1962 or 1963. He lived nearly ten more years, passing away in 1972 at the age of 80. In an amazing coincidence, Emil's birthday was the same day as Phil's, October 11.[61]

Emil, Jr. became a very successful and well respected tax accountant for the Denver and Rio Grande Western Railroad in Denver, where he began working full-time in 1948. This began a tenure that would last 43 years.[62]

His first position there was in the mail room, where he sorted and delivered mail. On a personal note, one of the people to whom he daily delivered mail was my grandfather, Mr. P. K. Yonge, who was the Director of Agriculture for the Denver and Rio Grande.[63]

While continuing to work for the railroad, full-time, Emil, Jr. attended Denver University at night from 1954 until 1960, earning a BSBA in Accounting. He then became an Auditor for Taxes and Mortgages for the Denver and Rio Grande, a position he held until his retirement in November, 1991.[64]

In 1967, when Mr. Miller donated $25,000 to build the original library building in Castle Rock, an article appeared in the Denver Post entitled "Douglas County to Start on Library." It showed a picture of Phil, and described how he, a successful and wealthy banker, had donated $25,000 as the seed money to finance the first Castle Rock Library. Anna saved that article and placed it in her album, later showing it to her son, Emil, and saying, "This man was once my beau."[65] Anna Weishaupl Walz died in 1977,[66] unaware of the full scope of Phil's philanthropy or the millionaire status he eventually acquired.

One thing which remains unclear during this time period is when Butch's mother, Augusta Ilch Miller, moved to Colorado. Even though pictures of her taken in Denver as well as in Elizabeth appear in Anna's albums during 1914 to 1917, her name does not appear in the Denver City Directories during any of those years. Her name does appear on the United States Census for Elizabeth,

Colorado during 1920 and shows that she was living in the household of her son, Philip Simon Miller, Sr.[67] It is likely she came either in 1906 with Butch and the family or in 1908 after Lena passed away. It is also not known when she died. She is not buried in Elizabeth or Castle Rock, she is not buried with Butch in Fairmount or in Crown Hill nor is she buried in Springdale Cemetery in Peoria.[68]

An interesting sideline to this mystery surrounding Grandmother Augusta is that to the best of anyone's recollection, Adam and Phil never mentioned her. They were both very private and humble men. Their early years and their family lives remained personal, almost confidential, not in a secret manner but rather in a sacred one. It is possible that the death of their mother when they were yet young boys may have contributed to their lifelong desire for privacy and developed in them traits of introspection and solitude where their personal lives were involved.

However, these may have simply been typical traits of the Kaestler family, because according to Gerd Adam, Jr., his father, Gerd Adam, Sr., who was Adam's and Phil's cousin, was also a very quiet and private man who spoke very infrequently about his family background or his early life. Apparently Uncle Frank was the only one with whom Gerd, Sr. would really talk and even after Uncle Frank's prodding, Gerd would only discuss his days in the Marines. Similarly, Uncle Frank was a very private person where his own life was concerned. Although he lived in Peoria and never married, he would only come two or three times a year to have dinner with Gerd's family. Despite the fact that he always had a job, nobody ever seemed to know what he did for a living.[69] When he died in 1948, he split his estate four ways: one-fourth each to Phil, Adam, and Gerd, Sr., and one-fourth divided equally between a church in Peoria and a Bible Institute.[70]

Endnotes

[1]Marriage License, Lena and Philip Simon Miller, Sr., April 20, 1892, Peoria, IL; and Death Certificate, Lena Miller, November 12,1908, Denver, CO.

[2]At the time of the 1920 Colorado Census, records show Augusta Ilch Miller as being 85 years old and her place of birth as Germany. This would make her birthday somewhere around 1835. It also shows the years of immigration or naturalization as unknown. United States Department of Commerce, Bureau of the Census, Fourteenth Census of the United States of America, State of Colorado, County of Elbert, Precinct #1 of Elizabeth, February 12-14, 1920, Sheet 6-B, Enumerator, George M. Wortman.

[3]Interview between Robert Oliver and the author, Castle Rock, CO, July 31, 1996.

[4]Obituary, Philip Simon Miller, Sr., Castle Rock Record Journal, September 20, 1940, p1.

[5]Marriage License, Lena and Philip Simon Miller, Sr; Death Certificate, Lena Miller; Last Will and Testament of Lina Kaestler Fischer, 1910; Kaestler family pictures courtesy of Gerd Adam Kaestler, Jr. and Norma Gish, Peoria, IL.

[6]Kaestler Family Tree compiled by Gerd Adam Kaestler, Jr.

[7]Death Certificate, Lena Miller; Last Will and Testament of Lina Kaestler Fischer, 1910; Last Will and Testament of Frank W. Kaestler, 1947; and Springdale Cemetery Records and Headstones, Peoria, IL.

[8]Kaestler Family Tree compiled by Gerd Adam Kaestler Jr.; and headstone, Lena Miller, Springdale Cemetery, Peoria, IL.

[9]IBID.

[10]IBID.

[11]IBID.

[12]Information Gerd Adam Kaestler, Jr., Peoria, IL.

[13]Letter and Kaestler Family Tree from Gerd Adam Kaestler, Jr. See Kaestler Family Tree.

[14]Marriage License, Lena and Philip S. Miller, Sr., April 20, 1892; Kaestler Family Tree; and obituary, Philip Simon Miller, Sr., Castle Rock Record Journal, September 20, 1940.

[15]IBID Marriage License.

[16]Douglas County News Press, April 6, 1988, p13.

[17]Douglas County News Press, August 30, 1979, p2.

[18]Birth Certificates, Adam Philip Miller, May 6, 1893 and Philip Simon Miller, Jr., October 11, 1895, Peoria, IL.

[19]Information, Gerd Adam Kaestler, Jr.

[20]Birth Certificate, Adam P. Miller, May 6, 1893, Peoria, IL.

[21]Kaestler Family Tree; and headstones Minnie Garrels and infant Lena Kaestler, Springdale Cemetery, Peoria, IL.

[22]Kaestler Family Tree.

[23]Birth Certificate, Philip S. Miller, Jr., October 11, 1895, Peoria, IL.

[24]Kaestler Family Tree; headstone Adam Kaestler Jr., Springdale Cemetery, Peoria, IL; and additional Information, Gerd Adam Kaestler, Jr.

[25]LeRoy Hafen, Colorado and Its People, Volume 1, p 644, Volume 2, p 400-401.

[26]Obituary, Philip Simon Miller, Sr., Castle Rock Record Journal, September 20, 1940 p l; obituary, Adam P. Miller, Douglas County News Press, written by his wife Dorothy Miller, March 23, 1983; and Denver City Directory, Volume 35, 1907.

[27]Denver City Directory, Volume 35, 1907.

[28]Beeler's Official Map of the City and County of Denver, 1913, courtesy of Emil Walz, Jr. and John Walker; and obituary, Adam P. Miller, March 23, 1983, Denver City Directory, Volume 35, 1907.

[29]Information according to the Archivist for the Denver Public Schools Attendance and Pupil Records Office, November 3, 1997.

[30]Beeler's Official Map of the City and County of Denver, 1913; Facts About Dora Moore School printed by Dora Moore School, 846 Corona Street, Denver, CO.

[31]Facts About Dora Moore School.

[32]Denver City Directory, Volume 36, 1908.

[33]Death Certificate, Lena Miller, November 12, 1908, Denver, CO.

[34]Kaestler Family Tree; headstone and cemetery records, Lena Miller, Springdale Cemetery, Peoria, IL; and additional information, Gerd Adam Kaestler, Jr.

[35]Denver City Directory, Volume 37, 1909.

[36]Denver City Directory, Volume 38, 1910; Beeler's Official Map of the City and County of Denver,1913; and Denver City Directory, Volume 39, 1911, address unknown for Lee Young.

[37]Denver City Directory, Volume 40, 1912; and Beeler's Official Map of the City and County of Denver, 1913, address unknown for T. F. Lynch.

[38]Denver City Directory, Volume 41, 1913.

[39]Denver City Directories, Volume 42, 1914, Volume 43, 1915, Volume 44, 1916; and Beeler's Official Map of the City and County of Denver, 1913.

[40]Denver City Directory, Volume 45, 1917. All dates and addresses from the Denver City Directories from 1907 until 1917 were researched and compiled by Emil, Jr. and Frances Walz.

[41]The site for the Auraria Campus was chosen in 1970 and the Ground Breaking took place in 1973. These buildings were demolished sometime during those early 1970's. The first classes were held in January, 1977. Information from Rosemary Fetter, Communications Director, Office of the Executive Vice President for Administration, Auraria Campus, Denver, CO.

[42]Layman, Fred Eyerman, Saint Elizabeth's Roman Catholic Church, Denver, CO, November 3, 1997; and Parish Coordinator, John Girten, March 24, 1998.

[43]All photos of Miller residences, Dora Moore School, St. Elizabeth's Church, Duffy's Restaurant, the old Sanderson location, and other remaining buildings were taken by Willis Buboltz, November, 1997 and May, 1998.

[44]The existence of these photo albums came to light in early 1996 when Mr. Walz wrote a letter to The Philip S. Miller Library and also to the Editor of The Douglas County News Press, and the Editor of The Castle Rock Chronicle. These albums opened up a whole new era in Mr. Miller's life and helped me piece together the years 1914 to 1917.

[45]Weishaupl Family Tree; History of Anna M. Weishaupl Walz, both by Emil Walz, Jr.; and letters November 7, 1997 and February 3, 1998.

[46]IBID; Family Tree and History.

[47]Denver and Rio Grande Western Railroad Map 1, Colo 1 C, June 30, 1919, courtesy of Emil Walz, Jr.; Beeler's Official Map of the City and County of Denver, 1913, courtesy Emil Walz, Jr. and John Walker; letter from Emil Walz, Jr., November 7, 1997, stating that the son of Anna's best friend, Emma Hurley, named Ray Harris, felt certain his mother, Emma, and Anna had attended Central School.

[48]History of Anna M. Weishaupl Walz, by Emil Walz, Jr.

[49]Denver City Directory, Volume 43,1915; letters from Emil Walz, Jr., November 9, 1997 and February 1, 1998; and history of Anna M. Weishaupl Walz, by Emil Walz, Jr.

[50]Interview between Emil, Jr., Frances Walz, and the author, Denver, CO, August 3, 1996; and first picture of Phil Miller in Anna Walz's Photo Album.

[51]Interview between Emil, Jr., Frances Walz, and the author, Denver, CO, August 3, 1996.

[52]Interview between Emil, Jr., Frances Walz, and the author, Denver, CO, August 3, 1996; and additional pictures in Anna Walz's Photo Albums.

[53]IBID.

[54]The final entry for Philip Sr., Philip, Jr. or Miller Meat Market on Champa St. appeared in the Denver City Directory, Volume 44, June,1916. No entry appeared in 1917, indicating they had moved out of the Denver area.

[55]Anna Walz's Photo Album.

[56]Interview between Don McBreen and Bette Saunders, August 1996, and follow-up letter; and interview between Don McBreen and Willis Buboltz, September 1996, and follow-up letter.

[57]Certification of Military Service, United States of America, Adam P. Miller, Personnel Records, National Archives, and Records Administration, St. Louis, Missouri; honorably discharged September 29, 1919; and obituary, Adam P. Miller, Douglas County News Press written by his wife Dorothy Miller, March 23, 1983.

[58]IBID Certification of Military Service; also, United States Department of Commerce, Bureau of the Census, Fourteenth Census of the United States of America, State of Colorado, County of Elbert, Precinct #1 of Elizabeth, January 26-27, 1920, Sheet 1-B; and February 12-14, 1920, Sheet 6-B, George M. Wortman, Enumerator.

[59]Letter from Emil Walz, Jr., February 23, 1998.

[60]Interview between Emil, Jr., Frances Walz, and the author, Denver, CO, August 3, 1996; history of Anna M. Weishaupl Walz by Emil Walz, Jr.; and letter from Emil Walz, Jr., February 1, 1998, Weishaupl Family Tree.

[61]Letters from Emil Walz, Jr., February 23, 1998 and March 30, 1998.

[62]IBID.

[63]Interview between Emil, Jr., Frances Walz, and the author, August 3, 1996, Denver , CO; and letter March 30, 1998.

[64]History of Anna M. Weishaupl Walz by Emil Walz, Jr., letters from Emil Walz, Jr., February 1, 1998, February 23, 1998, and March 30, 1998.

[65]Interview between Emil, Jr., Frances Walz, and the author, August 3,1996; Denver, CO; Denver Post Article entitled "Douglas County to Start on Library" by Fred Baker, August 1968.

[66]History of Anna M. Weishaupl Walz by Emil Walz, Jr.

[67]Refer to Endnote Number 2.

[68]Cemetery searches in Colorado: Elizabeth, Cedar Hill in Castle Rock, Fairmount and Crown Hill Memorial Park in Denver, 1995-1996; and cemetery records: Springdale Cemetery , Peoria, IL, April 14, 1998.

[69]Information Gerd Adam Kaestler, Jr.

[70]Last Will and Testament Frank W. Kaestler, December 18,1947; Peoria, IL; Kaestler Family Tree; and additional information, Gerd Adam Kaestler, Jr.

Frank Kaestler, nine months old, 1882, Peoria, Illinois.

Norma Gish and Gerd Adam Kaestler, Jr. Collection.

Frank Kaestler, 1924, the sole survivor of the original seven Kaestler children, Peoria, Illinois.

Norma Gish and Gerd Adam Kaestler, Jr. Collection.

SEE EARLY YEARS IN PHOTO SECTION.

THE SEARCH FOR LENA KAESTLER MILLER, PHILIP SIMON MILLER, SR., AND THE LADY WITH THE RAG MOP HAT!

One of the biggest challenges that confronted me as I wrote this book was trying to determine the location of the death and burial for Mr. Miller's mother and father, Lena Kaestler Miller and Philip Simon Miller, Sr., nicknamed Butch. All anyone knew about his mother was that she passed away from tuberculosis shortly after the turn of the century. No one seemed to know anything about the death of his father.

And so it was that the search for Lena Kaestler Miller and Philip Simon Miller, Sr., began in early 1996 in a snow-covered, country cemetery in Elizabeth, Colorado and would not end until many months later and 1500 miles away in the Kaestler Family plot in Springdale Cemetery in Peoria, Illinois. Before this search finally came to rest, my father, Willis Buboltz, had visited and explored cemeteries in Elbert County, Douglas County, Arapahoe County and Denver County.[1]

Based on information that Mr. Miller had given about his early years in Colorado everyone just assumed his parents were buried in Elizabeth and no one ever questioned him about it. It came as a total surprise to find no headstones and no burial information for either one of them. Elderly folks in the community, including a man named Mr. Hundley, who was in his nineties and who used to play cards with Butch, had no idea where they were buried.[2]

So, during early spring, as the green grass peeked through the melting snow, the search moved into Douglas County, to the peaceful grounds of Cedar Hill Cemetery, west of Castle Rock, where Philip and Jerry Miller were buried but most probably Lena and Butch were not. Again, but not surprisingly, there was no record of them at the cemetery or at Andrews Caldwell Gibson Mortuary in Castle Rock. The same held true at the cemeteries in Parker, Cherry Valley and Bear Cañon Cemetery of St. Phillip in the Field Episcopal Church in Sedalia.

But, anyone who knows Willie Buboltz, knows that when he sets a goal, he is relentless in his pursuit. Therefore, as spring flowers burst into full bloom, he pressed on into Arapahoe County, examining headstones in Littleton, Englewood and Aurora, while questioning records people, groundskeepers and caretakers in every cemetery he visited. He also checked records at Drinkwine Mortuary in Littleton. Again, as before, he found nothing.

Finally, with summer in full swing, he began the arduous task of exploring the many, immaculately manicured, big city Memorial Gardens of the Denver metro area. Day after day in the hot Colorado sun, cooled only by the occasional Rocky Mountain rainstorm that disappears as fast as it appears, he searched and questioned and discussed at Fairmount, Riverside, Park Hill and Crown Hill. When someone suggested that maybe Lena was Roman Catholic, he searched the headstones of Mount Olivet. After an unsuccessful quest of the big cemeteries, he silently walked the grounds of the small, private Church cemeteries, reading headstones, again to no avail. After weeks of hunting and inquiry he had found neither of them.

When the search of the Colorado cemeteries revealed no trace of either Butch or Lena, the logical progression was to attempt to locate any distant relatives who might be able to help solve the mystery of their whereabouts. With the last name of Miller, it seemed like an effort in futility. But the last name of Kaestler seemed to be somewhat unique, possibly not so hard to locate. To that end, my husband did a computer search for anyone with the last name of Kaestler, first in Mr. Miller's birth state of Illinois and then throughout the entire country. Three names appeared, two in Illinois and one in Florida! I was especially encouraged when the Illinois address was in Peoria—Mr. Miller's birth town! Immediately, I mailed an explanatory letter and a questionnaire to the Kaestlers on the list, hoping against hope for a good response.

As the search for Lena moved out of state, the search for Butch continued in Colorado when Douglas County residents and friends, Bette Saunders and Helen Daley, felt certain he was buried in Fairmount and Hazel Shoemaker felt certain that he was buried in Riverside[3]. My dad began to retrace his steps in those two cemeteries and, once again, the same records clerks told him the same thing, "No Philip Simon Miller, Sr. buried here."

One morning, at 7 a.m., my phone rang and a cheery Bette Saunders asked, "Have you checked Fort Logan National Cemetery?"[4] Up to that point I hadn't, but I immediately wrote to them and within four days they had written back. Once again, "No Philip Simon Miller, Sr. buried here."[5] The search had hit a snag. But I learned a long time ago not to give up.

Eventually, the following winter, I located Butch's obituary in a 1940 issue of the Castle Rock Record Journal.[6] It included not only his birth and death dates but the location of his burial, as well. He had died September 17,1940 in Colorado General Hospital in Denver and was buried in, none other than, Fairmount Cemetery, where my dad had already checked, twice, and been told, twice, that Butch was not there. The search concluded on an even more bizarre note when, after the snow melted and spring arrived, my dad returned to Fairmount and was told yet a third time that Philip Simon Miller, Sr. was not buried there! At that point, he produced the obituary which stated in black and white that Fairmount was, indeed, the place of burial. With this irrefutable evidence, they searched their records, again, and finally located the headstone. Bette Saunders and Helen Daley had been correct all along!

In the meantime, one of my inquiry letters regarding Lena had struck gold! I had received a phone call from Mr. Gerd Adam Kaestler, Jr., the man to whom I had written in Peoria, Illinois. As it turned out, he was Lena Kaestler Miller's great nephew and Mr. Miller's second cousin! Subsequently, he mailed me a copy of the Family Tree showing birth and death dates, additional family records and information as well as pictures belonging to his sister, Norma Gish. I could finally put a face to Lena Miller, this elusive woman for whom we had been searching so long. More importantly, however, was the picture verifying her burial plot in an area known as North Hill in Springdale Cemetery, 3014 North Prospect Road, in Peoria, Illinois.[7]

During the writing of this book there have been many days of elation. The days I found Butch and Lena were two of those days!!!!!

WHO WAS THAT LITTLE LADY WITH THE RAG MOP HAT?

As the search for Lena and Butch was just getting started, a man by the name of Emil Walz, Jr. wrote a letter to The Philip S. Miller Library, The Douglas County News Press, and Castle Rock Chronicle stating that he had pictures of Mr. Miller around the years of 1914 to 1917.[8] His mother, Anna Weishaupl, had dated Mr. Miller during that time. This was a stroke of great luck, because up until then, there were no pictures of Mr. Miller prior to his living in Castle Rock. Mr. Walz subsequently donated a tremendous group of these pictures to the Local History Collection at The Philip S. Miller Library in Castle Rock. The acquisition of these pictures has been an invaluable resource not only to me but to many other library patrons who have written and studied about Mr. Miller. Many of Mr. Walz's pictures appear in this book and I am grateful beyond words to him and his wife, Frances as well as to Johanna Harden, the Archivist of the Local History Collection, for the opportunity to have been able to include these pictures.

However, with the new pictures came a new mystery surrounding a new person! Frances Walz named her "the little lady with the rag mop hat!"[9] Indeed, as the pictures show, she was little and she always wore a rag mop hat! Because the pictures were taken in Denver and in Elizabeth with Phil and Adam and Butch, it was originally speculated (and hoped) that maybe this lady was Lena. However, for two reasons, that was just not possible. First, this lady was probably in her eighties at the time the pictures were taken and was simply too elderly to be Lena. Second, given the fact that Lena died shortly after the turn of the century, she could not have been alive between 1914-1917. So, who was this lady with the rag mop hat? How did she fit into the Miller family? How would I ever identify her?

By late summer, after my dad and I showed the pictures all over Castle Rock, with no luck whatsoever, it became obvious that this search, along with one for Butch and Lena, was suddenly hitting a dead end. But as I said before, I learned long ago never to give up. If I am supposed to find something, it will eventually appear.

During the writing of this book, I have developed some new, lasting and wonderful friendships. Emil and Frances Walz are two of those people and it is thanks to them that the identity of the little lady with the rag mop hat finally came to light.

One day in the fall of 1996, I received an envelope in the mail from Mr. Walz. He and Frances had decided to identify the lady with the rag mop hat![10] To that end they had gone to the National Archives in Denver to search the U.S. Census Records for Colorado and in the 1920 Elizabeth Census, they hit the jackpot! Enclosed were two large pages from the Census verifying that the lady was Augusta Ilch Miller, Philip, Sr.'s mother, Phil's and Adam's grandmother![11] It stated that she was living in Elizabeth with her son, her birthplace was Germany, and her age was 85, putting her birth date around 1835. Imagine my surprise and delight!! Later, when I located Butch and Lena's marriage license, sure enough, there was Augusta Ilch Miller, listed as the mother of the groom,[12] only much younger than in the pictures!

The information on these Census sheets proved invaluable not only with regard to Augusta, but to Phil, Adam, and Butch as well, because facts and information were listed on these sheets that I have never been able to find anywhere else. I have Emil and Frances Walz to thank for their perseverance, their never ending interest in the Miller family and their continued dedication to this project.

Augusta Miller, Mother of Philip Miller, Sr., Grandmother of Phil and Adam. The little lady with the rag mop hat! Circa 1916.

Local History Collection, Douglas Public Library District, Douglas County, CO.

Philip Simon "Butch" Miller, Sr., father of Philip, Jr. and Adam, Circa 1916.

Local History Collection, Douglas Public Library District, Douglas County, CO.

Endnotes

[1]All Colorado cemetery searches were done by my father, Willis Buboltz, during 1996 and 1997.

[2]Conversation between Mr. Hundley and Willis Buboltz, Elizabeth, CO, 1996.

[3]Information Bette Saunders, Helen Daley, and Hazel Shoemaker.

[4]Telephone call from Bette Saunders, Castle Rock, CO, August 14, 1996.

[5]Letter from Fort Logan National Cemetery, Denver, CO, August 20, 1996.

[6]Obituary, Philip Simon Miller, Sr., Castle Rock Record Journal, September 20, 1940, p 1; and headstone, Fairmount Cemetery, Philip Simon Miller, Sr.

[7]Information Gerd Adam Kaestler, Jr. and Norma Gish, Peoria, IL.

[8]Douglas County News Press, Commentary Page, January 28, 1996, p 5a; and Castle Rock Chronicle, letters to the Editor, February 28, 1996, p A2.

[9]Interview between Emil Jr., Frances Walz, and the author, Denver, CO, August 3, 1996.

[10]Letter from Emil Walz, Jr., August 19, 1996.

[11]United States Department of Commerce, Bureau of the Census, Fourteenth Census of the United States of America, State of Colorado, County of Elbert, Precinct #1 of Elizabeth, February 12-14, 1920, Sheet 6-B, Enumerator, George M. Wortman.

[12]Marriage License, Lena and Philip Simon Miller, Sr., April 20, 1892, Peoria, IL.

Kaestler Family Plot,
Springdale Cemetery, Peoria, Illinois.

front row left to right: Adam, Jr., Adam, Sr., Lina, Minnie
back row left to right: Willie, Emil, Mary, infant Lena, and Lena Miller (Mr. Miller's Mother).

Norma Gish and Gerd Adam Kaestler, Jr. Collection.

HE WHO FINDS A GOOD WIFE, FINDS A GOOD THING

Her real name was Jessie Ethel Stewart Miller but everyone knew her as Jerry. So unfamiliar was the name, in fact, that the post office would return mail addressed to Jessie Miller.

She told me once how she acquired the name "Jerry." When she was in grade school, the class had been assigned to read a book where the main character was a mean-spirited little girl named Jerry. The teacher decided that Jessie acted so much like that little girl in the book, they would give her the nickname "Jerry."

If she had been an overly sensitive, easily insulted child, this event could have possibly bruised her psyche and effected her self-esteem for the rest of her life. But, surprisingly enough, the name Jerry was fine with her because she never liked the name Jessie anyway! "Better a boy's name, than an old lady's name," she said.

However, anyone who knew Mrs. Miller, could never envision her as mean-spirited! She had a wonderful sense of humor and was regal, almost queenly in her mannerisms. In spite of their wealth and position in the community, she was never arrogant or over-powering. Instead she was kind, gentle, and humble. By her own admission, she was shy. Content to remain in the background, she felt more comfortable when her husband was in the forefront of things. An unpretentious and private woman, Jerry Miller preferred to focus on what she always felt was the most important thing in her life, helping Philip Miller become a success. However, the combination of living in a small town, as well as being married to one of the wealthiest men in that town, did not afford her much anonymity. Nevertheless, she preferred to think of herself and her husband simply as ordinary people who worked hard for things in which they believed. I disagreed with her, saying they may have been ordinary, but they did extraordinary things!

In the early 1970's, I owned a beauty shop in Castle Rock, The Powder Box Beauty Salon at 317 Third Street. Mrs. Miller was one of my regular customers—coming in every Friday afternoon at 2 o'clock. Much of the information in this book comes from those years of weekly beauty shop conversations.

Jerry Miller was a creature of habit. She always wore the same hairstyle and the same bright red nail polish. She also always smoked Pall Mall Red cigarettes! Year in and year out, those three things never changed. She was also one of my biggest tippers—fifty cents a week and a dollar when I gave her a permanent wave. And believe me, those were big tips for a beauty operator in the 1970's in Castle Rock, Colorado. The average was a quarter!

At the shop, everybody called her Jerry. My employees called her Jerry, the other ladies called her Jerry, and even the children called her Jerry. But not me! I could never call her Jerry. It would be too disrespectful. Having known her since I was two years old, she was Mrs. Miller to me, almost as if "Mrs." was her first name.

She once commented that she practically helped raise me. While that may have not been true in the literal sense of the word, it certainly represented how many years we had known each other. One of my earliest recollections as a child of about three is of Mr. Miller lifting me up to touch the soft furry head of a baby calf as Mrs. Miller held it perfectly still. Despite the long acquaintance, and after having done such personal things for her as cutting and curling her hair, filing and polishing her fingernails and once, even giving her a pedicure, I could still never call her Jerry.

One cold and snowy afternoon in October of 1973, she and I happened to be the only ones in the beauty shop. Because of the storm, most of the customers had canceled and everyone else had gone home. Usually Mr. Miller picked her up at 3:30, but on this particular day he deviated from his usual schedule and called us on the phone from the Bank at 3:15.

Due to the snowstorm, he had sent "all the girls home." But since it was Friday and the drive-up stayed open late, he, my dad and Mr. Oliver would remain at the Bank, "in case we have any last minute customers." He wanted to know if Mrs. Miller could stay with me at the shop until 6 o'clock? I was delighted! The prospect of visiting with her for three hours thrilled me immensely. So, as the snow piled up outside and the wind whipped against the windows, we sat and drank hot chocolate and smoked and she told me about her girlhood years.[1]

Jessie Ethel Stewart Miller was a Colorado girl. She was born on September 27, 1900 in Falcon,[2] a small railroad and agricultural community, located in El Paso County, approximately eighteen miles northeast of Colorado Springs. Her father, Alexander Stewart, had been born in Glasgow, Scotland in 1856.[3] Both his parents had been born in Scotland as well. They had come to this country in 1860 and had settled in the south.[4]

Her mother, Lucinda Irene Cummins, had been born in Camden, Arkansas on February 8, 1860.[5] Lucinda's father had been born in

North Carolina and her mother in Georgia.[6] Although the details of Lucinda and Alexander's marriage are not known, the 1900 Census shows they had been married twenty-four years, which would have put their marriage date around 1876.[7] Moving to Colorado in 1880,[8] they settled in an area which, in 1888, became known as Falcon. According to Historian, Mrs. Louise Solberg, of Falcon, this little town was established when it became a junction for two railroad lines, the Colorado and Southern Railroad, which came from Denver, down through Parker, Elizabeth, Elbert, Falcon and then headed south, and the Rock Island Railroad, which came from the eastern portion of Colorado through Burlington, Limon, Simla, Falcon and went on to Colorado Springs.[9]

Alexander worked as a Section Foreman for the Colorado and Southern Railroad, which meant he was a boss over a section crew which did routine work and track maintenance. Because one line came from the east and one line came from the north, a trestle was built at Falcon. Mrs. Miller said her father and his crew had helped build and maintain the C&S section of that trestle and the tracks at Falcon. When she was born in 1900, Alexander was forty-four and Lucinda was forty.[10] Jessie's only sister, Bernice Catherine, was born on January 18, 1903.[11] It appears that Lucinda used her middle name of "Irene", because she is referred to as Irene Stewart in the 1900 Census as well as other documents later in her life such as the Denver City Directory, funeral records for Alexander and her own headstone at Crown Hill Memorial Park in Denver.[12]

As with all pioneer families, they worked hard and strived to save as much money as they could, which in their case was very little. They were poor in terms of material wealth, but Mrs. Miller was never particularly bothered by this fact. On the contrary, she proudly said, "My father never owed any money to a living soul. That was the important thing!"

She commented that even though she and Bernie didn't have the clothes, toys or possessions, which many of their friends had during their childhood years, there was always food on the table and they never went hungry. Although they lived rather meagerly, often on a shoestring, "The necessities were there when we needed them."

This attitude of priorities, developed at such an early age, very likely contributed to the strength and fortitude she drew upon in her adult years, enabling her to weather the tough times. These initial, fundamental childhood experiences also intrinsically established in her mind what was important and what was not.

Unbelievable as it may seem, and despite the fact that her husband was one of the wealthiest men in Douglas County, she confided in me that she didn't have an electric washing machine, a dishwasher or a garbage disposal because she felt there were better ways to use their money. She publicly acknowledged this fact in an interview in 1980.[13] It was not until they sold the ranch and moved to a retirement community in Aurora, Colorado in 1983 that she finally would accept these amenities, and even then it was only because the condominium came furnished with them and she had no choice but to accept them!

There were more important aspects to life than "things," and to the Stewarts their faith was one of them. Alexander Stewart was a proper Scottish Presbyterian gentleman, while Irene was a fire and brimstone Southern Baptist. Although they didn't always agree on doctrine, they did agree that religious heritage was of utmost importance and this fact was reflected by the strict environment in which they raised their daughters. Both girls were baptized in the Community Church at Eastonville, which was about ten miles north of Falcon, and according to Mrs. Miller, "We attended church services whenever the doors were open and the snow wasn't too deep!" There are no records of these years, however, because the church burned and everything was destroyed.

Almost from the moment they learned to read, Jessie and Bernice were expected to study the Bible at home. They knew, from memory, the stories of Moses, Daniel in the Lion's Den, and the Three Hebrew Children. In Sunday school, they could quote scripture and verse better than many of the other children their age.

Mrs. Miller felt that this heavy religious indoctrination as a young child may have been the reason she strayed from the church as an adult. Although she was a woman of deep faith and inner strength, she didn't feel the need for organized religion in her life anymore.

It is not exactly clear where Jessie and Bernice attended elementary school or high school. From things Mrs. Miller said, I always just assumed it was in Falcon. In a letter to me during the writing of this book, Bernice's daughter-in-law, Shari Benedict, of Denver, said she was under the same impression. However, she also added that, "School was not a subject openly discussed in the family so we really don't know."[14] While researching the El Paso County schools during that era, in that area, I learned from Historian, Mrs. Louise Solberg, that Falcon had a school beginning in 1888, located directly next to the railroad tracks! It was apparently an elementary school because the first high school graduation in Falcon did not occur until 1920.[15] According to the El Paso County School Census Records of Eligible School Age Children for the Falcon District #49, Jessie Stewart did, in fact, attend school in Falcon during 1908 and 1909.[16] Additionally, another school document shows her father, Alexander Stewart, served on the Falcon School Board from September 9, 1901 to May 30, 1902.[17] These documents are in the possession of Mrs. Louise Solberg.

At some point in time, although no specific date can be verified, the family moved to Parker, Colorado in Douglas County.[18] Presumably this was a job related move because Parker was one of the small towns in which the Colorado and Southern Railroad had a station. According to copies of Douglas County School Census for Consolidated District #37, Parker, Colorado, now in the possession of former Parker resident, Mrs. Gertrude Clarke Kordziel of Golden, Colorado, Jessie Stewart attended school in Parker from the age of fourteen through eighteen during the years 1915 until 1919. Bernice Stewart was in the first year of high school in 1918.[19] A Parker Public School Program, which took place on Friday, May 12, 1916, lists Jessie Stewart as one of the soloists, singing "Song of Songs."[20]

PROGRAM

BY

PARKER PUBLIC SCHOOLS

AT 8:30

FRIDAY NIGHT, MAY 12, 1916

Cinderella		Played by Primary Children
Song	Springtime	Eleven Girls
Declamation	Home	Charles O'Brien
Recitation	On the Rappahannock	Zetella Tucker
Piano Solo	Valse	Gladys DuRay
Recitation	Mother	Lizzie Rueter
Recitation	Der Dog und der Lobster	Edwin Comer
Recitation	Dictating an Item	Callie Robertson
Song	Song of Songs	Jessie Stewart
Recitation	A Fellow's Mother	Richard Lewis
Recitation	Like Dad Did	Otto Rueter
Duet	Capriccio Brilliante	Emma O'Brien and Winnie Tallman
Recitation	Schlausheimer Pites Himself Mit a Dog	Vivian Fredinburg
Recitation	Swan Granderson Joins the Buffaloes	Ralph Sandstrom
Recitation	Riley's Bear Story	Mamie DuRay
Song	Song of the Flag	Eight Boys
Declamation	Character	John Robertson
May Pole Drill		Sixteen Children

GILBERT CARLSON COLLECTION

PARKER SCHOOL PROGRAM FOR 1916

From the book *Denver and New Orleans: In the Shadow of the Rockies*, by James R. Jones.

Courtesy of Sundance Publications, LTD. Denver CO.

As they grew older, Bernice became a tremendous tomboy while Jerry was the care-taker, always getting Bernie out of trouble.[21] Bernice could be described as assertive and authoritative while Jerry was soft spoken[22] and by her own admission, quiet and shy. Despite their differences in personalities they were "good pals" and shared a secret passion for dancing. Certain that their parents' religious beliefs would prohibit their ever attending a dance, they entertained themselves by quietly practicing, in stockinged feet, behind the closed doors of their bedroom. When they finally asked to go to a dance, their father shocked them by granting his permission. Unbeknownst to Mr. Stewart, this decision would ultimately change the future for his oldest daughter because it was, in fact, while attending a dance that she met her future husband.

Jerry Stewart met Philip Miller in the spring of 1919 at a dance in Parker, during her final year of high school. She was eighteen and he was twenty-four. She saw him from across the room and "immediately liked him." She thought he was terribly good looking and was especially impressed by his thick brown hair! But in those days, young ladies did not ask young men to dance. So, she smiled and waited for him to make the first move. He finally summoned up the courage to ask her to dance. She had a wonderful laugh and a sparkle in her eyes, and from then on they would go to a dance whenever possible. As spring turned into summer, they realized they were not destined to be just dance partners.

"We thought a lot alike," she said. "Our similar backgrounds of poverty and hard times immediately created a strong bond between us. Our goals for the future were the same," she told me. They were married that fall on November 3, 1919,[23] in Denver with their friends, Mr. and Mrs. Herman Seidler, as witnesses. By then, Jerry was nineteen and Phil was twenty-five. She showed me a picture of their wedding day, and I have always regretted not asking her for a copy of it.

The first few years of their marriage were spent in Elizabeth, where they lived in a small house on a few acres, which the 1920 Census referred to as a "farm,"[24] but what she jokingly called the haunted house because it was located just down the hill from a cemetery! She giggled as she told me that it was a rather depressing location, but, fortunately, they shared a sense of humor, which enabled them to transcend the gloominess of living by the cemetery, and have fun, whatever the situation. It was during this time that they adopted the nicknames, "Momma" and "Poppy," which they would affectionately call each other for the next 68 years!

She laughed as she reminisced about their outhouse, which was 75 feet away and had so many cracks between the slats that they would have to cover the walls with newspapers and old calendars to try and keep out the snow. Just when they thought they had it secured, a Colorado blizzard would hit, snow would blow in and they would have to shovel it out and recover the walls! It seemed appropriate that she related this story to me during a snowstorm!

They called the outhouse "Chick Sale's House," and she explained to me the story behind it. Before there was indoor plumbing everyone had an outhouse. In the early days of silent movies, a well-known comedian named Chick Sale capitalized on this fact by using an outhouse in his act. He would go into the outhouse, close the door and sit down. The wind would then blow the outhouse over and leave him sitting out there, all by himself, pants around his ankles, exposed to the world! People soon started calling the outhouse "Chick Sale's House."

She also reminisced about the very first car they owned after their marriage. They were so proud of it! Being their first big investment, they wanted to take good care of it and, since they didn't have a garage, they would park the car in the barn! One morning as he was leaving for work, Mr. Miller forgot to open the barn door and backed the car right through it! They were relieved to discover that there was more damage done to the easily repairable barn door than there was to the new car! Even then, their priorities were always very clearly defined!

It was also during these early years in Elizabeth that Mr. Miller's community service began when he worked evenings and Sundays to help build one of the town landmarks, the Elizabeth Chamber of Commerce Pavilion.[25]

During the summer of 1920, Mr. Miller was approached by two of his friends, Bill Faber and Karl Kleeman. Their desire was to go into the meat market business with him. Faber had been a rancher in Elizabeth before going into the service, but after his discharge he decided to leave ranching. Kleeman was a farmer in the same community who, quite simply, wanted out of farming.[26]

At this time, Mr. Miller was basically operating the meat market alone, as his father had become a dealer in cattle and pigs. Being a bit of a scrapper, Butch always enjoyed the wheeling and dealing better than being stuck behind the counter at the meat market. At any rate, Mr. Miller had always wanted to put a market in Castle Rock and another one in Kiowa. Faber's and Kleeman's offer seemed like a good opportunity to do just that.

After both men were trained in butcher shop operations and meat cutting, they formed a three-way partnership and opened two additional markets. In Kiowa was the Miller and Kleeman Meat Market and in Castle Rock was the Miller and Faber Meat Market.[27] The Elizabeth locale became the main branch, where Adam took care of the cattle and pigs while Butch and Phil did the buying and the butchering for all three shops. This was the first step of what Phil envisioned as the development of a successful chain of meat markets. He often remarked that he wanted to be a "big meat packer, a big guy." Proud of his father, Butch, and grandfather, John Miller, he had always wanted to continue in their footsteps.[28] Little did he realize that he ultimately would become a "big guy"—it just wouldn't be in butchering—it would be in banking!

While Mr. Miller was overseeing his three businesses, Mrs. Miller, now twenty years old, was experiencing the typical adjustments of a new bride. She missed her small, closely-knit family. Even though Parker wasn't that far away, she didn't see her parents too often and she would feel terribly lonely after they left. In 1920, she felt even more isolated when Alexander, Irene and Bernice moved from Parker to Denver.[29] It is not totally clear where they lived at first, however, Shari Benedict remembered that it was somewhere in the north part of town. The Denver City Directory shows that by 1922 they lived in a house at 2012 Meade Street, which was, indeed, in north Denver, within walking distance of Sloan's Lake Park.[30] During this time, Bernice met Charles Edwin (Ed) Benedict whom she would marry in October of 1921. He owned a company known as Allied Maintenance, which distributed paper and supplies to schools outside the Denver area and up into the Dakotas.[31]

With her family scattered and Mr. Miller working all the time, Mrs. Miller often felt as lonely and desolate as the wind swept prairie of Elizabeth. Coupled with the loneliness, was her constant fear for her husband's health. Haunted by thoughts of his mother, Lena's, early death from tuberculosis, she worried about him catching pneumonia, or worse, while working out in the rain or the snow or the dust. Intellectually, she knew that tuberculosis was not inherited, but emotionally, she was "just plain scared."

She told me that Phil had been quite ill during the influenza epidemic of 1918, leaving him with weakened lungs, and as a result, he was frequently sick during the first years of their marriage. These episodes led her to believe that he had inherited what she called "a tendency toward that sort of thing," even though influenza and tuberculosis were two completely different diseases. For nearly fifteen years, she "almost worried herself to death."

In September of 1934 an article entitled, "Close to Tuberculosis Cure," appeared in the local paper announcing that researchers back east had found a serum which offered promising results in the cure of tuberculosis.[32] This news calmed her fears somewhat, but she was never completely fear free until the 1940's when anti-tuberculous drug, streptomycin, was actually developed and marketed.[33] Additionally, she was always afraid that if Phil did become sick there wouldn't be enough money to get proper medical care. At that time she couldn't have known that he would live a robust life to the age of ninety-nine and they would become wealthy enough to afford any type of medical care they desired.

The summer of 1921 brought big changes for Phil and Jerry Miller as they faced the first of many business challenges that would confront them over the years. Bill Faber, the man running the meat market in Castle Rock, suddenly had to quit. Replacing him wouldn't have been all that difficult, had the partnership been just a little more sound. However, in planning for the future, they had incurred their first large debt when they became heavily involved in raising cattle and hogs for slaughter.

In order to buy out the partner in Castle Rock, and get themselves out of debt at the same time, Mr. Miller applied for a loan for $2,000 from a banker in Elizabeth. By modern standards, $2,000 is a small amount of money. But in 1921, it was a substantial sum and the banker, as they say, "turned him down flat". This put an abrupt end to any immediate plans he had for a chain of meat markets. It is likely that had he gone to Castle Rock to First National Bank or to Castle Rock State Bank, he would have received his loan. However, in demonstrating his philosophy of doing business in the community in which you live, he applied in Elizabeth, and was turned down.

This was an affront that profoundly affected both Mr. and Mrs. Miller—an experience that neither one of them ever forgot. Not only did the stroke of a banker's pen alter the course of their lives, it demonstrated to them, at a very young age, just exactly how cold and cruel the business world could be. However, their destiny apparently was in Douglas County and this event ultimately changed history.

Years later, during their early days in the banking business, this memory motivated them to develop a philosophy whereby they would always help the small business owners, if it were at all possible. Mr. Miller once always commented that he could never be a hardhearted banker. Good business sense was prudent. Hard heartedness was just plain mean. This was a philosophy he adhered to throughout his life, and instilled in his bank employees as well. When somebody would say he was a gentleman and a businessman, he took that as a supreme compliment. It was hard to balance the two, but he did it very successfully.

According to 1921 standards, all three meat markets were doing fairly well. Castle Rock and Kiowa were both county seats with enough people to patronize the meat markets. Although Elizabeth was a smaller town, the meat market there had been open nearly four years and had a solid base of return customers. There was no doubt in Mr. Miller's mind that each town could probably support its respective meat market if that was all that was necessary. However, with no loan and very little money to pay back the indebtedness, the future looked bleak. He knew that he was going to have to consolidate into one location. The choice of where to go and what to do weighed heavily on his mind.

He hated to give up any of his operations, especially the one in Elizabeth. When country life had lured them away from the city, Elizabeth had become a respite for Phil, his father and his grandmother. It had been there that the they joyously welcomed Adam home after World War I. It had been there that he and his partners bravely made their first venture into the business world. It had also been there that he owned his first home and carried his new bride over the threshold into their new lives. Elizabeth definitely held many fond memories.

Nevertheless, he truly felt he had no choice but to save the Castle Rock operation. He knew from a business standpoint that the long-range opportunities for a successful meat market were greater there than in either of the other two locations. Given his financial predicament, he would have to run it himself. For these reasons, he dissolved the partnership and sold his farm to pay off the debt. In August of 1921, Phil and Jerry moved to the big city of Castle Rock!

In the evenings they would stroll along the board sidewalks, lined with big beautiful trees growing to the middle of the street. The "business district" consisted of the few blocks surrounding the Courthouse Square and the building which would one day be "Mr. Miller's Bank" was not even built yet!

She continued with her reminiscing by telling me about Adam. In 1921 when she and Phil moved, Adam continued to farm on the prairies of Elbert County. His father and grandmother still lived there and he felt an obligation to remain near them. A few years after his grandmother passed away and his father moved to Castle Rock, Adam, at the age of thirty-eight, met a lively little lady by the name of Dorothy Dickson from Edgewater, Colorado. Her bubbly personality was a perfect match to his quiet nature and they balanced each other completely. Additionally, Adam was a big man, with broad shoulders while Dorothy was a petite little woman, barely tall enough to reach his broad shoulders and they made a very cute couple! They were married on June 30, 1931, in Denver, Colorado, with Phil as a witness.[34]

They moved to Parker and settled on a ranch in an area known as Hilltop. Dorothy often said that Adam grumbled at her because she didn't know how to make bread, and he insisted that one of his ranch hands teach her![35] They lived there, in a little white farmhouse, for the next six years while Adam continued to farm and raise livestock and Dorothy perfected her bread making skills!

In 1937, they purchased a larger ranch, with another little white farmhouse, at 9100 East Parker Road, just a few miles directly east of downtown Parker. They resided and ranched there for the rest of their lives, the next 45 years. Dorothy started teaching elementary school in Parker, a position she held for twelve years. I later learned that she was also very active in the Woman's Study Club of Parker, the Hilltop Social Club, as well as the Order of Eastern Star.[36] Adam's cattle business grew and he became a very successful and well respected rancher, raising and selling commercial cattle. He was also very active in the Masons and belonged to Douglas Lodge No. 153 A.F. and A.M. in Castle Rock.[37]

Shortly after getting married, Adam and Dorothy decided to become foster parents, and over the years they raised twenty foster children, all boys! This does not surprise anyone who knew them. Adam was a loving and kind man, funny and somewhat shy, yet with a wonderful personality, who could be strict when he had to be and soft when he wanted to be!! He was a typical father who enjoyed watching sports with his "foster sons"! Dorothy was outgoing and lively, cheerful and patient. As an elementary school teacher, she was not a bit intimidated by the seeming shenanigans of young boys and their propensity to become playful, rowdy and rough. In fact, she was quite aware of the needs and moods of growing boys, which made her a wonderful mother. Very willing to open the doors of her home and her heart, she happily anticipated each new arrival and quietly shed tears when one would leave.

Living and working on a ranch was a healthy environment for troubled boys, especially with "foster parents" who loved and cared for them the way the Millers did. For twenty years, mingling along with the whinnying and neighing of horses and the mooing of cows, the laughter of children could be heard drifting out over the fields of the ranch. Additionally Dorothy and Adam were very active in the Parker United Methodist Church and had a strong religious foundation in their lives, which they tried to instill in their "boys." Many of these now grown men owe their very existence to Adam and Dorothy Miller.

Dorothy's outgoing personality also made her a perfect "reporter" and she became well known for her newspaper column, "Mrs. Miller's Names in the News," which appeared weekly for over thirty years in the Douglas County News and later the Douglas County News Press. I found a poignant description in the News Press of how she kept Douglas County residents up to date on births and deaths, anniversaries and illnesses, graduations and visiting friends or relatives:

> "Her telephone chimed merrily day in and day out with calls relaying bits of information for her articles. Sitting at the kitchen table, she carefully composed each week's activities, in longhand, and mailed them promptly to the newspaper office."[38]

Over the years, Phil and Adam always remained close. Even in their adult lives, they affectionately referred to each other with their childhood nicknames. Phil calling Adam "Dutch" and Adam calling Phil "The Kid." Fortunately, they were never farther away from each other than the twelve-mile drive between Castle Rock and Parker.

Meanwhile, back at the beauty shop, repeated honking from horns in front of the shop ended our reminiscing and jolted us back into reality. Six o'clock had come, all too quickly. Bundled up and huddled together against the storm we made our way to the street where my dad's warm car awaited me and Mr. Miller's warm truck awaited her. As I helped her into the cab she asked, "Poppy, did you have any customers?" "Five," he replied. "Well, then," she said, "it was a good thing you stayed open."

As they drove away and I watched the snowflakes swirl in the glow of the red taillights, I remember thinking what remarkable people these two men and their wives were.

ENDNOTES

[1]The major source for most of the personal information contained in this chapter comes from this conversation which took place with Mrs. Miller in October 1973 at the Powder Box Beauty Salon, at 317 Third Street in Castle Rock, CO. Additional information comes from Mrs. Miller's niece, Shari Benedict and great-nieces, Melissa Benedict and Diane Benedict Fling all of Denver, CO, during the months of April and May of 1998. Further information comes from Historian, Mrs. Louise Solberg, Falcon, CO, May, 1998 and former Parker resident, Gertrude Clarke Kordziel, Golden, CO, May, 1998.

[2]Birth date for Jessie Ethel Stewart Miller is verified by the Birth Certificate of Jessie Ethel Stewart, State of Colorado, September 27, 1900; headstone Cedar Hill Cemetery, Jerry E. Miller, Castle Rock, CO; and Funeral Memorium Jerry E. Miller, November 5, 1987.

[3]Birth date for Alexander Stewart is verified by his headstone at Crown Hill Memorial Park, Denver CO. Birth location for Alexander Stewart is verified by the Birth Certificate of Jessie Ethel Stewart; also the Department of Commerce, Bureau of the Census, Twelfth Census of the United States, Schedule 1-Population; and State of Colorado, County of El Paso, Precinct #20 of Falcon, June 19-23, 1900, Enumerator Burke Potter.

[4]Department of Commerce, Bureau of the Census, Twelfth Census of the United States, Schedule 1-Population; and State of Colorado, County of El Paso, Precinct #20 of Falcon, June 19-23, 1900, Enumerator Burke Potter.

[5]Birth date for Lucinda Irene Cummins Stewart is verified by the Historical Records of Crown Hill Memorial Park, Denver, CO, Lucinda Irene Stewart, March 21, 1948; also her headstone showing Irene Stewart, March 22, 1948.

[6]Department of Commerce, Bureau of the Census, Twelfth Census of the United States, Schedule 1-Population; and State of Colorado, County of El Paso, Precinct #20 of Falcon, June 19-23, 1900, Enumerator, Burke Potter.

[7]IBID.

[8]IBID.

[9]Telephone conversations between the author and Historian, Mrs. Louise Solberg, Falcon, CO, May 26, 27, 28, 29, 1998.

[10]These ages appear on the Birth Certificate of Jessie Ethel Stewart, State of Colorado, September 27, 1900; Lucinda's age is further verified by Historical Records of Crown Hill Memorial Park, which shows her birth date as February 8, 1860.

[11]Birth date for Bernice Catherine Stewart Benedict is verified by funeral records of Bernice Catherine Benedict, Fairmount Cemetery, Denver CO, and Interment Records, Crown Hill Memorial Park, Denver, CO, January 28, 1994; and headstone Crown Hill Memorial Park, February 1, 1994.

[12]The Twelfth Census of the United States June 19-23, 1900 for Precinct #20 of Falcon, CO, lists her as Irene Stewart; The Denver City Directory, Volume 50, 1922, lists her as Irene Stewart; her name appears as Irene Stewart in Crown Hill Memorial Park, Denver, CO, Block and Lot Burial Record of Alexander Stewart, March 29, 1924; her own headstone at Crown Hill Memorial Park identifies her only as Irene Stewart, March 22, 1948.

[13] Douglas County News Press, August 30, 1980, p 7.

[14]Letters from Shari and Melissa Benedict, Denver, CO, May 12, 1998.

[15]Telephone conversations between the author and Historian, Mrs. Louise Solberg, Falcon, CO, May 26, 27, 28, 29, 1998.

[16]El Paso County Census Records of Eligible School Age Children for the Falcon District #49, 1908, 1909, courtesy of Mrs. Louise Solberg, Falcon, CO.

[17]Falcon District #49, Class Souvenir Program from the school year 1901-1902 lists Alexander Stewart as a member of the School Board, courtesy of Mrs. Louise Solberg, Falcon, CO.

[18]Lucinda Irene Stewart's Historical Record of Crown Hill Memorial Park states that she had lived in Denver since 1920 and her prior residence had been Parker, CO.

[19]Telephone conversation between Mrs. Gertrude Clarke Kordziel, Golden, CO and Ellen Buboltz, May 28, 1998 and June 9, 1998; and Douglas County School Census Records for Consolidated District #37, Parker, CO, 1914-1921 courtesy of Mrs. Gertrude Clarke Kordziel.

[20]Information Mrs. Louise Solberg, from the book Denver and New Orleans, In the Shadow of the Rockies, p 143, by James R. (Jim) Jones, used with permission of Sundance Publications, Ltd., Denver, CO.

[21]Letter from Shari Benedict, Denver, CO, May 12, 1998.

[22]Letter from Melissa Benedict, Denver, CO, May 12, 1998.

[23]Marriage License and Marriage Certificate, Philip S. Miller and Jessie E. Stewart; and State of Colorado, City and County of Denver, November 3, 1919.

[24]United States Department of Commerce, Bureau of Census, Fourteenth Census of the United States of America, State of Colorado, County of Elbert, Precinct #1 of Elizabeth, January 26-27, 1920, Sheet 1-B, Enumerator, George M. Wortman.

[25]Douglas County News Press, August 30, 1979, p 8.

[26]Douglas County News Press, August 12, 1980, p 2.

[27]Miller and Faber Meat Market Advertisement, Castle Rock Record Journal, June 24, 1921.

[28]Douglas County Express, August 29, 1979 p 22; Douglas County News Press, August 30, 1979, p 2 and August 12, 1980, p 2.

[29]Lucinda Irene Stewart's Historical Record of Crown Hill Memorial Park states that she had lived in Denver since 1920 and her prior residence had been Parker, CO; in a letter from niece, Shari Benedict in May of 1998, she told me that Alexander and Lucinda had bought a house in north Denver prior to 1921.

[30]This address appears in the Denver City Directory, Volume 50, 1922; it also appears in Crown Hill Memorial Park, Denver, CO, Block and Lot Burial Record of Alexander Stewart, March 29, 1924; Lucinda Irene Stewart's Historical Record of Crown Hill Memorial Park states that she had lived in Denver since 1920 and her prior residence had been Parker, CO; in a letter from niece, Shari Benedict in May of 1998, she told me that Stewarts had bought a house in north Denver prior to 1921.

[31]Letter from Shari Benedict, Denver, CO, May 12, 1998.

[32]Castle Rock Record Journal, September 28, 1934, p 7.

[33]History of Tuberculosis, Grollier Electronic Encyclopedia.

[34]Marriage License and Marriage Certificate, Adam P. Miller and Dorothy L. Dickson, State of Colorado, City and County of Denver, June 30, 1931.

[35]The source of most information pertaining to Adam and Dorothy Miller comes from the October 1973 conversation between Jerry Miller and the author. Additional information comes from the Douglas County News Press, Obituary of Adam Miller, March 23, 1983 and Obituary of Dorothy Miller, May 3, 1984.

[36]Castle Rock Record Journal, January 13, 1939 and March 17, 1939; Douglas County News Press, May 3, 1984, p 2.

[37]As a member of The Order of Rainbow for Girls, I knew Adam Miller personally and of his involvement in the Masons.

[38]Douglas County News Press, May 3, 1984, p 2.

LIVING IN THE HISTORIC CANTRIL COURTHOUSE! 1921-1925

After living on what had been a rather desolate, wind-swept prairie in Elizabeth, Mrs. Miller said Castle Rock, "Felt like we were in heaven."[1] And close to heaven they were. Living in a nice apartment on the second floor of the old Cantril Courthouse Building, on Fourth Street, they were blessed with heat, lights and "something resembling indoor plumbing!" The days of Chick Sale's House were gone! Now when they looked out the window they saw their meat market, diagonally across the street, nestled in a corner section of the lobby of the Keystone Hotel.

There is an interesting history surrounding this first place in Castle Rock Mr. and Mrs. Miller called home; it had once been the first Douglas County Courthouse, now known as the Cantril Courthouse! For many years, it was mistakenly believed that this building had been constructed in the 1860's in Franktown and was moved in 1874 to a lot on the southeast corner of Fourth and Wilcox Streets when Castle Rock became the county seat. These facts had been reported in the February 20, 1903 obituary of William Cantril, the builder of the building and also by Josephine Marr in her book, Douglas County, A Historical Journey.[2]

However, in 1995, Kent Brandebery, of the Douglas County Historic Preservation Board, discovered that, although the builder was, indeed, William Cantril, the two-story, wood frame building actually had been constructed in Castle Rock and not in Franktown. He located copies of the Minutes of Douglas County Commissioners Meeting from April 28, 1874 which detailed the contract drawn up between William Cantril and the Commissioners, for a "Courthouse for Douglas County, 20 feet by 40 feet by 20 feet high, at a cost of $1325.00."[3]

This contract identified the building site as Lot 18 in Block 19 in Castle Rock which was, indeed, the southeast corner of Fourth and Wilcox Streets at the location of what is currently Town and Country Barbers at 324 Wilcox Street. It further specified the size of the building, the height of each story, the size of the three downstairs rooms and the one upstairs room, as well as the height of the wainscoting, the amount of plaster, and the number of windows and doors. Subsequent minutes from May and June meetings reported an additional $25.00 expense for plastering, bringing the total cost to $1350.00 at the time of the final inspection when the building was completed on June 15, 1874.[5]

Six years later, in May of 1880, the little building was in danger of "blowing over" due to its "disproportionate height and lack of interior bracing." To rectify the situation, the Commissioners approved a 12-foot by 40-foot addition on the right side of the building, strengthening and supporting the existing structure. This addition contained three rooms and cost $375.00 to construct.[6] The now fortified building served the county well for the next ten years, until, ironically, directly across the street, construction began on the second Douglas County Courthouse. Famous for its beautiful stone design and structure, the new courthouse was completed in 1890.[7]

Usurped of its role as County Courthouse after sixteen years, the Cantril Courthouse became, for a while, the Castle Rock Journal Building. During this time it also housed a print shop. Its versatility continued, as from 1902-1904 the front room contained Castle Rock's first bank, The Douglas County Bank, which would later become The First National Bank.[8] Continuing its service to the community, it was even home to the post office until early 1920![9]

However, when I first began my research, there was a further mystery surrounding this little clapboard building. No one seemed to know where it had been located when Millers lived in it. Was it on the front of the lot at the original location or on the back of the lot where it currently stands at 310 Fourth Street? Unfortunately, by this time Mr. Miller had already passed away and I had forgotten to ask. In retrospect, I had forgotten to ask him many important things. I guess I always thought he would live forever and I had plenty of time.

Therefore, Bette Saunders and Willie Buboltz, went to work trying to locate the date the building was moved. My dad questioned Bob Oliver and Lowell Bush, the present owner of Town and Country Barbers, as well as a few of the "old-timers" while Bette questioned other people and enlisted the help of Laryce Nitch for a possible title search. Also, in her affiliation with the Castle Rock Historical Society, Bette mentioned the mystery to Starr Oberlin, President of the society.

In the meantime, Kent Brandebery kindly sent me the information verifying that the building had, in fact, been constructed in Castle Rock along with his article "Douglas County's First Courthouse." Shortly after that, Starr Oberlin located newspaper articles from two issues of the 1920 Castle Rock Record

Journal giving the dates and details regarding the relocation of the building from the front to the back of the lot!

According to these articles, it was during the fall of 1920 that the Cantril Courthouse was moved to the back of the lot, in order to clear the front corner of the lot for the construction of a new brick building which would house Mikolizik's Castle Rock Mercantile. At that time, the building was placed near the alley, facing north and remodeled into apartments where Mikolizik's lived on the ground floor.[10] In August of 1921, when Mr. and Mrs. Miller relocated to Castle Rock and moved into the upstairs apartment, the building had, in fact, been at its current location, on the back of the lot. Another mystery solved!

In the 1950's the building again became a newspaper office, this time for Kobolt Press. Over the years it has been used for many small retail shops, a locksmith shop as well as a photography studio, where, when my sister and I were small, we had our pictures taken! A small second addition was built on the left side of the first floor, next to the alley, during the early 1970's.

In 1996, Mr. Kent Brandebery began proceedings to have the Cantril Courthouse placed on The National Register of Historic Places. Unfortunately, it did not qualify due to the fact that, over the years, too many structural changes had been made.[11] However, it is on The Castle Rock Inventory of Historic Properties and is eligible for nomination to The Town of Castle Rock Register of Historic Landmarks.[12] The building still stands today at the same location and is utilized as a retail store.

The Cantril Courthouse on Wilcox Street. Mr. and Mrs. Miller would eventually live upstairs.

Local History Collection, Douglas Public Library District, Douglas County, CO.

ENDNOTES

[1]Conversation between Mrs. Miller and author at Powder Box Beauty Salon, Castle Rock, CO, October 1973.

[2]Castle Rock Journal, William W. Cantril Obituary, February 20, 1903, p 1; Josephine Marr, Douglas County, A Historical Journey, p 39; also Josephine Marr, "Castle Rock, 100 Years Old," Douglas County News, December 12, 1974.

[3]Douglas County Commissioner's Minutes, April 28, 1874, p 256; and Kent Brandebery, "Douglas County's First Courthouse," March, 1995, p 9, 10.

[4]IBID.

[5]Douglas County Commissioner's Minutes, May 26, 1874, p 261; Special Meeting June 15, 1874, p 264; and Kent Brandebery, "Douglas County's First Courthouse," March, 1995, p 12, 13.

[6]Douglas County Commissioner's Minutes, May 18, 1880; Susan Casey, "The Myth of the Moving Courthouse," Douglas County News Press, August 28, 1996, p 15a.

[7]IBID, Susan Casey.

[8]Castle Rock Journal, December 20, 1901, p 1 and November 21, 1902, p 1. Not to be confused with The Bank of Douglas County which Mr. Miller opened in 1939.

[9]Castle Rock Record Journal, July 6, 1917, p 1 and September 24, 1920; and letter from Bette Saunders, February 23, 1996.

[10]Castle Rock Record Journal, September 24, 1920 and December 17, 1920, courtesy of Starr Oberlin.

[11]Letter from Bette Saunders, February 23, 1996; letter from Kent Brandebery, March 16, 1996; and Susan Casey, "The Myth of the Moving Courthouse," Douglas County News Press, August 28, 1996, p 15.

[12]Telephone interview with Kent Brandebery, Douglas County Historic Preservation Board, Castle Rock, CO, March 17, 1998, and letter from Kent Brandebery, March 18, 1998; telephone interviews with Lionel Oberlin, the Castle Rock Historical Society, April 13, 1998 and June 10, 1998.

I could not have written this section without the help and research of Willie Buboltz, Bette Saunders, Starr and Lionel Oberlin, Kent Brandebery and Susan Casey.

The Cantril Courthouse was moved to its present location at 310 Fourth Street in 1920. Mr. and Mrs. Miller lived upstairs from 1921 until 1925.

Buboltz-Bodle Collection.

PERSEVERANCE PREVAILS: MORE MEAT AND A LITTLE COAL

On August 19, 1921, the Castle Rock Record Journal ran a front page article entitled "Change in Meat Business At Castle Rock." It announced that Mr. Miller had moved to Castle Rock to take over the Miller and Faber Meat Market, and that he had also purchased the meat business from two other existing Castle Rock stores, Shellabarger Company and Mikolizik's Castle Rock Mercantile.[1]

In an advertisement a few pages later Mr. Miller ran a personal announcement repeating the above facts and advising his customers that a full line of fresh and smoked meats would always be carried in stock. He ended the announcement with the statement, "I will strive to serve you to your entire satisfaction," and he signed it P.S. Miller, Jr.[2]

From the beginning of this venture, Mrs. Miller worked right along with her husband regardless of what was required or how hard it might have been. Bill Faber was now gone and the business was known as Millers Meat Market, a name which they were both determined to do proud.

They ran eye-catching advertisements, every week, during their early months in business.

"MEAT EATERS are the folks who do big things in this world. We carry a line of the best meats obtainable for our customers."[3]

"BARBEQUED STEERS are all right, but for a regular diet you will appreciate our juicy steaks and roasts."[4]

"CUSTOMERS ARE NOT SKINNED when they buy juicy steaks and tender roasts at Millers Meat Market."[5]

Advertisements from those early years also give us an idea of the vast price differences, in meat, between those days and today. Swift's Skinned Hams were twenty-seven cents a pound,[6] picnic hams were seventeen cents a pound,[7] pot roast was ten cents a pound and hamburger was a quarter![8]

By November of 1921, business had improved to the point that they actually found themselves growing out of their Keystone Hotel location. This was amazing growth, after only three months in Castle Rock, and as a result, they moved the meat market diagonally across the street into a storefront building, three doors from the corner, which is currently 320 Wilcox Street. At that time they also changed the name to Castle Rock Meat Market.[9] It was located directly next door to what later became and currently remains the historic and popular B & B Cafe, at 322 Wilcox Street, owned by Mrs. Pat Bradley.[10] 320 Wilcox Street was the location of Sign Design, owned by Steve Ramsour, from 1993 until mid-1998, when he moved to his new location at 109 Fourth Street.

While Mr. Miller did all the butchering and meat cutting in a slaughter house out on Lake Gulch Road, Mrs. Miller worked in the market grinding hamburger, rendering lard, slicing bacon, unpacking meat and waiting on customers.[11] She once remarked to me that although there wasn't much she could do in the slaughter house, she would go out there in the evenings just to lend "Poppy" moral support and they would often be there half the night.

In March of 1924, Mr. and Mrs. Miller experienced deaths in both of their families. Mr. Miller's grandmother, Lina Green Kaestler Fischer, passed away in Illinois at the age of 73. She was buried in the Kaestler Family plot in Springdale Cemetery in Peoria, next to her first husband, Adam, and surrounded by the six children and one grandchild she had survived. The bulk of her estate went to her only living son, Frank Kaestler, but she never forgot her Colorado grandsons, Adam and Philip, Jr., leaving them each $500.[12] Mrs. Miller's father, Alexander Stewart, passed away in Denver and was buried at Crown Hill Memorial Park.[13] He unfortunately never knew either of his grandchildren. Bernice's first child, Jim, was born just five months later, on August 10, 1924. Her second child, Shirley, was born in three years.[14]

In 1925, after living in the Cantril Courthouse for four years, the Millers moved three blocks west to a house at 310 Elbert Street.[15] When driving by that house today, it is bordered by Interstate Highway 25 on the west, which extends from the state line of southern Colorado, north through Denver to the Wyoming border. Across the street to the south is the Philip S. Miller Building, a Douglas County Administration Complex which was completed in 1997 in honor of Mr. Miller.[16] In 1925, however, I-25 did not exist, and other than a few more houses and a water tank, the area was mostly fields bordering East Plum Creek.

Although they had enjoyed apartment living, they welcomed the opportunity to have their own home, with a yard and neighbors and a front porch where they would sit and watch the Colorado sun setting in the west. Soon they purchased this house and would live there until 1950.[17] It also appears that sometime during these years Grandmother Augusta Ilch Miller also passed away because Mr. Miller's father, Butch, moved from Elizabeth to Castle Rock. It is unlikely that he would have moved had his mother still been alive. He lived with Phil and Jerry at this house while helping out at the meat market.[18] Soon, however, he and Jerry locked horns over something and in an attempt to keep the family peace, Phil gave his father the outside duties of buying animals and delivering meat.[19] Nevertheless, as the nickname suggests, butchering was in his blood and he could very often be found helping Phil at the slaughter house.

One night in late July of 1926, Butch was driving home, alone, from the slaughter house when he was involved in a car accident at the corner of Third and Wilcox Streets in front of the First National Bank Building. The next day the following headline appeared on the front page of the Record Journal: "Philip Miller, Sr. Injured Last Night."[20]

In describing the accident, the newspaper reported that as Dad Miller was crossing Wilcox, a six passenger sedan hit his car on the right rear, demolishing the right rear wheel and causing considerable damage to the left rear wheel and rear fender. The impact flipped his car around with such force that he was actually thrown out. To quote the article:

> "No bones were broken but the old gentleman was considerably bruised and the absence of loss of life or permanent injury was considered almost miraculous."[21]

Indeed, everyone considered it quite a miracle that he hadn't been killed. Mrs. Miller commented, years later, to me, "Phil's father was a tough old bird."

In 1928, Mr. Miller sold the meat market and opened a feed and coal business right down the street, in a long, low concrete building that had once been a livery stable and is now 413 Wilcox Street.[22] Known as Castle Rock Fuel and Feed, the new business wasn't primarily a feed store at this point in time, but rather a coal dispersing station.[23] It is not known what Butch did during this time but as before, Mrs. Miller worked right along with her husband. She ran the office, for no salary.[24] She took care of the paper work, did the accounting and continued to worry about her husband's health! This time it was coal dust she feared.

Interestingly, although the feed store is at a different location with a different name, it is still in existence today!

An early employee of Mr. Miller's in the fuel and feed business was Ben Saunders, a long-time resident of Castle Rock. Through these early years, a deep and lasting friendship was forged between the two men.

Ben Saunders was born September 26, 1914, in Sedalia, Colorado.[25] It wasn't too long before his family moved the ten miles north to Castle Rock and when it came time to go to school he attended grade school at the Cantril School, and high school at the Wilcox School.

Ben Saunders was a worker. In the mid-1920's, when he was still too young to drive and make deliveries, he worked at J.H. Woltzen's General Store as a stock boy. In the late 1920's, he went to work for Mr. Miller and remained a steady employee until after high school graduation in 1932. Then, according to Mr. Miller, as the Depression got worse, he couldn't afford to pay Ben's salary of $50 a month, so he had to temporarily let him go. During this time, the business became a one-man operation, as Mr. Miller loaded coal from a railroad car at the Denver & Rio Grande Western Railroad yard on Third Street into his own truck and then delivered it to each one of his customers. He charged $4.50 a ton, making only $1.00 profit for himself on each ton.[26]

The dollars added up too slowly, and he found himself going broke. Mr. E.G. Breslow, who ran the Denver & Rio Grande Western Railroad Depot in Castle Rock, and was reportedly the wealthiest man in town, came to the rescue by loaning the Millers enough money to keep the business afloat.[27] Years later, in an interview, Mr. Miller commented that he was "broke two times in his life."[28] This was one of those times.

Meanwhile, Ben had gone to work for Jake Kroll at his grocery store. Mr. Miller always felt badly about this turn of events and as soon as he paid off his loan to Mr. Breslow, the first thing he did was to rehire Ben. In light of what was to come, this was a fortunate move for both of them because in 1933, a new challenge arose as Mr. Miller was forced to take back the Castle Rock Meat Market.

Advertisements from the Castle Rock Record Journal show that at the end of May in 1933 a man by the name of Darrell Reum owned the meat market. By mid-July, however, Mr. Miller had apparently taken it over because subsequent advertisements reflect him as the owner.[29] Apparently, for awhile, Phil and Jerry ran the meat market and Ben ran the fuel and feed store. In 1935, Mr. Miller sold the Castle Rock Fuel and Feed Store to Ben Saunders,[30] finally assuaging the guilt he still felt at having to let Ben go a few years earlier.

The friendship and respect these men had for each other ran very deeply and this was not the last time they shared in a business interest. Ben Saunders would be one of the original stockholders when Mr. Miller opened The Bank of Douglas County in 1939. He would also be one of the men who would help construct the new building when Mr. Miller expanded The Bank of Douglas County in 1971.

After reacquiring the meat market, Mr. Miller remained in the butchering business for approximately the next five years at 320 Wilcox Street, the same location to which he had moved the store fifteen years earlier. While a new employee, Cliff Hawkins, ran the market, Mr. Miller took over all the butchering duties. He and Butch also bought and sold cattle, renting small pastures around town on which the animals could graze.[31] Additionally, he purchased a couple of horses, which he and Mrs. Miller would ride.

Close family friends Gill and Cecil Whitman moved to Douglas County from Happy, Texas, which was known as "The Town Without a Frown!," on April 4, 1936. They settled on a ranch southwest of Castle Rock on Highway 105. Cecil was anything but happy those first few years! They had no children at the time, and she remembered being so homesick that the mailman would tease her because she cried when he brought her a letter and she cried when he didn't bring her a letter![32]

It wasn't long before they became customers of the Castle Rock Meat Market. This was during the time Cliff Hawkins was running the store, but soon they met Phil and Jerry and began a lifelong friendship which would last nearly sixty years. They would go on picnics and have dinner together and this friendship helped ease Cecil's homesickness a bit!

Gill often commented how Castle Rock was so small in those early years that whenever a car with a Texas license plate would drive through town Phil would immediately call Cecil on the phone to tell her people were coming out to visit! That made her happy![33]

Despite the good times and good friendships, Mr. Miller often commented, "About the only thing I knew how to do in those days was work."[34] Even Sunday was not a day of rest, because according to H. G. "Pete" and Hazel Burgess, Phil and Jerry would spend Sunday cleaning the market and washing the windows.[35] They probably experienced more hard times during those years than most people do during a complete lifetime. It was the Depression, money was tight and life was just plain hard. Furthermore, it was during this time Mr. Miller and his father came to a parting of the ways in their business relationship.

In an interview in 1988,[36] Mr. Miller admitted that things were not always smooth and serene between father and son. Butch Miller had always been a scrapper and age never mellowed that characteristic. Rumor had it that during Prohibition, he ran bootleg whiskey between Douglas County and Elbert County, which was a dry county, although Phil would never verify that fact. However, it was not the shenanigans of the early days that drove a wedge between Phil and his father, but rather it was Butch's total lack of responsibility in later years. Phil remembered one incident which occurred soon after he reacquired the meat market. His father paid $75.00 for a Jersey dairy cow and two brothers in west Denver later offered Butch $100 for her. Phil wanted to keep her because she produced seven to eight gallons of milk a day, which he could sell at the market. But one hundred dollars was a lot of money, so Phil relented and they hooked her to the back of a wagon and headed for Denver.

By the time they reached the outskirts of town her hooves were so sore she could hardly walk and the Denver Police threatened to charge them with cruelty to animals. They bedded her down to rest in a barn in their old neighborhood at 11th and Champa, and later Phil discovered that their forty-mile trek had been totally unnecessary because the brothers had a cow trailer!

Butch liked to play poker, and he liked to drink. This combination resulted in the final parting of the ways between father and son. One day, after they had sold a large load of livestock in Denver, Butch got into a poker game and lost over $1,000 of their earnings. He came home with only $30.00 and Phil was furious. "I had worked like a dog for that money," he later said. A thousand dollars was a fortune during the Depression, and to Phil this loss was unforgivable. Following this incident, Phil ended his business relationship with his father.[37] They remained close, but they never worked together again.

After that episode Butch moved back to Elizabeth where he opened a pool hall. According to former resident, Don McBreen, his parents, Eunice and Bonnar McBreen, owned a cafe in Elizabeth during the mid-1930's and Butch's pool hall was two doors down. There was the cafe, a garage and then the pool hall.[38]

Don remembered an incident in 1935 when his parents had taken a vacation and left him and his brother, Bob, at home. They were teenagers at the time, and while their parents were gone they went in to Butch's hall to play pool. When their parents came home, Butch asked their father if, in fact, the boys had his permission to play pool. When the answer was no, the boys were in deep trouble! Butch told them never to try that again! He may have been a scrapper, himself, but he was not about to contribute to the delinquency of teenage boys! When the McBreen family got out of the cafe business in 1936, Butch and the pool hall were still there.[39]

Apparently, Butch lived the rest of his life in Elizabeth, running the pool hall and playing cards with his friends. It seems ironic that a man who so obviously liked to drink, spent his later years in a dry county. It is fitting, somehow, though, that he would spend his last years in the same little town where he spent so many years after first leaving Denver.

According to Phil, one day in early September of 1940, Butch wasn't feeling well and went to stay with them in Castle Rock where Jerry took care of him for several weeks. By September 16th he had become very ill and Phil took him to Colorado General Hospital in Denver where he was admitted.[40] Philip, Sr. died in Philip, Jr's. arms the next day, September 17, 1940, from heart complications at the age of 72.[41] Phil always said, "My father died in my arms."[42] The big, burly butcher who had come to Colorado back in the early 1900's to try and save his wife's life and had ultimately become both father and mother to Phil and Adam, was now gone. He had been a widower for thirty-two years. He was buried in Fairmount Cemetery in Denver on September 20, 1940.[43] "Dad Miller," as he had come to be known, left fond memories and funny stories in the minds and hearts of his many friends in both Castle Rock and Elizabeth. It was not until this time that Mr. Miller stopped writing "Jr." after his name. All his life, he had signed his name Philip Miller, Jr. as a sign of the respect and admiration he felt for his father.[44]

After Butch died in 1940 the pool hall never reopened, and the building remained empty until Charlie Davis eventually bought it and moved it west of Elizabeth, just across the Douglas County Line. Because Douglas County was not a dry county he opened County Line Liquor Store which remained at that location for many years to come.[45]

Meanwhile, Ben Saunders remained in the fuel and feed business until 1942. Although he never became an official Purina dealer, he soon started selling various Purina products. He added an ice route to the operation in May of 1935.[46] It is interesting to note that Ben delivered ice right up the street to the M & N Steakhouse, located in the Keystone Hotel, where at that time, his future wife,

Bette Gilbert, worked as a waitress, for fifty cents a day, during 1936 and 1937![47] His best friend, Jimmy Oltmans, was his primary employee while local high school boys such as Bob Oliver worked for him after school. It is very likely that Ben would have remained in the fuel and feed business, but military duty called and in a rather unique and humorous manner, both he and Jimmy wound up in the service.

According to Bette, this is the story Ben and Jimmy would tell:

They knew they were going to be "drafted" sooner or later, so they kept alert. One day, Jimmy went to the post office, peeked in his mailbox and saw his draft notice. He immediately went to the store and told Ben. They jumped in the truck, drove to Denver and enlisted in the Navy, leaving their draft notices in the post office for the next couple of days.

When the selective services officer, a rather stern man by the name of Henry Madan, tracked them down to see if they had received their draft notices they told him, "No, but it doesn't matter because we already joined the Navy." He informed them, in no uncertain terms, that they couldn't do it that way, to which they replied, "Sorry, we already have!" The Douglas County Service Record shows Jimmy's official enlistment date as January of 1942 and Ben's as August of 1942. Bette speculated that Ben was allowed some extra time to dispose of the feed store, which he did, selling it to Carroll Hier in the summer of 1942.[48]

Bette Gilbert had been born on Halloween in 1914 and was raised on a cattle and dairy ranch in Cherry Valley. Although she and Ben Saunders had been acquaintances in grade school and high school and he knew her from the M & N Steakhouse, they had never really struck up a friendship until Ben came home on leave in the spring of 1945. By that time Bette worked at the Rio Grande Depot in Castle Rock and when Ben came in to pick up his sea bag, they started talking. This talk resulted in "courting" and writing letters and when he was honorably discharged and returned home, they were married December 9, 1945. Ben went on to have a very successful career in the construction business.[49]

Prior to purchasing the Castle Rock Fuel and Feed from Ben, Carroll Hier had just completed three successful terms as County Assessor. During the next seventeen years, in addition to owning and operating the store, he would serve on the Castle Rock Town Board from 1946 to 1952 and be elected to two terms as Mayor from 1952 to 1956.[50]

However in 1942, his first official act as new owner was to establish it as a Purina franchise. He continued to operate under the same name at the Wilcox Street location until the early 1950's, when he moved into a building at 420 Third Street just east of what was then Richardson Lumber Company. In 1959, Carroll Hier sold Castle Rock Fuel and Feed to the Golden Feed Company. The new owners changed the name to Castle Rock Feed and Supply.[51]

The old building on Wilcox soon became the location of Hier and Price Well Drilling and remained such for many years. It was eventually rebuilt and is currently owned by John Sieber.

In the early 1960's, longtime Douglas County rancher, John Lowell, bought the Castle Rock Feed and Supply. At that time he was working for Jim Marr in the County Assessor's office, so he hired Frank Christensen to work at the store.[52] Frank Christensen soon hired the man who, without a doubt, holds the honor for the longest association with the feed store. That man was Bob VanPelt, who at that time was an employee at Martin Marietta and owned a ranch ten miles southwest of Castle Rock on Perry Park Road. He left Martin Marietta and began a tenure at the feed store which would last over thirty years and would take him from employee to eventual owner.[53]

In the meantime, John Lowell, had been elected County Assessor in 1962, a position he would hold until 1978. He had also purchased a second feed store in Franktown, known as High Plains Supply, which his son, Johnny, helped him run.[54]

However, in June of 1965, one of the worst natural disasters in the history of the state of Colorado occurred and subsequently changed many of our lives. The skies darkened and the rains came and the South Platte River and Plum Creek raged out of their banks, flooding large areas of Douglas, Arapahoe and Denver Counties. Tearing away at the earth, this flood left death and destruction in its wake, resulting in the loss of businesses and homes, as well as property and cattle, collectively valued in the millions of dollars in Douglas County alone, billions of dollars state-wide. John Lowell's ranch south of Castle Rock was in the path of that flood. So was Mr. Miller's.

Bruff Shea, Castle Rock Director of Parks and Recreation, related how one of his first jobs as a teenager was to help clear away the debris on Mr. Miller's ranch after the flood. "Mr. Miller hired a bunch of local boys and paid us a couple of dollars an hour."[55] He further recalled that Mr. Miller would come home at lunchtime and stand on the edge of the river bed and watch them work as they chopped up gnarled and twisted trees, hauled mud-soaked debris and roots and branches which had been tossed helter-skelter by the raging river. Miraculously, Mr. Miller didn't lose any cattle.

In John Lowell's case, however, the damage was so severe and the loss to his cattle and property was so extensive, that he was forced to sell his stores in order to devote more time to the repair and restoration of his ranch.[56] Consequently, in the late summer of 1965, he sold Castle Rock Feed and Supply to Paul Sutton, the owner of Valley Feed in Littleton, and J. A. Barton, the owner of South Side Feed in Englewood. They designated Bob VanPelt as their manager and very shortly he bought into the business. For the next twenty years he remained manager and co-owner until he and his wife, Bette, bought the store from Sutton and Barton and became full owners in 1985. Although their son, Ron, sometimes worked with his dad at the store, Bette never did, however, because in 1964 she was appointed Clerk of the District Court and Jury Commissioner, positions she held until her retirement in 1991. Later she helped out at the store if Bob needed her.[57]

In May of 1994, after thirty years at the feed store, Bob VanPelt was forced to retire because of health reasons. He and Bette sold the business to Bill and Wayne Bennington.[58] They soon added a line of clothing and changed the name to Castle Rock Feed and Western Wear.[59] At this writing, the store is still located at 420 Third Street.

It is interesting to realize that Mr. Miller's second business venture, which nearly went broke during the Depression, has survived the test of time. Thanks to a progression of good owners with good business sense, it has remained a thriving and vital enterprise in the ever changing business community of Castle Rock. Throughout the years, regardless of the owners, Mr. Miller remained a loyal customer to the feed store which had originally belonged to him.

In one of life's many mysteries, Mr. Miller outlived Ben Saunders who died in 1987[60] and Bob VanPelt who died in 1995.[61]

The slaughter house out on Lake Gulch Road still stands after 70 years!

Buboltz-Bodle Collection.

ENDNOTES

[1]The source for much of the personal information in this chapter comes from conversations between Mrs. Miller and the author at the Powder Box Beauty Salon, 317 Third Street, Castle Rock, CO, at various different times from 1973 until 1976; Castle Rock Record Journal, Aug. 19, 1921, p 1.

[2]IBID p 5.

[3]Advertisement, Castle Rock Record Journal, September 2, 1921.

[4]Advertisement, Castle Rock Record Journal, October 7, 1921.

[5]Advertisement, Castle Rock Record Journal, November 11, 1921.

[6]Advertisement, Castle Rock Record Journal, September 30, 1921.

[7]Advertisement, Castle Rock Record Journal, October 21, 1921.

[8]Douglas County News Press, August 30, 1971, p 1.

[9]Advertisement, Castle Rock Record Journal, November 25, 1921.

[10]Douglas County News Press Salute Section, "B & B Known For Its Food, Its History," February 28, 1996, p 32 C.

[11]Douglas County News Press, August 12, 1980, p 7.

[12]Headstone Lina Green Kaestler, March,1924, Springdale Cemetery, Peoria, IL; Kaestler Family Tree; and Last Will and Testament of Lina Green Kaestler Fischer, May 5, 1910.

[13]Crown Hill Memorial Park, Denver, CO, Block and Lot Burial Record of Alexander Stewart, March 29, 1924; also headstone Crown Hill Memorial Park, Burial date March 31, 1924.

[14]Stewart-Benedict Family Tree; birth date for James S. Benedict also verified by Diane Benedict Fling, November 8, 1997, and the Funeral Record of James S. Benedict, Fort Logan National Cemetery, Denver, CO, May 15, 1979; birth date for Shirley Benedict appears in the Historical Record of Crown Hill Memorial Park, July 13, 1961.

[15]Douglas County News Press, August 30, 1979, p 1.

[16]Douglas County News Press, September 10 and 17, 1997, p 3a.

[17]1950 Blueprints of the Miller Ranch courtesy of Mr. Ken Ash, Castle Rock, CO.

[18]Interview between Bette Saunders and the author, Castle Rock, CO, August 1, 1996; interview between Helen Daley and the author, Parker, CO, July 31, 1996 in which they both remembered Butch working at the meat market.

[19]Douglas County News Press, April 6, 1988, p 13.

[20]Castle Rock Record Journal, July 30, 1926, p 1.

[21]IBID.

[22]Douglas County News Press, August 30, 1979, p 2.

[23]Interview between Carroll Hier and Willis Buboltz, December 10, 1994.

[24]Douglas County Town and Country Squire, November 26, 1976.

[25]All information regarding Ben Saunders courtesy of Bette Saunders, letters, phone calls, and personal interviews at various times from 1992 until the completion of the book.

[26]Douglas County News Press, August 30, 1979, p 2.

[27]Douglas County Town and County Squire, November 26, 1976.

[28]Douglas County News Press, August 12, 1980, p 5.

[29]Advertisements, Castle Rock Record Journal: May 26, 1933, July 21, 1933, August 25, 1933, September, 15, 1933, October 6, 1933, and October 13, 1933.

[30]Interview between Bette Saunders and the author, June 3, 1996.

[31]Douglas County News Press, August 30, 1979, p 2; interview Willis Buboltz, May 15, 1994; Gill Whitman Dedication Speech, Philip S. Miller Bench, Douglas County Fair and Rodeo, August 3, 1996. On file in the Local History Collection, Douglas Public Library District, Castle Rock, CO.

[32]Interview between Gill and Cecil Whitman and the author, March 27, 1997, Castle Rock, CO.

[33]IBID Whitman Interview; also Douglas County News Press, August 12, 1980, p 8.

[34]Douglas County News Press, April 6, 1988, p 13.

[35]Letter from former Mayor, H. G. "Pete" and Hazel Burgess, November, 1996.

[36]Douglas County News Press, April 6, 1988, p 13.

[37]IBID.

[38]Interview between Don McBreen and Bette Saunders, August 1996; interview between Don McBreen and Willis Buboltz, September 1996; follow-up letters from Bette Saunders and Willis Buboltz, August and September 1996.

[39]IBID.

[40]Conversation between Philip Miller and the author Cherry Creek Care Center, Aurora, CO, August, 1991.

[41]Obituary, Philip Simon Miller, Sr., Castle Rock Record Journal, September 20, 1940, p 1.

[42]Conversation between Philip Miller and the author, Cherry Creek Care Center, Aurora CO , August, 1991.

[43]Headstone Philip Simon Miller, Sr., Fairmount Cemetery, Denver, CO, September 20, 1940.

[44]Conversation between Philip Miller and the author, Cherry Creek Care Center, Aurora, CO, August 1991.

[45]Letter from Bette Saunders, August 20, 1996.

[46]Castle Rock Record Journal, April 5, 1935.

[47]Telephone conversation between Bette Saunders and the author, June 11, 1998; also The Denver Post, Special article entitled "Famed Eatery To Be Revived" by Virginia Grantier, August 17, 1995.

[48]Letter from Bette Saunders, September 15, 1996; and interview between Carroll Hier and Willis Buboltz, December 10, 1994.

[49]Telephone conversations between Bette Saunders and the author during the writing of this book. Specifically June 3, 1996, July 18, 1997, and June 11,1998.

[50]Our Heritage-The People of Douglas County, John Carroll and Flora Hier, Written by Flora Bean Hier, p 118.

[51]Interview between Carroll Hier and Willis Buboltz, December 10, 1994; Castle Rock Chronicle, August 6, 1996, p B 9.

[52]Interview between John Lowell and the author, Castle Rock CO, March 18, 1997.

[53]Interview between Bette VanPelt and the author, Castle Rock, CO, March 7, 1997.

[54]Interview John Lowell, March 18, 1997.

[55]Interview between Bruff Shea, Director of Parks and Recreation, and the author, Castle Rock Town Hall, August 1, 1996.

[56]Interview John Lowell, March 18,1997.

[57]Interview Bette VanPelt, March 7, 1997.

[58]Interview Bette VanPelt, March 7, 1997.

59Castle Rock Chronicle, August 6, 1996, p B 9.
60Information Bette Saunders.
61Information Bette VanPelt.

Miller's Meat Market operated during 1920-1921 out of what was once the lobby of the Keystone Hotel. Currently it is The Castle Cafe at 403 Wilcox Street.

Buboltz-Bodle Collection.

320 Wilcox Street, home of Mr. Miller's Castle Rock Meat Market from 1921 until 1938, next to the famous B&B Cafe.

Robert and Helen Oliver Collection.

Ben Saunders in the Castle Rock Fuel and Feed Store, 1941.

Bette Saunders Collection.

413 Wilcox Street, location of the Castle Rock Fuel and Feed Store from 1928 to the early 1950's. It is now a modern office building owned by John Sieber.

Buboltz-Bodle Collection.

ELECTRICITY AND SEWER: NECESSITIES OF LIFE!

It seems almost impossible that the man who helped Castle Rock obtain an electrical system in the 1920's and a sewer system in the 1930's would be the same man who would help Castle Rock acquire a much-needed water supply fifty years later in the 1980's! However, as longtime friend and rancher, Bea Lowell, once commented, "When dealing with Phil Miller, nothing was impossible." His service to the community did, in fact, span well over 75 years, and continues to do so today—even after his death.

At the turn of the century in Castle Rock's history, there was no municipal electrical system. Residents bought kerosene and gasoline from a grocer for 20-25 cents per gallon to use in their lamps for lighting, and purchased wood and coal from a fuel and feed store for cooking and heating in their stoves and fireplaces.[1]

In 1902, the Board of Trustees boldly approved the installation of an acetylene gas plant.[2] It was located in the 200 block, between Perry and Wilcox Streets in the vicinity of what is now In and Out Shopping Center at 2nd and Wilcox.[3] Although there was one small, privately-owned system in Elizabeth, the Castle Rock Light, Heat and Power Company was reportedly the first municipal system to be installed in Colorado. It was financed entirely by local businessmen, who purchased stock in order to raise $2,500 to build the plant and nine blocks of mains.[4] Given the size of Castle Rock in the early 1900's this was considered a very progressive, if not risky, venture, and the Trustees, as well as the investors, were touted as innovative and brave.

Street lights were soon shining brightly on the eight corners of the downtown area, and J. E. Fetherolf became the first business owner to utilize the new service, impressively installing thirty jets in the Keystone Hotel, on the corner of Fourth and Wilcox Streets.[5] During the next year, gas fixtures were installed in many businesses and homes, and by the annual meeting in June of 1903 there were enough undivided profits to pay a dividend of 9%, which the stockholders prudently plowed back into the company.[6] Business continued to improve and this system successfully accommodated the community for the next twenty years. Bette Saunders remembered as a small child, around 1917, seeing those gas fixtures in her grandmother's home on the corner of Fifth and Wilcox Streets.[7] Mrs. Miller commented that their first Miller Meat

Market, located in the Keystone Hotel building in 1921, had acetylene gas lights.[8]

By the early 1920's the population of Castle Rock had grown and so had the need for electricity. However, Douglas County, overall, was still so sparsely populated that it was not a profitable venture for utility companies to install miles and miles of power lines for only a few homes.[9] Nevertheless, the demand for electricity had grown so strong that by June of 1920 a few business owners, such as those of the CourtHouse Cafe, started furnishing individual electric systems, known as an Alamo Lighting Plants, while other business owners threatened to follow suit.[10]

Newspaper articles show that over the next year the Trustees examined various possibilities for the establishment of an electrical system. They even secured bids for construction and arranged for the issuance of bonds for financing. The Record Journal succinctly summarized the collective opinion, "Castle Rock Wants Electricity! Let There Be Light!"[11]

By the time Mr. and Mrs. Miller moved to Castle Rock in August of 1921, the electricity issue was the topic of conversation. As a concerned business owner, Mr. Miller often attended Board meetings and, as a result, he was asked and then appointed to become a Trustee on the Board because, according to him, "That is how it was done in those days." His community involvement began at this point, and he often commented, "I joined everything when we moved to Castle Rock."[12]

In April, 1922, as public pressure increased, the Board of Trustees accepted a contract from E.I. DuPont De Nemours Company, a powder works plant located in Louviers, a small town about fifteen miles north of Castle Rock on Highway 85, to supply electric energy and power to the Town of Castle Rock.[13] In May, 1922, the Trustees authorized the installation of poles and lines between the two towns to begin in November, at a whopping cost of $5.00 per pole set in pasture land and $10.00 per pole set in cultivated land![14] Mr. Miller was always very proud of the fact that he was a Trustee on the original Board which implemented the DuPont electricity. However, this pride was somewhat overshadowed by the fact that he lost business because of his support for this issue. Ironically, when the electricity was finally established a strange twist of events transpired. Public acceptance was suddenly split!

While business owners were elated with this "new electricity", town and county residents did not share the same enthusiasm when they discovered the minimum charge was $1.50 per month, per house. Mr. Miller recollected that some of his customers were so angry that they came into the meat market and said, "Being as how you voted for the electricity, I'm going to pay my meat bill and not trade with you anymore."[15] Others complained that they had been "burning coal oil all their lives and they were going to continue to do so!" Mrs. Miller recalled that retired farmers and ranchers, living on fixed incomes, didn't know how they would pay this additional expense.[16] But human nature is nothing if not creative and Bette Saunders described how residents remedied the situation, "People learned to read their meters and when they were about to go over the number of kilowatts for the minimum $1.50 charge, they would stop using electricity and go back to their old lamps!"[17]

Six years later found Mr. Miller on the Board once again, after the death of Trustee, W. A. Shellabarger in March of 1928. Minutes show that he was nominated, voted on by the Board members and elected to fulfill the remaining term. His first meeting was April 4, 1928 at which time he was sworn into office.[18] It wasn't very long before the Board became involved in yet another electricity issue. Commonwealth Utilities Corporation of Limon, Colorado, applied for authorization to construct, operate and maintain an electric lighting and power plant in Castle Rock.[19] This system would eventually evolve in to the system in place today.

Town Board records show that over the next few months, as the Trustees examined this proposed system, Mr. Miller never once wavered in his support of Commonwealth Utilities. Recognizing the need Castle Rock had for a municipal system of its own, he repeatedly voted in favor of it despite the fact that in doing so he was taking money out of his own pocket—because by now he owned the Castle Rock Fuel and Feed Store and this electricity would inevitably be in direct competition with his own coal and fuel business.[20] His altruism was truly being put to the test. Was he willing, once again, to make personal sacrifice for the sake of public service? The answer was yes. It was always yes! He knew there was no way to stop progress, and in this particular situation, electricity was the utility of the future; coal and oil would eventually be utilities of the past. His philosophy was, "You have to move forward. You can't stand still." Generally speaking, he followed his own advice.

Unlike the controversy generated by the "new electricity" in 1922, the Commonwealth system was more enthusiastically accepted by business owners and residents alike, and in a special election on August 7, 1928, they officially voted their approval. Board members were pleased at this unexpected outcome, because although six years had mellowed most of the opponents, there were still some people who had remained openly opposed to the DuPont system and had not yet connected their homes to electricity. On October 3, the Town Board "Assigned to Commonwealth Utilities of Limon, all the existing contracts between E. I. DuPont de Nemours Company of Louviers and the Town of Castle Rock."[21]

Commercial and residential fees were established at that time. It is interesting to note that the minimum charge for lighting was still only $1.50 per month, per house. The rate schedule, for modern minds to ponder, was as follows:[22]

The rates for Commercial and Residential Lighting in kilowatt hours:

The first 40 KWH used per month, per KWH	13 cents
The next 60 KWH used per month, per KWH	12 cents
The next 100 KWH used per month, per KWH	11 cents
The next 100 KWH used per month, per KWH	10 cents
For all over 300 KWH used per month, per KWH	09 cents

Net minimum charge per month, under this schedule, $1.50

For sixteen years Commonwealth Utilities remained the major supplier of electric power in Castle Rock and surrounding parts of Douglas County, eventually serving 320 homes and businesses over forty miles of line. In 1944, the Intermountain Rural Electric Association (IREA) purchased Commonwealth Utilities and acquired the Douglas County operation. From then until the present, IREA has continued to supply electric power to the area. In 1980, Douglas County became a headquarters for IREA when a new building was constructed in Sedalia.[23]

Mr. Miller continued to be active on the Board during the remainder of 1928 and, according to Board Records, was reelected in April of 1929, serving on such committees as Police, Water, General and Ordinance. In April of 1930 he was reelected to a two year term,[24] and the Board became involved in yet another controversial utility issue. This time—a sewer system!

During the early 1930's, very few homes or businesses in Castle Rock had indoor plumbing. The ones that did were hooked up to a rather crude type of deep-well septic system. Most homes still had outhouses. The town hired a man to come around once a week to clean the septic systems and outhouses with what came to be known as the Honey-Dipper or the Honey-Pot.[25] Mr. Miller's opinion of this outdated system was well known. He used to say, "You might enjoy seeing that Honey-Dipper cleaning out septic systems, but I sure don't!"[26]

In August of 1930, members of the Board, wanting to modernize and sanitize the Town of Castle Rock, had authorized Town Engineer, Mr. A. A. Weiland of Weiland Engineering, to survey the area and to prepare maps and specifications for the possible construction of a sewer system.[27] In June of 1931 the Board authorized Weiland to finalize the plans.[28] On July 1, 1931, the Board introduced a preliminary order for the establishment of Castle Rock Sanitary Sewer District #1 and the construction of a sanitation system. The estimated cost of $28,406.90 was to be financed by bonds issued to the Town of Castle Rock, to be repaid by a newly assessed sewer tax of $.011 per square foot on each property within the new district.[29] Needless to say, Mr. Miller voted in favor of every aspect of this project!

Once again, public sentiment was mixed. While business owners accepted the idea very quickly, town residents, on the other hand, remained skeptical. According to Bette Saunders it wasn't so much that people were opposed to the sewer system; it was that no one had much money because of the Depression.[30] Prevailing attitudes always reflected the prevailing economic conditions. However, the Trustees would not be thwarted, and on September 9, 1931, they passed and adopted Ordinance Number 102-1931 establishing Sanitary Sewer District #1 of the Town of Castle Rock.[31] On October 14, 1931 they awarded a contract to build a sanitation system to the J. S. Schwartz Construction Company of Colorado Springs with a bid of $21,402.00.[32] Construction began immediately and residents soon watched as sewer pipes, mains and man holes appeared throughout town. At the November Board meeting, a representative from Schwartz announced that twenty-one men from the Castle Rock and Douglas County area were being employed and the project was right on schedule.[33] Mr. Miller was getting his wish! The days of the Honey-Dipper were numbered!

In April of 1932, in conjunction with the construction of the sewer system, the Trustees also approved the alignment, design and grades of streets, curbs, gutters, and sidewalks within Castle Rock. Mr. Miller was absent at that particular meeting and did not vote.[34]

By early summer of 1932 the sewer system was completed and on June 21, the final settlement was made with Schwartz. The total amount, including incidentals, cost of collection and interest, had come to $28,431.60, just a few dollars more than the original estimate.[35] Each property owner was notified and given thirty days to pay the assessed tax. If a property owner was unable to pay in one lump sum, which many could not do, a twenty month installment plan was arranged. Examples of the assessed amount, again, for the modern mind to ponder, were as follows:[36]

Assessed Sewer Tax, Sanitary Sewer District # 1:
Property 50 feet by 140 feet assessed tax $77.00
Property 25 feet by 140 feet assessed tax $38.50
Property 25 feet by 130 feet assessed tax $35.75
Property 25 feet by 125 feet assessed tax $34.38

By the time the sewer system was completed, Mr. Miller was no longer on the Board. His term of office had expired in April, and his final meeting had been on May 4, 1932,[37] one month prior to the actual completion of the sewer system. Although he was totally committed to the Town of Castle Rock and serving the community was to become his hallmark, he discovered politics was not for him. After years on the Board, at the same old wages—plenty of cussing and little credit—he chose not to run for another term. It is likely that had he chosen to do so, he could have been reelected to the Board, not only then but at any time in the future. He had been in Castle Rock eleven years and, despite the fact that he had been involved in controversial issues, his courage and community spirit earned him respect from Board members and townspeople and he was very well liked within the community. He had gained a reputation as a modern thinker, one who was not afraid to stand up for what he believed to be the best decision for the town.

However, the sewer issue, similar to the electricity issues, had not been without ramifications. As if history were repeating itself, he had lost business once again because of his support of yet another controversial town issue. Those were lean years and whether it was in the meat market or in the fuel and feed store, a loss of too much business could prove disastrous. He often commented that people's meat bills ran from two dollars to three dollars a month adding, "that was a lot of money."[38] Furthermore, Mr. Miller was the type of man who hated to lose even one customer because Castle Rock was small and every customer was a friend. He hated to offend his friends.

But in both the electricity and sewer issues, Mr. Miller believed that what the Trustees were doing was crucial to the future of Castle Rock. He knew that the efficiency of electricity far outweighed the dirt and dangers of coal and that a sewer system was absolutely necessary to curb the spread of disease. Therefore, he accepted his professional losses with his head held high, but he ultimately arrived at the decision that there were more positive ways to serve the community than in the political arena. He never regretted his terms as a Trustee, though, and, in a 1980 interview, he commented, "I think we accomplished a lot. We got electricity into the town and a sewer."[39]

More importantly, during his early years on the Board, Mr. Miller became acquainted with two ranchers who would impact his life through the coming decades. These men were Louis Higby, Sr. and Josef Winkler. The following chapter gives an account of their ranches and of the relationships that developed between these three men.

EPILOGUE TO SEWER SECTION

In 1936 the Record Journal announced that a WPA project in conjunction with the Colorado Department of Health would be put into effect in Castle Rock. More Sanitary Sewer Districts were established and additional Sanitation Taxes were assessed.[40] Bette Saunders recalled that shortly after that, sewer lines were installed in the alleys in blocks where previously there had been none.

On a personal note, she also remembered in the early part of 1939, her father connected her grandmother's house on the corner of Fifth and Wilcox Streets to the sewer system. Despite the fact that he hooked up the water, installed the bathroom and did most of the work himself, it still cost $500 which was quite an expense during post-Depression days! Years later, Bette discovered a sewer tax receipt for $50.00 dated in 1945, reflecting his final payment.[41]

In late August of 1939, the Board of Trustees placed a notice to property owners in the Record Journal announcing that, "All premises within the Castle Rock Sewer District must be connected by Nov. 1, 1939," and that owners failing to do so "will receive notice as required by law."[42] This requirement was not just some random request created by the Board but rather was sort of an 11th hour mandate made, for the safety of the public, under recommendation of the Colorado State Board of Health.[43] This illustrates the resistance people still felt toward the sewer systems, probably due to the terrible expense incurred in hooking up at that time in Castle Rock history.

ENDNOTES

[1]Castle Rock Journal, January 24, 1902, p 1; letter from Bette Saunders, May 21, 1996; and interview between Bette Saunders and the author, June 12, 1996.

[2]Our Heritage: The People of Douglas County, Anne Moore, p 354.

[3]Sanborn Maps, located by Bette Saunders at the Local History Collection, Douglas Public Library District, Castle Rock, CO. Reported to author in a letter May 20, 1996; additional conversation between Bette Saunders and the author June 11, 1998.

[4]Castle Rock Journal, January 21, 1902, p 1 and June 13, 1902, p 1.

[5]Castle Rock Journal, June 13, 1902, p 1.

[6]Castle Rock Journal, June 10, 1903.

[7]Letter from Bette Saunders, May 21, 1996.

[8]Conversation between Mrs. Jerry Miller and the author at Powder Box Beauty Salon, October 1975.

[9]Douglas County News Press, Pioneer Editions, February 27, 1988, p 5a and February 27, 1993, p 12a.

[10]Castle Rock Record Journal, June 11, 1920.

[11]Castle Rock Record Journal, November 4, 1921 and November 18, 1921.

[12]Douglas County News Press, August 30, 1979, p 9 and August 12, 1980, p 2.

[13]Record of Proceedings Board of Trustees, Town of Castle Rock, April 3 and 19, 1922.

[14]Town of Castle Rock Ordinance Number 93-94-1922, May 4, 1922; Record of Proceedings Board of Trustees, Town of Castle Rock, November 9, 1922.

[15]Douglas County News Press, August 30, 1979, p 9.

[16]Douglas County News Press, August 12, 1980, p 2 and August 30, 1979, p 9.

[17]Letter from Bette Saunders, May 20, 1996.

[18]Record of Proceedings Board of Trustees, Town of Castle Rock, March 7, 1928 and April 4,1928.

[19]Town of Castle Rock Ordinance Number 100-1928, August 1, 1928, adopted October 3, 1928.

[20]Record of Proceedings Board of Trustees, Town of Castle Rock, August 1, September 5, and October 3, 1928.

[21]Record of Proceedings Board of Trustees, Town of Castle Rock, August 1, September 5, and October 3, 1928.

[22]Town of Castle Rock Ordinance Number 100-1928, Section 4, August 1, 1928.

[23]Douglas County News Press, Pioneer Editions, February 27, 1988, p 5a and February 27,1993, p 12a; Intermountain Rural Electric Association Consumer Handbook, May 1997, p 2, courtesy of Richard W. Stith, Sedalia, CO.

[24]Record of Proceedings Board of Trustees, Town of Castle Rock, April 5, 1929 and April 5, 1930.

[25]Record of Proceedings Board of Trustees, Town of Castle Rock, March 7, 1928, April 29, 1929 and February 5, 1930.

[26]Douglas County News Press, August 30, 1979, p 9 and August 12, 1980, p 2.

[27]Record of Proceedings Board of Trustees, Town of Castle Rock, August 7, 1930.

[28]Record of Proceedings Board of Trustees, Town of Castle Rock, June 3, 1931.

[29]Record of Proceedings Board of Trustees, Town of Castle Rock, July 1, 1931.

[30]Letter from Bette Saunders, May 21, 1996.

[31]Record of Proceedings Board of Trustees, Town of Castle Rock, September 9, 1931; and Town of Castle Rock Ordinance Number 102-1931, September 9, 1931.

[32]Record of Proceedings Board of Trustees, Town of Castle Rock, October 14, 1931.

[33]Record of Proceedings Board of Trustees, Town of Castle Rock, November 4, 1931.

[34]Record of Proceedings Board of Trustees, Town of Castle Rock, April 12, 1932; Town of Castle Rock Ordinance Number 102, April 12, 1932; and Castle Rock Record Journal, April 15, 1932.

[35]Record of Proceedings Board of Trustees, Town of Castle Rock, June 1, 1932.

[36]Final Assessment Ordinance Number 106-1932, Castle Rock Sanitary Sewer District Number 1, July 8, 1932, p 1-6.

[37]Record of Proceedings Board of Trustees, Town of Castle Rock, May 4, 1932.

[38]Douglas County News Press, August 12, 1980, p 2.

[39]IBID.

[40]Castle Rock Record Journal, February 7, 1936.

[41]Interview between Bette Saunders and the author, Castle Rock, CO, August 1, 1996.

[42]Castle Rock Record Journal, August 25, 1939, p 5.

[43]IBID.

The Higby Store in Greenland built in 1906.

Louis R. "Dick" Higby, Jr. Collection.

Greenland Ranch in the 1950's.

Louis R. "Dick" Higby, Jr. Collection.

Louis, Sr. and Jennie Higby's home on Greenland Ranch, 1973.

Louis R. "Dick" Higby, Jr. Collection.

MR. HIGBY, MR. WINKLER, AND MR. MILLER

LOUIS R. HIGBY, SR. AND THE GREENLAND RANCH AND CATTLE COMPANY

When the name Higby comes to mind it is synonymous with Greenland, Colorado, where the family was recognized over the years for their successful ranch known as the Greenland Land and Cattle Company. This beautiful land was once described as nearly 17.5 square miles of plains, rolling hills, forests, lakes and mountains, a truly magnificent domain.[1] However, it is interesting to note that the Higbys were not always ranchers.

Louis Richard Higby, Sr. was born January 6, 1880 in Garden Grove, Iowa. He was the second of six children, the oldest of the four sons.[2] His parents, John William and Emily Marie, moved the family to Colorado from Iowa in 1888 settling on a homestead north east of Colorado Springs, near Peyton, in El Paso County.[3] Marie organized a school there, becoming the first secretary of the school board.[4] John went into partnership with the Russell Gates Mercantile Company, which was one of the first "chain store" operations in Colorado. Around 1892 or 1893 they moved to nearby Eastonville, where John operated a Russell Gates Mercantile Store.[5]

In writing about his father in Our Heritage: The People of Douglas County, Dick Higby recalled that two of Lou's favorite stories were about living in a tent on the homestead for the first year in Colorado and serving as a janitor at the Eastonville School[6] which he also attended. In 1899 Lou enrolled in Barnes Business College in Denver.[7]

By 1900, John William Higby decided to open his own business and moved the family to Monument, where they established Higby Mercantile Company and in 1906 a second store was established in Greenland.[8] The boys, Lou, Carl, John and William, helped their father run these stores. While William managed the Monument store, Lou did most of the managing of the Greenland store and also served as Postmaster of Greenland Post Office which was located at the back of the store.[9] Both stores remained family owned and operated for many years, even after the Higbys purchased their ranch. The Greenland store was sold in 1923.[10] The Monument store was sold around 1970.[11]

On December 4, 1907, Louis Higby, Sr. and Jennie Elizabeth Lake, from Clinton, Iowa, were married in Colorado Springs, Colorado. In 1909, when Lou was 29, the Higby family purchased the Greenland Ranch.[12] In writing about the history of the ranch, Dick Higby explained that it had been homesteaded between 1870 and 1875 and was established by Mr. Charles Kountz and Mr. Sheety of Colorado National Bank in Denver in 1880. The chain of ownership then went from Kountz and Sheety to the McMurtrie Land and Cattle Company to the Pollack Family and then to the Higby Family. The ranch consisted of 18,000 acres when they purchased it. In the beginning they raised Gallaway cattle, then Shorthorns and then Herefords.[13]

The business operation of the ranch became known as the Greenland Land and Cattle Company and remained under the ownership and management of the Higby family for nearly 70 years, developing a reputation as one of the most respected and well known cattle operations in the state of Colorado. After the death of John William Higby in 1916, Lou, along with his brothers, Carl, John, and William, continued the operation of the ranch.[14] In the 1920's Lou and Jennie had two sons: Louis Richard, Jr., known as Dick, and Charles Sebastian, known as Chuck.[15]

Lou, Sr. kept an active hand in the running of the ranch for many years.[16] By the time he passed away in December, 1966, it was largely being operated by his sons, Dick and Chuck and other family members who continued to run it for twelve more years. The Higby family sold the Greenland Land and Cattle Company in 1978.[17]

Lou Higby, Sr. met Phil Miller, Jr. when he was a customer at the Miller Market in Castle Rock during the early 1920's.[18] With their similar Midwestern backgrounds, coupled with their common interests, they discussed cattle ranching and business ownership and reminisced about the early years in their neighboring home states of Iowa and Illinois. They developed a fast friendship that would last a lifetime. Lou Higby was very active in the Masons as a member of Douglas Lodge No. 153 A.F. & A.M. in Castle Rock.[19] Shortly after becoming friends, he encouraged Mr. Miller to join. In March, 1924, Phil officially became a Mason and remained affiliated with Douglas Lodge No. 153 for the rest of his life.[20]

Years later they would work together and share in another common bond—banking. Lou Higby, Josef Winkler and Phil Miller would work tirelessly yet unsuccessfully, to reorganize a bank in the mid-1930's and again, successfully, to open one in the late 1930's.

Lou Higby would purchase the largest block of stock, and he would be the first President when The Bank of Douglas County opened in 1939. Josef Winkler would also purchase a large block of stock and become a Director.[21]

JOSEF WINKLER
GE RANCH-WINKLER CATTLE COMPANY

A successful Shorthorn cattle breeder and rancher, Josef Winkler had been born in Austria on August 8, 1888. He came to the United States in 1907 at the age of nineteen and moved directly to Douglas County to work on the GE Ranch, which was located about ten miles southeast of Castle Rock in the Lake Gulch/Castlewood Canyon area.[22] Originally homesteaded by the Honorable George Engle in 1860, this ranch had an interesting history.[23]

During the Indian War of 1864, when the Indians were roaming and raiding in the canyon, there had been a massacre on this property. George Engle, Lawrence Welty, Caspar Courts and Conrad Moschel were rounding up the GE Ranch's herd of Shorthorns when they were chased and attacked by thirty Indians. Mr. Engle and Mr. Courts escaped. Mr. Welty's life was spared, when his horse was shot and fell on him, allowing enough cover for him to crawl into the bushes, where he hid until he was able to make his way to safety. Conrad Moschel, however, was killed.[24]

When his body was discovered, he had a bullet in his head and a poisoned arrow in his back. He had been scalped in the Cheyenne tradition, with a two inch strip of skin removed from his forehead to the nape of his neck. He was buried there, in a grove of oak bushes, reportedly the first grave in Douglas County.[25] Forty years later, Conrad Moschel's nephew came to the canyon and recorded the incident for history by inscribing his uncle's name and date of death on a large rock above the grave.[26]

The event left an eerie mystique surrounding this beautiful canyon where history was made. One can visualize Indians perched high atop cliffs while settlers hid in caves. School children still come on field trips to the Winkler Ranch to see the place the man was chased and killed by Indians.[27]

After the death of his first wife, George Engle married Louisa Roracher who had come to this country from Austria and was Josef Winkler's aunt. When George Engle died, Louisa inherited the ranch. By the time Josef came to Douglas County, Louisa had married Charles Breuss and they were operating the ranch and raising the GE brand cattle.[28]

It seems that the Winkler family's destiny was on the GE Ranch. It wasn't long before Josef's three brothers, Florian, John and Norbert, immigrated from Austria to work with him. In 1919, Josef purchased the ranch from his aunt and uncle and changed the name to the Winkler Cattle Company. Josef Winkler also met his wife, Rose Paoli, at the GE Ranch. Born in Russell Gulch near Central City, she was a housekeeper for Louisa Breuss when he met her. They were married in 1921, and had seven children, George, Carl, Joe, Helen, Joan, Frances, and Rose, all of whom were actively involved in the ranch from an early age. Josef remained President of the corporation for over fifty years, and it is still family owned and operated today.[29]

As a closely knit family, loyalties were demonstrated when Norbert's wife died in childbirth, leaving three children, Bertha, Alfreda and Johnny. Josef and Rose raised those children right along with their own. Norbert left the ranch to homestead in Durango, Colorado where another relative lived. Josef's brother, John, settled in the Pacific Northwest.[30]

Philip Miller and Josef Winkler had met in the early '20's shortly after Mr. Miller moved to Castle Rock. Mr. Winkler had a very noticeable Austrian accent and would call Mr. Miller "Pheel."[31] With similar backgrounds in ranching, the two men became close friends. Frances Cannon told me she knew her father always thought of Mr. Miller as his best friend. The families would socialize, with the Millers often visiting at the Winkler Ranch.[32] Mrs. Miller once told me she enjoyed the Winkler children so much, she felt as if they were partly her own.[33]

Joe Winkler recollected his first meeting with Mr. and Mrs. Miller one summer day when they arrived at the family ranch on their beautiful horses. "Mrs. Miller remarked that our spring water was delicious because they had been drinking from local creeks and everything tasted like mud!"[34] Several years later, when the Millers decided to sell their horses, they prevailed on Joe's father, Josef, to buy them. Riggety Ann and Nikki became two of the ranch's most valuable stock horses.[35]

During the 1936 Denver Stock Show, Carl Winkler, Phil Miller, and Josef Winkler made headlines in the local papers!

The first headline was entitled, "Carl Winkler Wins Blue Ribbon for His 4-H Club Steer." Indeed, young Carl, who was not quite nine years old, won first place in the Medium Weight Shorthorn 4-H Class with his 950 pound yearling steer named Premier. Additionally, he won third place in the Open Class.[36] This event resulted in headlines for Mr. Miller, when he purchased the prize winning steer, had it butchered by Armour and brought the meat back to Castle Rock for a special Saturday sale in his meat market. In an article entitled, "Douglas County People Will Eat Prize Beef," the local paper proudly reported, "This was the first time that a Douglas County meat dealer had purchased a prize winning critter from the stock show for the local trade." The article invited residents to, "Give your palate a treat and your teeth a rest" by purchasing some of this prize winning meat.[37] The article referring to Josef did not have to do with Carl's prize winning steer, as had the first two articles. Instead, it reported on Josef's own prize winning Shorthorn steers and was entitled, "Edsel Ford Buys a Carload of Winkler Cattle."[38] The obvious question: What did Shorthorn cattle from Douglas County have to do with Ford cars in Detroit?

The Ford Motor Company used a large amount of soy beans in the manufacturing of various parts of automobiles, approximately a half a barrel per car. After the beans were harvested and threshed, there still remained a great deal of good, usable feed known as bean straw. Instead of wasting the excess, Edsel Ford would buy feeder calves to eat it, thus putting him in the cattle business, in a manner of speaking. Reportedly, by utilizing the by-product, Ford kept the expense of automobiles down at the lowest possible level.[39] Therefore, if you or a member of your family bought a Ford at a reasonable price in the mid-1930's, you more than likely had Josef Winkler, and his steers, to thank for it! Seems as if maybe Ford should have named one of his cars a Shorthorn or a Winkler in honor of that fact!

It bears repeating that in the late '30's when Mr. Miller was attempting to raise money to open The Bank of Douglas County, Josef Winkler was one of the first to make a commitment and buy a large block of stock. When the Bank finally opened in 1939, he became a Director and remained as such until 1944.[40]

Helen Longworth recalled how during World War II, all the boys were in the service and it was hard to get help on the ranch. George and Carl were in the Navy and Joe was in college at Ft. Collins and then enlisted. Consequently, the girls did much of the work. They would feed the cattle in the morning before going to school, and while they were gone their father would load the hay rack with bales and when they returned in the afternoon after school, they would haul hay again. She remembered they would work all weekend doing ranch chores, often herding cattle on horseback during blizzards. Helen joked that it was a privilege to go back to school on

Mondays! Frances and Helen also did the showing of cattle in the ring at the National Western Stock Show for about three years during the war.[41]

In 1947, Josef Winkler was chosen as Man of the Year in Livestock by the prestigious, pioneer publication, "The Record Stockman." It reported that when many people did not believe Shorthorns would ever come back and meet Angus or Hereford competitions, Josef Winkler proved them wrong. His Shorthorns met and topped the competition. He had reestablished credibility to a dying breed of cattle, an endangered species, so to speak, whose breeders were hanging on only because of a "loyal going down with the ship attitude." He was credited with giving new life to the breed, making Shorthorn owners proud, which resulted in a sensational rejuvenation of the breed.[42]

In addition, The Record Stockman wrote, "He almost single handedly created a new Shorthorn beef type. From a penniless immigrant he has made phenomenal success in the shorthorn cattle world showing his feeder calves and yearlings to top places in major livestock shows the past twenty-two years."[43] This pleased Mr. Miller tremendously because he knew the hard work and dedication Josef Winkler had spent on behalf of the Shorthorn breed.

After his wife, Rose, died in 1950,[44] he continued to run his ranch. In addition to his work at the local level in the Colorado Cattleman's Association and as a Director of the National Western Stock Show,[45] he was a member of the American Shorthorn Association, and served on the Board of Directors from 1961 until 1966, holding the office of Vice President in 1964 and 1965, and the office of President in 1966.[46] He was highly respected nationwide, for his exceptional Shorthorn cattle and his knowledge and expertise of the breed.

At the Grand Opening of The Bank of Douglas County after the expansion in 1971, Josef Winkler was honored as one of the original Stockholders and Directors.[47] When Josef Winkler died in May 26, of 1973,[48] Mr. Miller lost his dearest and closest friend, one with whom he had shared many good times, struggles, and successes. The family lost a wonderful and loving father and grandfather. The county lost a respected pioneer, a brave and courageous rancher, who, like Mr. Miller, lived a rags to riches story and left behind a legacy for his family and friends.

Strong friendships and lasting respect developed between the Winkler sons and daughters and Mr. and Mrs. Miller. Carl Winkler, who was a Douglas County Commissioner for many years, often referred to Mr. Miller as "a second father."[49] Frances and Helen became loyal employees of The Bank of Douglas County. Frances worked there for twenty-seven years, retiring in May of 1982. Similarly, Helen worked there for fourteen years, retiring in February of 1996. Joe, often traveled with the Millers on trips or to cattle shows.[50]

In summing up the relationship between the Millers and the Winklers, Frances Cannon commented, "They were very good friends of our family and were always there, for all of us."[51] Echoing her sentiments, Joe remarked, "They were lifelong mentors and dearest friends. I still miss those good old days when they rode into the ranch and changed my life and rewarded me to know and enjoy such beautiful people."[52]

Joe Winkler continues to run the Winkler Cattle Company along with his brothers-in-law, Bob Longworth and Bob Cannon. Carl Winkler passed away in January of 1989.[53] The next generation has become actively involved, working on the ranch, specifically Josef's great-grandsons, Joey and Jamie, the sons of his granddaughter, Karen Longworth Riesselman. Dr. Phil Riesselman is very active in 4-H and is a Director of the Douglas County Fair Board. The brand on the Winkler Shorthorn cattle still remains GE.

EPILOGUE TO HIGBYS AND WINKLERS

Although I went to school with all the Higbys, I knew the fathers, Chuck and Dick Higby, the best because of their work in Masons when I was in Rainbow Girls. It is a small world and Dick now lives across the street from my cousin's in-laws, Dr. and Mrs. John Buglewicz, in Florence, Colorado! I owe both Chuck and Dick a debt of gratitude for their assistance and information during the writing of this book. Chuck spent an afternoon with my father, answering my many questions. Additionally, Dick allowed me to use his photos, he wrote me many letters, and we had many phone conversations! He also helped in editing the Higby section of this chapter.

The Winkler family, on the other hand, has been a large part of my life for many years. I went to school with Phil and Karen. Phil always made me laugh and Karen was one of my closest friends. I spent many evenings at the Longworth home where her brother, Bobby, taught me to play pool! It would not be unusual to find us making banana splits or tuna fish and sardine sandwiches with her sister, Kendall, at midnight in Helen Longworth's kitchen. Actually, Helen would help us make these great concoctions and I know she

Mr. Josef Winkler, one of the first Directors from 1939-1944 and stockholders of the Bank of Douglas County.

Douglas County News, May 18, 1972, used with permission.

had as much fun as we did! Fran Cannon would take Karen and me shopping in Cherry Creek Shopping Center where we loved to try on hats! My father once gave Karen some age-old wisdom regarding men and I am sure she still remembers it!

This chapter could never have been completed without the help, encouragement, information and memories of Helen Longworth, Fran Cannon, and Joe Winkler. The Millers and the Winklers shared a loyalty and devotion to each other that went deeper than even friendship. They were integral parts of each others lives and this chapter is an important part of this book.

In the backyard of their Elbert Street house, Millers with the beautiful horses which Josef Winkler bought and named Nicky and Riggety Ann. Their blankets and saddles are still at the Winkler Ranch.

horses left to right: Nicky, Riggety Ann.

Robert and Helen Oliver Collection.

ENDNOTES CHAPTER 7

[1]Josephine Marr, Douglas County, A Historical Journey, p 191.

[2]Interview between Chuck Higby and Willis Buboltz, Castle Rock, CO, September 17, 1996.

[3]Our Heritage: The People of Douglas County, Higby Section, written by Dick Higby, p 118; interview between Dick Higby, and the author, Florence, CO, May 22, 1997; the actual location of the Higby Homestead was east on Highway 24 to County Road Ellicott and then in about 100 feet.

[4]Leroy Hafen, Colorado and Its People, Volume 3, p 24.

[5]Obituary, Louis R. Higby, Sr., Douglas County News, December 29, 1966; Our Heritage: The People of Douglas County, Higby Section, Written by Dick Higby, p 118.

[6]IBID, p 119.

[7]IBID, p 119.

[8]Interview between Chuck Higby and Willis Buboltz, September 17, 1996.

[9]Our Heritage: The People of Douglas County, Higby Section, written by Dick Higby, p 119.

[10]Interview between Chuck Higby and Willis Buboltz, September 17, 1996.

[11]William Higby went into politics, eventually becoming the Lieutenant Governor of Colorado. According to a letter I received from Dick Higby in May of 1997, a man by the name of Walter Van Fleet ran the Monument store during William's years in politics. William later turned over the management to his son, David, who sold it in the 1970's.

[12]Interview between Chuck Higby and Willis Buboltz, September 17, 1996.

[13]Our Heritage: The People of Douglas County, Higby Section, written by Dick Higby, p 119; and interview between Dick Higby and the author, May 22, 1997.

[14]IBID, p 119.

[15]Interview between Dick Higby and the author, May 22, 1997.

[16]Our Heritage: The People of Douglas County, Higby Section, written by Dick Higby, p 119.

[17]Interview between Chuck Higby and Willis Buboltz, September 17, 1996.

[18]IBID.

[19]Our Heritage: The People of Douglas County, Higby Section, written by Dick Higby, p 119; A.F. means Ancient Free and A.M. means Accepted Masons.

[20]Information letter from Shriner's Hospital to James Nelsen, Trust Attorney for Mr. Miller, October 4, 1996.

[21]The Bank of Douglas County Records, The Articles of Incorporation, Article V, August 1939; and Castle Rock Record Journal, August 25, 1939, p 1.

[22]Interview between Helen Longworth and the author, Castle Rock, CO, January 27, 1997; and interview between Frances Cannon and the author, Castle Rock, CO, April 14, 1998.

[23]Our Heritage: The People of Douglas County, Josef Winkler, written by Joe Winkler, p 314.

[24]Interview between Helen Longworth and the author, January 27, 1997; Douglas County News Press, September 11, 1996, "Time Traveler," by Ruth Miller, p 9 b.

[25]Castle Rock Journal, July 8, 1876, p 1, as recorded by Anne Moore in Our Heritage: The People of Douglas County, p 338.

[26]Interview between Helen Longworth and the author, January 27, 1997.

[27]Interview between Helen Longworth and the author, January 27, 1997; interview between Frances Cannon and the author, April 14, 1998; and Ruth Miller, "Time Traveler," Douglas County News Press, September 11, 1996, p 9 b.

[28]Our Heritage: The People of Douglas County, Josef Winkler, written by Joe Winkler, p 314.

[29]Interview between Helen Longworth and the author January 27, 1997; interview between Frances Cannon, April 14, 1998; Our Heritage: The People of Douglas County, Josef Winkler, written by Joe Winkler, p 314.

[30]IBID interviews between Helen Longworth, Frances Cannon, and the author.

[31]Conversation between Mr. Miller and the author Cherry Creek Care Center, Aurora, CO, August, 1991; and Douglas County News Press, August 30, 1979, p 3.

[32]Interview between Frances Cannon and the author, April 14, 1998.

[33]Conversation between Mrs. Miller and the author at Powder Box Beauty Salon, Castle Rock, CO.

[34]Letter from Joe Winkler, Castle Rock, CO, June 13, 1998.

[35]IBID.

[36]Castle Rock Record Journal, January 31, 1936, p 1.

[37]Castle Rock Record Journal, January 24, 1936, p 1.

[38]Castle Rock Record Journal, January 31, 1936, p 1.

[39]IBID.

[40]Castle Rock Record Journal, August 25, 1939, p 1; and Douglas County News, May 18, 1972.

[41]IBID interviews Helen Longworth and Frances Cannon; also The Record Stockman, 1947 Annual Edition, January 10, 1947, "Josef Winkler is Man of the Year in Livestock," article on file at the Local History Collection, Douglas Public Library District, Castle Rock, CO.

[42]The Record Stockman, 1947 Annual Edition, January 10, 1947, "Josef Winkler is Man of the Year in Livestock," article on file at the Local History Collection, Douglas Public Library District, Castle Rock, CO.

[43]IBID.

[44]Interview between Helen Longworth and the author, January 27, 1997.

[45]Our Heritage: The People of Douglas County, Josef Winkler, written by Joe Winkler, p 314.

[46]Information Dr. R.E. Hunsley, American Shorthorn Association, Omaha, Nebraska, March 27, 1997.

[47]Douglas County News, May 18, 1972.

[48]Obituary and Rosary Announcement, Josef Winkler, Douglas County News, May 31, 1973.

[49]Carl Winkler as quoted in the Douglas County News Press, August 12, 1980, p 2.

[50]Interview between Helen Longworth and the author, January 27, 1997; Interview between Frances Cannon and the author, April 14, 1998.

[51]IBID Frances Cannon, April 14, 1998.

[52]Letter from Joe Winkler, June 13, 1998.

[53]Interview between Helen Longworth and the author, July 6, 1998; Douglas County News Press, February 7, 1989; Carl Winkler headstone photo, Spring Valley Cemetery Photograph Album compiled by The Douglas County Historic Preservation Board, on file at the Local History Collection, Douglas Public Library District, Castle Rock, CO.

EARLY BANKING HISTORY IN CASTLE ROCK 1888-1932

"Do you have collateral?"

"No Sir! I ain't never been sick a day in my life!"

Fonzie to the Banker from an episode of "Happy Days."

In order to fully understand the impact Mr. Miller would have on the banking industry in Castle Rock and Douglas County, I believe it is necessary to look back at the history of banking in the area during previous years. The first banking establishment in Castle Rock was the C. H. Ellis Banking Company, which originated in 1888[1] when the population was around 315.[2] This small financial institution was not chartered and could be operated on a one man basis by Charles H. Ellis, who was also the President. It is not known where this bank was located.

In the early 1890's, an attempt was made to organize a National Bank in Castle Rock.[3] Although a formal committee was appointed to raise money and enlist stockholders, this venture never materialized past the planning stages. It is very likely that the necessary amount of capital stock could not be raised at this particular time in history for a community with such a small population.

On January 6, 1902, the institution which has been historically considered the first actual "bank" in Castle Rock opened for business, with an authorized capital of $30,000 and a paid up capital of $15,000. Chartered under Colorado law as The Douglas County Bank, it was housed in the front section of The Castle Rock Journal Building, which was located on the southeast corner of Fourth and Wilcox Streets.[4] As has been previously mentioned, this building was the first courthouse in Castle Rock, the Cantril Courthouse, but had been utilized for businesses since the completion of the new stone courthouse in 1890. Twenty years later, after it was remodeled and relocated, it became the first "home" of Phil and Jerry Miller when they moved to Castle Rock.[5]

Oddly enough, the principal stockholders of this bank were two men from Minnesota: Mr. B. B. Sheffield, the President and Mr. E. P. Brown, the Cashier. Reportedly both bankers of wealth and prominence, they had supplied the major part of the required capital to start this bank. Mr. Sheffield was President of Citizens Bank and half owner of Sheffield Milling Company, both in Faribault,

Minnesota. Mr. Brown had been the Cashier of the same bank in Faribault and also one in Alexander, South Dakota, before he was forced to move to Colorado for health reasons.[6]

While Mr. Sheffield remained in Minnesota, Mr. Brown operated the bank in Castle Rock with the help of three local men: Upton Treat Smith, the Vice President; Charles H. Ellis and Benjamin Quick, the Directors. Other local stockholders were Wallace Holcomb, G. W. Spitzer, Charles Woodhouse, Dr. J. B. Sandford, John Hillburger, Hugh Taylor, Julius Seidensticker, W. J. Thompson, W. B. Chamberlain, W. R. Kendall, Robert E. Palm, A. G. Webster, C. A. Woodhouse, Ulrich Sturdevant, Edward Hoffman, Frank D. Ball, Pleasant W. O'Brien, Charles Breuss, R. S. Alford and Chris Schneider.[7]

A few days prior to the opening of the bank, the new 4,000 pound, time-lock safe had arrived in Castle Rock, amid great chaos! While being unloaded from a Rio Grande freight car into a horse drawn wagon, the safe came down unevenly, tipping the bed of the wagon upward. This frightened the horses to the point that they ran away, pulling the wagon behind them. The safe then toppled to the ground, catching Mr. Ulrich Sturdevant, who was in charge of the team, on the toes. In the meantime, the wagon broke loose and crashed into a hitching post and a fence. The horses continued to run wildly around town, until they were finally caught and corralled in someone's back yard. The only damage to the safe was marred varnish, but Mr. Sturdevant remained lame for quite a while![8]

By 1902 standards, this new little bank was a prosperous one! Town and county residents immediately brought their banking needs to the "first real bank Douglas County ever had,"[9] and from the first day of operation the bank's business showed a steady and constant growth. Within not quite a year of operation, deposits totaled $60,000, an amount greater than had ever been expected. The loan activity also surpassed the projected figures.[10]

Therefore, it was not surprising when, in December of that same year, on a cold and snowy Saturday, the stockholders met and discussed a proposal for converting the organization into a National Bank.[11] The local paper reported that because of the success and growth of the previous year, the stockholders believed that by bringing the bank under National Banking Law it would become even more solid.[12]

THE FIRST NATIONAL BANK OF DOUGLAS COUNTY AT CASTLE ROCK

On the day after Christmas in 1902, a National Bank Charter, #6556, was granted by the United States Comptroller of the Currency to reorganize this bank.[13] As 1902 became 1903, The Douglas County Bank became The First National Bank of Douglas County at Castle Rock with a capital stock of $25,000 and for a time, anyway, was operated by the same group of men.[14] It is interesting to note that although Mr. Sheffield still held the office of President, he did not make his first trip to Castle Rock until May of 1903. The Castle Rock Journal reported that he and his new wife were on their wedding trip and only remained in town for twenty-four hours. Nevertheless, he was very pleased with the success of the bank.[15]

The First National Bank remained in the Castle Rock Journal Building at Fourth and Wilcox Streets during 1903 and most of 1904. Statements of Condition during June of 1903 showed capital structure at $26,000 while loans reached nearly $70,000 and deposits totaled $58,000.[16] As the bank grew and business increased, plans were drawn up and construction commenced on a new building, specifically designed to house the bank. Located on the northeast corner of Third and Wilcox Streets, at the opposite end of the block from the current location, it would be a simple transition for customers to make.[17]

During the summer heat of 1904, residents watched the two-story building take shape as workmen hauled lava stone and rhyolite from various Douglas County quarries to the site of the new bank. It was later reported that the construction costs were $7,000, which was a substantial sum of money in those days.[18]

When the building was completed in the fall, First National Bank occupied the largest area of the main level while The Telephone Exchange operated out of a small section in the back. The second story was designed as a meeting place for the Masons and other Fraternal Orders.[19] With an area of nearly 2000 square feet,[20] this building was one of the largest and most architecturally impressive stone structures in town.

The formal opening was on November 7, 1904 and all Castle Rock residents were invited to get their first glimpse of the impressive decor. The interior finish of the building was of hardwood, the counters were of marble and the railings were of wrought iron in a variety of beautiful designs.[21]

With the death of E. P. Brown in 1904, the managing group was reorganized. The new Officers at the time of the opening of the new building were: Charles H. Ellis, President; Upton Treat Smith, Vice President; R. J. Dobell, Cashier. The Directors were Benjamin Quick and Charles Woodhouse.[22] Charles H. Ellis would remain as President until 1910.[23]

It is not generally realized by newcomers, or often remembered by old-timers, that in 1887, the Methodist Episcopal Church, was originally located on the northeast corner of Third and Wilcox Streets, and was later moved in order that the bank building could be constructed. The story goes that in the spring of 1904 a property exchange took place between the Methodist Church and the First National Bank. The bank paid to have the church building moved to the southwest corner of Third and Perry Streets and gave the Church $125 as a bonus.[24]

In February of 1906, Mr. Thorwald H. Christensen exchanged the cold and snow of Minnesota for the cold and snow of Colorado to assume the position as the new Cashier of the First National Bank.[25] With two years of bank cashier experience at Security State Bank in Ellendale, this move began what would be a long tenure with First National. He would hold the position of Cashier as well as that of a Director, until 1933—as long as the bank was in existence.[26]

Over the years the officers changed periodically. In 1910, Mr. Robert Palm became President, Dr. W. A. Palmer became Vice President, while John Hillburger and Benjamin Quick were Directors.[27] After the death of Charles Ellis, the managing group was again reorganized. The Officers of this new group were W. L. Fales, President; Dr. W. A. Palmer, Vice President; T. H. Christensen, Cashier. The new Directors were Charles Breuss and C. A. Clarke. Other men connected with various aspects of bank operations over the years were Edward G. Seidensticker, Clarence Frink, Gilbert Palm, Josef Winkler and Charles "Bickey" Briscoe.[28]

It should be noted that in Colorado at the turn of the century there was minimal government interference and it was basically easy to open a bank.[29] There were simple and uncomplicated loan policies for bankers with virtually no impending problems for borrowers. The banking system, as it existed then, functioned in a satisfactory manner insofar as depositors felt their money to be safe and stockholders, while not making tremendous profits, were largely breaking even.[30]

Most bankers, especially those located in small rural communities, such as Castle Rock, didn't worry too much about business and economic conditions occurring outside their immediate area. They were interested in their own banks and their own customers. Probably the biggest concern facing small rural bankers in those days was competition, too many banks chasing the same dollar. First National was no exception.

PEOPLE'S BANK— STATE BANK OF CASTLE ROCK

In February of 1906, a privately-owned financial institution known as People's Bank opened for business in Castle Rock with a familiar name at the helm, President, Upton Treat Smith, most recently of First National Bank. Sedalia businessman, Jonathan House served as the Vice President and A. L. Meade, former bookkeeper of First National Bank, became the Cashier.[31]

Directors were W. W. Jones, C. L. Dickerson, John R. Campbell, Andrew Nickson, F. L. Montgomery, Sr. In addition to the Directors and Officers, other stockholders were Robert Cann, May Pierce Metcalf, John Vosko, George Robinson, Peter Smidt, Jacob Shutz, Eva B. Parker, Samuel R. Ditmars, John S. King, C. Berger, R.P. Conant, J. D. Wilson, Walter Sharp, John Kinner, and C. W. Reed.[32]

The capital stock was $10,000, and it was proudly reported, "With one exception, every dollar was paid by the enterprising citizens of our own Douglas County." The one exception was Elbert County banker, C.L. Dickerson from Elizabeth.[33] The newspaper welcomed the new bank, reporting:

"They are all conservatives and will without a doubt make a success of this new venture, With proper management this institution will be a valuable addition to the town and to Douglas County."[34] However, with First National firmly established and the limited population of Castle Rock at the time, there was not enough business to warrant two banks and the performance of this new institution did not meet the expectations of Directors and stockholders.

Two years later, in an attempt to inspire greater confidence and attract more business, People's Bank was reorganized in March of 1908 as The State Bank of Castle Rock.[35] (This should not to be confused with Castle Rock State Bank which opened in 1917.) New officers were Andrew Nickson, President; S. R. Ditmars, Vice President; M. J. Casey, Cashier. The Directors were W. W. Jones,

Walter Sharp, George Robinson, Robert Cann, U. T. Smith and Charles L. Dickerson.[36] Additional banking services were offered and a feeling of anticipation prevailed.

Despite reorganization, the growth was still unspectacular, and as a result, in November of 1909, controlling interest was purchased by United States National Bank of Denver under the leadership of that bank's President, Gordon Jones.[37] Well respected in the banking industry, his credits included ten years as a banker in Colorado and experience as a State Bank Examiner in Missouri. Currently, he was President of the Colorado Bankers Association and the expectation was that, with Mr. Jones overseeing the bank, it would prosper and grow. While Mr. Jones assumed the duties of President, the other Officers and Directors remained the same with the exception of one new member, M. M. Noyes.[38]

Although deposits did increase approximately fifteen thousand dollars over the next year,[39] it was still not enough of a financial gain to continue operating the bank. In December of 1910, The State Bank of Castle Rock ceased functioning and First National Bank absorbed all the remaining business.[40] Continued success seemed guaranteed for First National because it was, once again, the only bank in Castle Rock and would remain so for the next seven years. Indeed, with its solid customer base of farmers, dairymen, ranchers and businessmen, it continued to prosper and grow.

CASTLE ROCK STATE BANK

During World War I, another bank originated in Castle Rock. According to Colorado State Bank Commissioner's records, Castle Rock State Bank was issued Charter #336, during June of 1917 and the Certificate of Authority in July.[41] The new bank opened for business in August of 1917.[42] Organized by Judge, L. W. Cunningham of Colorado Springs, and Attorney, Harold A. Senter of Parker, the bank was located on the corner of Fourth and Wilcox Streets in the Enderud Building, in a room previously occupied by M. R. Eichling's Dry Goods Store.[43] The first Statement of Condition on September 11, 1917 shows Judge Cunningham as President and Mr. Senter as Cashier. In just a little less than a month from opening they had a Capital Structure of $12,500 with $300 in Unsecured Loans and $1,000 in Secured Loans. Additionally there were $2,500 in Personal Deposits and $1,115 in Time CD's, for a total of 3,615.00 in deposits.[44]

Soon W. L. Troutfetter, formerly an agent for the Cripple Creek District of the Allied Railroads became the Cashier[45] and Harold A. Senter became Vice President, a position he would hold until 1929.[46]

The Directors were L. W. Cunningham, W. L. Troutfetter, Fred B. Hood, George Robinson, Sherman H. Stream, Frank Dakan and C. M. Hurlbut. With only a few exceptions, this core group of men remained the managing force behind this bank for its fifteen years of operation.[47]

In 1922 George P. Stewart became the Cashier.[48] In 1925, J. P. Mikolizik and Andrew Christensen became Directors.[49] By November 1929, Andrew Christensen became Vice President, remaining in that position until the bank closed in November, 1932.[50] Also in 1929, Harold Senter became the Cashier and held that position until 1931,[51] when A. M. Schou took it over for the final months of operation.[52]

The advent of this bank was significant in many ways. Not only did it bring competition, once again, to First National Bank in Castle Rock, it demonstrated the belief held by certain town residents that the growth and economic base of the Castle Rock area might possibly indicate enough stability to support two banks.

By now the area was primarily agriculturally oriented with cattle and dairy farming reigning as two of the biggest industries. During the war years, food supplies were in great demand which stimulated the farming industry. At the same time, the demand for meat was so high that livestock ranchers prospered. One of the paradoxes of war is that while it creates devastation it also creates wealth and as the value of farm products increased there was sharp increase in land values. Colorado experienced prosperity during those years, and Douglas County farmers, ranchers and bankers shared in it. Between 1915 and 1920 loan activity as well as total assets and deposits, in banking institutions, statewide, increased tremendously.[53]

Although Castle Rock State Bank never reached or even paralleled the height in deposits, loan activity or capital structure of First National Bank, Statements of Condition from the new bank showed enough growth and stability during the remaining war years and throughout the early 1920's that the Directors made plans for the construction of a bank building in 1922. At this time, the Enderud Building, in which the room where Castle Rock State Bank was located, was moved 33.5 feet to the north.[54] A bank building was then constructed on the empty lot at 402 Wilcox during late 1922 and early 1923.[55]

It was also in December of 1922 that capital structure reached an all time high of $50,000.[56] After the opening of the new building, and presumably due to an increase in customers, deposits reached an all time high of $169,000 in October of 1924.[57] Following this peak, however, Statements of Condition for Castle Rock State Bank showed a slow decline in deposits over the next five years. This was due to the fact that agriculture, which had prospered during the war, suddenly found itself in overproduction, nationally, with a considerable reduction in demand, a situation that continued for a number of years, putting many banks in a downward spiral including Castle Rock State Bank.

Basic capital remained the same, however, from 1922 until 1929. After the Stock Market Crash in November of 1929, basic capital was reduced from $50,000 to $27,500.[59] The next two years saw yet a larger decline in deposits and loan activity.[60]

It was later reported that during this time, several of the Directors had voluntarily advanced substantial sums of money for the purpose of strengthening the bank and overhead expenses had been cut wherever possible. Prolonging the inevitable, they had even delayed closing the bank in the hope and belief that general financial conditions of the customers, mostly farmers and stock growers, would improve.[61] Despite all attempts to save this institution, Colorado State Bank Commissioner's records show that Castle Rock State Bank ceased operations on November 1, 1932.[62]

It was also revealed that the Directors of the bank had never profited a dollar since its organization and had it closed earlier they might have been able to recover some of their original investment.[63] Mr. J. D. DeLongchamps was appointed Receiver.[64] In March of 1935, The Record Journal reported that a 20% dividend check had been sent to depositors representing approximately $8,000 of the $40,000 on deposit when the bank closed.[65]

In 1936, the Town of Castle Rock bought the bank building for $2,000 plus accrued taxes of approximately $540. For the next three years the building was utilized as a Town Hall and Library.[66] The Castle Rock State Bank Building would eventually become home to The Bank of Douglas County, but that was years in the future. At this point in time, 1932, Mr. and Mrs. Miller were working across the street, operating the Castle Rock Fuel and Feed and struggling to survive the Depression right along with everyone else.

ENDNOTES

[1]When I was writing The History of Banking in Castle Rock for my 1967 history project, I interviewed Mr. Philip Miller and Mr. Josef Winkler. This information came from the notes of those interviews.

[2]A Century of the Colorado Census. Compiled by Suzanne Schulze, 1976. Revised 1977 on Microfilm Collection by Robert Markham, Michener Library, University of Northern Colorado, Greeley, CO, Table l. Population of Minor Civil Divisions 1910, 1900 and 1890, p 198.

[3]Josephine Marr, Douglas County, A Historical Journey, p 173.

[4]Castle Rock Journal, December 20, 1901, p 2, December 27, 1901, p 1, and January 17, 1902; and The Authentic History of Douglas County, Castle Rock Record Journal, December 16, 1921.

[5]See Chapter "Living in the Historic Cantril Court House!"

[6]Castle Rock Journal, December 20, 1901, p 1, January 3, 1902, p1, January 17, 1902, and November 21, 1902, p 1,2.

[7]Castle Rock Journal, January 3, 1902, p 1; Douglas County Bank Advertisement January 17, 1902 and November 21, 1902, p 2.

[8]Castle Rock Journal, January 3, 1902, p 1.

[9]Castle Rock Journal, November 21, 1902, p 1.

[10]IBID, p 1.

[11]IBID, p 5.

[12]IBID, p 1.

[13]The Authentic History of Douglas County, Castle Rock Record Journal, December 16, 1921.

[14]Castle Rock Journal, First National Bank Advertisement, January 2, 1903.

[15]Castle Rock Journal, May 15, 1903.

[16]Statement of Condition, First National Bank of Douglas County at Castle Rock, June 9, 1903, as reported in Castle Rock Journal, June 19, 1903.

[17]Douglas County Assessor's Office, Property Characteristic Report for 300 Wilcox Street , Castle Rock, CO, February 27, 1996.

[18]The Denver Post, November 6, 1904 article entitled "Castle Rock Bank Moves Into Handsome New Home Tomorrow," on file at the Local History Collection, Douglas Public Library District, Castle Rock, CO.

[19]Colorado Real Estate Review, November, 1904 article entitled "Douglas County Has New Bank," as reported in "Walk With Our Pioneers" by Josephine Marr, Douglas County News, July 29, 1971.

[20]Douglas County Assessor's Office, Property Characteristic Report for 300 Wilcox Street, Castle Rock, CO, February 27, 1996.

[21]The Denver Post, November 6, 1904, "Castle Rock Bank Moves Into Handsome New Home Tomorrow."

[22]Colorado Real Estate Review, November, 1904 article entitled "Douglas County Has New Bank," as reported in "Walk With Our Pioneers" by Josephine Marr, Douglas County News, July 29, 1971.

[23]Statement of Condition for First National Bank, as reported in Castle Rock Record Journal on January 12, 1910 showed that Charles H. Ellis was still the President. Statement of Condition reported on March 18, 1910 in the Castle Rock Record Journal showed that Robert E. Palm was the new President.

[24]Letter from Bette Saunders, September 10, 1994; Douglas County News Press Pioneer Edition, February 27, 1988, p 2a; Douglas County News, "Castle Rock 100

Years Old," December 12, 1974 shows photo of Methodist Episcopal Church built in 1887; and Authentic History of Douglas County, Castle Rock Record Journal, December 16, 1921.

[25]Castle Rock Journal, February 23, 1906, p 5.

[26]Castle Rock Record Journal, March 10, 1933 , p 1; also Genealogical Records of Thorwald Christensen Family, compiled by Ruth Christensen.

[27]Castle Rock Record Journal, March 18, 1910, and Statement of Condition, First National Bank.

[28]When I was writing The History of Banking in Castle Rock for my 1967 history project, I interviewed Mr. Philip Miller and Mr. Josef Winkler. This information also came from the notes of those interviews.

[29]Fred R. Niehaus, Seventy Years of Progress, History of Banking in Colorado 1876-1946, p 35.

[30]C. D. Bremer, American Bank Failures, p 37, 38.

[31]Castle Rock Journal, February 23, 1906, p 5.

[32]IBID.

[33]IBID.

[34]IBID.

[35]Castle Rock Record Journal, March 6, 1908, p 1; also State Bank of Castle Rock Advertisement, March 6, 1908.

[36]IBID.

[37]Castle Rock Record Journal, November 12, 1909, p 1.

[38]IBID.

[39]Statement of Condition State Bank of Castle Rock comparing deposits from November 10, 1909 to November 10, 1910 as reported in Castle Rock Record Journal, December 16, 1910.

[40]Castle Rock Record Journal, December 30, 1910, p 1.

[41]Colorado State Bank Commissioner's Records, Denver, CO, June, 1917 and July 19, 1917; and State of Colorado Official Certificate of Authority for Castle Rock State Bank, issued July 9, 1917, courtesy of Dr. Herman Anderson, Castle Rock, CO.

[42]Castle Rock Record Journal, July 20, 1917, p 1.

[43]Castle Rock Record Journal, July 6, 1917, p 1.

[44]Statement of Condition, Castle Rock State Bank, September 11, 1917. All Statements of Condition for Castle Rock State Bank beginning in 1917 as well as First National Bank of Douglas County at Castle Rock beginning in 1919 are contained in scrapbooks compiled by Mr. E.G. Breslow beginning in 1917. These scrapbooks also contain Statements of Condition and advertisements for The Bank of Douglas County beginning in 1939 and continuing until 1954. The scrapbooks became the property of Mr. Miller after Mr. Breslow passed away in 1967. Mr. Miller then gave my dad permission to give them to me when I started this project in 1992. They are still in my possession.

[45]Castle Rock Record Journal, July 20, 1917, p 1; and Statement of Condition Castle Rock State Bank, March 4, 1918.

[46]Statement of Condition, Castle Rock State Bank, November 25, 1929.

[47]Statements of Condition, Castle Rock State Bank, March 4, 1918 until November 1, 1932.

[48]IBID, June 30, 1922.

[49]IBID, April 6, 1925, December 31, 1925.

[50]IBID, November 25, 1929 until November 1, 1932.

[51]IBID, November 25, 1929 until December 5, 1931.

[52]IBID, December 5, 1931 until November 1, 1932.

[53]Fred R. Niehaus, Seventy Years of Progress, History of Banking in Colorado 1876-1946, p 67; and Statements of Condition, First National Bank of Douglas County at Castle Rock and Castle Rock State Bank.

[54]In an interview with Robert Oliver, Castle Rock, CO, July 31, 1996, he told me that to the best of his recollection, the Enderud Building was moved 33.5 feet to the north at this time, but he couldn't swear to it. Regardless of the actual date of the move, the Enderud Building remained at the "new" location, 33.5 feet to the north, until 1971 when it was demolished during The Bank of Douglas County expansion. See chapter "The Expansion of The Bank of Douglas County."

[55]Douglas County Assessor's Office, Property Characteristic Report for 402 Wilcox Street, Castle Rock, CO, April 25, 1996; and Statements of Condition Castle Rock State Bank, December 29, 1922, June 30, 1923. That building is still in existence today, eventually becoming The Bank of Douglas County from 1939 until 1996 when it was purchased by FirstBank Holding Company of Colorado and became The FirstBank of Douglas County after Mr. Miller's death. The original building is the south section and can be easily recognized by the round topped windows.

[56]Statement of Condition, Castle Rock State Bank, December 29, 1922.

[57]IBID, October 10, 1924.

[58]IBID October 10, 1924 until November 25, 1929.

[59]IBID December 29, 1922 until November 25, 1929.

[60]IBID June 30, 1930 until June 25, 1932.

[61]Castle Rock Record Journal, November 4, 1932, "Directors Close Castle Rock State Bank."

[62]Colorado State Bank Commissioner's Records, Denver, CO, November 1, 1932.

[63]Castle Rock Record Journal, November 4, 1932, "Directors Close Castle Rock State Bank."

[64]IBID.

[65]Castle Rock Record Journal, March 15, 1935, "Depositors Receive Dividends from Castle Rock State Bank."

[66]Record of Proceedings Board of Trustees, Town of Castle Rock, November 6, 1935, July 1, 1936; Castle Rock Record Journal, July 17, 1936 as appearing in Scholtz Scrapbook, Local History Collection, Douglas Public Library District; Castle Rock, CO; and letter from Bette Saunders, December 7, 1995.

First National Bank at 300 Wilcox Street was constructed in 1904.

Castle Rock Historical Society Collection.

Looking North on tree-lined Wilcox Street, 1925, First National Bank is on the right.

Local History Collection, Douglas Public Library District, Douglas County, CO..

F.D.R. AND F.N.B. ROOSEVELT AND REORGANIZATION 1933-1937

For the third time in Castle Rock banking history, First National was the only bank in town. It must be remembered that by the time Castle Rock State Bank opened for business in 1917, First National was an established bank having been in existence for nearly fifteen years, seven of which it had no competition. Supported by a solid group of loyal customers made up of businessmen, farmers and ranchers, the bank had a stable capital structure and a continual increase in deposits. Statements of Condition from 1920 to 1929 indicate that the aftermath of the war and the bottoming out of agriculture were not nearly as devastating to First National as they were to Castle Rock State Bank.

An all time high was recorded on December 31, 1929 with $71,000 in capital structure and $435,000 in deposits.[1] This is ironic in light of the fact that the Stock Market Crash had taken place just two months earlier. However, many rural banks which were not heavily invested in the stock market did survive. From 1930 until 1932, capital structure remained the same and the bank still showed a profit but there was a gradual decline in deposits, loan activity, owned government securities, stocks and bonds and real estate holdings.[2] This was due, of course, to the effects of the Depression.

In Douglas County, a predominantly agriculturally oriented area, ranchers, farmers and dairy owners who had experienced prosperity during previous years suddenly found themselves in overproduction with nowhere to sell their products. Farm land suddenly decreased in value and banks immediately found themselves holding loans on land worth virtually nothing, with very little hope of collection.[3] Small business owners suffered because money was so tight customers purchased only necessities. The seemingly secure economy of Douglas County was seriously threatened.

By 1933, when Franklin D. Roosevelt was inaugurated President, the United States was in the throes of the biggest economic breakdown the country had ever experienced. The Stock Market Crash had left thousands homeless, jobless, and penniless. Unemployment soared. Massive withdrawals by people attempting to pay their creditors drained the reserves and resulted in the closure of many banks, nationwide. Soon, what has come to be known as the Great Depression of the '30's was in full swing. One Montana banker, who was also a minister, said that he relied on the Lord to balance his books while another banker from the same state, admitted to depending on local bootleggers for most of his deposits![4] From the sublime to the ridiculous!

In his Inaugural Speech on March 4, 1933, President Roosevelt informed the American public that, "The only thing we have to fear is fear itself," further promising that "his greatest primary task was to put people to work and revive the economy."[5] To that end he would use the powers of the federal government to create various social and economic programs known as the New Deal. Further, he assured the country that there would be strict supervision of all banking, credits and investments; there must be an end to speculation with other people's money and there must be provisions for an adequate but sound currency.[6] To American citizens with their deflated economy and their deflated morale, Roosevelt's words were like manna from heaven.

On March 5, 1933, in his first official act as President, Roosevelt closed all banks in this country, effective March 6, 1933, in an attempt to avoid anymore massive withdrawals and a total collapse of the banking industry. Historically remembered as The Bank Moratorium or Bank Holiday of 1933, it lasted for one week.[7] It was during this Bank Moratorium that First National Bank was closed and the history of banking in Castle Rock was forever changed.[8]

The headline of the Castle Rock Record Journal on March 10th read "Banking Holiday is Put Into Effect By President Roosevelt." The article stated that Mr. Fales and Mr. Christensen from the First National had been to Denver every day to confer with bank officials and were keeping in touch with the latest developments of the situation.[9]

During the next week, the President and the Congress established the National Emergency Banking Law, empowering the Secretary of the Treasury to issue licenses allowing the reopening of banks considered to be in a sound financial condition.[10] Authority was then granted to Federal Regulators from the Comptroller of the Currency of the United States to determine which National Banks would resume business. State Banking Officials were given the authority to determine which State Banks would be allowed to reopen in each respective state. The Federal Deposit Insurance Corporation was also established at this time to insure deposits in reopening banks.[11]

These provisions were not just stop gap or quick fix measures, but rather were carefully calculated pieces of legislation designed to strengthen and protect the banking industry, not only then but in the future as well. More importantly, this legislation subsequently became the foundation for the Banking Act of 1933, which was approved June 16, 1933.[12]

On March 12, 1933, President Roosevelt, in the first of his many Fireside Chats, informed more than 60 million people, eagerly anticipating his speech in front of 20 million radios, that the Bank Moratorium would be lifted the next day. He very clearly stated, "Your Government does not intend that the history of the past few years shall be repeated. We do not want and will not have another epidemic of bank failures." Further, he assured the American public that it was safer to put their money in a reopened bank than under their mattresses.[13]

On March 13 and for the following three days, sound banks began reopening for business, first in twelve Federal Reserve Bank cities, then in large cities where the banks were considered "safe," and finally in smaller places all over the country where the banks were also considered "safe." Those judged "almost sound" were given financial assistance. Trading resumed on the Stock Market on Wednesday, March 15, after having been closed since March 3,[14] and gradually the country's financial community returned to some semblance of normality. By March 29, 1933, two-thirds of the banks that had been in existence in the United Sates prior to the Moratorium were again back in operation, controlling approximately ninety percent of the country's deposits.[15] This was either by merger, consolidation or reorganization, and in the case of strong institutions, reopening.

Specific banks which were not allowed to reopen were then placed in "Conservatorship" which meant that the remaining assets of the bank were "Conserved" or protected by a person appointed by the Regulators until a permanent solution could be determined.[16] If no solution was determined, the bank was then placed in "Receivership" which meant a person known as the "Receiver" was entrusted with authority either to reorganize the bank or to liquidate the assets and pay off depositors and other creditors.[17] Such was the case in Castle Rock.

In all probability, The First National Bank of Douglas County in Castle Rock would have been allowed to reopen had the Board of Directors simply complied with one request from the Federal Bank Regulators. The bank itself was in sound financial condition, definitely strong enough to reopen and continue in business.

Instead, the regulators were not happy with the actions and practices of one of the Directors and they had requested his removal from the Board. For the sake of propriety, I will not mention this gentleman's name nor what he had actually done. However, the remaining Directors, exhibiting great loyalty toward him, refused to comply with the request. Consequently, the bank was never allowed to reopen in its full scope as a banking establishment.[18]

On March 31, 1933, the Record Journal reported that Cashier, Thorwald Christensen had been appointed Temporary Conservator with Charles "Bickey" Briscoe as Clerk. The bank was open for restricted business only, under the National Emergency Banking Law. Although the assets and deposits were frozen, and no withdrawals or loans were being permitted, residents were nonetheless pleased to have a place to cash their checks and deposit their "few dollars."[19] The bank operated on this restricted basis for the next six months, and, although not a perfect solution, it was more satisfactory than having no bank whatsoever.

During that time a Reorganization Committee made up of L. R. Higby Sr., Josef Winkler, W. B. Chamberlain and Mrs. O. P. (Gussie) Weston had been attempting to re-establish normal banking services in Castle Rock through the Office of the United States Comptroller of the Currency which was the governing agency over National Banks. However, due to a deluge of business after the Bank Moratorium, it had taken much longer than expected to remedy the situation.[20]

In late October of 1933 a group of bank depositors met with the Reorganization Committee at the Courthouse. At that time the committee was expanded with the addition of members Colonel R. A. Anderson and George Leonard. S. F. Martin was elected Chairman with John Briscoe as secretary. A plan was set in motion to raise the necessary funds to reorganize First National and it was announced that the Comptroller of the Currency had slated "Castle Rock for a National Bank and every effort would be made to get one re-established soon."[21]

For the next few months the Reorganization Committee continued efforts to raise money in anticipation of restoring banking services to the area. Appeals were made to the Comptroller through Senators Alva Adams and E. P. Costigan and also through Representative Fred Cummings. Prospects for reorganization seemed less likely, however, when, in December, the bank was placed in Receivership and Mr. H. F. Avery was appointed permanent Receiver.[22]

On January 27, 1934, nearly one year after the moratorium, patience was running thin among residents and committee members alike, prompting Mrs. O. P. (Gussie) Weston, who was also the Douglas County Chairwoman of Women's Division of the Colorado NRA, to send a lengthy letter to President Roosevelt in which she wrote in part:

"The First National Bank of Douglas County in Castle Rock, Colorado was closed under the general banking moratorium and is now being liquidated through a receivership. After having had banking facilities for some thirty or more years, we have, for the past eleven months, been placed in a most unhappy and helpless position due to reasons beyond our control. I am convinced of the very serious need for adequate banking facilities located within our county, as well as the serious need for immediate release of frozen assets in the closed bank."[23]

She further outlined a detailed plan for reorganization designed by the committee and quoted the President from a recent speech in which he said, "Disorder is not an American habit. Self-help and self-control are the essence of American tradition."[24]

Roosevelt apparently took action because by the end of February, the Reorganization Committee had received telegrams from Representative Cummings, and Senators Costigan and Adams assuring their support.[25] During the first week of March, Deputy Comptroller, Gibbs Lyons, wrote letters to both Mr. Avery and Mrs. Weston, outlining a tentative plan for reorganization.[26] Who would have thought that a small rural bank in Castle Rock, Colorado would warrant so much attention?

For the next few months constant communications took place between the Reorganization Committee and Mr. Avery in Castle Rock, the Treasury Department and the Deputy Comptroller in Washington, the Chief National Bank Examiner in Kansas City, Representative Cummings and Senators Costigan and Adams, as details of the plan were arranged and accepted by all parties concerned. In July the finalized version was announced.

The plan called for the voluntary contribution of $10,000 from the shareholders of the old bank. It mandated the purchase of (or subscribing to) $20,000 worth of Common Stock with no less than $10,000 paid in new cash while the balance could be paid from deposits tied up in the old bank. Further, it required $10,000 in a surplus fund to be paid in cash.[27] It had been previously proposed, in March, that the new shares of stock be valued at $10.00 per share but be sold at $15.00 per share in order to create the surplus fund. This proposal was incorporated into the plan at this time.[28]

Shareholders in the closed bank were then asked to waive 20% of their frozen deposits in order to help raise the voluntary contribution of $10,000. Depositors and unsecured creditors were also asked waive 20% of their claims in order to restore the old bank to solvency.[29] Assets not taken over by the reorganized bank would be handled by designated trustees, as a trust fund, and when collected would be paid to the depositors who had waived their 20%.[30]

After the plan was publicly announced, efforts were doubled to raise money and the committee was once again expanded with the addition of E. G. Breslow, S. E. Livingston and Mrs. George Nickson. It was also at this time that Mr. Miller was officially named to the Reorganization Committee,[31] although he had been diligently working behind the scenes since the onset. His willingness to take a stand on important issues, coupled with his integrity and his honesty, had earned him the respect of many Castle Rock businessmen and townspeople alike and they held his opinions in high regard.

The proposed plan for reorganization seemed feasible and on July 20th, the Record Journal printed an article explaining how everyone would reap the benefits. Shareholders, who at the moment shouldered all the liability and stood to lose the most money, would, after waiving their 20%, be released from their liability and would hold shares in the newly reorganized bank.[32]

Depositors would, after waiving their 20%, receive 65% to 70% of their deposits which had been frozen for a year and a half, and which totaled considerably more than the average amount being paid in bank liquidations under receiverships in Colorado at that time.[33]

Douglas County ranchers and farmers, faced with foreclosure on mortgages still being held by the old bank, and the forced sale of cattle on a depressed market, would likely receive extensions under the reorganization plan, thus saving many ranches. The same held true for homeowners and other borrowers, who, owing money on notes to the old bank , were also facing foreclosures.[34]

While the Reorganization Committee labored, the Record Journal, in weekly front page articles, faithfully reported each new event, emphasizing positive progress, and encouraging community support with slogans such as “Active Cooperation of All is Needed,”[35] “If We Say We Can’t, We’re Licked Before We Start, If We Say We Can, We’ll Do It,”[36] and “Help Now or Howl Later.”[37] These articles helped gain public support as well as ease public frustration, because, by then, a year and a half had passed since the moratorium and depositors had still not been allowed to withdraw any of their money.

There was no difficulty obtaining support within the business community because everyone was weary of the inconvenience of no bank. To quote Mr. Miller, "It was terrible to try and do business without a bank. We would take turns going to Littleton to get silver and currency for our businesses."[38] The Record Journal very bluntly reported, "The difficulty of doing banking at distant points and the forcing of cash to distant places is slowly choking our community to death."[39]

The first indication that the plan was going awry came in August of 1934, when the Reorganization Committee requested an extension from the Comptroller, who granted it, but urged haste in completing the plan.[40]

In September the Committee sent a report to the Comptroller stating that only approximately $6,000 of the necessary $10,000 voluntary contribution from the shareholders in the old bank had been pledged. However, $11,000 had been pledged for common stock in cash and from frozen deposits in the old bank. The Reconstruction Finance Corporation would subscribe to $30,000 of new stock. Finally, of the approximate $36,000 waiver on the part of the depositors, only $29,000 had been secured.[41] Although the committee was making progress, they were falling short of the goal.

While the Reorganization Committee renewed efforts to raise the final amount, the Record Journal tried to motivate people into getting involved:

"If you are a depositor in the old First National Bank and you want this plan to succeed, assuring a bank at Castle Rock, you should join in now and help in every way you possibly can. A display of real cooperation is needed right now."[42]

However, the paralyzing effects of the Depression were still being felt. Money was tight. Fear was rampant. The required amount ultimately could not be raised. In the final analysis, people wanted their frozen deposits, in hand, more than they wanted a bank in town.

Finally, during November of 1934, in light of the fact that reorganization would not occur, the Comptroller of the Currency issued checks in the amount of $152,900 to depositors of the closed First National Bank. This represented approximately 85% of the frozen deposits, reportedly the largest percentage of the first dividend to be paid out to depositors in any closed bank in Colorado.[43]

In May of 1935, as liquidation proceedings continued, Mr. H. F. Avery, the Receiver, died suddenly of a heart attack.[44] In his place, Mr. John Q. Adams was appointed Receiver.[45] He remained in this position for two years, overseeing the liquidation process, until resigning to take over a bank in Golden in May of 1937. Reuben Todd of La Junta was then appointed Receiver for the final stages of the liquidation process.[46] In June, 1937, with his job as Clerk for the Receiver completed, Charles "Bickey" Briscoe went to work for First National Bank of Englewood.[47]

On July 9, 1937 all remaining assets of First National Bank of Douglas County in Castle Rock were sold to Charles L. Mann of Denver for a bid of approximately $4,000. The Record Journal reported that although the assets totaled about $68,000, many of these assets were old and worthless accounts.[48] Charles L. Mann would reappear, at a later date, in Castle Rock banking history.

No doubt, Mr. Miller was disillusioned and disheartened that the efforts to reorganize First National Bank had failed, but he was not a man who dwelt on defeat. He was a realist who understood economics. He knew that while fifteen dollars per share was a tremendous amount of money for stock men, farmers and businessmen to invest, for the average person, struggling to survive, it might as well have been a million!

More importantly, Mr. Miller understood human nature and once again he knew that progressive ideas could not be resisted forever. After all, he had witnessed this same human nature, first hand, just a few years earlier, during the establishment of the electric and the sewer systems. It was through these experiences, hard fought though they might have been, that he learned to trust in his own instincts, believe in the integrity of the people and concentrate on the future of the community.

He may have lost the immediate battle but he certainly hadn't lost the war. His next undertaking would, once again, be for the establishment of a bank. Only this time, he would win!

EPILOGUE TO FIRST NATIONAL BANK BUILDING

After First National Bank permanently closed, Lou Higby, Sr. was instrumental in securing the building for the Masons. They had been meeting upstairs since it had been constructed in 1904 and it was a logical progression that they should own it. Mr. Higby successfully took steps to acquire it from the Receiver, Reuben Todd. On July 15, 1937, Mr. Higby deeded The First National Bank Building to Douglas Lodge No. 153 A.F. and A.M.[49]

Since that date, it has remained under continual ownership of the Masons and is utilized as a meeting place for the Masons, the Order of Eastern Star and the Order of Rainbow for Girls. The Castle Rock Historical Society also holds meetings and special events there. During the 1960's, as a member of the Order of Rainbow for Girls, I never could get used to having potluck dinners in what used to be the lobby of a bank!! Somehow, it just seemed disrespectful!!

In August of 1993, the building was designated as a Historic Landmark during the First Annual Castle Rock Historic Day, sponsored by the Castle Rock Historical Society. During the ceremonies a Plaque was presented by State Representative, Jeanne Adkins, to commemorate the event.[50] It was installed on the side of the building and remains there to this day. In 1995 the building was placed on The National Register of Historic Places.[51]

The building has been owned by Douglas Lodge No. 153, A.F. & A.M., since 1937.

Buboltz-Bodle Collection.

ENDNOTES

[1]Statement of Condition, First National Bank of Douglas County at Castle Rock, December 31, 1929.

[2]IBID, March 27, 1930 until December 31, 1932.

[3]Fred R. Niehaus, Seventy Years of Progress, History of Banking in Colorado 1876-1946, p 67.

[4]Lynne Pierson Doti and Larry Schweikart, Banking in the American West, p 105.

[5]Kenneth S. Davis, FDR: The New Deal Years 1933-1937, A History, Inaugural Speech, p 29-33.

[6]IBID, p 31.

[7]Fred R. Niehaus, Development of Banking in Colorado, p 61.

[8]The date of Suspension for First National Bank of Douglas County at Castle Rock was March 6, 1933 as recorded on a Statement of Condition, June 30, 1934, printed in the Record Journal, July 27, 1934. Also on Statement of Condition, December 31, 1935, printed in the Record Journal, December 1935 or January 1936. The printing date is unclear.

[9]Castle Rock Record Journal, March 10, 1933, p 1; also a Record Journal article entitled "Lions Hear About Banking Situation; Fishing; Mesa Verde," March 10, 1933.

[10]Fred R. Niehaus, Development of Banking in Colorado, p 62.

[11]IBID.

[12]IBID.

[13]FDR First Fireside Chat on Banking, March 12, 1933, Public Papers and Addresses of FDR Volume 2, 1933; and Kenneth S. Davis, FDR: The New Deal Years 1933-1937, A History, Fireside Chat, p 60.

[14]IBID p 60, 61.

[15]Herbert Feis, 1933: Characters in Crisis, p 109, Fred R. Niehaus, Development of Banking in Colorado, p 62.

[16]Thomas Fitch, Dictionary of Banking Terms, Second Edition, p 142.

[17]IBID p, 497.

[18]Interview with my father, Willis Buboltz, May 1994; when I was writing The History of Banking in Castle Rock for my 1967 history project, I interviewed Mr. Philip Miller and Mr. Josef Winkler. This information was also contained in the notes from those interviews.

[19]Castle Rock Record Journal, March 31, 1933, p 1; June 25, 1937, p 1.

[20]Castle Rock Record Journal, October 27, 1933, p 1.

[21]IBID, p 1.

[22]IBID, May 3, 1935, obituary, H. F. Avery. He is also identified as the Receiver in numerous articles in the Castle Rock Record Journal from December,1933 until his death in 1935.

[23]Letter to President Roosevelt from Mrs. O. P. Weston reprinted in the Castle Rock Record Journal, March 2, 1934, p 1, 2.

[24]IBID p 2.

[25]Telegrams from Cummings on February 20, Costigan on February 28 and message from Adams, also reprinted in the Castle Rock Record Journal, March 2, 1934, p 2.

[26]Castle Rock Record Journal, March 16, 1934, p 1; this letter was also reported as having been written February 23, 1934 in the previously mentioned article on March 2, 1934, Castle Rock Record Journal, p 2.

[27]Castle Rock Record Journal, July 13, 1934, p 1, 8.

[28]IBID March 18, 1934, p 1.

[29]IBID July 13, 1934, p 1, 8.

[30]IBID.

[31]IBID.

[32]IBID, July 20, 1934, p 1,2.

[33]IBID.

[34]IBID; Also August 3, 1934, p 1.

[35]IBID August 3, 1934, p 1.

[36]IBID August 10, 1934, p 8.

[37]IBID August 17, 1934, p 1.

[38]Douglas County News Press, August 30, 1979, p 2, 3

[39]Castle Rock Record Journal, July 20, 1934, p 1.

[40]IBID August 10, 1934, p 1.

[41]IBID September 14, 1934, p 1.

[42]IBID.

[43]IBID November 2, 1934, p 1.

[44]IBID May 3, 1935, "Mr. H. F. Avery Dies of Heart Attack".

[45]IBID May 10, 1935, "John Q. Adams Appointed Receiver of First National Bank".

[46]IBID May 2, 1937, "John Q. Adams Resigns as Receiver of First National Bank".

[47]IBID June 25, 1937, p 1, "Charles Briscoe Now Working for Englewood National".

[48]IBID July 16, 1937, "Remaining Assets of First National Bank Sold".

[49]Warranty Deed, #68875, Louis R. Higby, Sr. to Douglas Lodge #153 A.F. and A.M., July 15, 1937, Douglas County Clerk and Recorder, Castle Rock, CO, Book 88, p 369.

[50]Castle Rock Historical Society First Annual Castle Rock Historic Day, Program of Activities, August 28, 1993, courtesy of Bette Saunders and Starr Oberlin.

[51]Castle Rock Historical Society Annual Newsletter, January, 1996, written by President, Starr Oberlin, courtesy of Bette Saunders.

Louis R. Higby, Sr.,
first President of
The Bank of Douglas County,
1939-1943.

Louis R. "Dick" Higby, Jr. Collection.

THE HISTORY OF THE BANK OF DOUGLAS COUNTY

"To me the greatest virtues for being successful are to be honest, hard working and conservative."
Philip S. Miller

Although Mr. Miller entered the business world as a butcher at around the age of seventeen, he didn't become a banker until the age of forty-four. People often marvel that one of the soundest, safest and most successful banks in Colorado was founded by a butcher! But it was true and it would change the course of history in Castle Rock and Douglas County.

In early 1938, a group of businessmen, who by then were totally weary of the inconvenience of no bank, approached Mr. Miller about trying to raise money, once again, to open a new bank. By this time he was back in the meat market business, having sold the Castle Rock Fuel and Feed to Ben Saunders. As a business owner himself, he recognized the need for a bank.[1] Undaunted by his earlier experiences with the townspeople during the establishment of the electricity and sewer, as well as the previous attempt to reorganize First National Bank, he labored untiringly in his attempt to secure capital for yet another bank. Quietly and calmly, as was his nature, he assured his customers and friends alike that it was not only practical but also possible to open a bank in Castle Rock. As before, there was no difficulty obtaining enthusiasm within the business community. Even the average residents recognized the need and were cautiously optimistic. But gaining community support and gaining financial support were two different things altogether, especially for "a little butcher boy!"[2]

The goal for this new establishment, as it unfolded, was to open a privately-owned, independent, State Bank, with independent being the optimum word. Three facts pointed in that direction. First, it would be easier to open a State Bank than it would be to open another National Bank. The recent events with First National Bank had already proven that fact. Second, dealing with the Colorado State Bank Commissioner would be far less complicated than dealing with the Comptroller of the Currency. Third, and probably most important of all, the amount of start up capital required to open a State Bank in Colorado at that time was $25,000, which was considerably less than the amount required to open a National Bank.[3]

Two of the first people Mr. Miller approached were his friends Lou Higby and Josef Winkler. As has been mentioned in other chapters of this book, Lou Higby immediately committed money for the largest single block of stock purchased by any one shareholder and when The Bank of Douglas County finally opened in 1939, he was elected President, a position he held until 1943. Likewise, Josef Winkler committed to a large block of stock and became a Director, a position he held until 1944.[4]

In order to raise money to purchase his shares, Mr. Miller sold his meat market to Mr. Fred White of Denver in December of 1938[5] and all his cattle in 1939 for $45 a head for cows and $20 a head for calves.[6] He was forty-four years old and this time there was no turning back! The butcher had found a new business—banking! It was a brave move, given the financial condition of Castle Rock and the recent banking crisis. But he was willing to take the risk. His decision would ultimately have an effect upon hundreds and thousands of people over the next half century and would help transform Douglas County and Castle Rock.

One new man directly involved in the organization of The Bank of Douglas County was Mr. H. B Dopf, a banker from Nebraska who had moved to Castle Rock during the early part of 1939 in the hopes of opening a bank. According to Mr. Miller, "Mr. Dopf needed help with financing and other things and some people had sent him to see me." They joined forces and soon Mr. Dopf had purchased a large block of stock. Mr. Miller often commented that when they organized The Bank of Douglas County, Mr. Dopf was the only one with any banking experience and when it opened, he became Cashier.[7] He also helped when it came time to find the location for the new bank.

On June 23, l939, Mr. Dopf met with the Board of Trustees of the Town of Castle Rock at a special meeting to request leasing the Town Hall on the corner of Fourth and Wilcox Streets to be utilized, once again, as a bank. This seemed a logical location because it had previously housed Castle Rock State Bank. The Board agreed to lease the building to The Bank of Douglas County for a term of three years, for the remarkable rent of $35.00 per month with an option to purchase for $3,500.[8] No one could have predicted that The Bank of Douglas County had just found a home where it would remain for almost six decades, and that in this building Mr. Miller would create a financial empire and amass a fortune. From beneath the shadow of

The Rock would emerge one of the most successful banks in Colorado history.

By the time the bank opened, Mr. Miller had raised $25,000 dollars in capital stock.[9] With the exception of one man from Golden and three from Denver, the majority of the twenty-seven stockholders were Douglas County ranchers, farmers and businessmen. There was also one woman. The complete list of the first stockholders of The Bank of Douglas County was as follows: L. R. Higby, Sr., Josef Winkler, P. S. Miller, Jr., H. B. Dopf, Ben Saunders, Harold Senter, J. H. Kroll, E. G. Breslow, H. H. Gandy, Norman H. Smith, Paul V. Pattridge, Harland Palm, Gilbert Palm, Mrs. Anna Palm, Charles Doepke, Frank Doepke, Guy Anderson, J. A. VanLopik, Fred M. Smith, Henry Singer, Andrew Nickson, Ross King, George Robinson, A. L. Friendthal, E. S. Tripplett, C.A. Sturdevant, A. E. Kuhnke.[10] Speaking years later, Mr. Miller once said to me, "Many of these boys were not just stockholders, they were loyal friends—Lou Higby, Josef Winkler, Ben Saunders, E. G. Breslow, Jake Kroll, Norm Smith. They knew we needed a bank in Castle Rock and they were not afraid to go out on a limb with me to make it happen."[11] He also related a very interesting story with regard to the naming of the bank.

Years earlier, there had been a bank in Parker, Colorado known as Bank of Douglas County, which had long since closed. Mr. Miller, Mr. Higby and Mr. Winkler liked the name because they wanted the new bank to be recognized as a financial institution which served all of Douglas County and not just the town of Castle Rock. However, they couldn't be granted the Certificate of Authority with a name that had already been used, despite the fact that bank which had used the name was out of existence. In order to be allowed to use that name, they had to somehow make a slight change, to create a different name. Mr. Miller suggested they simply add the word "The" in front of Bank of Douglas County. That explains why, on all documents over the life of the bank as well as all references to it in this book, the word "The" is always capitalized, designating it as an official part of the title of the bank as well as a pivotal word in the history of its beginning.[12]

The Bank of Douglas County opened on Monday, August 28, 1939.[13] The prior two weeks had been spent finalizing the details. On Monday, August 14, the stockholders held a meeting and elected the following men to the Board of Directors: Louis R. Higby, Sr., Philip S. Miller, Jr., H. B. Dopf, Henry Gandy, Harlan Palm, Josef Winkler and Norm Smith. The Board members then elected Officers for the ensuing year: Louis R. Higby, Sr., President; Philip S. Miller, Jr.,

Vice President and H. B. Dopf, Cashier.[14] The Record Journal reported:

> "Sentiment is very strong for the Bank and it will, without a doubt, receive hearty local support and patronage. The folks who are in this organization are all successful and will, without a shadow of a doubt, make a success of the new venture."[15]

It was also announced that Mr. Miller, as Vice President, would be in charge of the Bank.[16]

On Tuesday, August 15, the Officers went to Denver to the Colorado State Bank Commissioner to make application for the Certificate of Authority and Charter. Everything was in order and the Certificate was granted the following week on Monday, August 21, 1939.[17] It was also during this week that application was made for membership in the Federal Deposit Insurance Corporation, which at that time insured individual depositors of member banks up to $5,000. This, of course, was granted, although word was not officially received until January of 1940.[18]

View from the Bank of the famous Stone Douglas County Courthouse which was destroyed by fire in 1978.

Kenneth Flansburg Collection.

CERTIFICATE OF AUTHORITY

STATE OF COLORADO

OFFICE OF STATE BANK COMMISSIONER

I, Maple T. Harl State Bank Commissioner of the State of Colorado, do hereby certify that THE BANK OF DOUGLAS COUNTY of Castle Rock County of Douglas State of Colorado has complied with all the provisions of Chapter 44 of the Session Laws of the State of Colorado of 1913 "An Act Relating to Banks and Banking" and all Acts amendatory thereto that it has a paid in Capital of $ 25,000.00 and that said bank is authorized to conduct the business of banking under the laws of this State.

In Testimony Whereof I have hereunto subscribed my name and affixed the official seal of the office of State Bank Commissioner of Colorado at Denver, Colorado, this 21st day of August 1939.

CERTIFICATE NUMBER 433

State Bank Commissioner

ROCKY MOUNTAIN BANK NOTE CO-DENVER

The Bank Of Douglas County Certificate Of Authority.

Courtesy of Dr. Herman Anderson and Mr. Buddy Douglass Castle Rock CO.

No. 15715

Federal Deposit Insurance Corporation

Washington, D.C.

Hereby Certifies That

The Bank of Douglas County

located in Castle Rock

in the State of Colorado

is an insured bank under the permanent plan for the insurance of deposits by the Federal Deposit Insurance Corporation, with maximum insurance of $5,000 for each depositor, as provided by Act of Congress.

In testimony whereof, witness my signature and the seal of the Corporation this 9th day of Jan 1940

Attest:

Secretary

Chairman of the Board of Directors

The Bank Of Douglas County
Federal Deposit Insurance Corporation Certificate.

Courtesy of Dr. Herman Anderson and Mr. Buddy Douglass, Castle Rock CO.

Four days before the opening of the Bank, the Record Journal followed up, in a great show of civic pride, with a front page article entitled:

THE BANK OF DOUGLAS COUNTY
WILL OPEN NEXT MONDAY
"The announcement that the doors of
The Bank of Douglas County would open in Castle Rock on August 28 is themost important piece of news as well as the most welcome, that has come to the people of Douglas County for a long time! Greetings to The Bank of Douglas County.
May it live long and prosper!"[19]

From newsprint to God's ears!!

The first deposit in this new bank was made by Mr. P. D. Dunn, the President of Littleton National Bank. A loyal friend with great respect for Mr. Miller, he had driven to Castle Rock on the morning of August 28 and was actually standing outside the door, waiting for The Bank of Douglas County to open on the historic first day of business.[20] Gill Whitman described Mr. Dunn as a big, tall, good old guy and explained the extent of Dunn's admiration for Mr. Miller, "Even though we were customers of Littleton National, when Phil opened The Bank of Douglas County, Mr. Dunn told us to 'Go help Phil Miller!' And we did!"[21]

Although Bank Statements of Condition show immediate growth in deposits, by Mr. Miller's own admission, "Times were tough." In an interview with the Douglas County News Press in August of 1979 and again in 1980, he remembered once during those early years when he was forced to ask that the stockholders to go through a stock assessment.[22] Sometimes, when a bank isn't making much money, the stockholders are offered the opportunity to put in more capital by purchasing more shares, on a pro rata basis, according to how many shares they own. For example, if a stockholder owns five shares, he or she is allowed to buy five more shares. This increases the capital of the bank. However, at the time, Mr. Miller just felt badly because he had to ask his friends to "pour" more money into the bank! Since quite a number of people had invested a few dollars each, it comes as no surprise that at one time there were as many as forty-seven stockholders.[23]

Frequently, in many small towns, the banks were controlled by wealthy citizens who lent money only to their wealthy friends who probably didn't need it, never extending credit to the common man. It was also an unfortunate fact that in the early days of our history, banks serving farmers and ranchers suffered the most. Mr. Miller was determined never to let either of those things happen in Douglas County. And they never did! It is an incredible fact that The Bank of Douglas County never posted a loss since opening the doors. Although Mr. Miller often said he lost money in the beginning, it must have been very minimal, because Statements of Condition reflect a steady rise in profit as the capital structure and total deposits continually increased. Never was there a time when they decreased, even during those early days. The majority of loans were agricultural and one of his most important goals was to serve the farmers and ranchers in every way possible.

From the beginning, this small country bank, the only one in Castle Rock, could fundamentally be considered a success. The first Statement of Condition, in October, 1939, showed approximately $30,000 in deposits, which was a formidable figure for that time in history as well as an impressive amount because the Bank's doors had only been open a little less than two months![24] In December, 1939, the first personnel change occurred as a new man, Harry Lowe, was designated by the Board of Directors to fill out the unexpired term of Cashier when H. B. Dopf moved away.[25]

By March, 1940, the deposits had more than doubled, reaching $79,000,[26] and the Directors were making plans to purchase the bank building they were renting. On April 2, with a vote of 115 to 8, voters had overwhelmingly passed an Ordinance allowing the Town of Castle Rock to sell the building to The Bank of Douglas County for $3,500.[27] Expressing appreciation for both these important milestones, the Directors issued a public thank you in the paper on April 15th. It read, in part:

NOTE OF THANKS

"The Bank of Douglas County wishes to thank the voters of the Town of Castle Rock for their support and cooperation in enabling us to purchase the banking quarters which we are now occupying and also to thank all the people of Douglas County for their confidence, support and patronage which has enabled us to show this growth."[28]

From the time The Bank of Douglas County opened, Mrs. Miller again worked along with her husband. Gill Whitman humorously described their "jobs" in a speech at the Philip Miller Bench

Dedication ceremony during the 1996 Douglas County Fair and Rodeo. He said, "Phil was the President and Jerry was the Vice President and on the weekends they were both the janitors!"[29] In point of fact, former Mayor, "Pete" Burgess and his wife, Hazel, recalled Jerry working as a Teller during the week and on weekends they remembered Phil and Jerry washing the windows, only now they were the windows of a bank and not a meat market.[30]

Mr. Miller would joke that during the week they were business people, dressed in nice clothes, serving the public and on the weekends, they were the Bank janitors, at which times they would put on grubby clothes and dust and mop the floors, wash the windows, clean the bathrooms, and clean out the coal furnace! During those early years, Mr. Miller's salary was $125.00 a month. He often reminisced how he, as a major stockholder, earned less money than the Cashier who earned $150.00 a month! However, since Mrs. Miller earned $50.00 a month, they felt they were really in the money![31]

In a letter to me during the writing of this book, Joe Winkler related how his father, Josef, had, at that time, been designated to make the semi-weekly run to Central Bank in Denver to pick up coins and currency to facilitate the local operations. On occasion Joe would be along and when they arrived back at the Bank, and when the money was secured in the safe, Jerry insisted they go to the Miller's for dinner. He recalled how she always prepared the most elegant meals with no apparent effort. Before and during dinner Mr. Miller tried to solicit advice from his father, Josef. "Joe, what do think about this or that?" Josef, who had complete confidence in Mr. Miller, would reply, "Pheel, you are the boss—follow your own good instincts and everything will be fine."[32]

However, according to Mr. Miller, at one point in time, when all forty-seven stockholders were expressing different opinions on policy and procedure, he seriously considered quitting the banking business altogether and resuming his previous vocation of butchering.[33] Being a calm, non-confrontational type of person, dealing with meat instead of money seemed very tempting during those first few years! But, he took Josef's advice, he followed his own instincts and in December of 1943, the pressure eased when Mr. Miller took on a partner, Mr. Charles L. Mann, a banker from Denver.[34] At this time, Statements of Condition reflect that, since opening in 1939, Capital Structure had increased approximately $6,000 for a total of nearly $37,000 while the growth in deposits had reached nearly $600,000.[35]

Mr. Miller and Mr. Mann both purchased enough shares of stock so that after the transaction was completed they each held 50%.[36] This began a successful seven year business partnership which Mr. Miller always referred to as the "nicest relationship." Charlie Mann was President and Mr. Miller was Cashier and later Vice President. Echoing Phil's sentiments, Gill Whitman described Charlie Mann as a nice, friendly, personable kind of guy.[37] This was not the first time Charlie Mann had been involved in banking in Castle Rock. It might be remembered that six years earlier, in 1937 during the final liquidation of First National Bank, he had purchased all the remaining assets and accounts for $4,000.[38]

Also in December of 1943, Mr. Miller gave his wife ten shares of stock and she became a Director, a position she would hold for the next forty years, until 1983, when health problems, including the loss of her eyesight, would make it impossible for her to continue. During all those years, remarkably, she never missed a monthly Board of Directors meeting.[39]

In 1947, Mr. C. B. Grout purchased ten shares of stock and became a Director.[40] Both Mr. Grout's and Mrs. Miller's acquisitions were in accordance with the corporate by-laws which, at that time, dictated that in order to be a Director, one must be a shareholder. Mr. Miller then became Vice President, Mr. Grout became Cashier and Mrs. Miller became Assistant Cashier.[41]

On May 10, 1950, Mr. Miller purchased all of Charlie Mann's stock and became majority stockholder, owner and President of The Bank of Douglas County.[42] At that time Mr. Grout became Vice President and Cashier.[43] During the previous seven years Capital Structure had increased by $82,000 bringing it to a total of nearly $120,000, while deposits had grown nearly $800,000, crossing the one million dollar mark in 1946.[44] At the age of 55, when many men might be contemplating only ten years until retirement, Mr. Miller took on a new challenge—to make this bank one of the strongest and safest banks in the country.

In order to purchase Charlie Mann's stock, Mr. Miller naturally needed a loan of a fairly sizable amount and, because there were still no other financial institutions in Castle Rock at the time, he went to Denver to apply for this loan. He had plenty of collateral: the house in Castle Rock and his and Jerry's majority shares in the Bank. However, he had no cash in hand, and, as if history were repeating itself from the days of the meat market in Elizabeth, the first bank he approached, First National Bank of Denver, turned down his loan application.[45] As a close, anonymous, friend remembers:

"From that day forth, Phil never had any use for First National Bank of Denver. However, at a later date, he placed $50,000 on deposit with them in the name of The Bank of Douglas County and kept it there for many years, to show them he was as big as they were."

His loss at First National Bank of Denver became his gain at Central Bank and Trust Company of Denver, for not only did he receive his loan, but it was during this time that Mr. Miller met that bank's President, Mr. Elwood Brooks, and they began what would become a lifelong business relationship as well as a close personal friendship. This association would also benefit Mr. Miller in another way for it was through Elwood Brooks, that Mr. Miller met a bright young banker who hailed from a little town in northern Wisconsin and who worked for Mr. Brooks at Central Bank and Trust.[46] That man was my dad, Mr. Willis Buboltz.

The interior of The Bank from 1939 until 1971 with glass surrounding the Teller area and the famous "Jail Bars" at the Teller Windows!

Dona Sherlock Collection.

ENDNOTES

[1]Conversation between Mr. Miller and the author Cherry Creek Care Center, Aurora, CO, August, 1991.

[2]Douglas County News Press, August 30, 1979, p 3.

[3]IBID.

[4]The Bank of Douglas County Records, The Articles of Incorporation, Article V, August 1939; Douglas County News, May 18, 1972; conversation between Mr. Miller and the author Cherry Creek Care Center, August 1991; also see Chapter "Mr. Higby, Mr. Winkler, and Mr. Miller".

[5]Scholtz Scrapbook, Local History Collection, Philip S. Miller Library, Castle Rock, CO; and Castle Rock Record Journal, December 2, 1938, p 2.

[6]Douglas County News Press, August 12, 1980, p 2.

[7]Douglas County News Press, August 30, 1979, p 3.

[8]Record of Proceedings Board of Trustees, Town of Castle Rock, Special Meeting, June 23, 1939.

[9]The Bank of Douglas County Records, The Articles of Incorporation, Article IV, August 1939.

[10]The Bank of Douglas County Records, The Articles of Incorporation, Article V, August 1939.

[11]Conversation between Mr. Miller and the author Cherry Creek Care Center, August 1991.

[12]IBID; also interview with my father, Willis Buboltz, May 1994.

[13]The Bank of Douglas County Records, Daily and Weekly Ledger Sheets, August 28, 1939 to September 2, 1939; and Colorado State Bank Commissioner's Records, August, 1939.

[14]Castle Rock Record Journal, August 18, 1939; also Scholtz Scrapbook, Local History Collection, Douglas Public Library District, Castle Rock, CO.

[15]IBID.

[16]Castle Rock Record Journal, August 25, 1939, p 1.

[17]Colorado State Bank Commissioner's Records, August,1939; Certificate of Authority Number 433, State of Colorado granted to The Bank of Douglas County, August 21, 1939, courtesy of Dr. Herman Anderson and Mr. Buddy Douglass.

[18]Castle Rock Record Journal, January 9, 1940; Federal Deposit Insurance Corporation Certificate Number 15715, granted to The Bank of Douglas County, January 9, 1940, courtesy of Dr. Herman Anderson and Mr. Buddy Douglass.

[19]Castle Rock Record Journal, August 25, 1939, p 1.

[20]Conversation between Mr. Miller and the author Cherry Creek Care Center, August 1991; also thanks to Mr. Max Brooks, former President of Central Bank and Trust Company in Denver for remembering Mr. Dunn's initials.

[21]Interview between Gill and Cecil Whitman and the author, Castle Rock, CO, March 27, 1997.

[22]Douglas County News Press, August 30, 1979, p 3; and Douglas County News Press, August 12, 1980, p 5.

[23]Douglas County Express, August 29, 1979, p 22.

[24]Statement of Condition, The Bank of Douglas County, October 2,1939.

[25]Statement of Condition, The Bank of Douglas County, December 29, 1939.

[26]Statement of Condition, The Bank of Douglas County, March 26, 1940.

[27]Town of Castle Rock Ordinance, April, 1940, p 1-3.

[28]Statements of Condition, The Bank of Douglas County, October 2, 1939 and March 26, 1940; and Castle Rock Record Journal, April 5, 1940, p 8.

[29]Speech by Gill Whitman at the Philip S. Miller Bench Dedication Ceremony, August 3, 1996, Douglas County Extension Office at the Douglas County Fairgrounds on file at the Local History Collection, Douglas Public Library District, Castle Rock, CO.

[30]Letter from former Mayor H. G. "Pete" and Hazel Burgess, Castle Rock, CO, November, 1996.

[31]Douglas County News Press, August 30, 1979, p 3.

32Letter from Joe Winkler, Castle Rock, CO, June 13, 1998.

[33]Douglas County Town and Country Squire, November 26, 1976.

[34]The Bank of Douglas County Records, December 1943 and May 1950.

[35]Statements of Condition, The Bank of Douglas County, October 2, 1939—December 31, 1943.

[36]The Bank of Douglas County Records, December 1943 and May 1950.

[37]Interview between Gill and Cecil Whitman and the author, Castle Rock, CO, March 27, 1997.

[38]Castle Rock Record Journal, July 16, 1937.

[39]Statements of Condition, The Bank of Douglas County, December, 1943—December, 1983.

[40]The Bank of Douglas County Records, May 1947; and Statement of Condition, December 31, 1947.

[41]Statements of Condition, The Bank of Douglas County, December 31,1947 and December 31, 1948.

[42]The Bank of Douglas County Records, May 1950.

[43]Statement of Condition, The Bank of Douglas County, December 30, 1950.

[44]Statements of Condition, The Bank of Douglas County, December 31, 1943—April 24, 1950.

[45]Conversation between Mr. Miller and the author Cherry Creek Care Center, August 1991.

[46]IBID.

My favorite table with the cubby holes and the glass top.

Robert and Helen Oliver Collection.

Mr. Miller at his desk in the front left office, 1960.

Robert and Helen Oliver Collection.

Interior of The Bank and Mr. Miller at his desk, 1962.

Robert and Helen Oliver Collection.

MY DAD: MR. WILLIS BUBOLTZ

Unlike Mr. Philip Miller, Mr. Willis Buboltz did not come to Colorado as a young boy; he came as a soldier during World War II at the age of twenty. Born in Green Bay, Wisconsin on a cold, snowy morning the day after Christmas in 1923[1] to Olga and Reuben Buboltz, he was only the third generation born in the United States into a proud heritage of German-Lutherans who had emigrated to this country in the mid-1800's and settled in northern Wisconsin.[2]

Reuben was born January 17, 1894 in Brillion, Wisconsin,[3] and although his father, Charles Buboltz, was a well known auctioneer, Reuben did not follow in Charlie's footsteps. Instead, he began a career in banking in 1911 at the age of seventeen as a clerk at the First National Bank in Brillion. In 1917 he moved to Milwaukee to be First Assistant Cashier of the Bay View Commercial and Savings Bank, where he remained until the early 1920's.[4] He then returned to the north country and worked at The Bank of Navarino, a small town twenty miles west of Green Bay, where he and Olga lived when Willis was born.

Five months later, Reuben moved his family to Wrightstown, a little village on the Fox River ten miles south of Green Bay, where they lived four doors north of the Lutheran Church. He had been hired by the Farmer's and Trader's Bank as Cashier and Director. This was to be his final professional move, for he would hold these positions for the next forty years.

On Willis' first birthday, Reuben and Charlie placed before him a silver dollar, a book and a piece of bread. This was an old family tradition which determined whether a child's life's work would be finance, education or agriculture. To the delight of his father and the chagrin of his grandfather, Willis immediately grabbed the silver dollar, indicating that he, too, would become a banker![5]

Olga Buboltz was tall and thin, with soft, light brown hair which she wore in a "bun." She was a fun loving, high spirited young woman with an infectious laugh, an outgoing personality, and a zest for life. She enjoyed her son, and would play with him for hours, taking numerous pictures of his infant years and recording his antics and accomplishments in his baby book. Willis would grow up to resemble his mother in stature and facial features, and would develop her personality and outlook on life.

Reuben was a very friendly person, but he was much quieter than Olga. A proper, conservative banker he found relaxation in gardening and fishing, hobbies Willis would ultimately enjoy years later. Olga's congenial personality balanced Reuben's reserved demeanor and they truly brought out the best in each other. Once, when she impulsively climbed a tree to rescue a stray kitten, Reuben said she was "acting foolishly." However, his smiling eyes revealed the affection and admiration he felt for his wife.

In November of 1926, one month before Willis' third birthday, the happiness of this family was shattered when Olga contracted pneumonia and died suddenly, leaving thirty-two year old Reuben to raise his son alone. Shortly thereafter, Olga's sister and her husband, Meta and Art Mattes, invited Reuben and Willis to live with them in their large, comfortable house in nearby Greenleaf. Reuben gratefully accepted this offer because it ensured that while he was at the bank during the daytime, Willis would be well cared for and have the continuity of a loving, secure childhood.[6]

Many "firsts" took place in his young life during the next three years in Greenleaf, and "Aunt Mae," as Willis called her, continued her sister's tradition of writing in the baby book and taking pictures of this cute, smiling little boy. In the quiet tree-lined back yard he built his first snowman, rode his first bike, played with his first wagon and witnessed, for the first time, kittens and puppies being born. If there were any after effects from Olga's death, they certainly never showed. The love and stability of the family and the wonder and innocence of childhood apparently eased much of the trauma. Weekends found Reuben and Willis and various family members fishing and swimming in the Wisconsin lakes or attending auctions with "Big Grandpa Buboltz." Willis started first grade in Greenleaf when he was only five years old, because according to what Aunt Meta wrote in his baby book, "There was no kindergarten here."[7]

In September of 1929, Reuben married Mathilda Caroline Stuht,[8] and for the second time in their lives, he and Willis moved to Wrightstown, this time into a large and spacious apartment above the post office where Mathilda worked as Postmistress, a position she would hold until retirement. Despite her full-time job, Till embraced her new life as wife and mother with inherent German-Lutheran family devotion. A wonderful cook and homemaker, she made certain Willis was immaculately, Sunday-best dressed every day for school with a nutritious lunch in his pail, and when Reuben came home to eat every day at noon, there was a hot meal on the table which she had run up the stairs thirty minutes earlier to prepare!

She loved Willis as if he were her own son, never wanting him to think of her as a step-mother. Given his young age when Olga died,

Till was, in fact, the only mother he ever remembered. Likewise, this smiling little boy with the friendly personality became the only son she would ever know, and a special blessing to her as well, for it was later discovered that she was unable to have children.

Mathilda was the total opposite of Olga. Short and chubby, conservative and quiet, her propriety and privacy would have never allowed her to climb a tree to rescue a stray kitten! Nevertheless, she enjoyed fishing and camping and the three of them spent happy weekends and summer vacations on the lakes of northern Wisconsin, where she baited her own hook and helped Reuben and Willis clean fish!

The family weathered the Depression better than most, thanks to Reuben's years of diligent saving and the fact that they both had secure jobs. The post office remained open, and while many banks in Midwest farming communities failed, Farmer's and Trader's survived. It was one of the few rural banks in Wisconsin allowed to reopen immediately after the 1933 Bank Holiday, largely due to the foresight of the Directors who had never heavily invested in the stock market and had adopted a very conservative loan policy several years earlier.

By 1934, Wrightstown had become religiously divided with the Roman Catholics living on the west side of the river and everybody else, mostly the Lutherans, living on the east side. It is not quite clear if this was the result of Depression hardships or Church differences. Nevertheless, the town was very definitely split. Attempting to bridge the gap between the two groups, Reuben bravely bought a house on the west side of town, four doors south of the Catholic Church, and they became one of first Lutheran families to move across the river. This bold move earned him untold respect from townspeople, and strengthened public relations at the bank. Many of the west-side Roman Catholics who typically drove six miles to Kaukauna to do their banking, became customers of the east-side Farmer's and Trader's Bank in Wrightstown! Eventually, the town became religiously integrated, not only in the residential areas but within the business community as well.

Not long after they bought the house and moved across the river, Mathilda's mother died, and her older, unmarried sister, Emma, came to live with them. Although she, too, was a devout Lutheran, honored her German heritage and shared Till's devotion to Willis and Reuben, Emma had an uncanny ability to see the humorous side of life and to take things much less seriously than did her sister. The presence of a huge tree in the back yard of the family home in Wrightstown illustrates this fact.

On one of their many fishing trips to northern Wisconsin, Willis found a little pine tree, approximately one foot tall, which he decided he wanted to take home. As they were getting ready to leave, he dug it up and proudly carried it to the car, where his mother, lovingly but firmly, told him he had to replant it in the ground. Emma felt Mathilda was being too strict, so she mischievously whispered to Willis to put it under his jacket and take it with him. When they got home, Mathilda unzipped the jacket and there was the tree! Recognizing Emma's influence in the situation, she did not scold or punish her son.[9]

The next day, Reuben planted the little tree in the backyard where Willis proudly watered it and watched it grow. Today that tree is one of the largest and most beautiful in the whole town—a testimony to the fact that Aunt Emm believed a little boy's happiness was more important than propriety or the seeming dictates of right and wrong.

Willis completed elementary and secondary school in Wrightstown. With a very strong work ethic ingrained in him from childhood, he always had an after-school and summer job. He mowed lawns, delivered newspapers and milk, and during his teenage years, operated a horse driven threshing machine at a pea vinery. After high school graduation in 1939, he enrolled in Lawrence College in nearby Appleton, studying business and economics. Adhering to an unwritten rule that relatives could not be employed at the Farmer's and Trader's Bank, he was never allowed to work with his father. Had it not been for this rule, his banking career probably would have started much earlier than it did. Instead, he worked at Allis Chalmers to help pay college expenses, and when his draft notice appeared in 1943, he enlisted in the Army.

Following basic training at Camp Buttner, North Carolina, he was transferred to Denver and assigned to a unit slated to become the Air Corp Finance Unit. This unit never came to fruition, however, and the men were put on permanent KP duty at Fort Logan, which at that time was an Army Base and not a mental health facility as it is today. They worked twelve hours on and twelve hours off with weekends free. It was during one of those free weekends that he met Eleanor Yonge on a blind date, which had been set up by two friends who felt they would make a nice couple because they were both tall!

Interestingly enough, she was the first woman to call him Willie and he was the first man to call her Ellen and they soon discovered they had much more in common than being tall! They dated for three months and became unofficially engaged when he was reassigned to the Army Engineers and shipped overseas in the summer of 1944. While Willie went to war, first to serve in Belgium for a year and then in Germany for another eighteen months, Ellen finished college at Denver University. They became officially engaged in April of 1946 when he returned after the end of the war. They were married in October of the same year in Denver.[10]

While Ellen taught 7th Grade at Grant Junior High in Englewood, the "Silver Dollar Prediction" came true, as Willie went to work at Central Bank and Trust Company in Denver, embarking on a career in banking which would last nearly fifty years. His natural abilities as a banker, his inherent sense of economics and his relaxed diplomacy with customers impressed Central's President, Elwood Brooks, who, during the next six years, promoted him from an entry-level position as a Teller to Manager of the Bookkeeping and Proof Department.

Additionally, his knowledge and expertise earned him a position in a group of bankers from Central who helped organize and open new banks in small rural communities throughout Colorado and New Mexico such as Home State Bank in Loveland, Englewood State Bank in Englewood, Arkansas Valley Bank in Pueblo and First National Bank in Farmington, New Mexico. At twenty-nine years old, my father's future in banking was definitely secure, and it would take a very special person to get him away from Elwood Brooks and Central Bank. That person was Philip Miller.

During the first week of May in 1952, Mr. Brooks asked Willie to go to The Bank of Douglas County in Castle Rock to prepare a Call Report. This was a report which lists deposits and loans, profits and losses, assets and liabilities, as well as income and stockholder dividends. It is, in essence, a balance sheet for a bank. In today's banking procedures, a Call Report is more commonly referred to as a Statement of Condition, and is filed twice a year on the last day of June and December. However, in the early 1950's, a Call Report was prepared at any given time when either someone from a Federal or State Banking Regulatory Agency, or the Correspondent Bank requested or "called" for it. In this particular instance, Central Bank was the Correspondent Bank for The Bank of Douglas County, and when Mr. Brooks requested the report, Mr. Miller had no one available or qualified to do it. The man responsible, Mr. C. B. Grout, had recently resigned his Directorship as well as his position as Vice President and Cashier.[11] Mr. Brooks, therefore, had to send someone from Central Bank and my father was chosen because of his familiarity with rural banking procedures. The events which transpired over the next four days would ultimately alter the course of many lives.

Willie Buboltz was slender and tall, six foot six inches, to be exact, and Mrs. Miller told me years later that the first thing Mr. Miller thought when they met was, "This boy would be a hell of a basketball player. What is he doing in banking?"[12] As they worked together over the next four days, this question was very clearly answered as the same qualities which had impressed Elwood Brooks for the past six years impressed Mr. Miller now. It soon became apparent that Willis Buboltz would fit into the immediate, as well as long range, plans for The Bank of Douglas County. However, Mr. Miller knew that Willie had a prominent position as Manager of the Bookkeeping and Proof Department, and that within the hierarchy of Central Bank, other opportunities awaited him. It was doubtful that he would abandon a promising future at one of Denver's most prestigious top three banking institutions to come to Castle Rock and work in a country bank. On the fourth day, with the Call Report completed, despite his preconceived notions that my dad would turn him down, Mr. Miller invited him out for a drink and then offered him a job![13]

Facing the crossroads in life never presented a problem for my father. With his philosophical outlook, decisions, large or small, came very easily, and it didn't take him long to make up his mind. From a personal standpoint, he was a small-town boy at heart who wanted to raise his family in the same manner in which he had been raised. By this time I was two years old, and it wouldn't be long until my sister was born. He and my mother felt Castle Rock would be a good place to raise children.

From a business standpoint, he enjoyed working at Central Bank, and the previous six years under the tutelage of Elwood Brooks had provided him with invaluable experiences. However, Denver was entering an era of big growth and development and metro area banks were scrambling for a piece of the action. He knew that Castle Rock's proximity to Denver would eventually result in growth and development there as well, but his experiences with rural banking had taught him that those changes would occur on a smaller scale over a longer period of time, thus allowing Castle Rock to retain its small town charm and rural atmosphere. It somehow seemed more challenging to him to be at the forefront of the changes which would take place as Castle Rock grew than to fight the inevitable politics which would eventually engulf the banking industry as Denver grew. History confirmed the truth of these predictions and the wisdom of his decision.

From a professional standpoint, he knew that he and Mr. Miller would work well together. Their shared Midwestern roots in neighboring states of Illinois and Wisconsin had instilled in them similar values and standards, creating a mutual understanding of German frugality and rural conservatism. Consequently, their views on banking were very closely related and while not always in total agreement, they respected each other's opinions, and were enough alike in their thinking to be compatible. By this time, Capital Structure had grown to $138,000 and total deposits had reached $1,500,000 reflecting Mr. Miller's exceptional ability as a banker and a businessman in a small town.[14] Additionally, my dad felt a comfortable rapport with Mr. Miller. The same age as Reuben, there were similar character traits between the two men: their quiet reserve, their humble integrity and their unwavering commitment to their respective communities. Mr. Miller's altruistic endeavors in Castle Rock were reminiscent of when Reuben moved the family to the Roman Catholic side of the river twenty years earlier in Wrightstown.

Willie's tree still grows inWrightstown.

Kenneth Flansburg Collection.

Elwood Brooks reluctantly accepted my dad's resignation and told Mrs. Miller, "I knew I was gonna lose Willie to Phil!"[15] But the three men remained lifelong friends and business associates as the two banks shared a Correspondent Banking relationship for many years to come. On May 14, 1952,[16] after moving us to Castle Rock, taking a twenty five dollar cut in salary and investing half of his savings to purchase enough shares of stock to become a Director, my dad went to work for Mr. Miller as Vice President and Cashier. This move began a tenure at The Bank of Douglas County which would last 42 years. He had come a long way since the days of the pea vinery in Wrightstown, Wisconsin.

ENDNOTES

[1]Birth Certificate, Willis Charles Buboltz, State of Wisconsin, December 26, 1923.

[2]The source of most of the personal and professional information for this chapter comes from interviews with my parents, Willis and Ellen Buboltz, during the writing of this book as well as earlier conversations with Mrs. Miller at the Powder Box Beauty Salon between 1973-1976. Additionally, many of these facts are my own recollections and knowledge because they were part of our family history which I had learned in childhood.

[3]Birth Certificate, Reuben Louis Buboltz, State of Wisconsin, January 17, 1894.

[4]DePere Journal-Democrat, DePere, Wisconsin, June 29, 1961, p 8.

[5]This fact is documented in the Baby Book of Willis Buboltz, written by Olga Buboltz, December 26, 1924.

[6]These facts are all documented in the Baby Book of Willis Buboltz, written my Meta Mattes during the years 1926 through 1929.

[7]IBID; also pictures in Baby Book of Willis Buboltz.

[8]Marriage Certificate, Reuben Louis Buboltz and Mathilda Caroline Stuht, Town of Wrightstown, State of Wisconsin, September 23, 1929.

[9]Aunt Emm and Grandma Buboltz related this incident to me at such an early age, I don't remember the date! It was repeated over the years by many family members, and the tree still stands today as proof!

[10]Marriage Certificate, Willis Charles Buboltz and Eleanor Adelaide Yonge, City and County of Denver, October 15, 1946.

[11]Statements of Condition, The Bank of Douglas County, March 31, 1952, June 30, 1952.

[12]Conversation between Mrs. Miller and the author, Powder Box Beauty Salon, Castle Rock, CO, August 1974.

[13]IBID.

[14]Statement of Condition, The Bank of Douglas County, March 31, 1952.

[15]Conversation between Mrs. Miller and the author, Powder Box Beauty Salon, Castle Rock, CO, August 1974.

[16] The Bank of Douglas County Records, May 1952.

THE MILLER RANCH AND SHORTHORN CATTLE A NEW HOME; A NEW HOBBY

The acquisition of my dad might have been one of the most important changes of the early 1950's for Mr. Miller but it was not the only one. The first year of the same decade, the Millers moved "out in the country," to a place that would not only change their lives and their address, but would broaden their areas of interest, as well.

When Mr. and Mrs. Miller first moved to Castle Rock back in 1921, they discovered a ranch which they liked very much. Given their financial situation, they, of course, couldn't even consider buying a ranch and besides that, it wasn't for sale. Known as the Briscoe Ranch, it consisted of 933 acres and was located "out in the country", approximately two miles south of downtown Castle Rock. They kept their eyes on this ranch for many years to come, driving out there each weekend, planning and hoping it would eventually belong to them![1] The owner, George Cole Briscoe, had been a multi-talented man.

Cole Briscoe, as he preferred to be called, moved to Douglas County in 1879 from Illinois and is credited with being one of the original pioneers of the area. He first homesteaded about five miles south of Castle Rock on land, which contained an abundance of clay pits. He helped establish the clay mining industry, which ultimately contributed to the growth and development of both the town and county.[2]

Not only did his thriving clay pits cement him firmly in Castle Rock's upper echelon of society; his tireless efforts on behalf of education in Colorado had won him respect and admiration in the political arena. He frequently served as one of the delegates from Douglas County to the Democratic State Convention and in the late 1890's he was elected to the Colorado House of Representatives. During the Legislative Session of 1899, he presented House Bill #114, known as the Colorado High School Bill, which provided legislation for the establishment of a county high school system created and funded by the state. Under the new plan, a high school tax would be assessed and admission would be free to any resident of the county.[3]

The bill received immediate support from colleagues on capital hill, as well as from taxpayers statewide, and during the Legislative

Session of 1900 it passed both the Colorado House and the Senate. Soon the Colorado High School Law was enacted, resulting in the development of updated curriculum and the establishment of new and free high schools in many areas of Colorado.[4]

Years later, Cole Briscoe's son, Charles "Bickey" Briscoe, commented on the positive results of his father's stand on education in Douglas County. "The formation of a county high school was a significant event in the area's history. It brought ethnic groups together. The Germans, Swedes, English and resident Yanks came to understand each other. There were intermarriages and family ties began."[5]

In 1919, Cole and Ina Briscoe purchased the 933-acre parcel of land from John Pleasant O'Brien and named it the Briscoe Ranch.[6] Eventually, that same land would become the Miller Ranch.

However, twenty-four years later, when the Briscoe Ranch finally went up for sale in early 1943, the timing was all wrong for Mr. Miller to buy it because he had all his money, "every nickel," tied up in The Bank of Douglas County, which he had helped open in 1939. His good friend, Josef Winkler, himself a stockholder and a Director of the Bank, was aware of Mr. Miller's financial situation and kindly offered to lend him money to help buy the ranch.

One day at Cherry Creek Care Center, Mr. Miller related the story to me, with tears in his eyes. He said that Mr. Winkler had come to their home on Elbert Street one evening in early 1943 and said, "Pheel, I hear you want to buy that Briscoe Ranch." When Mr. Miller told him he couldn't come up with the full amount, Mr. Winkler said, "Pheel, I'll see that you get the extra money," and he did.[7] On March 2, 1943, at a regular monthly meeting of the Douglas Agency Company, the real estate company that was listing the land, Mr. Miller made an offer to purchase the Briscoe Ranch and the Board of Directors voted to accept it. The transaction was finalized on April 21, 1943.[8]

Mrs. Miller often said that Josef Winkler was one of the nicest men who ever drew breath. She said there wasn't anything he wouldn't do for them and when the time came to help him, they did.[9]

The land on the ranch was beautiful. It had grassy meadows and rolling hills, over which the Miller cattle would eventually roam. Groves of oak and maple trees swayed in the breeze, while ponderosas and lodge poles contributed the smell of pine. In the winter, snow would flock the trees and blanket the land and the wind would blow it into great glistening snowdrifts, often giving the appearance of large, white dunes.

In the summer, bright, colorful wildflowers would dot the landscape for as far as the eye could see while the cactus and yucca would give the impression of a desert. Twisted sagebrush and scrub oak lined East Plum Creek as it meandered through the central section of the property and then cut west while sparkling streams and tributaries provided irrigation for the grasslands and water for the future herds.

Although they would own this ranch for the next forty years, the Millers did not immediately move out there. Opening the Bank and buying the ranch had left Mr. Miller with some large debts, and he wanted to be more financially secure before building a new home and moving out to the ranch. He especially wanted to repay his good friend, Josef Winkler. In order to accomplish these goals, they continued to live in their house on Elbert Street for the next seven years. It was during this time that Mrs. Miller's mother, Lucinda Irene Stewart, died in Denver on March 20, 1948 and was buried in Crown Hill Memorial Park next to Alexander. At 88 years old, she had been a widow for exactly twenty-four years and died the same month as had her husband.[10] It was also during these years that Mrs. Miller's, nephew, Jim Benedict met and married Shari Ann Nicholls, January 11, 1950. They would have four children: James born January 10, 1951, Charles born December 5, 1953, Diane born July 28, 1955 and Melissa born November 9, 1966.[11] In a letter to me in May of 1998, Shari related fond memories she had of the early years.

"I met Phil and Jerry prior to marrying Jim. I thought the world of them both. They took me in as one of the family from the very beginning. We spent a lot of time with them when we were first married. They were very good times. I always considered Phil and Jerry to be the kindest, most gentle people."[12]

By the spring of 1950, the Millers felt financially secure enough to make plans to move to the ranch and had a house designed, to their specifications, by well known Aspen, Colorado architect, R. B. Hurst.[13] According to Mrs. Miller, they had a difficult time locating an architect who could understand their ideas. They wanted the house built at a specific angle on the property so they could have a view on all sides. Mr. Hurst could visualize exactly what they wanted.[14] When it was completed the single-level ranch house, with its dark brown exterior wood, gave the appearance of a large and impressive log cabin sitting out in the middle of this beautiful land.

The inside walls were built with "wormy cypress," a very elegant paneling which was quite a rarity in those days. Mrs. Miller was always proud of the fact that hers was one of only two homes in the county constructed with it.[15] Gill and Cecil Whitman described it as a gray wood which came from the southern part of the United States and actually had visible worm holes in it![16]

In a corner of the kitchen there was a breakfast nook with windows facing north and east, giving an unobstructed view of Castle Rock and the surrounding hills and plateaus. The dining room and adjoining living room had large picture windows and offered an even more panoramic view than did the kitchen. They used these rooms frequently for entertaining as evidenced by the presence of a large oak table surrounded by many chairs. Joe Winkler recalled that Jerry was a marvelous cook and the ultimate hostess.[17] Cecil Whitman remembered how she often used avocados in her recipes![18]

The thickly carpeted master bedroom included a walk-in wardrobe area with built-in closets and drawers extending from floor to ceiling and wall to wall. There was also a private bathroom with a tub, shower, and sink. The second bedroom, almost as large as the master bedroom, was also carpeted, had a wardrobe area and a bathroom. In point of fact, this was probably one of the few houses in all of Douglas County at that time which had two bathrooms! They had come a long way since the days of Chick Sale's House!!

In the large, comfortable living room and adjoining dining room there were smooth, shiny hardwood floors that reflected the glowing firelight from the stone fireplace. Their furniture was natural wood and overstuffed leather, which would withstand the rigors of ranch life and fit into their budget as well as their country surroundings. They were, after all, simple people. The house and furnishings were not ostentatious. There was a hint of the western motif in the throw rugs on the floor and pictures on the wall. Although Mrs. Miller once commented to me that they were not marble and crystal-chandelier type people, she had "poise, refinement and culture."[19] This was definitely reflected in the charm and uniqueness which made their home one of the most elegant in the area. The aroma of wood and leather permeated throughout the house, creating an atmosphere both warm and inviting.[20]

Because of all the large picture windows and the design of the house, they had a sweeping view of Pikes Peak and the southern mountain ranges, which could be enjoyed from inside as well as outside. Over the years, it was not unusual to find one of a handful of Denver Bankers sitting on the comfortable, shady, back porch, visiting with Mr. and Mrs. Miller. Mr. Elwood Brooks, President of Central Bank and Trust, or Mr. Frank Goldy, the Colorado State

Bank Commissioner, would frequently journey to Castle Rock to the Miller Ranch for an afternoon of quiet contemplation, far from the hustle and bustle of the big city.[21]

Bankers from small towns, as well, would find retreat and relaxation as they pondered banking issues from their own respective areas. Russ Jennings, President of Middle Park Bank, would often drive from as far away as the mountains of Granby, while Fred Aurand, President of Bank of Manitou, would journey from his mountain town west of Colorado Springs. If the truth were to be known, as the years went by, many important business decisions were made by many important men, over a glass of iced tea in the peace and solitude of the Miller's porch, with Pikes Peak glistening in the sun and the sounds of Shorthorn cattle echoing from a distant pasture.[22]

To the north, the view was quite different. There was the precipice of Castle Rock itself, visible for miles, towering high above the rolling hills and prairie lands, while beneath it, the little country town was nestled in the protective shadow of The Rock. During the next thirty-three years, Mr. and Mrs. Miller watched, through their very own windows, this sleepy little village waking up and growing up, as it changed and expanded and developed into a successful, financially sound and economically profitable town. They watched it grow out over the surrounding hills and up the foot of The Rock. And although it never grew out to meet them, it came close.

Moving to the ranch allowed the Miller's to develop a new hobby! Through their friendship with Mr. Winkler, Mr. Miller had developed an interest in Shorthorn cattle. Soon he purchased a pen of registered Shorthorn calves, although not from Josef Winkler, who raised and sold commercial Shorthorns. Mr. Miller only wanted to show his cattle in the ring as a hobby! This "hobby" eventually developed into a long and successful tenure of raising registered Shorthorns.[23]

Although Mrs. Miller wasn't raised on a ranch, had never been around cattle or even witnessed a calf being born, she soon learned the difference between an Angus and a Shorthorn and could discuss the cattle business with the best of them. From feeding the calves to cleaning the barn, she willingly and happily pitched in with the "chores." She also helped out when they started showing the cattle, by learning to groom, to curry, to walk and to train them.

Her new found interest soon gave way to a strong commitment as well as a deep affection for these animals. Many evenings she would bring them in from the fields and get them settled in the barn, often taking time to play with them, giving them cotton cakes and apples and sugar treats. In fact, she spent many hours with her pets. They each had a name and she knew which calf belonged to which "Momma" cow.[24] It was not unusual to find her in the barn, late at night, sometimes in the midst of a snowstorm, helping her husband with a sick animal or with an especially hard delivery during calving season.[25] Despite her demure size, ranch life toughened her and made her strong. She could often be seen completely surrounded by a herd of what her great niece, Melissa Benedict of Denver, later referred to as "great horned creatures!"[26]

Melissa's mother, Shari Benedict, remembered an incident, which occurred while she and her three oldest children, James, Chuck, and Diane were having lunch on the patio at the ranch one summer day. "Aunt Jerry spotted a rattlesnake slithering in the grass. She went inside, grabbed a straw broom and proceeded to beat the snake to death or at least into unconsciousness! Then she picked it up and threw it over the hill. This tiny little woman, up against a poisonous snake! That is something we all still talk about!"[27]

The most incredible thing about Jerry Miller was that she loved this life! These animals were her "babies," her "gals." She was no more afraid of them than she was of that snake! And whether she was out in the bone-chilling cold of the Colorado winter or in the sweltering summer heat of the barn, she never complained. In fact, she enjoyed it all. Mr. Miller used to tease her and say she even loved to shovel manure!

She often told a story about that very subject! One morning, after Mr. Miller had gone to the Bank, she decided to play with the "gals" and then clean the barn. Now, this in and of itself was not unusual because she would frequently clean the barn. The thing that made this time a noticeable event was that not long after she began pitchforking out the stalls, Mr. Miller came home, unexpectedly, accompanied by the President of the Shorthorn Cattle Association and his wife. There stood Mrs. Miller with straw in her hair and dirt on her face, wearing blue jeans and rubber boots and holding a shovel full of manure!

Mr. Miller was terribly embarrassed. His sense of propriety would not allow him to even entertain the thought that this incident was funny, and he proceeded to tell her so after their visitors had gone. Mrs. Miller, on the other hand, exhibiting her fabulous sense of humor, told him that she thought it was funny and that everyone else would, too! Over the years she delighted in telling that story, often at the beauty shop, and, truth be known, everyone who has heard it has always thought it was funny—as well as very typical—of both Mr. and Mrs. Miller![28]

In this modern day and age when women pump their own gas, change their own tires, and often operate their own ranches, Jerry Miller would be considered an enigma. She never even learned to drive! She once started, but just about the time she was getting comfortable behind the wheel, she read an article about a woman in Denver who injured some people in a car accident and that was the end of her driving days. She decided to stay home and mind her own business. That way she and everybody else would be safe.[29]

Consequently, this created an interesting scene when it came time to feed the herd. Since Mrs. Miller didn't drive, she would be seen riding in the back of the truck, throwing off bales of hay to the animals, come rain or shine, snow or sleet, while Mr. Miller would be riding in the nice comfortable cab! People would often tease him that he really had his wife well trained! I asked her one time if she ever drove that truck. She said that, weather notwithstanding, she could never learn to shift those gears! And, of course, they always had a standard transmission because it was more economical.

The Millers never showed the cattle themselves; they frequently traveled to shows while a hired professional handler by the name of Delbert Mathias from Greeley, Colorado, would show the cattle in the ring.[30] As the years went by, Miller Ranch Shorthorn cattle became well known and well respected all over the country, winning many awards. They exhibited, nationwide, in most of the large, well known stock shows and one year some of their champion bulls and champion heifers were not beaten. One of their most widely known, and best loved, champions was Gold Max, a 2,000 pound Shorthorn bull, who won many awards over the years. In addition to being a Colorado State Fair Champion, he also won championships at cattle shows in Oklahoma, Kansas and other states as well.[31] He was so tame he would nudge Mrs. Miller if he wanted her attention or a treat!![32] Mr. Miller affectionately joked that "we lost our shirts to those animals!"[33] But they enjoyed raising cattle, they enjoyed the traveling and their "babies" became like big, burly pets to them. Of course, winning in the ring, which occurred plenty of times, was an added thrill!

Often, because Phil was so busy at the Bank, Gill and Cecil Whitman would help him with the cattle. Gill remembered, "Usually we would take eight or ten or even twelve of his calves out to our ranch to halter break them. These were calves that he was going to show and we would keep them for about six weeks and teach them to be led around the ring. They weighed 450-500 pounds each. We did this two or three times."[34]

"One time Phil brought us some bulls he was going to sell and they were the kickingest things we had ever seen. We couldn't walk by them without them kicking at us! They weighed between 600-700 pounds each! We had to halter break them so they could be sold!" Sometimes when Mr. Miller had little calves with crooked horns, Gill would go out to the ranch and cut the horns for him. Additionally, Gill Whitman and Harlan Lowell built a block barn, by hand, for Mr. Miller, on the ranch. This was the type of loyal and dedicated friendships that existed in Castle Rock and Douglas County in those days.[35]

Gill also remembered one time when a new veterinarian came to town. Mr. Miller always liked to give new people a chance. He made an appointment for the vet to come out to the ranch and as luck would have it, Mr. Miller could not get away from the Bank at the scheduled time. So he called Gill, who went out and met the veterinarian.[36] That man was Dr. Herman Anderson, who would become a Director of The Bank of Douglas County many years in the future.[37]

With the exception of an occasional traffic noise from the distant highway, Mr. and Mrs. Miller were greeting by the sights and sounds of nature every morning for almost thirty-five years as the sun rose silently, gently over Haystack Hill and the mountains east of the ranch. Maybe they would hear a painful wail of a mother cow nearing a delivery or the soft whimper of a new-born baby calf.

Maybe the wind would gently sway the trees, and the birds would chirp.

In the spring there was the smell of wild flowers.
In the summer there was the quiet patter of rain on the roof.
In the fall, there was the rustle of autumn leaves.
In the winter, there was the gentle floating of snow flakes.

Mr. and Mrs. Miller had a feel for nature that only ranch people can understand:

The silence of the country; the solitude of the land;
horses pawing in the dirt; cattle munching contentedly,
unconcerned with life.
Mrs. Miller's baby cottontail rabbits,
hopping around the back door,
waiting for their daily treats.

These were the things that kept the Millers peaceful and centered and able to face each day; able to amass a fortune; able to become millionaires; able to withstand personal tragedy. When niece, Shirley Benedict, (Bernice's daughter) died only a few days before her thirty-fourth birthday, on July 12, 1961, following heart surgery,[38] Mrs. Miller was devastated by the loss. She had been very fond of Shirley[39] and in the weeks after the funeral, she found comfort and solace in the animals and the peacefulness of the ranch. Likewise, when Mr. Miller had stressful days at the Bank, of which there were many over the years, or when he suffered personal tragedy in his life, he always knew there was a refuge at the ranch, where he could work off the tension, commune with nature, and "talk to the animals!"

And some days, when a Colorado snowstorm would be raging outside their windows, it would be so cold they would want to stay in bed under the big warm comforter. But they never indulged themselves in the luxury. This was the life they had chosen, for all seasons. One cold, snowy January day somebody at the Bank suggested to Mr. Miller that he ought to take Mrs. Miller on a cruise to the nice warm Bahamas, to which he replied, "I would rather take her to the National Western Stock Show!" And he probably did!

Eventually, the two miles between the ranch and the Bank would become industrialized, residentialized and commercialized. The silence would be broken by the sounds of bulldozers; jackhammers and earth diggers as the developers turned hillsides into houses and gravel into gold.

But that would be many years in the future. Gratefully, for Phil and Jerry Miller, during their years at the ranch, the overall atmosphere, beauty and mystique of the land remained intact, unspoiled, undisturbed, undeveloped.

Miller Ranch Registered Shorthorn sign seen upon entering the ranch, 1955.

Robert and Helen Oliver Collection.

ENDNOTES

[1]Conversation between Mrs. Miller and the author at Powder Box Beauty Salon, Castle Rock, CO, August 1974.

[2]Obituary, Charles "Bickey" Briscoe, November 13, 1996, Douglas County News Press p 1,2; Josephine Marr, Douglas County: A Historical Journey, p 159, 160, 162.

[3]IBID, Josephine Marr, p 146, 147. Prior to this time, grade schools were generally supported by tax dollars and attendance was free but the high schools in existence often charged tuition to students who lived outside town or the district.

[4]IBID Josephine Marr, p 147.

[5]Obituary, Charles "Bickey" Briscoe, November 13, 1996, Douglas County News Press, p 1, 2.

[6]Warranty Deed, John Pleasant O'Brien to George Cole Briscoe, February 11, 1919, Douglas County Clerk and Recorder, Castle Rock, CO, Book 57, p 213-215.

[7]Conversation between Mr. Miller and the author at Cherry Creek Care Center, Aurora, CO, August 1991.

[8]Douglas County Abstract Company, Castle Rock, CO as appearing in the Records of the Douglas Agency Company; Corporation Warranty Deed to Philip S. Miller, April 21, 1943, Douglas County Clerk and Recorder, Castle Rock, CO, Book 94, Page 458 and Book 96, Page 256.

[9]Douglas County News Press, August 30, 1979, p 8.

[10]Historical Record, Crown Hill Memorial Park, Lucinda Irene Stewart, March 21, 1948; also headstone Crown Hill Memorial Park, Irene Stewart, Burial date, March 22, 1948.

[11]Dates courtesy of Diane Benedict Fling, Denver, CO, April 1998; also see Benedict Family Tree.

[12]Letter from Shari Benedict, Denver, CO, May 12, 1998.

[13]Blueprints dated 1950 of the Miller Ranch house, courtesy of Mr. Ken Ash, Castle Rock, CO, August 1, 1996.

[14]Douglas County News Press, August 30, 1979, p 9.

[15]IBID.

[16]Interview between Gill and Cecil Whitman and the author, Castle Rock, CO, March 27, 1997.

[17]Letter from Joe Winkler, Castle Rock, CO, June 13, 1998.

[18]Interview between Gill and Cecil Whitman and the author, March 27, 1997.

[19]Letter from Joe Winkler, Castle Rock, CO, June 13, 1998.

[20]In addition to the blueprints, descriptions of the house came from Gill and Cecil Whitman, Bob Oliver, Willis and Ellen Buboltz and my own recollections.

[21]Interview with my father, Willis Buboltz, May 24, 1994.

[22]IBID.

[23]Conversation between Mr. Miller and the author at Cherry Creek Care Center, Aurora, CO, August 1991.

[24]Letter from Joe Winkler, Castle Rock, CO, June 13, 1998.

[25]Conversation between Mrs. Miller and the author at Powder Box Beauty Salon, Castle Rock, CO, August 1974.

[26]Letter from Melissa Benedict, Denver, CO, May 12, 1998.

[27]Letter from Shari Benedict, Denver, CO, May 12, 1998.

[28]Conversation between Mrs. Miller and the author at Powder Box Beauty Salon, Castle Rock, CO August, 1974; also Douglas County News Press, August 12, 1980, p 7.

[29]IBID.

[30]Interview with my father, Willis Buboltz, May 24, 1994.

[31]Douglas County News Press, August 12, 1980, p 2.

[32]Douglas County News Press, August 12, 1980, p 8 and August 30, 1979, p 9.

[33]Conversation between Mr. Miller and the author at Cherry Creek Care Center, Aurora, CO, August 1991.

[34]Interview between Gill and Cecil Whitman and the author, March 27, 1997.

[35]IBID.

[36]IBID.

[37]Statements of Condition, The Bank of Douglas County, June 1994 to December 1995.

[38]Death date for Shirley Benedict verified by Historical Record of Crown Hill Memorial Park, July 13, 1961; also headstone Crown Hill Memorial Park, Shirley Benedict, Burial date, July 15, 1961; and letter from Shari Benedict, Denver, CO, May 12, 1998.

[39]Interview between Gill and Cecil Whitman and the author, March 27, 1997.

Miller's animals were so tame they could be fed by hand. Here Dona Sherlock gives treats to three of the herd! 1957

Dona Sherlock Collection.

Mr. Miller standing in the midst of part of his herd by East Plum Creek on a section of the ranch. 1972

Robert and Helen Oliver Collection.

My favorite picture, one of "the gals" eating hay! 1955

Robert and Helen Oliver Collection.

THE PHILIP S. MILLER INSURANCE AGENCY

Philip Miller diversified into cattle raising and insurance. The former was a hobby. The latter was a moneymaker!

The early 1950's became quite a pivotal time for Mr. and Mrs. Miller, not only in their personal lives but in their professional ventures as well. Shortly after purchasing Charlie Mann's stocks and assuming majority control of The Bank of Douglas County, Mr. Miller bought an insurance agency, which had been in existence in Castle Rock since 1904. Originally the Castle Rock Insurance Agency, it later became the Rock Bottom Insurance Agency, and was well known for its advertisements of a diapered baby with the agency name printed across its bottom! In later years it had been owned by Sturdy Lawonn, and at the time Mr. Miller purchased it the agency was under the management of a large regional insurance group known as Garrett-Bromfield.[1]

The Rock Bottom Insurance Agency of the early 1900's, which eventually became Mr. Miller's, should not be confused with The Rock Bottom Insurance Agency of the 1960's located in the 300 block on Wilcox Street. They were two separate businesses operating at two separate times during Castle Rock history. According to former Castle Rock Junior High Principal, Jack Williams, he and Castle Rock resident, Stan Mikelson, opened the Rock Bottom Insurance Agency on Wilcox Street in 1961. William's father-in-law, Vinton Lord, later bought out Stan Mikelson's share. Mrs. LaVaun Williams, Mrs. Glenva Lord and Mr. Rudy Rennecker operated the agency until it was sold in 1968.[2]

Mr. Miller renamed his new business the P.S. Miller Insurance Agency. As a convenience to his customers, he relocated it in the lobby of the Bank and employed a full-time insurance sales person. Although there were other insurance agencies in Castle Rock at the time, Mr. Miller believed in providing his customers with an on-the-spot-agency whereby they could purchase automobile, homeowner and fire insurance at the same time they obtained their loans. This one-stop-shopping proved to be an extremely successful strategy. The P.S. Miller Insurance Agency showed a profit immediately, and continued to do so for years to come.[3] It remained in operation under his ownership for the next three decades, and is still in existence today as part of Co West Insurance Group.

The first person to work for Mr. Miller at the insurance agency was Mrs. Edwina Colton, who remained there until the summer of 1954.[4] The second person to work at the insurance agency was Robert Oliver, and interestingly enough, this was not the first time he had worked for Philip Miller. Twenty-five years earlier, Mr. Miller had given nine year old Bob Oliver his first paying job![5]

In 1926, around the age of five, Bob Oliver had moved with his parents to Douglas County where they lived on the W.F. Turner Ranch located just south of Tomah Road and Highway 105. This was a 920-acre stock ranch, which his Grandfather Oliver purchased in 1927. Bob attended first grade at a one-room schoolhouse in West Plum. In 1928, when he was seven years old, the family moved to Castle Rock where they lived for the next two years in a house on Cantril Street just west of the school. Another move to a house on Elbert Street in 1930 proved to be a life-changing event for him, because across the street and two houses south lived Philip and Jerry Miller.

Both in their thirties, Mr. and Mrs. Miller spent most of the time operating their business, the Castle Rock Fuel and Feed, which was located in a long low building at what is now 413 Wilcox Street. Since they had no children of their own, they enjoyed this quiet, yet intuitive, neighborhood boy with sandy brown hair. Although he was too young to work for them at the store, it wasn't long before he was mowing their lawn and washing their car for which he was paid fifty cents each. These were jobs he continued throughout high school, not only for Millers, but for several others in town for as the 1930's progressed so did the Depression, and in those days it was necessary to do whatever there was. The experiences of these years initiated not only a business relationship, but a close friendship between the three of them, which would span more than sixty years.

Bob did finally work at the Castle Rock Fuel and Feed. However, it wasn't until the summer of 1937 when he was fifteen years old, and by that time Mr. Miller had sold the business to Ben Saunders and gone back to work at the meat market. Bob remembers driving a dump truck for Ben, delivering ice to various Castle Rock residents. One particularly unforgettable day he was driving up a small, hilly street when 300 pounds of ice slid out of the back of the truck! It was slippery and wet and dirty but somehow he got it got it all loaded back in the truck. What made this event even more memorable was the fact that he didn't have a driver's license yet!

Although he never worked in the meat market, he would frequently help Mr. Miller move sides of beef from the slaughterhouse on Lake Gulch Road to the meat market on Wilcox Street. He also helped Cliff Hawkins butcher one beef.

In April of 1940, with only two months remaining in high school, Robert went to work, part-time, at The Bank of Douglas County where Mr. and Mrs. Miller and Harry Lowe were the only other employees. Bob remembers helping Mr. Miller clean the stoker and dust the counter tops.[6] Hazel and Pete Burgess remember him washing the Bank's round-top windows.[7] After graduation, he attended business college in Denver in the morning and continued to work at the Bank in the afternoon as a teller and a bookkeeper. When his schooling was completed, he became a full-time employee.

In July of 1942, Bob enlisted in the Air Force, but continued to work at the Bank while on reserve until January of 1943 when he was called to active duty. As a member of the Officers' Personnel, he was soon sent overseas, where he served in North Africa, Sicily, Italy and Germany. After the war ended in December of 1945, Bob returned to Castle Rock and Mr. Miller welcomed him back to the Bank where he worked for the next year. On November 27, 1946 he married Helen Mueller, a local Douglas County girl, who had been raised in Sedalia on the Rattle Rock Ranch.

In January of 1947, Bob Oliver went to work for the Bureau of Reclamation on the Colorado-Big Thompson Canyon Project, a federal government venture designed to divert 310,000 acre feet of water by means of a thirteen-mile tunnel underneath the Continental Divide from Grand Lake to Estes Park. This project entailed the construction of a network of power plants, transmission stations and canals, as well as Horsetooth Reservoir, Green Mountain Reservoir and Carter Lake. When completed, it supplied water for irrigation to land in the South Platte Valley between Fort Collins and Loveland which eventually would become one of the largest and most successful farming and ranching areas in northern Colorado.[8]

Over the next seven years, while living first in Loveland and then in Estes Park, he worked on various aspects of the project. From an entry-level position as a clerk typist, he was soon promoted to the Personnel Department of the Construction Division and later became an Administrative Assistant for the Power, Operation and Maintenance Division. It was also during this time that his daughter, Carol, was born.

In all probability, Bob Oliver would have had a very successful future with the Bureau of Reclamation. However, in the summer of 1954, not wanting to relocate out of Colorado, he turned down a transfer to South Dakota and moved his family back to Castle Rock. During his absence Mr. and Mrs. Miller had built a new home on the ranch and had also purchased the insurance agency. Consequently, the Olivers moved into in a vacant house on the Miller ranch and Bob replaced Edwina Colton at the P.S. Miller Insurance Agency. By the end of 1954, he had successfully completed classes and had become a Licensed Insurance Agent. This job change resulted in a lifelong career in insurance and banking, and a thirty-year employment stint with Mr. Miller.

Meanwhile, back at the ranch, Mr. and Mrs. Miller, still with no children of their own, welcomed their new neighbors. They enjoyed the laughter of six-year old, curly haired Carol, reminiscent of the early days on Elbert Street when Bob was a young boy not much older than his daughter was now. Bob and Helen, neither of them strangers to ranch life, felt comfortable there and it was a good atmosphere in which to raise a child.

When he was not working at the insurance agency, Bob was working at the ranch and over the next four years he and Helen helped Phil and Jerry take care of what had been described in 1953 by the Douglas County News as "one the finest herds of Shorthorn cattle in the country."[9] In addition to the daily ranch chores of cleaning the barn and stalls or grooming and feeding the animals, Bob remembers devising a way to get large amounts of hay out into the pasture during the winter months:

> "I built a heavy wooden, three-foot-square platform
> which Mr. Miller and I would mount on the tractor lifts,
> load with bales of hay and haul out to feed the cattle.
> When we were not using the platform for snow hay, I
> trained one of the prize Shorthorns to stand on it with
> all four feet!"[10]

Frequently he could also be seen out in the pen coaxing a 2,000 pound bull to walk up two brick steps! Although neither of these exercises were required for the show ring, they definitely proved that you can teach an old bull new tricks!

More than just neighbors, Bob and Helen Oliver were very devoted to Phil and Jerry Miller. The close friendship and deep respect between the two families continued even after the Olivers built a home and moved into Castle Rock in 1958. Many years later

Mrs. Miller commented, "Although the Olivers moved only a few miles away, Poppy and I felt as if we had lost part of our family."[11]

Over the next twenty years the agency continued to grow, representing such well known insurance companies as Scottish Union, Continental Insurance Group and Travelers. Under Bob Oliver's management, it became a Full Line Agency expanding services into life, accident and health insurance as well as business, livestock, farm, ranch and aircraft insurance, selling surety and fidelity bonds and credit life for the Bank.[12] During many of the early years, The P.S. Miller Insurance Agency was located in the lobby of the Bank. I remember Mr. Oliver's desk was in a cubicle directly on the right upon entering the Bank. Later, as business increased, the "insurance office" was located in various areas of the building.

In addition to his insurance related responsibilities, Mr. Oliver always had duties involving the Bank. After his early days as a teller, he became supervisor over the line, frequently responsible for the hiring and firing of tellers as well as other Bank employees. He also held the position of Assistant Cashier from 1966 until 1971.[13]

When the bank building was remodeled in 1971, Bob Oliver left the insurance business to become a Vice President and Loan Officer in the newly expanded Bank. At that time Marge Lappin took over management of the agency in a separate room on the north end of the building which had been specifically designed to house it.[14] In the late 1970's, Mr. Miller relocated the insurance agency across the parking lot, east of the Bank, into the duplex apartment building which he owned and had converted into office spaces. This marked the first time in twenty-five years that the agency was located outside the confines of the bank building![15]

In 1978, along with his obligations as a Vice President of the Bank, Bob Oliver became Cashier. In 1979, a long held goal was realized when he became a member of the Board of Directors, serving as Secretary, until his retirement in December of 1983.[16] It is interesting to note that the years from 1979 until 1983 represented the first time since 1952 in which The Bank of Douglas County operated with four directors. For the previous thirty-three years there had been only three: Mr. and Mrs. Miller and Mr. Willis Buboltz.[17]

Another insurance agency employee who has experienced a very impressive career, is former Castle Rock resident C. Bryan Ruth, who entered the insurance business as a clerk at the Philip S. Miller Agency during 1978 while studying to get his agent license. After becoming licensed, he was promoted to an insurance salesman at the agency where he remained for several years. After leaving Castle Rock, he earned a Bachelors Degree in Criminal Justice and Criminology and worked in Denver, Honolulu and San Francisco as an Insurance Adjuster and Investigator for such companies as Commercial Union, American International Group as well as Crum and Forster, where he is currently employed in San Francisco as a Supervisor of the Special Investigations Unit. In this capacity, he frequently works with federal, as well as state and local, law enforcement officers from around the country.[18]

EPILOGUE TO THE P. S. MILLER INSURANCE AGENCY

In October of 1981, shortly after turning 86 years old, Mr. Miller made a heartfelt but necessary decision to sell his nearly-thirty-year old insurance agency. The following month, Mr. Ernie Bergamo, a local man with a strong insurance background, purchased the Philip S. Miller Insurance Agency and changed the name to Douglas County Insurance Services. Initially, he operated it out of an office at 222 Front Street and later moved it to 118 Third Street next to The Old Stone Church Restaurant.[19] Under his ownership, the agency has continued to grow and expand. Douglas County Insurance Services is now part of Co West Insurance Group and is located at 703 B Wilcox Street in Castle Rock.

P.S. Miller Insurance Office was once in this front right cubicle. Willis Buboltz's office was directly behind.

Robert and Helen Oliver Collection.

ENDNOTES

[1]Douglas County News Press, Pioneer Section, February 5,1980 and January 29, 1982, p2; Douglas County News Press Pioneer Edition, February 27, 1988 p 4a; and interview with my father, Willis Buboltz, May 15, 1994.

[2]Interview between Jack Williams and Ellen Buboltz, Aurora, CO, July 19, 1997.

[3]Interview with my father, Willis Buboltz, Castle Rock, CO, May 15, 1994.

[4]IBID.

[5]All information regarding Bob and Helen Oliver courtesy of Bob Oliver during an interview with the author, July 31, 1996 Castle Rock, CO and extensive letters and questions during August and September, 1996.

[6]Douglas County News Press, August 12, 1980, p5.

[7]Letter from former Mayor, H. G. "Pete" and Hazel Burgess, November 9, 1996.

[8]Leroy Hafen, Colorado and Its People, Volume 2, p 125.

[9]As reported in the Douglas County News Press, August 12, 1980, p 2, "Finest Shorthorns".

[10]Interview between Bob Oliver and the author, July 31, 1996.

[11]Conversation between Mrs. Miller and the author, Powder Box Beauty Salon, Castle Rock, August 1974.

[12]Interview between Bob Oliver and the author, July 31, 1996; and interview with my father, Willis Buboltz, July 31, 1996.

[13]Statements of Condition, The Bank of Douglas County, December 1966 through December 1971.

[14]Statement of Condition, The Bank of Douglas County, December 31, 1971.

[15]Interview with my father, Willis Buboltz, November 11, 1994.

[16]Statements of Condition, The Bank of Douglas County, December 1978 through December 1983.

[17]Statements of Condition, The Bank of Douglas County, December 1952 through December 1983.

[18]Interview between C. Bryan Ruth of San Francisco, CA and the author, June 1, 1997.

[19] Douglas County News Press Pioneer Firms, January 29, 1982, p 2 and Douglas County News Press Pioneer Edition, February 22 , 1988, p 4a.

Original ranch house where Olivers lived from 1954 to 1958.

Robert and Helen Oliver Collection.

Robert Oliver training one of Miller's prize shorthorns, M.R. Marksman, to stand on a three-foot-square platform! 1956

Robert and Helen Oliver Collection.

M.R. Marksman walking up two brick steps! 1956

Robert and Helen Oliver Collection.

FROM DAIRIES TO DEVELOPERS

In order to understand fully how Mr. Miller and the Bank impacted Douglas County, it is necessary to look back at the changes that took place, within the county and the economy, during the years he was in business.

As has been mentioned earlier, when The Bank of Douglas County opened in 1939 the loans were primarily agricultural. Small business and home loans were frequent, too, as Castle Rock grew and more new businesses opened. However, the majority of borrowers were still farmers and ranchers either growing wheat, or raising cattle, horses and sheep. These industries had been steadily progressing and by the time my dad went to work for Mr. Miller in 1952 the Castle Rock area had become the center of a prosperous farming, stock raising, and dairying district. Agriculture was the central hub around which lives and livelihoods revolved. The majority of loans were General Agricultural Loans.[1] This trend continued for many years to come as these small farms and ranches evolved into family-owned enterprises, handed down from generation to generation, some still in existence today.

At that time in history the whole Castle Rock-Douglas County area was abundant with grazing land, contributing to the success of these industries. One never had to drive far to see cattle grazing. Also, since Douglas County was strategically located between the South Platte Watershed and the Arkansas River Watershed, irrigation was plentiful as well as available. In addition, both the South Platte and the South Fork Rivers carried substantial water supplies year round, making the area suitable for crop growing and offering sufficient water supplies for cattle. In point of fact, there was a considerable amount of land in Douglas County available for agricultural purposes, which had not been cultivated yet, leaving many opportunities for the future.[2]

It is hard to believe that in those early years it was frequently considered risky to lend money for automobiles and appliances, or to lend money to farmers, first time homebuyers and even returning servicemen. Mr. Miller believed, however, that average people were what made a community grow and the success or failure of a banking institution hung in the balance of how often these people came in the Bank and how well they were treated. He strived to meet even their most basic financial needs and to always give a fair deal, if it were at all possible. He bent over backwards to help people, advertising in the local paper for car loans, home loans and loans for the newfangled electric gadget destined to change the world—the television![3]

In those days, it was more difficult for small banks in rural areas to make money than it was for banks in larger areas. Consequently, the rule of thumb for small banks was to charge higher interest rates on loans and pay lower interest rates on savings accounts. Because of a lack of competition, the banks could follow this traditional practice with little or no fear of major repercussions.

This was, however, not Mr. Miller's way of doing business. He knew that while this policy might work successfully in small banks in larger towns, in a rural agricultural community such as Castle Rock, it could spell financial disaster. He could clearly see this situation from both sides of the coin, as a rancher and a cattleman as well as a banker. So, he kept the loan interest rates as low a possible while the interest on savings accounts remained moderately as high as possible. He was a master at not undercutting himself or the Bank while still keeping the customers' needs in mind. In 1953, for example, The Bank of Douglas County paid 2% interest on savings and this was considered a good rate![4]

Likewise, he had a keen ability to judge human nature when it came to loaning money for new or existing businesses and his dedication, belief and commitment to the small business owners paralleled his commitment to that of the farmers and ranchers. He very seldom ever made a bad judgment call. In remembering those early days of the Bank, Mr. Miller once commented how people would come in for loans to get started with "only a little something" to offer as collateral. But these were good, solid, hard working people, which, in Mr. Miller's opinion, was equally as important as collateral. He recalled financing a couple who wanted to buy the old hotel, citing that, "They worked from daybreak until midnight to make a go of it and they were a success." Mr. Miller not only believed in giving a person a loan, he believed in giving a person a chance.[5]

In 1953, the Bank offered a new service to help the grain farmers. It was known as a Commodity Credit Corporation Loan and was implemented to coincide directly with the wheat harvest.[6] The Commodity Credit Corporation was an agency of the federal government operating under the Department of Agriculture. The intent of the loan was to aid those grain farmers who were in the export business by allowing banks to give them guaranteed loans so they could receive an immediate advance of money for their grain crops at harvest time.[7]

In the mid-1950's, the government dealt a crushing blow to the dairy industry by dictating stringent dairy requirements, necessitating major changes in the way the small dairymen were doing business. Consequently, dairy farmers either could not, or simply would not, spend the kind of money the government was demanding to exact these changes.[8]

In Douglas County, as in many successful dairy areas across the country, numerous small, privately-owned family dairies either sold out to, or consolidated with, the larger commercial cattle businesses which supplied dairy products to the food industry as well as to feed lots on a large scale. These new commercial dairy cattle loans amounted to millions of dollars, as the typical small dairy loans of the previous years dropped to nearly nothing because there was no longer a demand for them. Not only was this a terrible jolt to the small dairy owners, it resulted in a drastic decrease in dairy loans in the loan portfolios of most small banks. On the other hand, it created a boon to many larger banks, who saw this as an opportunity to make big bucks by taking advantage of the new government edict and helping large dairies buy out the small ones.[9]

Because Mr. Miller carried quite a few small dairy loans in his portfolio he was tremendously concerned for his customers and for the Bank. He viewed this as another step in government intervention, and instead of idly sitting by while the larger dairies tried to swallow up the smaller ones in Douglas County, he refinanced and extended the dairy loans, allowing these families the time to decide whether or not to hold, fold, or walk away.[10] Some very successful dairy families in Douglas County remained and weathered the storm, so to speak, refusing to be driven out. One of the most well-known and successful operations in Douglas County was the Kelty family dairy in Franktown, which stayed in business for years and years to come.[11]

The late '50's and '60's represented decades of increased growth in population and small businesses in the Castle Rock area. This necessitated more residential and business loans than ever before, as the influx of people resulted in new businesses. It seemed that even then people were migrating from the Metro-Denver area, south to Castle Rock, where the small-town atmosphere prevailed and it was safe enough to leave the back doors unlocked and the car windows rolled down!

From the beginning of his career as a banker, Mr. Miller never shied away from helping a newcomer to the community—a fact that was always reflected in the Bank's loan policy. Countless numbers of people will attest to that fact. Dr. H. R. "Hal" Gannon, now retired, remembered, as a young dentist, coming to Castle Rock from Iowa in the mid-1950's with all his belongings and his dental equipment in a U-Haul trailer. When he approached Mr. Miller for a loan to open a new practice, he didn't even know how much money he needed! "Mr. Miller told me to go out and buy what I needed and then come back in and sign the note."[12] This commitment, to a customer he barely knew! But Hal Gannon was a man Mr. Miller immediately and instinctively trusted. He was honest and sincere, obviously a hard worker to have made it through medical school at a very young age. Furthermore, the town needed a dentist!

Once again, Mr. Miller's instincts were correct, his trust was never misplaced. Over the years the dental practice grew, and Mr. Miller watched, almost like a proud father, as Dr. Gannon excelled not only in the dental profession but also in real estate and land development. What started out as a business relationship that first day in the 1950's evolved into a close and loyal friendship between the two families which lasted until Mr. Miller's death in 1995.

Dr. Gannon was frequently quoted as saying, "The fact that Mr. Miller helped so many people he didn't know and didn't have to help is one of the main factors in Castle Rock's continued progress."[13] History has proven this statement to be true.

Likewise, if Mr. Miller trusted a customer, he would often send a check for a loan through the mail. Freddie Smith, former Mayor of Castle Rock, remembered Mr. Miller doing just that, years ago, when he was a young boy and his family was ranching outside of Franktown. "My folks would call Mr. Miller up when they needed a loan and the check would come through in the mail. That's how people did business then. Their word was good. They didn't have all those credit reports and such."[14]

People familiar with Mr. Miller's background, believe his experience with the Elizabeth banker in the early 1920's, when he was turned down for a loan on his meat markets, coupled with the fact that he had been raised "really poor," later resulted in his passionate almost obsessive commitment to provide a bank to serve small businessmen, ranchers, and farmers.

This also might explain why throughout his banking career he remained very independent. Although it was not in this man's character to do anything illegal, immoral or unethical, he refused to be reigned in by government gibberish or bureaucratic babble. As a result, over the years, Mr. Miller frequently locked horns with the Bank Examiners, who repeatedly requested that he raise the interest rates on agricultural loans. He was so concerned about the well being and financial condition of the farmers and ranchers in the county, he refused to comply with the requests and would not raise the rates. This steadfast faith in and commitment to the farmers and ranchers helped Douglas County develop into and remain one of the most successful agricultural areas in the state. Harry Truman once said "Farmers and ranchers need luck and a crazy banker." Mr. Miller always liked that philosophy and considered himself to be crazy, crazy like a fox![15]

Neither would he conform to certain changes occurring within the banking industry. When BankAmericard became the rage all across the nation and most Denver Banks were offering the service to their customers, Mr. Miller refused to pay the required $25,000. He waited, patiently, and in a few years Colorado formed its own group. Known as Mountain States Bankcard Association, it marketed Master Charge (which later became MasterCard) and he signed on. Eventually, Rocky Mountain Bank Card Systems offered Visa and, once again, Mr. Miller signed on.[16]

He was very conservative in the loan policies and there was one big requirement: The borrower had to show the ability to pay. As one employee once put it, "He was a kind and generous man but he was a businessman first,"[17] and as my dad said on more than one occasion and in more than one interview, "If Mr. Miller felt there was no ability to repay a loan, the answer would always be no. He never over obligated himself or the Bank."[18] That is one of the secrets of his success. Bad loans, like bad meat, could ruin a business!

Carl Winkler once said that Mr. Miller really liked people and that is why he helped so many. But there are two sides to every coin. "He was a hard boiled businessman, but his actions were always justified. He was always fair and people respected him for that. He never turned anyone down without a legitimate reason."[19]

Similarly, Gill Whitman believed Mr. Miller was an ideal businessman, especially as a banker, because it gave him the opportunity to help people.

"I remember one time when Phil helped a gentleman by the name of Fred White. Fred had this old car that would barely make it back and forth to the Winkler Ranch, where he worked. Fred finally found a used Ford for $400 at Burgess Motors, and he asked Phil for a loan. Phil said, 'Well, okay, go ahead and get it.' The guy paid Phil back $20.00 a month, but as long as you regularly paid back something, Phil was happy! He helped many young married kids who needed a home or a better car or even a TV. If they were working, he would help them."[20]

This is not to say that there were never any problems. Occasionally, there were repossessed items in our basement or a repossessed car in our garage. One memorable time, I rode with Dad as he pulled a 60-foot, repossessed house trailer, all the way from the Kansas state line to Castle Rock, hooked to our station wagon with only a boat hitch! The owners had defaulted on their loan and pulled the trailer across the state line erroneously thinking if it were in Kansas it couldn't be repossessed in Colorado. We couldn't go over twenty-five miles an hour but with the help of both the Kansas and Colorado State Patrols, we finally made it to Castle Rock at 3 a.m.! Dad stayed awake on the porch until the sun came up to make sure no one would try and steal it back. Later that day he pulled it out to Mr. Miller's ranch and they eventually sold it to a construction company.[21] However, these episodes were few and far between because bad loans and deadbeat customers were not common place at the Bank in those days.

Around the late '60's and early '70's another change occurred in the business climate that would impact Castle Rock and Douglas County and permanently alter, forever, life as we knew it up until then. Enter the Real Estate Developers. Although real estate development was booming, statewide, nowhere was it quite so apparent as it was in Douglas County. Perhaps the proximity to Denver made it so prevalent and so newsworthy. Maybe the rolling hills and green meadows, or the views of valleys and streams were the main attractions. More than likely it was that the calm, country atmosphere, the smalltown friendliness and the smog-free air drew people from the big city. Whatever the reasons, the phenomenon began and it has really never stopped, to this day.

Large ranches and farms, which up until then had been successful family enterprises, were suddenly worth big money as real estate development began to change grazing land into housing and scrub oak into shopping centers. Many farmers and ranchers saw this as an opportunity to make a fortune, thanks to the increased value of their land, and consequently they sold out. More areas which had previously been agricultural and grazing land, subsequently became housing developments, with the new buzz word being "subdivisions," such as Glover Subdivision to the south, Beverly Hills to the north, Monta Vista Estates to the west, some with large lots and homes such as Happy Canyon, and Surrey Ridge to the north and Yucca Hills to the southwest. Lavish condominium and golf course communities such as the Pinery in Parker and Perry Park south of Sedalia were constructed during these years. With this growth came big changes in commercial real estate, and the development of two new shopping centers.

These new changes also resulted in an upsurge in population throughout the entire Douglas County region. No longer a sleepy little country town, Castle Rock was becoming a "suburb" of Denver. Mr. Miller was flexible enough and business minded enough to change with the times, and he was smart enough to realize that Castle Rock was prime territory where people would inevitably want to move. Always keeping one eye on the immediate business and one eye on the horizon enabled him to remain stable and move forward as the agricultural businesses slowly shifted toward residential and commercial businesses while the focus of the economy went from rural to urban.

Although this real estate boon started out as a small movement with the involvement of mostly local realtors and developers, it wasn't long before the popularity of Castle Rock and its proximity to Denver had attracted large land developers from outside the county, and sometimes even outside of the state or the country. However, during those years, The Bank of Douglas County never catered to the big developers, instead choosing to support and finance the local real estate people, the hometown men and women. The recollection of one successful realtor echoes the sentiments of the others, "Many of us wouldn't be where we are today and the town or county wouldn't have the homes or businesses if it weren't for The Bank of Douglas County. It is a recognized fact, that the Bank was instrumental in the growth and development around Castle Rock and Douglas County during these years."[22] Mr. Miller was frequently honored by the Douglas-Elbert Board of Realtors, for his commitment to both counties and was awarded "Senior Citizen of the Year" several times.[23]

It is very important to mention that there were quite a few families, however, who would not sell out their birthright, electing instead to keep their principles and their land intact, valuing open space and family heritage more than money and progress. Some of these are still in existence today, successfully being operated by younger family members. Gill Whitman described the situation very accurately when he said, "Phil never listened to the big developers. But a farmer or rancher would go in the Bank with some idea he wanted to try and Phil would listen!"[24] These are further indications of his independence as a banker and his loyalty to his customers.

It is also interesting to note that Mr. Miller never got involved in speculative land deals as did many bankers nationwide. Despite the fact that he had more money, personally, than most developers did at that point in time and could have made a fortune as a land developer, he never had any aspirations along those lines. He never purchased any land other than what he already owned on his ranch. As Castle Rock grew and the developers moved in, Mr. Miller spent his money in a different way. He prepared for the future by remodeling and expanding The Bank of Douglas County!

Only photo showing Enderud Building, The Bank of Douglas County, and Senter Building. Notice the brass plaques on either side of doors.

left to right: Enderud Building, The Bank of Douglas County, Senter Building.

Robert and Helen Oliver Collection.

ENDNOTES

[1]Willis Buboltz as quoted in Impact Newspaper, June 7, 1985, p 1.

[2]Yearbook of the State of Colorado 1919, Denver, CO, July 15, 1919, p 75-77.

[3]Douglas County News, Bank Advertisements, October 22, 1953 and November 5, 1954.

[4]Douglas Count News, Bank Advertisements, July 16, 1953 p 7, July 23, 1953, and September 10, 1953.

[5]Douglas County News Press, August 12, 1980, p 2.

[6]Douglas County News, Bank Advertisement for Commodity Credit Corporation Loans, July 16, 1953, p 6.

[7]Thomas Fitch, Dictionary of Banking Terms, Second Edition, p 135; additional information Willis Buboltz.

[8]Interview with my father, Willis Buboltz, May 1994.

[9]IBID.

[10]IBID.

[11]This is the family of Sandy Kelty Shea, owner of Kurly Q Beauty Salon in Castle Rock and wife of Bruff Shea. The Kurly Q Beauty Salon was once The Powder Box Beauty Salon, which I owned in the early 1970's and where I fixed Mrs. Miller's hair. Although the shop is currently located at 703 Wilcox Street, the phone number is still the same as when I had it!

[12]Dr. H. R. Gannon as quoted in the Douglas County News Press, August 12, 1980, p 2.

[13]IBID.

[14]Former Mayor, Freddie Smith, as quoted in the Douglas County News Press, August 12, 1980, p 5.

[15]David G. McCullough, Truman.

[16]Interview with my father, Willis Buboltz, May 1994.

[17]Anonymous employee as quoted in the Douglas County News Press, August 12, 1980, p 5.

[18]Willis Buboltz as quoted in Impact Newspaper, June 7, 1985, p 1 and the Douglas County News Press, August 12, 1980, p 5.

[19]Former County Commissioner, Carl Winkler as quoted in the Douglas County News Press, August 12, 1980, p 2.

[20]Speech by Gill Whitman at the Philip S. Miller Bench Dedication Ceremony, August 3, 1996, Douglas County Extension Office at the Douglas County Fairgrounds; and interview between Gill and Cecil Whitman and the author, Castle Rock, CO, March 27, 1997.

[21]My personal recollections.

[22]Former Mayor, Freddie Smith, as quoted in the Daily News Press, January 12, 1980, p 1 and Douglas County News Press, August 12, 1980, p 5.

[23]One of the Senior Citizen of the Year Awards is on file at the Local History Collection, Douglas Public Library District, Castle Rock, CO.

[24]Speech by Gill Whitman at the Philip S. Miller Bench Dedication Ceremony, August 3, 1996, Douglas County Extension Office at the Douglas County Fairgrounds; Interview between Gill and Cecil Whitman and the author, Castle Rock, CO, March 27, 1997.

Exterior 1971. Remodeling begins. Enderud Building comes down, scaffolding goes up.

Robert and Helen Oliver Collection.

Interior 1971. "Jail Bars" come down in the Teller area.

Robert and Helen Oliver Collection.

Interior 1972. Teller area completely remodeled and moved forward.

Robert and Helen Oliver Collection.

Exterior 1972. Remodeling completed, tripling the size of the building. New offices to left. Brass plaques are still there!

Douglas County News, May 18, 1972, used with permission.

THE EXPANSION OF THE BANK: BIGGER AND BETTER!

Castle Rock was a diamond in the rough. Mr. Miller and The Bank of Douglas County were going to make it shine.

In 1971, Mr. and Mrs. Miller decided it was time to expand the bank building. Capital structure was approximately $1 million, deposits had exceeded $8 million, and loan activity had reached more than $3 million.[1] Additionally, the number of employees had quadrupled since the early days, and the insurance company had grown out of its various cubicles.

Castle Rock, too, had grown considerably during the previous thirty years. From the sleepy little town of the 1920's and 1930's it was now one of the fastest growing bedroom communities in the state of Colorado. New businesses spread out from the enlarged downtown area, and new homes were cropping up every year within the city limits. As was stated in the previous chapter, outlying subdivisions had brought in an additional influx of people. The Bank was at the forefront of much of this progress.

Mr. Miller knew the growth and development would continue. At this time, Castle Rock's only bank was The Bank of Douglas County and he wanted to be prepared to meet the town's needs. Furthermore, he wanted to help usher the town, and the county, through the crucial changes that a growing community experiences over the years. He was proud of the contributions that the Bank had made toward the ongoing growth and development in the area, and wanted to continue serving his customers and the community.

Incredible as it may seem, Mr. Miller was 75 years old at this time! In remarkably good health, his mind remained as sharp as it was in his 50's. Margaret Olson remembered how energetic Mr. Miller was when she started working there in August of 1971, just prior to the expansion, "He was in his 70's when I started and I thought he was about 50!"[2] He always attributed his stamina to good, hard work, at the Bank as well as on the ranch. Even at 75 years old, he followed his own tried and true philosophy, "You have to keep moving forward. You can't stand still."

So, it was, that in the fall of 1971, the silver haired, impeccably dressed, grandfatherly patriarch was standing straight and tall, pouring over blueprints for the new building and mapping out a future for The Bank of Douglas County which would continue through the next twenty-five years. Mrs. Miller once said he would never retire. The Bank was his baby and he had fed it and nurtured it and watched it grow into full maturity. Now he would watch it grow some more.

The first challenge he faced after deciding to expand was whether or not to remodel at the present location on the corner of Fourth and Wilcox Streets or to construct a new building on his property at the south end of town. Mr. Miller knew that eventually the south end of Castle Rock would be another business area with retail shops and stores, an ideal location for a bank. Additionally, there was a five-acre piece of property on his ranch, which he and Mrs. Miller had always believed might be a good location for a new bank building or a satellite drive-up facility.[3]

In retrospect, both of these predictions have come true. The south end did indeed become a booming business area, with shops and businesses and the Library, which bears his name. When it came time to sell the ranch in early 1980's, he kept the five-acres, which subsequently went into his estate, when he died. In 1996, FirstBank of Douglas County, which bought the Bank after Mr. Miller's death, purchased the five-acres from his estate, in anticipation of possibly building an additional branch.[4] During the early part of 1998, a new branch building was, in fact, constructed on the very land which Mr. Miller had saved for so many years for just that purpose.[5]

However, in 1971, after much discussion and thought, Mr. and Mrs. Miller concluded that the timing was not quite right to move south and decided to keep the Bank at its current location. Plans to remodel and expand the existing building began as Mr. Miller hired three local men to head up the project, Chuck Prescott as the Contractor, Andy Anderson as the Architect, and Russ Kostroski as the Engineer.[6] Ben Saunders, with his many years of construction experience and his loyalty to Mr. Miller, was also an important part of the remodeling and expansion project.

Before that job could even begin, the surrounding buildings needed to be removed or razed. This immediately created the second challenge he had to face: What to do with those buildings, which included the two-story frame Enderud Building directly to the north of the Bank on Wilcox, the red brick Senter Building adjoining the southeast corner of the Bank facing Fourth Street and the two Pottenger apartment buildings which ran parallel to each other and were located directly east of the Bank on the alley. He needed these adjacent lots cleared, in order to expand the existing bank building, while one apartment building would have to be moved for the construction of a drive-up area and two new remote units.[7]

Now, it must be noted that Mr. Miller was not one to arbitrarily tear down buildings. But, he was not going to spend a fortune on moving expenses either. His German frugality would still dominate, especially with an expensive project such as remodeling the building. Business was business!

Therefore, after many discussions with the contractors and the building owners in which they explored the feasibility and cost of moving these buildings versus the cost of destroying them, The Bank of Douglas County bought the buildings. Mr. Miller then had the Enderud Building and the Senter Building demolished. He sold the front, west section of the Pottenger apartments for $1,000.00 to business owner, Jerry Reddy, who moved it to the south end of Castle Rock and placed it on a foundation behind his liquor store at 3 South Wilcox Street. Mr. Miller kept the back, east section of the apartments behind the Bank and eventually converted it into commercial office space.[8]

With the buildings gone, and the lots cleared, the work began! The actual construction took place from October of 1971 until April of 1972. The existing building was the core around which the new addition was constructed, like the eye of a tornado around which the all the activity whirled! The expansion largely took place to the east and north sides of the building, where two complete new sections were added to the existing structure, almost tripling the size.

Internal changes took place also. In the new section on the north end, all new offices were added, with Mr. Miller's of course, the first on the left where customers were used to seeing him sit! Directly next to Mr. Miller's were three more offices, Bob Oliver's, Dona Sherlock's, and my dad's. These all had windows looking out over the lobby and the teller counters and my dad's additionally had a window facing east, with a view of the drive-up area. The new Bank was furnished with the most up to date desks, filing cabinets, and credenzas and my dad had a terrific new, high backed, cushioned chair. Also, in the farthest north end of the building was a new room which, for a few years, housed the P.S. Miller Insurance Agency.[9]

In the original Bank, the safety deposit box vault was directly in front of you on the back wall of the lobby as you would walk into the Bank. The money safe was off to the right, located in a not so visible vault behind the teller windows. As a small child, I can remember, in awe, walking into the safety deposit box vault, staring at all those shiny, locked boxes in the wall, perfectly aligned from floor to ceiling like little drawers in a big closet. With the smell of metal and money surrounding me, I would tiptoe so that my shoes wouldn't echo off the floor or the tin boxes. I can also remember the excitement when I was allowed to go into the money vault! This is where all the money in the world was stored, or so I thought! The first lesson Dad ever taught me at the Bank was, "Do not ever go into the vault and close the door!"[10]

The location of these vaults themselves has never been changed and still remain the same today. However, their usage changed when during the remodeling, the money safe was moved into the safety deposit box vault and the money vault became the safety deposit box vault with an additional 350 boxes added. This change was necessitated by the fact that the teller area was relocated across the old lobby in front of the old safety deposit box vault making it more convenient as a money vault. New rooms were added for operations and bookkeeping in the area of the old teller windows, making the old money vault a more convenient location for the safety deposit boxes. Some of those 350 boxes were never rented, but Mr. Miller wanted to be prepared.[11]

Other structural changes within the Bank were made which indicated that the times they were a changing! My earliest recollection of the Bank was having to stand on tiptoes to get a drink out of the old round marble water fountain in which the water was always warm and always came out in a trickle. That was gone, replaced with the more modern, aluminum water cooler, always with cold water and always with strong pressure![12]

The teller "cages", which actually resembled jail cells, were also gone. In their place was a modern, open counter where tellers helped customers with their business transactions. Former Castle Rock resident, Jane Reddy Olsen, remembered how she always liked those teller cages when she was a small child and was so sorry to see them go during the remodeling.[13] Many people expressed the same sentiments! The wooden gates, which separated the offices and teller area from the lobby, had been removed a few years earlier for the sake of safety. Many children of that era remember those swinging wooden gates as one of the main attractions in the Bank! Many parents remember them, too, because they pinched an occasional little finger!

The large front entry doors, which swung both ways were also gone, replaced with the more energy efficient and modern entry door. One very well-known and respected rancher in Douglas County, who shall remain nameless, reminisced how he, as a small boy, got his fingers caught between one of those old swinging doors. The only way to get his fingers out was for Mr. Miller and my dad to remove the door with a screwdriver! To this day, he still has the scars to prove it!

One special link to the past was the tall, oak wood table which had money displayed under its glass top and little cubbyholes for deposit and withdrawal slips. It stood in the lobby to tickle our memories and bring a smile to our lips. For me, it represents the realization of some of my earliest childhood goals. I was so small when my dad began working at the Bank that I could not even reach those cubbyholes! One of my first goals was to grow tall enough to be able to reach my hands into those cubbyholes. I needn't have worried! By the time I was five I could reach in and pull out the deposit books, which at that time had purple carbon paper in them. I also remember the light blue counter checks, obsolete today, but very much used back then. They had the Bank logo, a little Castle Rock, imprinted on them, and I still cherish the one I have today.

Having conquered my desire to *reach* the top of the table, I next wanted to *see* the top. I knew, in my heart of hearts, that treasures galore awaited my scrutiny. By about age seven I not only attained the necessary height to see what was up there, but also proved myself correct! As I viewed the old notes, money and currency I felt that I had, without a doubt, found the end of the rainbow!

The large, round top windows survived the remodeling, too, although the panes were replaced with energy efficient, security glass. I was glad because those windows held an amazing amount of memories for me. My first recollection is that the surrounding moldings were painted turquoise and I have pictures from that era. The two windows on the southwest corner were to my dad's office. The south window faced Fourth Street with a view looking south at the main business block. The west window faced Wilcox Street with a view of the Courthouse Square to the left and the Keystone Hotel straight across the street. I would often walk up to Dad's windows, cup my hands around my eyes, and peek in to see if he was there sitting at his desk in his swivel chair with its wooden slats. If he was, I would knock and he would turn in the chair and wave back at me. Sometimes, he would wink. I knew never to knock on the window if he was helping a customer. Walking down to the Bank and looking in his windows was one of my greatest joys. It was something I did from the time we moved there, holding hands with my mom until I eventually was allowed to walk there alone, apparently signaling my maturity.

The next window was Mr. Oliver's and was located on the front of the Bank, south of the door, also facing Wilcox Street. I always looked in his window, but never knocked. The window on the north side of the door was Mr. Miller's, and then just beyond that there was another door which went directly into his office but which he never used. These also both faced Wilcox Street and I never knocked or even looked through them! Although he never would have minded, he was the boss, after all, and I had respect for his window and his door!

I remember the first time I was invited in to the hallowed walls of his office. As I sat in the big, brown leather chair, my feet barely skirted the floor. He had pictures of cows on the wall and cow statues and trophies displayed around his office. I didn't know they were registered Shorthorn cattle, worth a fortune in money or meat. To me, in childish understanding, they were just cows. As I ran my hands over the smooth leather arms of the chair, I can remember looking up at him and innocently asking, "Do you milk those cows everyday?"

His face broke into a smile and then he laughed and his eyes twinkled and he answered, "No, Sweetheart, those are not milk cows." He always called me "Sweetheart." The last time I ever saw him in Cherry Creek Care Center, when he was ninety-something and I was forty-something, he still called me "Sweetheart!"[14]

However, as the old and familiar disappeared, the new and innovative appeared. On the south side of the building on Fourth Street, an Automatic Teller Machine was installed.[15] History was made, as they say, because The Bank of Douglas County was the first place in Castle Rock to have such a system. People could now get money in the middle of the night, on weekends or holidays by simply driving to the Bank, inserting a little card and, like magic, cash appeared. Of course, it could be used for deposits, too, but as human nature would have it, more people used it for withdrawals than they did deposits! I must admit that, to this day, I have never in my entire life used an ATM. I don't even know my access code or my ID "pin" number! To me, banking is not banking unless there is a human involved, somewhere, somehow at the other end of the transaction!

Another bit of Castle Rock history was made that year: The Bank of Douglas County implemented drive-up banking![16] This was probably one of the greatest conveniences ever offered! On the east side of the building there was now a drive-up window coming directly from the Bank and two remote units. Customers could do their banking from the car by either putting their transactions in the drawer at the window or in the plastic tube at the remote unit and send it, miraculously, through a tunnel down under the pavement, in through the basement and up to the teller. On paydays, or Friday afternoons, cars could be seen lined up all the way around the block. A "dummy window" was built at this time on the north end of the east wall, directly behind my dad's office, because, once again, Mr. Miller wanted to be prepared for the future. Eventually this second window was activated when the additional remote units were installed during the late 1970's.[17]

The convenience of drive-up banking was incredible. Women could do their banking while the kids slept in the car. Men in dirty overalls and greasy boots could do their banking without having to go home and clean up first. Teenagers could sport through, cashing their part-time job paychecks, while hiding cigarettes under the dash. On cold, snowy winter days or rainy, summer afternoons, customers could remain warm and dry in their cars while doing banking business with the aid of a little tube, a mechanical drawer, and a smiling voice echoing from the speaker.

In addition to the most up-to-date security system with time locks on all the vaults and safety features on the windows and doors, cameras were also placed throughout the Bank at strategic points. This followed a recent order by the FDIC that all banks, nationwide, must have a camera system.[18] Wall to wall carpet had also been installed, not only for appearance sake but for safety sake, too.

Finally, the old brick on the outside of the building was sandblasted clean to match the newly installed brick. It was quite a transformation! When looking at the front of the building today, it is hard to tell where the old stopped and the new began because the remodeling blended the two so perfectly. The old section is the right side of the building, symbolized by the six round top windows, while the new section is the left side of building, where the Enderud Building once stood. On the south end, facing Fourth Street, the ATM was located in the area where the Senter Building once stood. The drive-up window on the east side of the building was part of the new addition near the new teller area. In the drive-up area, the two original remote units were located where the west Pottenger apartment building stood, the additional remotes were located where the east Pottenger building was removed a few years later.

Probably the most innovative and ultimately the most humorous remodeling marvel was designed specifically for the winter months. Underneath the new sidewalks surrounding the Bank and drive-up area in the back, a heating coil system had been installed, which would prevent ice from forming after the snow had been shoveled or had started to melt. This was the first place in town to have such a modern and convenient system, not to mention the safety it imparted to Bank customers and employees.

Soon after it was installed, a Colorado snowstorm blew through, and the next day after shoveling and sweeping, Mr. Miller activated the coils. They worked perfectly! There was no icy film on the sidewalks, no slippery spots due to runoff, no spinning tires in the drive-up area. Everything functioned according to plan and the new system was the topic of conversation throughout town. Jim Folkestad remembered, a month or so later, asking Willie Buboltz how the new coils worked. My dad told him that they worked fine, and everyone was pleased—until the first electricity bill arrived in the mail! Mr. Miller took one look at the amount due and said, "Never turn those coils on again!!" And no one ever did! Modern convenience lost out to German Frugality![19]

On May 13, 1972 the Grand Opening was celebrated from 10 a.m. until 4 p.m. and was enjoyed by many, many Bank customers, old friends, Bankers from Denver and Colorado Springs and surrounding areas. The first 400 ladies received free carnations. Hundreds of door prizes were awarded. There was something for everyone: Series E Savings Bonds in the amount of one hundred, fifty, and twenty-five dollars; cameras; radios; picnic jugs; clocks; coffee pots; and record albums were all given away.[20] Mr. and Mrs. Miller were on hand to greet their guests as were all the Bank employees. Everyone expressed awe at the beautiful new building, with its spacious lobby, large offices and lovely furnishings. The transformation was truly amazing! Adding to the festivities, two highly honored guests were in attendance from the early days, Josef Winkler and Ben Saunders. Delicious food and drinks were served and that day has always been remembered by many of us as one of the highest and happiest points in the history of Castle Rock and The Bank of Douglas County. It was also the beginning of a new era, for the Bank and its employees.

SEE 1972 BANK GRAND OPENING IN PHOTO SECTION.

ENDNOTES CHAPTER 15

[1]Statement of Condition, The Bank of Douglas County, December 31, 1971.

[2]Letter from Margaret Olson, Castle Rock, CO, December ,1996.

[3]Interview with my father, Willis Buboltz, May, 1994.

[4]Douglas County News Press, March 20, 1996, p 2a.

[5]Information Senior Vice President, Buddy Douglass, FirstBank of Douglas County, Castle Rock, CO, April 9, 1998; and Douglas County News Press, April 8, 1998, p 1.

[6]Interview with my father, Willis Buboltz, May 1994.

[7]IBID.

[8]IBID.

[9]Personal recollections of the new bank building.

[10]Personal recollections of the early bank building.

[11]Interview with my father, Willis Buboltz, May 1994.

[12]Personal recollections.

[13]Interview between Jane Reddy Olsen and the author, Prescott Valley, Arizona, September 1996.

[14]All of the above sections are personal and wonderful memories of my childhood years and experiences regarding The Bank of Douglas County, my dad, and Mr. Miller.

[15]Interview with my father, Willis Buboltz, May 1994.

[16]IBID.

[17]IBID.

[18]IBID.

[19]Interview between Jim Folkestad and the author, Castle Rock, CO, January 1997; and interview with my father, Willis Buboltz, May 1997.

[20]Douglas County News, May 18, 1972.

Willie Buboltz, Vice President and Cashier, 1972.

Buboltz-Bodle Collection.

Robert Oliver, Vice President, 1972.

Douglas County News, May 18, 1972.
Used with permission.

Dona Sherlock, Assistant Cashier, 1972.

Dona Sherlock Collection.

COMPETITION AND PHILANTHROPY: MR. MILLER AT HIS BEST

The Mid 70's and Early 80's

The expansion and remodeling brought a whole new look to the Bank, a more modernistic, futuristic look. It was not a country bank anymore, because Castle Rock was no longer a little country town. But while the building and the look may have changed, this merely symbolized that they were growing right along with Castle Rock. The service and the commitment to the community by the employees and the Millers were still as important as ever.

Saturday hours were once again resumed (after having been on hiatus since 1951) with the drive-ups open from 8 a.m. until noon. Daily hours were also expanded. While the lobby was still open from 9 a.m. to 3 p.m., Monday through Friday, the drive-ups remained open until 5 p.m. on weekdays and 6 p.m. on Fridays.

In January, 1973, Willis Buboltz became Executive Vice President and Cashier. He would remain Executive Vice President for the next fifteen years.[1]

On June 18, 1975, First Bank opened at 221 Wilcox Street with Mr. Mel Sorensen as President.[2] This brought competition to The Bank of Douglas County for the first time in thirty-five years! However, Mr. Miller welcomed this new bank. With all the growth and development occurring in the area there was definitely enough business to support another bank. Additionally, the conservative nature of Mr. Miller and the Bank caused them to exercise a philosophy that one bank does not have to take all the loan business of a community. The two banks had a very compatible business relationship and the officers and directors had great respect for each other.[3]

Despite the competition, The Bank of Douglas County continued to grow. The hours were expanded with the lobby still opening at 9 a.m. but remaining open until 4 p.m. on weekdays. The drive-ups were now open daily from 8 a.m. to 5 p.m. and until 6 p.m. on Fridays. Saturday drive-up hours remained 8 a.m. to noon. Within a few years it was necessary to hire some more people and do some internal rearranging. The P.S. Miller Insurance Agency was moved across the parking lot into the second apartment building. This didn't last too long, however, because as the customer base and the Bank continued to grow, by the late 1970's, it became time to expand once again, this time in the area of the drive-up facilities. Plans were designed for two additional remote units, and this meant that the second apartment building would finally have to be removed.[4]

It has been previously mentioned that Mr. Miller was very independent. More importantly, he was equally ethical and honest. He would always ask, "Is this a rule, a regulation or a law?"[5] If something was a law, he followed it to the letter, in spite of the fact that he may have totally disagreed with it. However, if it was simply just a random rule or a ridiculous regulation, that was a different story. Sometimes those could be circumvented!

A perfect example of his independent spirit involved the tearing down of the second apartment building. There was a town regulation that, as the building owner, he had to obtain required permits, at a fee, which, to his frugal way of thinking, was totally exorbitant. Consequently, he refused to obtain the permits.

One Saturday immediately after the noon closing of the Bank, Arlie Gordon and his crews, who had obtained their required permits, began the task of bulldozing the apartment building. By six o'clock that evening , all that remained was a flat, grated lot, cleaned and cleared and ready for construction.

The following week Mr. Miller received a fine for failure to purchase the proper permits, which he gladly paid, because the amount of the fine was much cheaper than the price of the permits! He may have been frugal but he was honest enough to pay the consequences. He later commented to me, with a grin on his face, "It wasn't the price so much as it was the principle!"[6]

During May of 1979, the family experienced the death of Bernice's son, Jim Benedict, of Denver at the age of 55. Because of his military background, he was buried in Fort Logan National Cemetery.[7] Shortly thereafter, I saw Mrs. Miller in the Bank and expressed my sympathy. She sadly commented, "Poor Bernie, she outlived both of her children. But thank the good Lord she has grandchildren and great grandchildren living nearby."[8]

In a letter to me during the writing of this book, Jim's daughter, Melissa, remembered the kindness and generosity "Uncle Phil" demonstrated to both her and her mother, Shari, after her father's death:

"The year my father died, times were very hard. The hospital bills had stacked up and it made life very difficult for my mother. My brothers and sister were grown and on their own at this time. For

Christmas, Mother and I both received checks from Uncle Phil. These gifts were very much appreciated and such a surprise."[9]

In August of 1979, an important milestone took place in the history of the Bank as it reached its 40th year in business since opening August 28, 1939! Significant also, was the fact that it was the longest continuously operating bank in the history of Castle Rock or Douglas County. The 40th Anniversary was recognized with an Open House at the Bank and a well deserved tribute to both Mr. and Mrs. Miller in the local paper with a series of impressive articles written by Dianna Gordon.[10] Congratulations and best wishes were also printed from business people and friends, alike. Mr. Mel Sorenson, President of First Bank of Castle Rock, wrote a letter, publicly expressing his congratulations and indicating his admiration and respect for Mr. and Mrs. Miller and their contributions to the community. It read:

> Dear Mr. and Mrs. Miller: Congratulations on the 40th Anniversary of The Bank of Douglas County. Thank you for all your efforts in helping the people of Castle Rock and Douglas County over the last forty years. The growth and vitality of our area is a testament to the hard work of you, your officers, and staff. Our best wishes are extended to you for continued health and success. Signed, Warm Regards, Melvin J. Sorensen, President.[11]

In an editorial appropriately entitled "Movers and Shakers of Past Made Present Possible," Jim Adkins, Editor of the Douglas County News Press wrote:

"As communities grow and evolve from the small towns of America 50 or 60 years ago, new residents and even old-timers often forget the tremendous efforts of the movers and shakers of those decades. Such are Phil and Jerry Miller."[12]

He went on to list their many contributions, from the early days in the meat market and the feed store to the Town Board and then later, their most formidable accomplishments being the Bank and the Library. He added that two of the most important things to Mr. Miller were good economic health for the community and progressive development. In conclusion he wrote:

"It is appropriate that in August 1979 as The Bank of Douglas County celebrates its 40th Anniversary that in celebrating that event the Millers are recognized. Without their tireless efforts and foresight, many things that are taken for granted in Douglas County would not be. We and others salute the Millers for those years."[13]

It was indeed a very special time for the employees, the town and the proud owners! At this time Mrs. Miller was 79 and Mr. Miller was 84. They still lived at the ranch and Mr. Miller still came to work every day. In less than three months they would celebrate their 60th Wedding Anniversary.

On December 28, 1979 the Bank achieved another milestone, technologically speaking. Though Mr. Miller had fought it to the bitter end, on that date the Bank began its conversion to computer-based bookkeeping. Although they had used posting machines for years, they still did much of their transactions by hand. Scheduled to go "on-line" on January 1, 1980, Mr. Miller felt that this change would somehow diminish the "personal touch" he had always strived for at the Bank. He nonetheless realized that computers were the wave of the future and not just a passing fad. On the first day of a brand new decade, he and his Bank moved from the era of the posting machine into the era of the computer.[14]

The '80's will be remembered as the decade when the bottom fell out of the banking industry! But not for The Bank of Douglas County! As deregulation, greater competition, high costs of money and a shaky nationwide economy caused banks all over the country to close their doors, The Bank of Douglas County was still growing and showing a profit. My dad once commented, "The Bank made money hand over fist during the '80's!" This can be contributed, once again, to the conservative loan policy as well as to the wisdom and good business sense of Mr. Miller, his Board of Directors and his Loan Officers. In a 1985 interview with Impact Newspaper, Willie Buboltz described their policy, "We require twenty-five percent down on an auto loan. We are to the point where we require a down payment on everything. We feel customers are less likely to walk away from something if they have equity in it."[15]

Despite the fact that Douglas County had become a hotbed for the land developers and the housing industry, the Bank loan portfolio still reflected that 10-20% of the outstanding loans were agricultural, proving that in spite of the subdivisions and the golf courses, farming and ranching remained strong economic forces in the county, and reflected Mr. Miller's never ending commitment to ranchers and farmers.

It must not be overlooked that when Mr. Miller moved to Castle Rock in 1921 there were only twenty-five businesses. By 1980 there were between 550 and 600, with the majority of them having been financed by The Bank of Douglas County. Many of them were family owned and operated and passed down from grandfathers to fathers to sons. One of Mr. Miller's greatest pleasures was knowing that he helped somebody "get started." He was proud of the contributions that the Bank made toward the development of the business community. He was equally as committed to the small business owners as he was to the ranchers and farmers. Expressing awe at the loyalty, which ran so deeply toward him and the Bank, Mr. Miller once said, "The sons have carried on some of the businesses and they are some of the greatest supporters and largest depositors in the county."[17]

The thing that was so remarkable about the success of this Bank was the fact that it was a small-town bank as opposed to a large city bank. Yet, it frequently had more total assets and more total equity with a more stable loan portfolio than did many larger city banks. In addition, it was consistently ranked as one of the safest institutions in the United States. For example, in The Bank Safety Directory, which reports the nationwide rating of all banks, The Bank of Douglas County was given a safety index of 142 points, which in the banking industry, translated into "exceptionally strong" and was the highest rating given. It was one of only 35% of the banks in the US rated that high.[18] Given the dismal state of affairs the banking industry was in during that whole decade, banks which were succeeding and showing a profit were few and far between! In addition to the consistently high nationwide rating, The Bank of Douglas County also ranked in the top ten banking institutions in Colorado, for growth as well as for safety, during the previous thirty years.

One of Mr. Miller's most philanthropic gestures toward Castle Rock took place in late 1979 but was not announced until January of 1980. He donated the water rights from 204 acres of his ranch to the Town of Castle Rock. He had recently sold that section of land and, under Colorado law, water rights are retained by the seller and can be sold separately.[19] In order to fully understand the significance of this donation, it is necessary to review the fundamental facts about water and what was happening to it in Castle Rock during these years.

Water is measured in acre-feet. One acre-foot equals approximately 325,850 gallons of water.[20] Mr. Miller's donation consisted of approximately 300 acre-feet and provided nearly 100 million gallons of water, enough to supply an estimated 600 homes. In 1980 the dollar value of these water rights was estimated to be between $125,000 and $400,000.[21] In today's market, they are worth millions.

Under normal circumstances, this donation would have been considered a huge philanthropic gesture, but these were not normal circumstances, which made it even more benevolent. At the time of Mr. Miller's donation, Castle Rock was in the midst of a water shortage, which had been created by the large-scale growth and development in the area during the previous few years. As a result, in the summer of 1979, the Town Board had been forced to place a moratorium on the annexation of land surrounding the town due to "uncertainty about whether Castle Rock had sufficient water supplies."[22] Since he was very aware of this water shortage, Mr. Miller had been contemplating his donation since selling his land. As the gravity of the situation increased, the decision was not a difficult one to make.

Although the donation was made in late 1979, it was not made public until January 17, 1980 in a front page article entitled, "Banker Gives Water Rights to Castle Rock."[23] At that time, Mayor Freddie Smith announced this charitable gesture saying, "Water rights are a very salable item today. Mr. Miller could have sold them to Aurora or Chatfield, yet he donated them to Castle Rock. I can only say thanks. I'm going to guarantee you we're going to protect those water rights." Mr. Miller commented, "Castle Rock has been good to me. At one time I would have asked for something in return but now I don't need it."[24]

In retrospect, it remains unclear what might have happened had Mr. Miller not donated that water to the town. It is feasible that the town, out of necessity, might have been forced to ration water, so short was the supply. In all likelihood, future development, whether business or residential, might have come to an abrupt halt. Furthermore, to purchase equivalent water rights at that time would have resulted in an enormous expense to the Town of Castle Rock. But, thanks to Mr. Miller, none of that ever transpired. Motivated solely to benefit the town and its people, his unselfish gesture once again solved the immediate problem. Castle Rock received a desperately needed water supply, the annexation moratorium was lifted and the way was cleared for future business and residential development.[25]

In an interview in August of 1980, Freddie Smith commented on the water rights and summed up Mr. Miller's dedication to the town and county:

"By giving the water rights to the town he wanted to make sure the water was protected, to make sure it was handled the way he wanted it to be handled. Those are million dollar rights, and he just gave them to the town."[26]

"He's always looked out for the town, for the county. He has done more than any one individual. I guess maybe he adopted the county and town as his family. It's been good to him, and he's been good to it. It's a mutual relationship. He's put a lot of money into the county and the banking business has been good to him. He's not a selfish person."[27] Further he commented, "For years the Officers of The Bank of Douglas County managed our money, the town's money, and showed us how to make money. We didn't know anything about it."[28]

It is interesting to note that at this time Mr. Miller was 85 years old and 69 year old Ronald Reagan was running for President! Freddie Smith then made one of the most notable and poignant statements ever spoken, "I look at Phil Miller and honestly think I might be able to vote for Reagan. I thought Reagan was too old, but you look at Phil and *he* could run the country!"[29]

While the water rights donation was a one-time act of generosity, Mr. Miller's support and philanthropy in other areas was ongoing and far reaching. This is best reflected with his efforts regarding The Town of Castle Rock, The Douglas County Fair and Rodeo, and The Douglas County Public Library System. The following three chapters focus on these important entities to which Mr. and Mrs. Miller were both highly dedicated.

My favorite photo of Mr. Miller at his desk in 1980.

Douglas County News Press, August 12, 1980, used with permission.

ENDNOTES

[1]Statements of Condition, The Bank of Douglas County, January 31, 1973 until December 31, 1988.

[2]Information regarding FirstBank of Castle Rock verified by Sr. Vice President, Buddy Douglass, FirstBank of Douglas County, April 9, 1998.

[3]Interview with my father, Willis Buboltz, May 1994; and conversation with Mr. Miller and the author at Cherry Creek Care Center, Aurora, CO, August 1991.

[4]IBID Willis Buboltz.

[5]IBID Willis Buboltz.

[6]Conversation with Mr. Miller and the author at Cherry Creek Care Center, Aurora, CO, August 1991.

[7]Death date for James S. Benedict verified by Diane Benedict Fling, November 8, 1997, and the Funeral Record of James S. Benedict, Fort Logan National Cemetery, Denver, CO, May 10, 1979 , burial date, May 15, 1979.

[8]Conversation with Mrs. Miller and the author at The Bank of Douglas County, May 1979.

[9]Letter from Melissa Benedict, Denver, CO, May 12, 1998.

[10]Douglas County News Press, August 30, 1979, articles written by Dianna Gordon, p 1, 2, 3, 8, 9.

[11]Douglas County News Press, August 30, 1979, letter from Mel Sorensen, p 5.

[12]Douglas County News Press, August 30, 1979, "Movers and Shakers of Past Made Present Possible," Editorial written by Jim Adkins, p 4.

[13]IBID.

[14]The Bank of Douglas County Records, December 28, 1979 and January 1, 1980.

[15]Willis Buboltz as quoted in the Impact Newspaper, June 7, 1985, p 1, also Statements of Condition, The Bank of Douglas County, January 1980 to January 1990.

[16]IBID; also Interview with my father, Willis Buboltz, May 1994.

[17]Douglas County News Press, August 12, 1980, p 2.

[18]Weiss Research Inc, Bank Safety Directory, A Complete Listing of U.S. Banks and Their Safety Ratings.

[19]The source of information and quotations regarding Mr. Miller's water rights donation to The Town of Castle Rock comes from the Daily News Press, January 17, 1980 in an article written by Gail Anderson entitled "Banker Donates Water Rights to Town," p 1, 9.

[20]IBID p 9.

[21]IBID p 1.

[22]Minutes of Regular Meeting, Town of Castle Rock, June 21, 1979; and Daily News Press, January 17, 1980, p 1.

[23]Daily News Press, January 17, 1980, p 1.

[24]IBID.

[25]Minutes of Regular Meeting, Town of Castle Rock, November 1, 1979.

[26]Freddie Smith as quoted in the Douglas County News Press, August 12, 1980, p 5.

[27]IBID.

[28]IBID.

[29]IBID.

RICHARDSONS, RAMSOURS, MILLERS, AND THE TOWN HALL

During the early 1980's, Mr. Miller acquired a building on the southwest corner of Fourth and Perry Streets in Castle Rock. Previously known as The Ramsour Building, it more recently had been converted into offices, one of which had housed the P.S. Miller Insurance Agency prior to 1981. The history of this building spans nearly a century and intertwines three well-known and successful Castle Rock families—The Richardsons, The Ramsours and The Millers.

In the early 1900's there was a Douglas County Mercantile located at 400 Third Street on the southeast corner of Third and Perry Streets, a Castle Rock Hardware Store located at 318 Wilcox Street, and a empty little warehouse on the southwest corner of Fourth and Perry Streets.[1] In March of 1937,[2] Mr. Clyde Richardson, a former lumber yard owner from Parker, bought the hardware store from Joe Lacey and the empty little warehouse, where he soon opened a lumber and implement business. In 1938,[3] his son, Duane, moved to Castle Rock and went to work at the hardware store while Clyde operated the lumber and implement business, which by then stocked International Harvester Farm Machinery, served as a warehouse for the hardware store, and functioned as a separate lumber operation. They called their combined businesses The Castle Rock Hardware, Lumber and Implement Company.[4] It should be noted that at this time Mr. Miller owned the meat market. The Bank of Douglas County did not open until August of 1939.

In January of 1942, recognizing the need which a growing community such as Castle Rock had for a larger lumber operation, Clyde Richardson purchased the Douglas County Mercantile at 400 Third Street, through an estate sale, and opened Richardson Lumber Company.[5] Although he purchased the building and the contents, the lot consisting of approximately one half of a city block, was leased from the Denver and Rio Grande Western Railroad. According to Duane's daughter, Kathy Reis, her dad worried every time the lease came up for renewal.[6] Worry notwithstanding, Richardson Lumber Company would remain at that location for the next 42 years.

In 1943, as his son prepared to enter the Army,[7] Clyde sold the Castle Rock Hardware Store, lot, stock and barrel, and converted the Lumber and Implement Company into a warehouse and storage area for Richardson Lumber Company. While Duane went to war, Clyde ran the lumber yard with the help of Duane's wife, Eleanora, who went to work there as the bookkeeper.[8] When Duane returned home in 1946, the three of them worked side by side to make Richardson Lumber Company one of the most successful businesses in the town of Castle Rock.

The hardware store at 318 Wilcox Street later became a Gambles Store. It was owned by Jay and Kay Williams from 1957 until 1966 when it was bought by their son and daughter-in-law, Ed and Glenda Williams, who operated it until 1978 when they closed the store. At that time, Attorney, Jim Folkestad bought the building and converted it into additional office space in order to expand his law practice at 316 Wilcox.[9]

Sometime during the 1950's, three brothers by the name of Ramsour moved into Castle Rock. They started a business of their own, and became regular customers of Richardson Lumber Company and The Bank of Douglas County. Glen Ramsour always credited Clyde Richardson and Phil Miller with helping the Ramsour Brothers get their start in Castle Rock. While Clyde would advance them a line of credit for needed materials, Phil would advance them small loans for needed capital.[10] The struggles of these early days cemented a professional relationship between the three businesses as well as established a lifelong friendship between the three families.

Ramsours eventually purchased the old warehouse building and the lot at Fourth and Perry Streets from Clyde Richardson and, in 1967,[11] constructed a larger facility which became the base of operations for Ramsour Brothers Construction Company. This firm grew to be one of the most successful, sought after general contractors in Colorado and neighboring states, specializing in million dollar highway construction projects and bridge building.

While Ramsour Brothers Construction was growing and expanding in its own specific niche, Richardson Lumber Company was becoming the largest and most successful lumber operation in Castle Rock. With an excellent reputation and very little competition,[12] the business grew and expanded. Two large multi-level sheds were constructed along the east side of the building as well as the back west side of the lot, increasing the capacity for lumber storage and offering greater convenience to customers. Over the years, as business continued to increase, more storage sheds were added throughout the lot.

In January of 1969,[13] Duane purchased Richardson Lumber Company from Clyde, who was ready to retire. Eleanora Richardson told me that when Phil Miller loaned Duane the money to buy the lumber yard, Duane was so grateful he paid off the loan as fast as he could! She described Mr. Miller as always being a very generous man. She further remembered that he trusted his instincts about people and if he believed in someone, he would always help out. He always believed in Duane.[14]

Similarly, a few years later when Richardsons built a large and beautiful residence up on hill overlooking the town of Castle Rock, Phil Miller, once again, loaned them the money.[15] Mr. Miller's instincts were never wrong where Duane Richardson was involved. So certain was he of Duane's integrity that the initial commitments to both of these transactions were handled with a telephone call and a handshake.

In June of 1984, Duane and Eleanora sold Richardson Lumber Company to Larry Holmberg and Kenny Ritter.[16] This event came about after the untimely and tragic death of longtime employee and close family friend Robert Neal on New Years Eve earlier that year. The new owners changed the name to Douglas Lumber but remained at the same location until May of 1986, when they moved the lumber yard to its current location on the west side of town at 1335 N. Park Street.[17]

Meanwhile, Ramsour Brothers had grown and expanded to a larger facility north of Castle Rock, and in a 1980 interview Glen Ramsour reminisced about his thirty-year association with Mr. Miller and The Bank of Douglas County, "I've known Mr. Miller for thirty years and all I know about him has been good. He has been an awfully good asset for the county..."[18]

He credited Mr. Miller's friendliness and desire to help others as secrets of the Bank's success:

"You go in to the Bank and he's sitting at his desk. If there is no one there you can go in and sit down and chat with him. He has always taken time to visit with people who come in the Bank. I think he tried to help everyone. When the town was small and he knew everyone, I think he probably even helped a few deadbeats, too."[19]

On a more personal note, Ramsour fondly recalled, "Mr. Miller has been awfully good to me. We didn't have anything when we came here but I never went out of that Bank without getting what I came in for."[20] Like Duane Richardson, Glen Ramsour was another man in whom Philip Miller always believed.

Therefore, it somehow seemed right that in the early 1980's, the building and the property on the corner of Fourth and Perry Streets, which once belonged to Richardsons and then belonged to Ramsours was acquired by Mr. Miller. Despite the fact that the acquisition of this building offered him a number of profitable options, he characteristically chose philanthropy over profit and, on June 10, 1982, donated the building and the property to the Town of Castle Rock.[21] Attorney Jim Folkestad remembers the day:

"Both Mr. and Mrs. Miller were there. It was one of the last times I ever saw her. There was a big ceremony and he turned over the deed and the keys to the Town. Then we all went over to the Old Stone Church Restaurant and had a big meal and it was quite a celebration, quite a festival. The Town immediately began using the building as a Town Hall, because at that time there was quite a need for space and buildings to locate the municipal offices."[22]

On June 21, 1982, the Mayor of the Town of Castle Rock and the Douglas County Board of Commissioners joined together to issue a Proclamation expressing appreciation for the donation. It read:

PROCLAMATION
R-82-51

WHEREAS, Mr. and Mrs. Phil Miller have through the years generously supported the Town of Castle Rock and Douglas County; and

WHEREAS, in yet another exhibit of generous support, Mr. and Mrs. Phil Miller have donated the building located at the corner of Fourth Street and Perry Street to the Town of Castle Rock.

WHEREAS, the Mayor of the Town of Castle Rock has issued a proclamation to express appreciation for the donation and to recognize the efforts of the Millers to better the Town of Castle Rock and Douglas County.

NOW, THEREFORE, BE IT PROCLAIMED that the County of Douglas joins the Town of Castle Rock in expressing appreciation for the donation and in recognizing the efforts of the Millers to better the Town of Castle Rock and Douglas County.

This Proclamation was signed by County Commissioners Dr. W. G. Duncan, Carl A. Winkler, John P. Orcutt and attested to by Douglas County Clerk and Recorder, Carroll Hier.[23]

Mr. and Mrs. Miller regarded this unexpected recognition as very kind but totally unnecessary. They had donated the building as a benefit to the town and no thanks were required.

In the early part of 1983, renovations began on this building to convert it, officially, into a Town Hall.[24] Over the years it has been occupied by many entities of the Town of Castle Rock such as the Town Board and the Fire Department. It is currently the home of the Castle Rock Police Department.

In May of 1998, as I was finishing this book, groundbreaking took place for a new police station on the southeast corner of Second and Perry Streets. The Douglas County News Press reported that Developer, Mr. Brad Brown, planned to "renovate the old police station, once it was vacated, converting it into offices and retail space."[25]

EPILOGUE TO RICHARDSONS

Kathy Richardson Reis, to this day, is my best friend in life. During my teenage years in Castle Rock I spent equally as much time with her family as I did with my own, and Duane and Eleanora Richardson became like second parents to me. Many of my happiest recollections occurred while with the Richardsons.

Kathy taught me how to drive an old Vespa motor scooter we had nicknamed Granny, which I promptly drove into a stone wall at Cedar Hill Cemetery because I forgot where the brakes were located! Then, bravely, she taught me how to drive a car out on Ridge Road. As she held on, white knuckled, I tried to learn to shift gears in her poppy red 1965 Mustang without burning up the clutch. Although my parents never admitted it until years later, they were very grateful that she had spared them the insanity of having to teach me themselves!

I learned to water ski in Fort Collins, Colorado with Kathy and Eleanora cheering me on from the boat. As Duane pulled me out of the cold water of Horsetooth Reservoir, I remember the feeling of freedom and exhilaration as I looked up at the green trees etched against the blue Colorado sky. I have the Richardsons to thank for that memory.

Eleanora Richardson was invaluable to me as I wrote this chapter. Although it is further back in the book, it was the first chapter to be totally completed. She died ten months later and I was so grateful that I had the opportunity to work with her and learn from her wisdom, expertise, and memories. Kathy has helped me continually, with information and pictures but more importantly, with never-ending support and encouragement! The Richardsons are in this book, not only because they were a big part of my life, but because they were a big part of Mr. Miller's life as he was of theirs, as well.

In another one of life's many mysteries, Philip Miller outlived both Duane Richardson, who passed away January 18, 1990 and Glen Ramsour, who passed away March 10, 1990.[26]

Clyde and Duane Richardson's first business.

Douglas County Fair Book, 1938, p4. Local History Collection, Douglas Public Library District.

ENDNOTES

[1]Douglas County News Press Pioneer Edition, January 29, 1982, p 2; Our Heritage-The People of Douglas County, Clyde Richardson, written by Clyde Richardson, p 241.

[2]Scholtz Scrapbook, March 12, 1937, Local History Collection, Philip S. Miller Library, Castle Rock, CO.

[3]Douglas County Daily News Press, May 23, 1984, p 1.

[4]Interview between Eleanora Richardson and the author, Castle Rock, CO, May 15, 1996; and Castle Rock Record Journal, August 26, 1939, p 5.

[5]Our Heritage-The People of Douglas County, Clyde Richardson, written by Clyde Richardson, p 241.

[6]Interview between Kathy Reis and the author, Fayetteville, Arkansas, April 5, 1996.

[7]Interview between Eleanora Richardson and the author, May 15, 1996; and Douglas County News Press Pioneer Edition, January 29, 1982, p 2.

[8]Interview between Richard Lee, brother of Eleanora Richardson, and the author, Castle Rock, CO, March 25, 1997.

[9]Interview between Glenda Williams and the author, Castle Rock, CO, June 4, 1997; interview between Jim Folkestad and the author, Castle Rock, CO, January 30, 1997.

[10]Glen Ramsour as quoted in Douglas County News-Press, August 12, 1980, p 8.

[11]Douglas County Assessor's Office, Property Characteristic Report for 318 Fourth Street, Castle Rock, CO, April 25, 1996.

[12]Moore Lumber opened in 1978, Douglas County News Press Pioneer Edition, February 27, 1993, p 2a.

[13]Douglas County Daily News Press, May 23, 1984, p 1; interview Eleanora Richardson, May 18, 1996.

[14]Interview between Eleanora Richardson and the author, Castle Rock, CO, May 18, 1995.

[15]IBID.

[16]IBID; also Douglas County News Press, June 15, 1984, p 3.

[17]Douglas County News Press Pioneer Edition, February 27, 1988, p 2c.

[18]Glen Ramsour as quoted in Douglas County News Press, August 12, 1980, p 8.

[19]IBID.

[20]IBID.

[21]Deed, Philip S. Miller to Town of Castle Rock, June 10, 1982, recorded June 11, 1982, Douglas County Clerk and Recorder, Castle Rock, CO, Book 443, p 691.

[22]Interview between Jim Folkestad and the author, Castle Rock, CO, January 30, 1997.

[23]Douglas County Board of Commissioners, Proclamation R-82-51, June 21, 1982 on file at the Local History Collection, Douglas Public Library District, Castle Rock, CO.

[24]Douglas County News Press, March 2, 1983, p 1.

[25]Douglas County News Press, June 3, 1998, p 3a.

[26]Information Kathy Reis; and information Steve Ramsour.

Clyde Richardson's storage warehouse, during the mid-50's which Ramsour Brothers eventually bought and rebuilt into the Ramsour Building.

Duane and Eleanora Richardson Collection.

Mr. Miller acquired the building and donated it to the Town of Castle Rock in 1982. Here in 1983 it is being remodeled into a Town Hall.

Douglas County News Press, March 2, 1983, used with permission.

The building later became the longtime home of the Castle Rock Police Department.

Buboltz-Bodle Collection 1995.

MR. MILLER AND THE DOUGLAS COUNTY FAIR: PEOPLE AND EVENTS

The Douglas County Fair and Rodeo is a myriad of different entities, events, activities and even buildings, all to which Mr. and Mrs. Miller were both very dedicated. Their support spanned seventy-five years and encompassed 4-H, The Douglas County 4-H Livestock Sale, The 4-H Council, The Fair Association and Fair Board, The Douglas County Young Farmers and Homemakers, Kirk Hall and The Whitman Lowell Pavilion. Some of these entities continue to receive money since Mr. Miller's death in 1995 through his Perpetual Charitable Trust.

Mr. Miller's involvement in the Douglas County Fair dates back to 1921, when he placed his first advertisement in the annual Fair Book.[1] It was a simple little ad, because they had just moved to Castle Rock and taken over the meat market and, as he told me years later, "I didn't have the time or the money to get creative. I think that first ad cost me two dollars and fifty cents, but I couldn't swear to it."[2] Nevertheless, over the next 75 years of his business career, some very eye-catching and unique advertisements appeared in the Fair Book as Mr. Miller continued his steadfast practice of advertising The Castle Rock Meat Market, The Castle Rock Fuel and Feed and The Bank of Douglas County. Even though an official livestock auction was not part of the fair in the early days, Mr. Miller frequently made arrangements with ranchers at the fair to purchase their animals, which he would butcher and sell at the meat market.

From its inception in the 1890's, support has always been strong for the fair.[3] In fact, over the years it has become a mainstay of community life in Douglas County, a testimony to the stability and spirit of ranching and farming lifestyles. Even during the Depression, when money was tight and morale was low, the fair was still held. If cancellations did occur they were never due to lack of interest, but rather to droughts or crop failures or epidemics or wars. Such was the case during the middle of World War II, when, out of respect for the soldiers, the fair had been canceled.

But John Hammond, who was Sheriff, believed it was important to offer the community some type of entertainment in spite of the fact that the fair had been canceled. Consequently, Hammond, Vernon Wyatt, Charlie Kirk and Phil Miller donated around twelve hundred dollars to sponsor a combined rodeo, horse show and chariot race. While county residents owning race horses and show horses volunteered their animals for the events, ranchers brought in feed and supplies. Gill Whitman remembered donating two truckloads of hay. The organizers hired a judge from Wyoming to judge the horse show.[4] Charlie Kirk once commented proudly, "We financed it ourselves and if there was money to be lost, we lost it ourselves."[5] People didn't always lose money, though.

Cecil Whitman remembered during the chariot races, "Somebody would run around with a couple of handful of bills taking bets on the side and would raise maybe fifty to one hundred dollars for the purse!"[6] In describing the popularity of the chariot races, Charlie Kirk said, "You couldn't have gotten anybody to move with a stick of dynamite until those chariot races were over!"[7] By sundown the festivities would be finished, but the day was a good morale builder. This county pride and volunteer spirit resulted in a combined rodeo, horse show and chariot race which ran successfully two years in a row during the middle of the summer as a replacement for the fair.

The second year it rained and hailed and was very cold. Gill Whitman remembered that when the rain quit, J. B. Godley, who was kind of the boss that year, put on his yellow slicker and got on his horse, Patches, and said, "The show must go on!" Pretty soon, Hap Godley, Les Godley and Benny Esquibel were out there pushing calves around in the mud. If anyone had dampened spirits, they didn't last for long!

Despite the great success of this substitutionary event, when the war was finally over, it was a little hard to regain support and build up momentum for the fair and 4-H after the years on hiatus. Returning servicemen were concerned with marriage, jobs, and starting families. Even ranchers and farmers had other things to think about as the end of the war signaled a decline in demand and price of meat and foodstuffs. Furthermore, in 1946, just as the Rodeo Association of America had officially been added to the activities, the fair had to be canceled at the last minute due to the polio epidemic.[8] During the following years, the Extension Service and the Fair Board members worked long and hard organizing the Fair and judging the events. Charlie Kirk, who was the County Agricultural Agent at the time, recruited 4-H members and operated on a budget of only $200.00.[9] These were lean times, both in the areas of community involvement and financial support.

To quote Mr. Miller, "The fair was just about to die out."[10] This seeming lack of interest bothered him tremendously, because he believed very strongly that the children of the county deserved a chance to learn about animals. He felt that one way they could do this was to have the opportunity to raise and feed their animals and then display and sell them at the fair. For the sake of the children, Mr. Miller and J. B. Godley decided to save it!

J. B. Godley was a rancher and an auctioneer in the county and, according to Mr. Miller, "A real go getter." Mr. Miller explained that, in the evenings and on weekends, at their own expense and on their own time, the two of them solicited donations from the people of Douglas County for financial support of the fair. At the same time they dug deep into their own pockets to personally contribute money. Additionally, they collected prizes from the local merchants so that the children who won with their 4-H entries would have something to show for their efforts. "We used our own money and our own gas and we worked darn hard," he said.[11] Their work paid off. In addition to raising money and prizes, they brought awareness to the community regarding the plight of the fair.

Shortly after that, a group of ranchers and businessmen decided it was time to make some improvements on the fairgrounds. Many areas were in disrepair due to lack of use and maintenance. Therefore, as with the chariot races during the war, these people pooled their money and resources, donated supplies and materials, and volunteered hundreds of man hours and labor to complete the many projects necessary to bring the fairgrounds back in working order. The main entrance off Lewis Street was constructed, old buildings were repaired and repainted and new posts and fences replaced old ones. Gill Whitman remembered how he and others spent hours and days building the cattle barns and exhibit halls. At the urging of none other than J. B. Godley, a new arena was constructed and wooden chutes were installed.[12] It is interesting to note that during World War II, two original barns were used to store straw. The straw was stuffed in to mattresses by women and children, and then shipped overseas to the servicemen.[13]

According to Gill Whitman, Mr. Miller never did any of the physical labor at the fairgrounds, but he donated money for the improvements anytime he was asked. Additionally, if they needed materials or supplies he would go to Richardson Lumber, pay for them and have them sent out to the fairgrounds immediately. This was during the early years of the Bank and he kept a pretty close watch over it.[14] Furthermore, much of the work was done on Saturdays making it impossible for him to participate because this was also during an era when the Bank was open on Saturdays.[15]

Although he was maybe not on the front-line trenches where the sweat was being shed and the nails were being hammered, he was always behind the scenes, quietly donating money and offering support and supplies. The experiences of this time resulted in a lifelong devotion to the Douglas County Fair and to 4-H for both Mr. and Mrs. Miller.

It is very important to note that the repairs, improvements and additional buildings were all built with private money. To quote Gill Whitman, "It was not the county's money. It was the people's money. They donated it and they worked for nothing. That's the kind of people we had here."[16] The volunteer spirit has always been the bedrock for all support, improvements, and events that have taken place over the years at the fairgrounds.

At that time in history, the fairgrounds were out in the country. There was only one entrance—down the dusty, unpaved, tree-lined, Lewis Street. Bordering the south end of the fairgrounds was the Miller Ranch. In early 1950's Mr. Miller sold the Fair Board some land on his ranch, to straighten up the boundaries of the fairgrounds. He charged $25.00 per acre. According to Gill, Phil said, "Well I gotta charge you something, how about $25.00 an acre?"[17]

It is hard to believe that those very same fairgrounds are now surrounded by apartments to the east, shopping centers to the west, and Plum Creek Golf Course, elegant housing and the Philip S. Miller Library to the south. The only thing that remains the same is Lewis Street, to the north, only now it is paved! With a 10-15 year Master Plan already on the drawing board, massive changes and expansion will result in the Douglas County Fairgrounds and Castle Rock Regional Park. A modern rodeo complex will be built to accommodate fair activities and sporting events while maintaining the rural atmosphere and preserving the heritage of the fairgrounds.[18]

In 1951, J. B. Godley was killed in a car accident.[19] Shortly after that the arena was dedicated to him and a flagpole erected in memory of his many years of service and commitment to the Douglas County Fair and Rodeo.[20] It is very likely that had he lived, he would have been very involved in another big project at the fairgrounds—the establishment of the Douglas County 4-H Livestock Sale.[21]

In 1959, three well-known and well respected Douglas County men got together and organized the Douglas County 4-H Livestock Sale. These men were auctioneer, Charles Sherlock, and ranchers

John Lowell and John Paulk.[22] They believed a livestock sale would help the children raise money, as well as generate more interest and support for the Fair. Mr. Miller's devotion was evidenced again by the fact that he purchased the first Grand-Champion Hog at the first Sale in September of 1959. Years later, he was given a commendation for that purchase.[23]

For the first few years of the Sale, Charles Sherlock did the auctioneering. The community experienced great sadness when he passed away in 1964,[24] never knowing the full impact that this Sale, which he helped organize, would have on the future of 4-H and the Douglas County Fair. Revenues from the Sale have increased from $10,000 at its inception to present day totals of more than $100,000 per sale.[25] During the writing of this book, John Paulk passed away, in March of 1998.[26]

Every year, at the Livestock Sale, Mr. Miller, acting as a representative of the Bank, would frequently buy animals at more than the going rate so the children could make a little extra profit. It would also not be unusual for him to buy animals at the Sale and then return them to the owner either for resale or slaughter. Over the years, Mr. Miller and The Bank of Douglas County became two of the largest financial supporters of the Sale, with purchases totaling in the hundreds of thousands of dollars. Additionally, employees of The Bank of Douglas County clerked the Sale for the first fifteen to twenty years it was in existence.[27]

Although he purchased his share of championship animals over the years, it was more customary to find him bidding on, and buying, animals which were not necessarily of championship quality. Tilting his cowboy hat back and scoping out the crowd, he would watch the bidders and listen to the bids, carefully calculating the totals in his head to make sure that the champions were getting the appropriate prices. When he was satisfied that they were, he would then choose seven or eight animals which were maybe smaller in size or weight, younger and less mature—animals which would not normally bring in the big money. Then, he would purposely "bid the price up" on each animal, as high as he could before purchasing it. This would increase the amount of money the child would make on the final sale of his or her animal. Bea Lowell believes that this practice can be perceived as Mr. Miller's way of helping the children whose animals were not commanding the high prices.[28]

This was typical of Mr. Miller's philosophy of determining the greatest good for the greatest number of people. In this case, he deemed it more prudent to "spread the wealth" by purchasing several animals at a higher than expected price instead of bidding on one championship animal where the proceeds would benefit but one child.

His generosity found him frequently paying more than the market price for beef so the kids could make a little more money on their animals. John Lowell remembered when fat steers were only selling for 30 cents a pound, Mr. Miller would often buy the kids' steers at 40 and 60 cents a pound, then send them on to the yards and get only about 30 cents back.[29] He might have lost money at the slaughter house, but that was just fine with Mr. Miller. He felt that although each animal might not always be equal, each child always deserved an equal chance at a fair price.

One day somebody yelled, "Donate that animal back to the 4-H Council for resale," and although it can never be verified, many people believe that somebody might have been Phil Miller! Regardless of who yelled it, the practice of donating the animal back for resale became routine, generating thousands of dollars more each year. The 4-H Council has always been highly dedicated to awarding educational scholarships to young people in the county, and income from the resale of these animals helps, in large part, to fund the scholarships. Former Fair Board President, Karen Serafini, explained the dynamics of this, "The first time the animal is sold, the Livestock Sale gets a small percentage but the rest of the money goes to the child. After all the animals have been sold, the ones which have been donated back are resold a second time and the money from the second sale then goes to the 4-H Council for the scholarship fund."[30]

From then on, Mr. Miller donated every purchase he made back to the 4-H Council. Even after his health would not allow him to participate in the Sale anymore, a representative from The Bank of Douglas County, usually Willie Buboltz or Bob Oliver, would attend each year and purchase animals on behalf of Mr. Miller and the Bank, always donating them back to the Council for resale. This practice continued even after his death in 1995, when at the Sale less than two months later, my dad was still honoring Mr. Miller's longstanding custom of helping the kids by purchasing their animals and donating them back to the Council. In 1996, he continued the tradition in Mr. Miller's memory, only in the name of the Philip S. Miller Library, because by then The Bank of Douglas County had been sold.[31]

Over the years, it became a common practice for major bidders to play a friendly little game of competition with each other during the

Sale. Glen Ramsour, Duane Richardson, Bob VanPelt and Phil Miller, among others, would see "who could out bid who" and which organization would spend the most money at the Sale! Whoever spent the most money wouldn't let the rest of them live it down until the following year at the Sale when the competition would start all over again! Duane Richardson once joked that Phil Miller was the only man in the county who could bid a rabbit up to $500.00 and get away with it!

The results of this generosity were not only reflected in the amount of money the children made, but also in the overall totals of the Sale as a whole. According to Bea Lowell, Mr. Miller and The Bank of Douglas County were instrumental in helping the Douglas County 4-H Livestock Sale to yield more dollars per animal, as well as to generate the highest total auction revenues over any other county in Colorado. This was an honor held for many, many years.[32] The Douglas County 4-H Livestock Sale has continued to grow, and is one of the most successful in the state.

I have seen the lists of purchases, and would like to share each and every name with you. That of course, would be space prohibitive. Suffice it to say, however, that thanks to Mr. Miller and the Bank, many young people in Douglas County have been able to finance their college years and/or begin a career in ranching. It is impossible to make so much as an educated guess as to how many young people this would include.

Because Mr. Miller's involvement in the Sale spanned more than thirty years, it very often happened that he would purchase animals from 4-H members who were the children or grandchildren of ranchers from whom he had purchased back in the old days!! He could often be heard proudly telling a youngster, "I bought a rabbit (or a steer or a pig or a lamb) from your Daddy or Mommy twenty-five years ago when he or she was just about the age you are now!" The little one would giggle in disbelief!

Mr. Miller often commented, "I am happy to support the fair. It is wonderful to see the kids with their little rabbits, chickens, lambs, hogs and cattle. I get great pleasure out of it. When I got started in 4-H, I loved the kids and wanted to do something for them."[33] Although approached many times, Mr. Miller never served on either the Douglas County 4-H Council or the Douglas County Fair Association. Instead, he was more content to work behind the scenes where he was always one of the most dedicated supporters of every aspect of the fair, devoting immeasurable amounts of time, money and effort on behalf of the kids.

Kirk Hall and the Whitman-Lowell Pavilion were two other projects which Mr. Miller donated money to help build although they were built more than twenty years apart. They, once again, demonstrated the community spirit which prevailed when the people of Douglas County decided to get things done at the fairgrounds.

In the early 60's it became apparent that there was a definite need for an all-purpose facility at the fairgrounds. This facility would be utilized for fair and 4-H activities, displays and exhibits, meetings and county functions, public gatherings and an election hall. Completed in 1964, named Kirk Hall in honor of County Extension Agent, and longtime Fair Board member, Charles Kirk, the building was entirely built by financial pledges and donations of goods and services, materials and labor. There was no loan money involved, whatsoever.[34]

Although Kirk Hall was a project taken on by the Young Farmers and Homemakers, it was the brainchild of John Lowell. As longtime 4-H leaders, as well as a Fair Board member and officer, he and his wife, Bea, were involved in almost every aspect of the fair, from the livestock sale to the hamburger booth! Realizing the benefits a building such as this would provide, but at the same time being completely aware of the exorbitant construction costs, he decided to do an experiment. At his own expense, he printed pledge cards and sent one home with each 4-H member. The idea was to determine exactly how much support, if any, could be generated to finance a new building.

The response was astounding! Not only were pledges received, but, to his delight, offers were made for goods, materials, and supplies as well as services, labor and manpower! This was not surprising, however, because the people of Castle Rock and Douglas County have a history of pulling together out of the goodness of their hearts to provide hard work and support for a necessary project. As always, Mr. Miller was one of the staunchest and strongest supporters of this project. During the months in which the construction took place, he frequently donated money in the name of the Bank. To quote Bea Lowell, "He gave us anything we asked for."[35]

As construction progressed, it is interesting to note that the cinder block was donated by different people throughout the county. When the building was completed there was a shortage of twenty blocks, and it still remains that way today.[36] Over the years, Kirk Hall has been enlarged and expanded several times. Not only is it an exhibit hall during the fair, it is the central hub where fair-goers often congregate to visit and enjoy delicious hamburgers from the Food Booth. During the rest of the year, Kirk Hall serves as an all-purpose facility for many county functions. Charlie Kirk always said it should have been named in honor of John Lowell![37]

Meanwhile, the Livestock Sale continued to grow and it soon became obvious that a permanent location was needed specifically to house it. Up to this time, the Sales were always held in the rodeo grounds or behind the livestock barns where bidders would sit on bleachers, sometimes pelted by late summer rainstorms! I can remember a couple of times the animals and their owners were almost ankle-deep in mud, nearly forcing the cancellation and emphasizing the need for a covered facility. At the 1988 Fair, a new building, The Whitman-Lowell Pavilion, named in honor of longtime Douglas County ranchers, fair supporters and Board Members, Gill and Cecil Whitman and John and Bea Lowell, was dedicated for the purpose of holding the Livestock Sale and various livestock shows.[38] This was particularly appropriate since John Lowell was one of original organizers of the Livestock Sale in 1959.

The success of the Whitman-Lowell Pavilion was largely due to the efforts of Larry Carnahan, who was President of the Douglas County Fair Board at that time. As before, with Kirk Hall, most of the work was done by donation or at cost with volunteer manpower hours and labor, supplies and materials. The Douglas County 4-H Council contributed $27,000 toward its construction[39] and Mr. Miller also made a generous donation in the name of The Bank of Douglas County.[40] Once again, the community support and volunteer spirit enabled this much needed pavilion to become a reality. According to Gill Whitman, when the building was completed there had been an unexpected overrun on the construction costs. Mr. Miller gave the County Commissioners a no-interest loan through the Bank. After a few months, he made another large donation to retire the debt on the loan.[41]

Another fair oriented organization of which Mr. Miller was tremendously supportive is the Douglas County Young Farmers and Homemakers of America, who sponsor the Food Booth each year at the Douglas County Fair. This booth is operated all day, every day during the fair by members who fry hamburgers, grill buns, dole out pickles, onions, ketchup and mustard and generally work very hard. I can remember when I was a kid, the booth was in a wooden and aluminum stand before it was permanently located in Kirk Hall. Regardless of the location, this Food Booth has become renowned for its delicious, mouthwatering hamburgers. Mr. Miller used to say he never could eat just one, and that was true. He always bought four or five or six, which he and Mrs. Miller would either eat there or take home and share later. Mr. Miller's support of this organization came in an entirely different and very unique way, however. Every year at the fair, regardless of how much the cost of his hamburgers, he would always pay with a twenty dollar bill and tell them to keep the change! In the "old days," when hamburgers were "two bits," that was a pretty good chunk of change![42]

In a poignant statement, Gill Whitman expressed his feelings about those years, "When we would get through with the fair, the sun would be getting ready to set. We would go into the shade behind the barn and visit, Joe Winkler, Phil, myself. We'd talk about things that happened a long time ago. It was great truth and it was interesting. Those were the greatest few hours of our lives!"[43]

EPILOGUE TO THE DOUGLAS COUNTY FAIR

During the 1960's there were three concession booths situated directly behind the rodeo stands, just across from Kirk Hall: a cotton candy booth operated by the Rainbow Girls; a sno-cone stand operated by the Episcopal Church Youth Group; and a popcorn stand operated by the DeMolay Boys, usually Charles Bowman and Bryan Ruth. As members of both the youth group and the Rainbow Girls, Kathy Richardson Reis and I always worked both booths, sometimes finishing our shift in one and climbing over the counter directly into the next to begin our following shift! Year after year Mr. Miller would always buy cotton candy for Mrs. Miller to eat during the rodeo, and I always made it especially fat for her! One of my most colorful memories of Mr. Miller is watching him saunter across the dusty fair grounds in his cowboy hat and boots, carrying a pink fluffy wad of cotton candy for his wife! Years later, during one of our many beauty shop conversations, Mrs. Miller laughingly admitted that the hamburgers and the cotton candy were two of her favorite things about the fair! They may have been wealthy but they were, after all, human!

Whitman-Lowell Pavilion on the Douglas County Fairgrounds named in honor of Gill and Cecil Whitman and John and Bea Lowell.

Buboltz-Bodle Collection.

ENDNOTES

[1]Douglas County Fair Book Advertisement, 1921, p 70. On file at the Local History Collection, Douglas Public Library District, Castle Rock, CO.

[2]Conversation between Mr. Miller and the author, Cherry Creek Care Center, Aurora, CO, August 1991.

[3]Wendy Thomas, "A Walk Through Time," Douglas County Fair and Rodeo Book, 1996, p 50.

[4]Interview between Gill and Cecil Whitman and the author, Castle Rock, CO, March 26, 1997.

[5]Wendy Thomas, "Fair Survives Drought and Depression," Douglas County Fair and Rodeo Book, 1996, p 82.

[6]Interview between Gill and Cecil Whitman and the author, Castle Rock, CO, March 26, 1997.

[7]Wendy Thomas, "Fair Survives Drought and Depression," Douglas County Fair and Rodeo Book, 1996, p 82.

[8]IBID.

[9]Karen Serafini, "Charlie Will Not Be Forgotten," Douglas County Fair and Rodeo Book, 1997, p 30.

[10]Wendy Thomas, "Ranching Ties," Douglas County Fair and Rodeo Book, 1996, p 80.

[11]IBID Wendy Thomas, p 80; and Douglas County News Press, August 12, 1980, p 5.

[12]Interview between Gill and Cecil Whitman and the author, March 26, 1997; and Wendy Thomas "Fair Survives Drought and Depression," Douglas County Fair and Rodeo Book, 1996, p 82.

[13]Karen Serafini, "More Than Just Pickles," Douglas County Fair and Rodeo Book, 1997, p 75.

[14]Interview between Gill and Cecil Whitman and the author, March 26, 1997.

[15] The Bank of Douglas County Records, Castle Rock, CO, August 29,1939 to March 10, 1951.

[16]Wendy Thomas, "Fair Survives Drought and Depression," Douglas County Fair and Rodeo Book, 1996, p 82.

[17]Interview between Gill and Cecil Whitman and the author, March 26, 1997.

[18]Karen Serafini, "Master Plan," Douglas County Fair and Rodeo Book, 1997, p 40-41.

[19]Wendy Thomas, "Fair Survives Drought and Depression," Douglas County Fair and Rodeo Book, 1996, p 82; and Karen Serafini, "More Than Just Pickles," Douglas County Fair and Rodeo Book, 1997, p 75.

[20]IBID.

[21]In the mid-1970's, a new arena with metal chutes was constructed. This project was largely engineered by Carl Winkler who was a Fair Board Member, County Commissioner and Rodeo Superintendent. Gill Whitman was also a Fair Board Member and County Commissioner at that time.

[22]Interview between Bea Lowell and the author, Castle Rock, CO, February 9, 1996.

[23]John Lowell as quoted in Douglas County News Press, August 12, 1980, p 9; and copy of Commendation on file at the Philip S. Miller Library, Castle Rock, CO.

[24]Interview between Dona Sherlock and the author, Castle Rock, CO, July 30. 1996, April 16, 1998.

[25]Wendy Thomas, "Kids Benefit From County Fairs," Douglas County Fair and Rodeo Book, 1996, p 84.

[26]Obituary, John Paulk, Douglas County News Press, April 1, 1998, p 7a.

[27]Interview with my father, Willis Buboltz, Castle Rock, CO, August 3, 1996.

[28]Interview between Bea Lowell and the author, Castle Rock, CO, February 9, 1996.

[29]John Lowell as quoted in Douglas County News Press, August 12, 1980, p 9.

[30]Interview between Karen Serafini and the author, Parker, CO, February 4, 1998.

[31]Interview with my father, Willis Buboltz, Castle Rock, CO, August 8, 1996.

[32]Interview between Bea Lowell and the author, Castle Rock, CO, February 9, 1996.

[33]Wendy Thomas, "Ranching Ties," Douglas County Fair and Rodeo Book, 1996, p 80.

[34]Interview between Bea Lowell and the author, Castle Rock, CO, February 9, 1996.

[35]IBID.

[36]Karen Serafini, "More Than Just Pickles," Douglas County Fair and Rodeo Book, 1997, p 75.

[37]IBID.

[38]IBID.

[39]IBID.

[40]Interview with my father, Willis Buboltz, Castle Rock, CO, August 3, 1996.

[41]Interview between Gill and Cecil Whitman and the author, Castle Rock, CO, March 26, 1997.

[42]My own recollections; Also interview with my father, Willis Buboltz.

[43]Interview between Gill and Cecil Whitman and the author, Castle Rock, CO, March 26, 1997.

Kirk Hall on the Douglas County Fairgrounds named in honor of Charles Kirk.

Buboltz-Bodle Collection.

MR. AND MRS. LIBRARY

Although Mr. and Mrs. Miller will be remembered for their many acts of benevolence, generosity and philanthropy, probably the one most recognized will be the Philip S. Miller Library. No one could have ever known the impact this man and his wife would have on Douglas County when they moved to Castle Rock in 1921. Forty-five years later they would finance a library.

When Mr. and Mrs. Miller first came to Castle Rock, the only library available to the public was operated by the Douglas County Women's Club with volunteer members opening it one afternoon a week.[1] Articles in the Record Journal indicate that it was located in a room in the Courthouse and was open on Thursday afternoons. Library cards were available to anyone over the age of twelve and two books could be checked out per card.[2]

Mrs. Miller once told me that the library was one of the first places she went when they moved to Castle Rock. She was one of the first people in town to get a library card and she faithfully checked out two books each week, which she promptly read and returned the following week, so she could check out two more! Although she would have liked to volunteer at the library, her time was taken up at the meat market and then at the fuel and feed store, so initially she was unable to do so. A few years later, she was able to arrange it.

Apparently the library remained in the Courthouse, possibly occupying a couple of different rooms, until February of 1936 when, according to another article in the Record Journal, it was moved to a room in the Cantril Grade School Building. At that time, the library day was changed from Thursday afternoons to Tuesday afternoons.[3]

As has been previously mentioned in another part of this book, the Town of Castle Rock purchased the Castle Rock State Bank Building on the corner of Fourth and Wilcox Streets in July of 1936. The bank had recently closed and the building had been sitting vacant. The Town was now converting it into a Town Hall with permanent rooms for the library.[4]

After what the paper aptly described as "the library's varied and moving career," (it had been shuffled and shifted every place but the local saloon!) members of the Women's Club voiced their enthusiasm as they relocated, once again, from the Cantril School to their new and, hopefully, permanent quarters, conveniently located in the middle of downtown Castle Rock. With easy access for all residents, the new Town Hall was attractive with natural lighting from the large picture windows. The Town offices had much more room for storage and work space and the library rooms offered eye-catching areas to display and arrange the books as well as comfortable chairs in which to sit and read. Renovations had taken place on the outside and the old roof had been replaced, making the building one of the nicest looking in town.[5] Bette Saunders remembered checking out books with her grandmother during 1937 when the library was in this location.[6]

On September 11, 1936, the Women's Club held an Open House and Tea in honor of the new Library and Town Hall. Despite the fact that this was supposed to be a celebration and not a fund raiser, a nice sum of money was collected from the many people in attendance for the purchase of new books.[7] Mrs. Miller attended the Tea, and told me years later that she was so pleased with the library's new location because it was "just down the street from the meat market!" At that time she began volunteering one afternoon a week because Cliff Hawkins was running the meat market and she felt freer to take off for a few hours. Since library day had once again been changed from Tuesday back to Thursday, she could be found volunteering on Thursday afternoons at the library, a job she thoroughly enjoyed and eagerly anticipated each week.

In March of 1937, the Douglas County Women's Club held a "Birthday Party" for their "Pet Child, The Library". It had been sixteen years since its inception, and they celebrated this milestone with an afternoon gathering of food, fun, and games with over thirty club members in attendance.[8] It was truly a miraculous feat that the library had remained in existence for so many years, despite the financial ups and downs of the 1920's and 1930's and the many relocations the library had been forced to make. However, the success was due to the commitment and dedication of the members of the Douglas County Women's Club. Without them, without their devotion and without their hard work, it is doubtful whether or not this little library would have survived the first year, let alone the next fifteen!

In August of 1939, some major changes took place, not only for the library but for the Millers as well! Mr. Miller had helped open The Bank of Douglas County and the Board of Directors had rented the Town Hall and turned it, once again, into a bank building. Instead of working there as a library volunteer, Mrs. Miller became a paid employee of The Bank of Douglas County. In 1940, The Bank of Douglas County purchased the building from the Town of Castle Rock.[9]

It is not quite clear where the library was located after this time. Mrs. Miller once said that for a couple of years the books were stored in the large, dungeon-like basement of the Bank. An article in the Castle Rock Record Journal, dated March 13, 1942, reported the Douglas County Women's Club held another Open House and Tea on March 5, 1942 in honor of the library's moving to another location in the City Hall. The article further stated that the books had been "transferred from the Bank Building to the new site," thus verifying what Mrs. Miller had told me.[10]

The Women's Club continued, successfully and faithfully, to operate the library until February of 1956 when, minutes of the monthly meeting indicate a majority vote to turn the library over to PTA # 38 and that consideration be given to County Librarian, Mr. Robert Metzler and also to the Douglas County High School when it came time to distribute the books.[11] The "Pet Child" was now nearly thirty-six years old, and the only reason the Women's Club would even entertain the thought of giving it up was that they were making plans to disband the organization in the fall. The members who had worked for so long and so hard to make the library a success wanted to make sure it would remain in existence and be placed in capable hands.

During the summer of that year, the children's books were placed in what was a small County Library located in an upstairs room of the Courthouse. Those of us who were children of reading age in the mid-1950's remember very distinctly going there and checking out books from Mr. Metzler. Also in the fall of that year, the high school level and adult books were given to the Douglas County High School on Wilcox Street, where my mother, Ellen Buboltz, was the High School Librarian.[12] In October of 1956, after a unanimous vote, the Douglas County Women's Club disbanded.[13]

But the '60's were comin' and the times they were a changin' and by the end of the next decade, thanks to Mr. and Mrs. Miller, Castle Rock was going to have a full-fledged library!

In 1961, a new Douglas County High School was completed north of Castle Rock on Front Street. At that time the Wilcox School became the Douglas County Junior High School.[14] My mother stayed at that location, became Junior High Librarian and organized the new Junior High Library until 1963, when Mrs. Fleta Nockels took over the position.[15]

During the school year of 1963, the Colorado State Department of Education provided a Bookmobile for the county for one year. Although the Douglas County schools had libraries of their own, especially the high school and junior high, the more remote areas of the county often had a very limited supply of available books to be checked out. For this reason, the Bookmobile was an important step in getting reading materials to the smaller schools in the county and was met with great enthusiasm. By this time my mother had been hired as the County Elementary Librarian and Bookmobile Librarian as well. Mr. Roy Woodworth was the Bookmobile driver, and they followed a set schedule where they took the Bookmobile to all the elementary schools in the county on a regular basis every two weeks.[16]

It must be recognized that in the early 1960's places such as Parker, Larkspur, Cherry Valley, Franktown, Sedalia, Plum Creek, Louviers and Gann (which is no longer in existence) were very small areas, with very few people living there and small schools. Many ranching and farming families lived farther out in the country and the students were bussed to the schools. When the new high school was completed in 1961, high school and junior high school students were all bussed to Castle Rock. It is hard to imagine, in this day and time, when these areas are so built up with growth, development, schools, people and businesses, that during the early 1960's, some of these places were in areas of the county that could almost be considered remote, especially in the middle of the winter when access was sometimes rather limited. For the Bookmobile to come rolling in was an exciting event not only for the students but for the adults who came to check out books, as well.

In the meantime, due to lack of space at the Courthouse, the County Library had been moved into the basement of our house at 619 Fifth Street in Castle Rock! Additionally, library books from the various elementary schools from around the county had also been consolidated there. I guess they figured if Mom was the librarian, they might as well put the books in her basement! The school district provided materials and carpenters who installed fluorescent lighting, built wooden shelving and brought in large work tables and chairs. This was, of course, in the days before computers, so metal and wooden card catalog cabinets were also added, thus transforming our basement into a library! When my mother wasn't on the Bookmobile, she was working, downstairs, with a loyal staff of library volunteers who would come once a week to help sort, catalog and organize the children's and elementary school books.[17]

This dedicated group of volunteers called themselves "Parents for Books" and they worked diligently for the library. Every year they sponsored a Library Tea and local art exhibit at the High School where they invited an author or a librarian to review a current book. This was always a successful event with the proceeds going for new library books. With a small grant, my mother also began to develop an adult section by purchasing current best sellers.[18]

This one-room library remained and grew throughout our basement for the next five years and formed the nucleus of what eventually became the Douglas County Public Library. My sister Shelley and I felt we were the luckiest kids in the county. Whenever we needed a book for school, wanted to read something special, or required an encyclopedia, all we had to do was run downstairs! I truly believe that those years of constant availability of reading materials and books, instilled in both of us a love of reading and a thirst for knowledge and history that has stayed with us until this very day.[19]

It should be noted that this was not a library where people came to check out books. Generally speaking, it was more like a central distribution point where teachers needing specific information might come to look through the materials or call and have special books delivered on the next Bookmobile visit. Additionally, all new or donated books were processed and cataloged through this point before being distributed to the schools. This little library also became the main provider of books for the first Douglas County Bookmobile!

Following the success of the one year Bookmobile program from the Colorado State Department of Education, the Douglas County School Board arranged for the conversion of a school bus to be used as a Bookmobile for Douglas County and my mother, in her capacity as County Librarian remained the Bookmobile Librarian.[20] I will never forget the first day the new Bookmobile slowly backed up to our basement garage! It was a pinkish gray color with big black steps that folded down from the back. My sister and I helped Mom and a group of library volunteers carry boxes to the new Bookmobile and place books on the newly constructed shelves for what seemed to be hours! But it was such an exciting project, we were thrilled to be a part of it! We were really making history that day![21]

This routine was repeated every week during the school year, only on a smaller scale, in order to keep the shelves replenished and stocked as the Bookmobile would make trips to all the elementary schools throughout the county. Despite the help of all the volunteers, the work in the "basement library" continued to grow and popularity of the Bookmobile increased. Mrs. Helen Serrell was hired as Assistant Librarian for my mother and part-time Bookmobile Librarian as well.[22]

A year or two later, the Castle Rock PTA organized a Summer Reading Program with approximately 800 books in a room at the

Cantril Grade School Building. It was open once a week and became an immediate success. Between forty and sixty students would show up to check out books every time it was open.[23]

1966 until 1969 were pivotal years toward a new library in Castle Rock. At the State level, a research group had recently been hired to analyze Colorado's library facilities. The group's recommendation was that the State be divided into six systems with books being pooled and shared and used cooperatively between the six areas in order to save duplicate costs of purchasing the same books. This meant that a small library could be opened at much less expense! Possibly even in Castle Rock![24] One of the areas, The Plains and Peaks Public Library System, was just forty miles south in Colorado Springs!

At the local level in Douglas County, a meeting was called in March of 1966 to determine the public's opinion with regard to the possible development of a new and permanent library. Present at this meeting were the school superintendent, teachers, principals, presidents of civic organizations, Chamber of Commerce Representatives and County Commissioners as well as various county residents. Additionally, Mrs. Evelyn Brewster, the area Consultant for the State Department of Education Library, spoke about how to successfully accomplish the formation of a library. She offered two important ideas which were ultimately implemented.[25]

She suggested that the County Commissioners appoint a Library Planning Commission to study the needs and feasibility of a library, as well as to learn about funding and other technical details. Additionally, she recommended the development of The Friends of The Library, a group to gain support, both publicly and financially, for the new library. By the end of this meeting, $80 had been raised and The Friends of the Library was unofficially born![26]

On March 30, 1966 a Charter Steering Committee met at the Courthouse to begin formal organization of The Friends of the Library. By the end of this meeting, by-laws had been formulated, permanent committees had been appointed, a slate of officers was in the process of being prepared, fund raising had been discussed at great length and the first regular meeting was scheduled for April 19, 1966.[27]

At the April 19th meeting, officers were elected, with Mrs. Nicky Mead as President. The other officers were: First Vice President, Mrs. Betty Prince; Second Vice President, Mrs. Bert Jones; Third Vice President, Mr. Walter Hale; Secretary, Mrs. Betty Walker; Treasurer, Mr. Gordon Seyfried. This group of officers made up the Executive Board of the Friends.[28] During the course of the evening,

Mrs. Mead read the Purpose of the Friends of the Library Organization:

> "The purpose of this organization shall be to maintain an association of persons interested in the Douglas County Library System; to focus Public attention on library services and needs, to encourage and assist in the development of adequate physical facilities for the library system; to formulate procedures by which gifts, endowments, valuable records, documents and desirable materials may be acquired for the library; to interpret to the citizens the needs and services of the library and to stimulate the use of the library to the fullest extent."[29]

The incredible thing about this organization was that by the first Executive Board Meeting on April 28, 1966, less than a month after their official formation, they had gained 143 individual memberships at $1.00 per member; they had nearly $200 already deposited in an account in The Bank of Douglas County; they had received endorsements from schools, churches and service organizations, with further requests for information and speakers. Work on the tax exempt status and the state charter was going full speed ahead. Additionally, fund raising projects had already begun![30]

During the days, weeks and months of the development of the Friends of the Library, Nicky Mead and my mother worked very closely together in order to complete the many details and technicalities necessary. My mother was still County Librarian and the library was still in our basement! It became a habit of theirs to call each other two or three nights a week between five and six o'clock. Their reasoning was, they knew that at that time, they would both be home fixing dinner and they could talk and cook and bring each other up to date on what was happening with the Friends. Good thing we had long phone chords because this was years before cordless phones had been invented! Nevertheless, it became a standing joke in our family that no one ever called home between five and six because we all knew the line would be busy with Mom and Nicky discussing the library![31] It was definitely that important—in both our households. Years later, Jay Mead recalled that, after Mr. Miller became involved in the library, his mother would write "Miller" instead of "Mead" on his lunch sack in honor of Mr. Miller![32]

In June of 1966, the Douglas County Commissioners followed the advice of Evelyn Brewster and appointed a Douglas County Library Planning Commission. The purpose of this commission was threefold: to make a study of library facilities throughout the county, to learn what federal or state funding may be forthcoming and to determine what local costs might be incurred. They were given six months to gather their information. Members were James Rathbone Falck of Sedalia, Dr. John Hannon of Parker, Charles Higby of Larkspur, Russ Kostroski of Franktown, Ina Lagae of Castle Rock, Tom Naylor of Castle Rock, Jean Riesselman of Plum Creek, Nicky Mead of Castle Rock as Ex-officio member, being President of the Friends.[33]

Meanwhile, the Bookmobile was still running throughout the county on its summer schedule, loading out of our basement once a week, with more and more patrons visiting at each location. The popularity of the Summer Reading Program at Cantril School continued to grow. The Friends of the Library sponsored a Beef Barbecue which raised $550 and a Book Sale which raised over a thousand dollars. It became more obvious, with each passing week, that books and reading and a new library had evolved into very important issues in Douglas County![34]

In November, the Douglas County Library Planning Commission, after working all summer preparing surveys, charts, projections and budgets, presented a plan for suggested library development to the Douglas County Commissioners. In light of all the public support and fund raising which was continually taking place and based upon the information, facts, and recommendations of the Library Planning Commission, The Douglas County Commissioners appropriated $5,000 from the General Fund for the Year 1967 to be used to start a public library![35]

As fund raising continued and the Friends of the Library grew, the possibility of a library for Douglas County was finally becoming a reality. In April of 1967 the Douglas County Commissioners adopted a Resolution for the establishment of the Douglas County Public Library and appointed a five member Board of Trustees: Nicky Mead and James McKay, of Castle Rock, Anne Weaver of Parker, Betty Prince of Larkspur and Beryl Livengood of Louviers.[36]

But the best was yet to come! Mr. and Mrs. Miller had been quietly following the developments of the past year with regard to the establishment of a library. Later that same week, on April 27, just a few hours prior to the Board's first meeting, Nicky Mead was given a letter from Mr. and Mrs. Miller announcing their donation of $25,000! That evening she read the letter to the Board. It said in part:

> "Kindly use this letter as a commitment from us for a donation of $25,000 for the construction of a new library building. We wish this money to be all used for building purposes and not for land or remodeling of an old building."[37]

Needless to say, the Board was overwhelmed by this generosity and what it ultimately meant for Castle Rock. A new library!! In light of this magnificent donation, plans went full speed ahead to find a temporary location for a library and hire a librarian. Almost simultaneously, the search began, in earnest, for a permanent location to build the first Douglas County Public Library. By early June 1967, the old Plateau Gas Building at 311 Third Street had been chosen as the temporary quarters.[38] At that time the School Board discontinued the Bookmobile and shifted the books to the temporary library. Although my mother was asked if she would like to apply for the job of Douglas County Public Librarian, she did not accept the offer, having already made plans for a leave of absence from the District to pursue an additional degree at Denver University.[39] Mr. Alden Briskey was hired as Librarian and began his duties July 1, 1967.[40] Also during that summer, the County Library, which was still in our basement, was moved to the new location. It was a sad week indeed, when we helped pack up and carry everything out of our "basement library," book by book, box by box.

The Millers' donation made it possible for the county to apply for matching funds and in July, a Library Services and Construction Grant through the cooperation of the Colorado State Library was approved and provided approximately $24,000 toward the construction of a new building.[41]

The enthusiasm surrounding the development of the library was beginning to spread! City-wide and county-wide, nearly everyone was becoming involved. Throughout the summer, additional book drives and fund raisers were held not only by the Friends of the Library but by the Parents for Books, as well as by various civic, community and school organizations. The largest was a drive by the Friends which collected over two thousand books![42] The newspaper reported that Nicky Mead was hauling so many books her car looked like a bookmobile![43] The National Honor Society of the Douglas County High School made the new library their project for the coming school year and many of the members spent long hours during the hot summer helping transport books which the school district had lent to the new library.[44]

While the Trustees attended to official business and red tape, volunteers spent many hours organizing and cataloging donated books, which continued to be delivered daily. It is important to mention that all donated books were used in one form or another. If there were some unsuitable for inclusion in the permanent collection due to condition or age, they were auctioned off at a later date and the money was used to buy more books.[45]

The big day finally arrived, August 10, 1967: the day for which people had worked, waited, and prayed! The Douglas County Public Library opened at 311 Third Street with no evidence whatsoever that the building had ever been anything but a library, so thorough was the transformation! Free library cards were immediately issued, and the turnout was phenomenal! Even though it was only open Tuesday, Thursday and Saturday, a steady stream of library patrons checked out books each week and the Saturday morning Children's Story Hour was a huge success.[46]

As part of the Plains and Peaks Library System, headquartered in Colorado Springs, The Douglas County Public Library would participate in an inter-library loan program along with other member libraries of Elbert, Lincoln, Park, Teller, and El Paso counties.[47] In October, Douglas County was given the use of a Bookmobile from the Plains and Peaks Library System during the second and fourth weeks of each month. This was helpful for the outlying areas, especially during the winter.[48]

Another milestone occurred for the new library in September of 1967. After considering many locations for a permanent site, the Library Board of Trustees and the Douglas County School Board came to an agreement whereby the School Board would sell the Library Board three 50-foot lots on the corner of Third and Gilbert Streets, at a cost of $6,000. Located just four blocks east of the temporary library, these lots had been a playground for the Cantril Elementary School which was just a half a block away.[49] Additionally, this corner had a spectacular view of The Rock!

Despite the fact that Mr. and Mrs. Miller had hoped for a downtown location on the Courthouse Square, they were pleased that a site had been purchased and that construction could soon begin. The location was important, but getting the library built was the overriding factor. In October, Architect, Maxwell Saul, of the Denver Architectural firm Hatami, Saul and Tanaka, was chosen to design the new library. Mr. Saul was selected because of his experience in the field of library architecture throughout Colorado, specifically in Louisville, Lafayette, Boulder and Northglenn.[50]

By March 1968, the design was approved by the Library Board of Trustees. The first floor of the building would have approximately 1800 square feet, including a spacious adult wing and a special children's wing. Additionally, there would be workshop and office spaces plus a meeting room. A finished basement would provide areas for reference books and additional storage. Also included in the design were provisions for future expansions.[51]

The historical Groundbreaking for the Douglas County Library on Gilbert Street took place on Saturday, August 10, 1968, with Mr. Miller proudly turning the first shovel full of dirt! In attendance at the ceremony were the contractor, Charles Prescott, Jr.; Mayor, H. G. "Pete" Burgess; County Commissioner, Hank Kimbrough; Library Trustee, Nicky Mead; and Librarian, Alden Briskey. Members of the Friends of the Library and Board of Trustees as well as a host of library volunteers and interested, devoted citizens were also on hand for the ceremony. Construction began the following Monday.[52]

Work on the new building progressed rapidly and, on September 28, 1968, members of the Masonic Lodge held an impressive Dedication Ceremony during which they placed the cornerstone for the new library. In a proud tradition of supporting public education, the Masons frequently place cornerstones in new educational buildings. Members of the Most Worshipful Grand Lodge of Colorado A.F. and A.M., as well as members of the local Douglas Lodge No. 153, participated in this commemoration, which began with a procession in front of the Douglas Lodge No. 153 at the corner of Third and Wilcox Streets in downtown Castle Rock. While the Jr. High Band, directed by Mr. Harold Sloan, played at the library site at Third and Gilbert Streets, the Masons marched up the hill to begin the Dedication Ceremony.[53]

After a speech by the Most Worshipful Grand Master, Stewart A. Shafer, a permanently sealed, metal box was placed in the cornerstone space, located on the southeast corner of the library building. This box contained the following important items pertaining to the Library as well as to the Masons:

An American Flag; a copy of the Douglas County News from August 25, 1967 showing the Groundbreaking Ceremony for the Douglas County Library; a copy of the 1968 Colorado Masonic Directory with a list of the officials participating in the laying of the cornerstone; a copy of the Bulletin of the Colorado Masonic Craftsman; a Letter to the People of Douglas County describing the events that lead to the building of the Douglas County Library; and Four Coins dated in the year 1968, a half dollar, a quarter, a dime, and a penny, signifying the year the cornerstone was placed.[54] Finally, the cornerstone, which read "Douglas County Public Library, Laid by Most Worshipful Grand Lodge, A.F. and A.M. of Colorado, September 28, 1968," was lowered into place in front of the box.[55] This particular day was especially important to Mr. Miller because he and his brother, Adam, were both members of the Douglas Lodge No. 153 and were both in attendance.

By the end of November, the new Douglas County Library on Gilbert Street was completed. In order to allow for the transfer of all books and supplies to the new location, the temporary library at 311 Third Street was closed on November 30th.[56] Members of the community, including the Board of Trustees, the Friends of the Library and countless volunteers pitched in to help make the move go as smoothly as possible. The elementary school children decorated the library in the Christmas spirit. Teachers, students and parents helped out, as well as Senior Citizens who sorted and shelved books. It was a total community effort and everyone worked extremely hard in preparation for the opening on December 10th.[57]

It was a typical crisp, cold but clear, sunny day when the Douglas County Public Library at 303 Gilbert Street opened its doors for the first time at one o'clock on Tuesday, December 10, 1968.[58] Many patrons were on hand to check out books, as well as to view the new and beautiful, 2200 square foot facility. Mr. and Mrs. Miller came by later in the afternoon and were both pleased at the new library—their adopted project of which they were proud to have been a part. It was another example of their never-ending commitment toward the progress of the community and the education of the youth. Mrs. Miller told me years later that she felt on that day, that next to the Bank, the Library was their most important contribution. Throughout the winter and early spring, attendance increased and more books were checked out than ever before. Fund raising never stopped as the Friends of the Library and the Board of Trustees continued working toward the success of this new library.

Although it opened to the community in December, the official Library Dedication Ceremony did not occur until the spring of 1969. Waiting, in anticipation that the Colorado weather would cooperate, the dedication was scheduled for April 26, 1969.[59] Hopes for a sunny spring day were realized and under clear blue skies with The Rock looming in the background, the Douglas County High School Band, directed by Mr. Kent Brandebery, opened the ceremony at two o'clock with a medley of concert selections. This was followed with a brief invocation by Reverend Sigurd Burch of the First United

Methodist Church in Castle Rock. Next Nicky Mead, President of the Board of Trustees, presented a poignant welcoming speech, in which she said:

WELCOMING SPEECH

"Three years ago, the Douglas County Library was a dream. Today we dedicate a new building with a collection of 8,000 books and thousands more available. Three years ago during National Library Week we began the first organized effort to establish a county public library. Today, during National Library Week we honor those who helped our dream come true."[60]

Mrs. Mead then introduced the Library Board of Trustees, Douglas County Board of Commissioners, and Officers of the Friends of the Library. Mr. and Mrs. Miller were introduced and officially honored. At that point in the ceremony, a large and impressive portrait of Mr. Miller was presented, as a gift to the library, from local artist and photographer, Eugene Everitt of Everitt Studio in Castle Rock.[61] "Red" Everitt, as he was nicknamed due to his red hair, was without a doubt one of the finest portrait photographers in Colorado and it was truly an honor for Mr. Miller to be recognized in this way and for the library to receive this gift. The portrait was later placed in the adult wing of the library, but for this Dedication Ceremony, it remained in the entry for everyone to view. To this day, it still hangs in the library as a tribute to Mr. Miller and a remembrance of that historic day.

Charles Larsen, President of the Friends of the Library, then presented a Plaque honoring Mr. and Mrs. Miller which read: "Douglas County Public Library acknowledges the generous gift of Mr. and Mrs. P. S. Miller." Underneath was listed the name of each Library Trustee.[62] Mr. and Mrs. Miller were both humble and private people despite the fact they were often in the public eye due to their benevolence and generosity. They were both visibly touched by this show of appreciation and honor bestowed upon them. In their minds, they were just giving back to the County which had so richly given to them and they never, ever expected public recognition in return. It deeply touched their hearts because of their love of the community.

Following a Dedication Speech by Justice Herbert Schauer, Douglas County Commissioners Henry Kimbrough, Russell Higginson and Warren Christensen officially accepted the new Douglas County Library Building. Everyone agreed with Commissioner Kimbrough's sentiments when he said:

"In accepting this beautiful library, I must pause to pay tribute to the many people who have made it possible for us to be here today. Although every level of government—school district, city, county, state and federal—has cooperated and assisted with this undertaking, it is in no sense a government project. I prefer to call this a people project. This is the American system at its very best."[63]

That having been said, Henry Kimbrough then cut a large gold ribbon as Russell Higginson permanently placed the Plaque honoring the Millers in the vestibule of the library signaling that the Open House was officially underway. Over 250 people attended. Refreshments were provided by the Friends of the Library with additional help and support from organizations all over the county: The Hilltop Social Club, The Martha Club, Parker Home Extension and The Parker Sirens.[64]

Librarian, Alden Briskey was quoted as saying there were more than 6800 books on the shelves including 2000 children's books with 1200 more still being processed and cataloged.[65]

Special art exhibits, drawings, paintings and sculpture by Junior High Art students were on display as well as a history of Douglas County organized by, Historian, Mrs. Josephine Marr. Of particular note, however, was an album entitled "The Birth of the Library." It contained a chronology of all library publicity and articles representing everything that was done and every step that was taken from the beginning idea for a library to the final completion and opening. This book, exhibited by Mrs. Ellen Buboltz, won Honorable Mention in the prestigious, international competition, The John Cotton Dana Publicity Awards Contest, and subsequently became the property of the American Library Association. The citation on the award read, "For winning community support for establishing of public library service in a sparsely populated area."[66]

Although the library was completed, nobody rested on their laurels, so to speak. In the fall of that year, The Friends of the Library sponsored "The Douglas County on Parade Home Tour". The success of this project resulted in an annual event which continued for several years and raised thousands of dollars for the library. Another popular annual event began in the early 70's at the upscale Echo Hills Country Club in Perry Park. Also, sponsored by the Friends of the Library, it was a lavish dinner with entertainment in honor of the benefactors and volunteers while raising money at the same time. Over the years guest speakers included the famous Colorado radio personality, Pete Smythe, and the Denver media man, Woody Paige.[67] Mr. and Mrs. Miller always attended this successful, yearly fund raiser and were frequently honored at the event.

From bake sales to book drives, fund raisers were sponsored by civic, county, and school organizations. There was always a need for materials, supplies, shelving, landscaping and, of course, a never-ending need for books! Library patrons continued to increase and the popularity of the library grew. Incredibly, by 1971, there was already a need to begin planning an expansion. Mr. and Mrs. Miller were, once again, the first to make a donation of $5,000 to begin the new campaign.[68]

By 1975, plans were underway for a 3600 square foot addition and matching funds had been awarded. Van Schaack Realty held an auction and the Friends of the Library raised $2,000.[69] At the Groundbreaking Ceremony in July, Mr. and Mrs. Miller donated an additional $5,000.[70] By February of 1976, the new addition was completed, almost doubling the size of the library. Adult and children's sections were expanded, storage areas were added downstairs and an elevator operated between the two floors. On January 22, The Board of Trustees had designated a new room as The Philip S. and Jerry E. Miller Community Room. The plaque read: "In Recognition of Their Continuous Contributions to the Community and the Douglas County Public Library." Underneath was listed the name of each Library Trustee.[71] A Grand Opening was held on February 2nd and one of the highlights of that ceremony was the hanging of Mr. Miller's portrait and the plaque in the new Miller Community Room.[72]

Although the new addition was completed, it opened lacking a few necessities! There was a shortage of shelves and furniture, but probably most noticeably missing was carpet in some of the new areas. Mr. Miller soon donated an additional $3,540 toward carpeting and with fund raisers by the Friends of the Library additional shelves and furniture soon appeared.[73]

In the meantime, Castle Rock continued to grow and so did the patronage and popularity of the library. In 1980, Mr. and Mrs. Miller, in another charitable gesture, donated an additional $25,000 to the Castle Rock Library![74] At the Library Board of Trustees meeting in June, the Trustees formally passed a Resolution and announced plans to rename the Castle Rock Library in honor of Mr. Miller. The Resolution read as follows:

RESOLUTION

"It has been resolved that the library in Castle Rock be renamed for Philip S. Miller because of his initial and continuing interest and support for the libraries of Douglas County. The Castle Rock Library will be henceforth known as the Miller Branch in Castle Rock. The formal Dedication Ceremonies and Open House are being planned for August 9, 1980."[75]

Mr. and Mrs. Miller were present for this reading, but they had no idea of the Resolution or the proposed name change for the library. They had simply attended the meeting, as they frequently did, visiting the branch libraries throughout the county. After the reading of the Resolution, Board Secretary, John Carlson told Mr. Miller, "Most people are still convinced that if it weren't for you, we still wouldn't have a library." As always, Mr. and Mrs. Miller were very humbled and honored. Mr. Miller commented, "It makes me feel good that I was able to do this, not just for Castle Rock but for the whole county."[76]

On August 9, 1980 a gala celebration was held at the Castle Rock Library on Gilbert Street to officially honor the Millers and to formally change the name and rededicate the library to Mr. Miller. Peggy Hybiak, a Library Trustee, read a proclamation citing the many financial gifts from the Millers over the years. Additionally she stated, "Philip S. Miller wisely established a standard of excellence for future growth in Douglas County by stipulating that his gift be used for capital construction to provide a permanent building to house the library."[77]

In keeping with this special tribute, the week was designated Philip S. Miller Week, when he was honored as Douglas County's Outstanding Citizen. The paper reported, "This is an honor he richly deserves for his untiring efforts to make Douglas County and Castle Rock better places to live."[78] Coincidentally, it was the same week as the Douglas County Fair and Rodeo, and what an appropriate time to pay tribute to the man who, for so many years, had provided contributions and longstanding support to 4-H and the Fair as well. The Douglas County News Press ran a special section dedicated to Mr. and Mrs. Miller, with impressive articles written by Dianna Gordon in which she interviewed friends and employees. One article entitled "Quiet Hero" perfectly described Mr. Miller! He was indeed a "Quiet Hero!"[79]

In January 1983, Mr. and Mrs. Miller donated an additional $30,000 to the library[80] as discussions began regarding the need for a new building in Castle Rock.[81] The population growth, as well as the increased number of library patrons, simply could not be accommodated anymore by the Miller Branch at the Gilbert Street location. It was no longer large enough, and all the allotted expansion area in the original design had been utilized. From 1968 until 1983 this location had served the public well. The expansions had met the immediate needs and the library was indeed a huge success. Therefore, the logical progression was to build another, larger library building and, consequently, the search for a new site began.

It is very important to note that the site which was eventually chosen for the new library was located on property that had once been part of Mr. Miller's ranch. However, when the search for a new location began, Mr. Miller didn't own that land anymore. By this time he and Mrs. Miller had moved into Tremont, a retirement community in Denver and had sold most of their land, not realizing that eventually part of it might be a prime spot for the library. However, the Library Board of Trustees, the County Commissioners, the Friends of the Library, and everyone connected with the project felt it was absolutely mandatory that the library which carried Mr. Miller's name be built on property which Mr. Miller used to own. Mr. Miller always apologetically said that if he still owned it, he would just donate it! But since he didn't, other steps had to be taken. Therefore, in order to alleviate this situation and obtain the desired section of property, the County and the landowner made a straight across trade. According to Bruff Shea, Director of Parks and Recreation, land the County owned adjacent to the ball park by the fairgrounds was traded to the landowner while the section of property once owned by Mr. Miller was traded to the County to build the library.[82]

In 1985, as plans progressed for the construction of the new library on the old Miller property, Mr. and Mrs. Miller donated $100,000 toward the project! This was matched by a federal government grant enabling plans to go forth in earnest.[83] That year Mr. Miller was honored as the Library Benefactor of the Year by the Colorado Library Association. This is a prestigious award given each year to a person who, through his or her benevolence, has improved the quality of library service throughout the state. The award read: "Colorado Library Association Library Benefactor Award 1985, Presented to P. S. Miller, For Outstanding and Unwavering Support of The Douglas County Library."[84] He was a well deserving recipient and was always very proud of this particular award.

In 1986, The Miller Branch on Gilbert Street was sold to a Day Care Center and all library operations were temporarily moved into a warehouse near Park Street on the west side of town. The library remained at this location for the next year as construction continued at the new site. The Philip S. Miller Library on Plum Creek Boulevard was completed in October of 1987.[85]

Lynn Robertson, who was the Branch Manager at that time, recalled an emotional and heartfelt experience she and Mr. Miller shared a few weeks prior to opening. "We were still in a state of chaos," she remembered. "Books were in boxes, shelving had not arrived. Mr. Miller walked in and he was in awe! Although he had come out to see the building in progress, this was the first time he had seen the completed project."

"I will never forget the moment," she continued. "Tears were coming down his cheeks. Then I started to cry. It was all coming together. We had been through so much."[86]

The new library contained 15,000 square feet with large areas for adult, as well as children's, books and a huge reference section. With ample work room, storage space and office areas, this building was, and still is, an impressive library. At that time a new computer system was implemented. Known as Dynix, it showed the card catalog, listed all available books and put holds on requests.[87] With high ceilings and windows all around, library patrons could look out on land which used to be part of the Miller Ranch. One of the most poignant statements I have ever read was written by Jamie LaRue and Cindy Murphy in a special section of the Douglas County News Press entitled "Twenty Who Made A Difference" in January 1995, when Mr. Miller was one of the honored twenty. They wrote, "His cattle grazed on the lands where the Library named in his honor now stands."[88]

On October 24, 1987, another Grand Opening was celebrated at the new Philip S. Miller Library! Eight hundred invitations were mailed and later indications were that over three fourths of those invited had attended.[89] This was truly a wonderful day for the county and the town. It was a tremendous accomplishment, thanks to the generosity, once again, of the Millers. Although Mrs. Miller was not able to attend, her presence and spirit were felt there by everyone.

On February 25, 1988, The Daily News Press ran a headline which made people look twice to make sure their eyes weren't playing tricks on them! It said, "Miller Gives $510,000 to Library."[90] Their eyes were not playing tricks, because, in the largest donation he had ever made, Mr. Miller donated enough money to retire the remaining debt on the Philip S. Miller Library! However, in presenting this donation he placed two stipulations on it. The first being that the library be permanently known as the Philip S. Miller Library, not the P. S. Miller Library.[91] People often thought that he did this because he didn't like his initials! But that was not the reason as my dad, Willie Buboltz, explained, "There was another man in the county with the same initials named Miller and Phil wanted to make sure there would be no confusion in the future as to whom the library was named for and from where the money had come."[92] The second stipulation was that the debt be completely paid off as soon as possible. Mr. Miller was 92 years old at this time, and it was very important to him that this debt be paid off during his lifetime, which it was.[93]

In 1990, Mr. Miller was once again honored as the Library Benefactor of the Year by the Colorado Library Association. The award read: "Colorado Library Association Benefactor Award, 1990, To Mr. Philip Miller, For His Generosity and Outstanding Support of Colorado Libraries."[94] He was very honored to have been given this award a second time, especially, at the age of 94!

In March 1990, Mr. Jamie LaRue was hired as Library Director. Thanks to his efforts and a massive campaign for the creation of an independent library district, voters, in November, had approved the establishment of The Douglas Public Library District to coincide with the county boundaries.[95] Also in 1990, the Douglas County Historical Society disbanded and donated all their archival materials to the Philip S. Miller Library.[96] This included an incredible amount of printed information, pictures, research, newspapers, and historical resources with regard to Douglas County. This donation, plus other historical materials previously acquired, formed the foundation of what would soon become the Local History Collection.

In 1992, The Douglas Public Library District earned the Colorado Public Library Excellence Award. During that year, it became the first Dynix public library in the state to go on the Internet providing public availability to the Access Colorado Library Information Network.[97] Later that year the west wing of the Philip S. Miller Library was renovated and in November, the Douglas Public Library District Local History Collection was officially recognized.[98]

This is a special area of the library which contains history, photographs, scrapbooks, maps, special collections of valuable resources such as Fair Books, newspapers, and often one-of-a-kind materials of historical value to Douglas County and Castle Rock. It is truly one of the most important sections of the library because it contains local roots and history. In September of 1993, the Josephine Lowell Marr Research Room was dedicated specifically to house the Local History Collection.[99] Since that time, a second room became necessary. This collection is efficiently supervised and very carefully organized by Archivist, Johanna Harden. Without her help and the information and pictures from the Local History Collection, I would have never been able to complete this book.

It is important to note that in 1995, several years after the deaths of Mr. Miller's brother Adam and his wife, Dorothy, a $55,000 bequest from their estate was used to help build the current Parker Library. The main meeting room is named in their honor signifying the contributions and commitment they demonstrated over the years on behalf of the Parker Library. A picture hangs on the wall in their memory.[100]

In August of 1997, The Douglas Public Library District celebrated another milestone, its 30 Year Anniversary! It didn't seem possible that thirty eventful and historical years had passed since Mr. and Mrs. Miller made that first $25,000 donation which resulted in the building of the first Douglas County Public Library. It had also been thirty years since the temporary library had opened at 311 Third Street in August 1967. The occasion was celebrated with a special section in the Douglas County News Press entitled "Thirty Years of Opening Windows to the World," which detailed the history of the library district and its impact on the county. It also gave tributes to Mr. Miller and Mrs. Mead. The Friends of the Library had special hospitality tables set up at each library throughout the county to observe this important event.[101]

One of the highlights of the 30 Year Anniversary was a collector's edition postal cancellation, which had been designed to commemorate thirty years of library operation. The public was invited to purchase the commemorative stamp or to bring their mail to the Philip S. Miller Library on Saturday, August 23, where Postal and Library employees applied the anniversary cancellation to the outgoing mail.[102] This unique cancellation showed the original, thirty year old logo on the left side as well as the current logo on the right side. The August 23, 1997 date was placed in the center, surrounded by an oval in which was written Douglas Public Library District, Castle Rock, CO 80104. The motto underneath read, "Thirty Years and Still Bookin' Good." According to Archivist, Johanna Harden, "The Douglas Public Library District is the first one in the state to offer an anniversary stamp cancellation. We are making history in Colorado and we are writing a chapter in local history books," she said.[103]

Douglas Public Library District
30th Year Stamp Cancellation.

Courtesy of Local History Collection, Douglas Public Library District, Castle Rock, CO.

Although this chapter focuses mainly on the Philip S. Miller Library in Castle Rock, it must be noted that Mr. and Mrs. Miller's original donation sparked interest county-wide and ultimately resulted in the development of branch libraries throughout Douglas County. In the early stages, some of these libraries were very small, were operated completely by volunteer staff, and very often the buildings did not even contain a telephone! This demonstrated how strongly people felt about the need for the libraries and how willing they were to pull together to work toward that end. The dedication shown during subsequent years is obvious by the many libraries now in existence in Douglas County.

According to Jamie LaRue, Library Director of the Douglas Public Library District, as of 1998, the Library District consisted of two types of libraries: full service libraries, operating seven days a week and "satellite" libraries operating approximately eight hours a week. The full service libraries are: Philip S. Miller Library at 961 South Plum Creek Drive in Castle Rock, Parker Library at 10851 South Crossroads Drive in Parker, Oaks Mill Library at 8827 Lone Tree Parkway in Littleton, and Highlands Ranch Library at 48 West Springer Drive in Highlands Ranch. The "satellite" libraries, which have computer connections and book delivery, are located within Douglas County School District elementary schools at Cherry Valley and Roxborough. Additionally, the Louviers Library is open in the Louviers Village Club House Monday and Thursday from 3-7 p.m.[104] Mr. and Mrs. Miller would definitely be pleased!

EPILOGUE TO MR. AND MRS. LIBRARY

The impetus and motivation for the library came from a variety of people. Rosemary Metzler, an English teacher in the Douglas County Public Schools, continually reminded Mr. Miller how important a library would be for the future of Douglas County as well as for its students.

A businessman in Denver once told Mr. Miller that building a library would be the finest thing he could ever do for the people of Douglas County—that a library system would do more than anything else he could ever contribute.

But if the truth were to be known, it was his wife, Mrs. Jerry Miller, who encouraged and cajoled and gently persuaded him to seriously consider donating money to build the first library.

Jerry Miller was quite a reader. Dona Sherlock and my mother, Ellen Buboltz, remembered this for as long as they knew Mrs. Miller. She recognized the value of literature and good writing as well as recreational and pleasurable reading. My mother distinctly remembered one time at a dinner party, Jerry mentioned that whenever she finished her housework and had dinner ready, she would read, while waiting for Phil to come home. Anytime during the day, when she had a few spare moments, she would read a few pages of whatever book she had at the time. It was relaxing for her and she enjoyed reading very much. Someone said to her at the dinner party that night, "Jerry, you can't read very many books that way," to which she replied, "Oh yes I can! You would be surprised how many books I read that way!"

The interesting thing is that despite Mrs. Miller's love of books and reading, Mr. Miller did not share the same enthusiasm. To sit down and read a Zane Gray western novel held absolutely no interest for him whatsoever! He was not a recreational reader. Conversely, though, as Gill Whitman remembered, Mr. Miller would read everything he could get his hands on about cattle raising, ranching, breeding and feeding. Similarly, my dad recalled that Mr. Miller constantly studied about banking and finance. He would keep current on all the new legislation, statewide and nationwide, while always being aware of the events and changes occurring in the large Denver banks. On a more humorous note, Mr. Miller did enjoy reading the cartoon book, "Cowpokes". He always got a "kick out of it" and often had copies under the glass on his desk of one or two cartoons he particularly liked!

Where the library was concerned, I think it would be safe to say, in the final analysis, that it was a combined effort between the two of them. Mrs. Miller maybe pushed and prodded a bit but Mr. Miller ultimately made the decision and the donation. Together they would have done anything for that library, as evidenced by the hundreds of thousands of dollars they donated during their lives and the fact that the Douglas County Public Library shares in the Perpetual Charitable Trust.

Many people have said that the library should have been named the Philip S. and Jerry E. Miller Library. Chances are, Mrs. Miller would have never allowed that to happen. Even though she may have been the inspiration and the driving force behind his greatest deed, The Philip S. Miller Library, she would have always insisted that he receive all the acknowledgement, all the accolades, and all the recognition.

In 1978, Nicky Mead moved to Denver and took a job at the Virginia Village Branch of the Denver Public Library.[105] Although she left Douglas County, she kept a close eye on the growth and development of the library system to which she had been so devoted. She brought to the Denver Public Library the same dedication and innovation, being the first to suggest the now thriving Denver Public Library Docent Program. She retired in 1993 but the recognition continued. In 1994 she was honored at a groundbreaking ceremony for a new Denver branch library and in the same year she received the Colorado Library Association's Lifetime Achievement Award, for her work in both the Douglas County Public Library and the Denver Public Library.[106]

Nicky Mead passed away on Christmas Day in 1995.[107] On February 22, 1997, the Virginia Village Branch of the Denver Public Library dedicated the Genevieve Nichols Mead Community Room in her honor.[108]

Miller Boulevard sign stands against a backdrop of fluffy white clouds and blue Colorado skies.

Buboltz-Bodle Collection.

ENDNOTES

[1]Joanne Ditmer, "Forty Years Later, A Library," The Denver Post Empire Magazine, July 27, 1969.

[2]Castle Rock Record Journal, October 4, 1929 and October 25, 1929; and Cindy Murphy and Sally Maguire, "Birth of A Library," Douglas County News Press, August 20, 1997, p 4e.

[3]Castle Rock Record Journal, February 7, 1936.

[4]Record of Proceedings Board of Trustees, Town of Castle Rock, November 6, 1935, July 1, 1936; Castle Rock Record Journal, July 17, 1936 and September 11, 1936 as appearing in Scholtz Scrapbook, Local History Collection, Douglas Public Library District, Castle Rock, CO; also see Chapter "Early Banking History in Castle Rock, 1888-1932".

[5]Castle Rock Record Journal September 11, 1936, as appearing in Scholtz Scrapbook, Local History Collection, Douglas Public Library District, Castle Rock, CO.

[6]Letter from Bette Saunders, December 7, 1995.

[7]Castle Rock Record Journal, September 11, 1936.

[8]IBID, March 19, 1937; also appearing in Scholtz Scrapbook, Local History Collection, Douglas Public Library District, Castle Rock, CO.

[9]See Chapter "The History of The Bank of Douglas County".

[10]Castle Rock Record Journal, March 13, 1942; also appearing in Scholtz Scrapbook, Local History Collection, Douglas Public Library District, Castle Rock, CO.

[11]Minutes of the Meeting of the Douglas County Women's Club, February 17, 1956, on file at the Local History Collection, Douglas Public Library District, Castle Rock, CO.

[12]Interview with my mother, Ellen Buboltz, February 1996.

[13]Minutes of the Final Meeting of the Douglas County Women's Club, October 12, 1956, on file at the Local History Collection, Douglas Public Library District, Castle Rock, CO.

[14]Information Douglas County School District Administration Office, Castle Rock, CO.

[15]Interview with my mother, Ellen Buboltz, February 1996.

[16]IBID.

[17]IBID; additionally much of this information came from my own recollections of those years when the library was in our basement.

[18]Interview with my mother, Ellen Buboltz, February 1996.

[19]My own recollections.

[20]Interview with my mother, Ellen Buboltz, February 1996.

[21]My own recollections.

[22]Interview with my mother, Ellen Buboltz, February 1996.

[23]IBID.

[24]Joanne Ditmer, "Forty Years Later, A Library," Denver Post Empire Magazine, July 27, 1969.

[25]IBID.

[26]IBID.

[27]Ellen Buboltz, "For Those Who Like Books," Douglas County News, March 31, 1966.

[28]Minutes of the First Meeting, Friends of the Library, April 19, 1966, as reported in the Douglas County News, April 21, 1966.

[29]IBID.

[30]Minutes of the First Executive Board Meeting, Friends of the Library, April 28, 1966, as reported in the Douglas County News, May 5, 1966.

[31]My own recollections.

[32]Jamie LaRue, "Library Bindings," January 3, 1996.

[33]Arapahoe Herald, June 14, 1966; and Douglas County News, June 16, 1966.

[34]Interview with my mother, Ellen Buboltz, February 1996.

[35]Ellen Buboltz, "For Those Who Like Books," Douglas County News, November 17, 1966; Denver Post, November 2, 1966; and Littleton Independent, November 4, 1966.

[36]Douglas County Board of Commissioners Resolution, Special Meeting April 18, 1967 as reported in the Douglas County News, April 20, 1967; Denver Post, April 22, 1967; and Littleton Independent, April 27, 1967.

[37]Letter from Mr. and Mrs. Philip Miller to Douglas County Library Board of Trustees, April 27, 1967, on file at the Local History Collection, Douglas Public Library District, Castle Rock, CO; Douglas County News, May 4, 1967; Littleton Independent, May 4, 1967; and Minutes of the Douglas County Library Board Meeting April 27, 1967 as reported in Parker Press, May 4, 1967.

[38]Ellen Buboltz, "For Those Who Like Books," Douglas County News, June 8, 1967.

[39]Minutes of the Douglas County School Board Meeting April 1967, as reported in the Douglas County News.

[40]Douglas County News, June 29, 1967.

[41]Rocky Mountain News, October 13, 1967; Alden Briskey, "The Library Notebook," Douglas County News, November 23, 1967; Denver Post, May 4,1969; and Parker Press, May 8, 1969.

[42]Douglas County News, June 16, 1967.

[43]Parker Press and Douglas County News, June 1, 1967.

[44]Douglas County News, article and photo of National Honor Society Members carrying boxes of books to new library, June 1, 1967.

[45]Parker Press and Douglas County News, June 1, 1967.

[46]Douglas County News, August 10, 1967 and August 17, 1967.

[47]Douglas County News, Diagram and description of the Plains and Peaks Library System, April 25, 1968.

[48]Alden Briskey, "The Library Notebook," Douglas County News, September 21, 1967 and October 5, 1967.

[49]Meeting between Douglas County Library Board and Douglas County School Board, September 27, 1967 as reported in Douglas County News, October 5, 1967; Alden Briskey, "The Library Notebook," October 12, 1967; and Littleton Independent, October 12, 1967, Section 2, p 1.

[50]Rocky Mountain News, October 13, 1967. This article is on file at the Local History Collection, Douglas Public Library District, Castle Rock, CO.

[51]Douglas County News and Parker Press, March 21, 1968; Rocky Mountain News, March 25, 1968; and Denver Post, March 25, 1968.

[52]Photo of Groundbreaking Ceremony, Douglas County News, August 15, 1968; and photo on file at the Local History Collection, Douglas Public Library District, Castle Rock, CO.

[53]Parker Press, October 17, 1968, p 3; and photos of Cornerstone Ceremony on file at the Local History Collection, Douglas Public Library District, Castle Rock, CO.

[54]Douglas County News, October 10, 1968; and photos of Cornerstone Ceremony on file at the Local History Collection, Douglas Public Library District, Castle Rock, CO.

[55]Douglas County News, Library Souvenir Edition, May 15, 1969 shows the Cornerstone in the photo section. On file at the Local History Collection, Douglas Public Library District, Castle Rock, CO.

[56]Douglas County News, November 28, 1968.

[57]Alden Briskey, "The Library Notebook," Douglas County News, December 19, 1968.

[58]Cindy Murphy and Sally Maguire, "Birth of a Library," Douglas County News Press, August 20, 1997, p 4e.

[59]Douglas County Public Library Dedication Program, April 26, 1969 as printed in Douglas County News, April 24, 1969.

[60]Welcoming Speech by Mrs. Nicky Mead at Douglas County Public Library Dedication, Saturday, April 26, 1969 as reprinted in the Parker Press, May 8, 1969, p 1.

[61]Douglas County News, Library Souvenir Edition, May 15, 1969, p 1, photo of Eugene Everitt and Nicky Mead with the Miller portrait on file at the Local History Collection, Douglas Public Library District, Castle Rock, CO. The actual portrait hangs in the Philip S. Miller Library, Castle Rock, CO.

[62]Douglas County News, Library Souvenir Edition, May 15, 1969, p 1, also photo section shows Charles Larsen presenting Mr. Miller with Plaque; photo and copy of the Plaque on file at the Local History Collection, Douglas Public Library District, Castle Rock, CO.

[63]Library Acceptance Speech by County Commissioner, Henry Kimbrough, Douglas County Library Dedication, April 26, 1969, as reprinted in the Douglas County News, Library Souvenir Edition, May 15, 1969, p 1.

[64]Douglas County News, Library Souvenir Edition, May 15, 1969, p 1.

[65]Denver Post, May 4, 1969.

[66]Douglas County News, Library Souvenir Edition, May 15, 1969, p 1 and photo section; photo also on file at the Local History Collection, Douglas Public Library District, Castle Rock, CO; Parker Press, May 8, 1968, p 1; Cindy Murphy and Sally Maguire, "Birth of a Library," Douglas County News Press, August 20, 1997, p 4e.

[67]Cindy Murphy and Sally Maguire, "Birth of a Library," Douglas County News Press, August 20, 1997, p 4e.

[68]IBID.

[69]IBID.

[70]Douglas County News, July 17, 1975 photo of Nicky Mead presenting a $5,000 check on behalf of Mr. and Mrs. Miller to Board President, Roger DeVries.

[71]Copy of the Plaque on file at the Local History Collection, Douglas Public Library District, Castle Rock, CO; Douglas County Press Squire, February 5, 1976; Cindy Murphy and Sally Maguire, "Birth of a Library," Douglas County News Press, August 20, 1997, p 4e.

[72]Douglas County Press Squire, February 5, 1976.

[73]Cindy Murphy and Sally Maguire, "Birth of a Library," Douglas County News Press, August 20, 1997, p 4e.

[74]IBID.

[75]Record of Proceedings Douglas County Library Board of Trustees, June 17, 1980 on file at the Local History Collection, Douglas Public Library District, Castle

Rock, CO; Douglas County News Press, June 20, 1980; and Parker Press, June 20, 1980.

[76]Douglas County News Press, June 20, 1980; and Parker Press, June 20, 1980.

[77]Douglas County News Press, August 12, 1980, p 1.

[78]IBID, p 4.

[79]IBID, Dianna Gordon, p 2, 5, 7, 8, 9.

[80]Douglas County News Press, January 29-30, 1983.

[81]Cindy Murphy and Sally Maguire, "Birth of a Library," Douglas County News Press, August 20, 1997, p 4e.

[82]Interview between Bruff Shea, Director of Parks and Recreation, and Willis Buboltz, Castle Rock, CO, November 1995.

[83]Cindy Murphy and Sally Maguire, "Birth of a Library," Douglas County News Press, August 20, 1997, p 4e.

[84]Copy of Library Benefactor Award, 1985, on file at the Local History Collection, Douglas Public Library District, Castle Rock, CO.

[85]Cindy Murphy and Sally Maguire, "Birth of a Library," Douglas County News Press, August 20, 1997, p 4e.

[86]Jamie LaRue, "Library Notes," Douglas County News Press, March 18, 1992, p 2.

[87]Cindy Murphy and Sally Maguire, "Birth of a Library," Douglas County News Press, August 20, 1997, p 4e.

[88]Jamie LaRue, "Twenty Who Made a Difference, Philip Miller," Douglas County News Press, January 21, 1995, p 16b.

[89]Library Board of Trustees, Minutes of Special Meeting at Miller Branch, October 6, 1987, p 2, on file at the Local History Collection, Douglas Public Library District, Castle Rock, CO.

[90]Daily News Press, February 25, 1988, p 1, 3.

[91]IBID.

[92]Interview with my father, Willis Buboltz, May 1994.

[93]Daily News Press, February 25, 1988, p 1, 3.

[94]Copy of Library Benefactor Award, 1990, on file at the Local History Collection, Douglas Public Library District, Castle Rock, CO.

[95]Cindy Murphy and Sally Maguire, "Birth of a Library," Douglas County News Press, August 20, 1997, p 4e, 5e.

[96]Telephone conversation with Kent Brandebery, Douglas County Historic Preservation Board, Castle Rock, CO, March 17, 1998.

[97]Cindy Murphy and Sally Maguire, "Birth of a Library," Douglas County News Press, August 20, 1997, p 5e.

[98]IBID.

[99]IBID.

[100]Douglas County News Press, Parker Section, November 1, 1995, p 2b, photo of Adam and Dorothy Miller is also on file at the Local History Collection, Douglas County Public Library District, and the Parker Library.

[101]Douglas County News Press, August 20, 1997 p 5a; "Thirty Years of Opening Windows to the World," Douglas County News Press, August 20, 1997, Section E, p 1-8.

[102]IBID.

[103]"Thirty Years of Opening Windows to the World," Douglas County News Press, August 20, 1997, p 2e.

[104]Information courtesy of Jamie LaRue, Library Director, Douglas Public Library District, April 14, 1998.

[105]"Thirty Years of Opening Windows to the World," Douglas County News Press, August 20, 1997, p 7e.

[106]Jamie LaRue, "Library Bindings" Douglas County News Press, January 3, 1996.

[107]Obituary, Nicky Mead, Douglas County News Press, December 30, 1995.

[108]Invitation to the Dedication of the Genevieve Nichols Mead Community Room at the Virginia Village Branch of the Denver Public Library, February 22, 1997.

You Are Invited to the Dedication of the

Genevieve Nichols Mead Community Room
at the
Virginia Village Branch of the Denver Public Library

Saturday, February 22, 1997 • 10:30 a.m.
1500 S. Dahlia St. at E. Florida Ave.
Denver, Colorado
(303) 757-6662

TTY for persons who are deaf or hearing-impaired, (303) 640-6375.
If you would like to schedule an interpreter, call at least one week in advance of the event.

Buboltz-Bodle Collection.

SEE DOUGLAS COUNTY PUBLIC LIBRARY IN PHOTO SECTION.

PROSPERITY AND TRAGEDY: THE BITTERSWEET DECADES

The 80's and 90's

Amidst all their philanthropic endeavors and while the Bank continued to prosper, the 80's and 90's became decades of sadness and change for the Millers in their personal lives. On March 7, 1983, Mr. Miller's brother, Adam, passed away at Camellia Care Center in Aurora, at the age of 89, only two months short of his 90th birthday.[1] Over the years the two brothers had remained very close, their lives often running on parallel paths. Both of them owned ranches and raised cattle, and although Phil's was a hobby and Adam's was his livelihood, they were both very well respected in agricultural circles around the country. Despite the fact neither of them ever had any children, their shared a strong devotion for the youth of Douglas County as well as the libraries in their respective towns. As his only living relative on the Miller side of the family in Colorado, Mr. Miller felt the loss of Adam very deeply.

Additionally that year, Mrs. Miller was beginning to lose her eyesight, a condition attributed to macular degeneration. Although it started out slowly, it inevitably would result in almost total blindness. This was very devastating to Mrs. Miller because one of her lifelong enjoyments had been reading. My mom began bringing her "Books-On-Tape." Mr. Miller's health was still fairly good although he often said he was "failing," and it was approaching the time in life when moving to a retirement community was becoming a necessity, albeit an unwelcomed one, but nevertheless a reality. It was also during this time that Mr. Miller began selling off the remaining parcels of his beloved ranch to local real estate men in whom he placed great trust.[2]

Unlike present-day Castle Rock, where there are numerous housing options for senior citizens in good health, some even on land which Millers once owned, in 1983 the choices were very limited. There was one nursing home, which they did not need and one senior apartment house directly behind the Bank, which Mrs. Miller did not want! She said, "It would be too easy for Poppy to walk across the parking lot to the Bank and stay all day!" This was semi-retirement and he was only planning to come to work once a week and she was hoping to hold him to his word![3]

They didn't really like the idea of leaving Castle Rock, but in the near future, as Mrs. Miller's eyesight deteriorated, they would need to live in a place where medical help was readily available, if necessary. After looking at numerous retirement communities in the south Denver and Aurora area, they decided to move into Tremont at 10200 East Harvard Avenue in south Denver. Located right off Parker Road, near 1-225, there was easy access for the drive to Castle Rock when Mr. Miller wanted to go to the Bank. One very big advantage to Tremont was that it had twenty-four hour medical on-call services and a dining area where, if Mrs. Miller did not feel like cooking, they could go eat, with no dishes to wash and no mess to clean up!

Phil and Jerry Miller left Castle Rock on July 4, 1983, after living there 62 years. They had lived in town from 1921 until 1950 and at the ranch from 1950 until 1983, so it was not an easy move for either one of them to make. But after 64 years of marriage, they still had each other, their sense of humor and their sense of adventure, which was a good thing because Tremont was a totally different type of living than that to which they were accustomed. From the big spacious ranch house with the beautiful views out of every window, surrounded only by the sounds of nature, they had, almost overnight become city dwellers, living in a condominium with a view of a courtyard and buildings, surrounded by the sounds of traffic and airplanes![4]

It was also the first time, as has been previously mentioned, that there was a garbage disposal and a dishwasher, appliances Mrs. Miller had happily lived without all those years at the ranch. Now she had no choice! They were built in! The rooms were of nice size and they brought their favorite leather and wood furniture. Mementos such as trophies, plaques and photos of their prized Shorthorns represented their many years of cattle raising and made them feel closer to home! On one wall Mr. Miller proudly displayed many years of financial statements attesting to the growth and success of the Bank.[5]

In October of 1983, Mrs. Miller's sister, Bernice's husband, Ed, passed away and was buried in Crown Hill Memorial Park in Denver.[6] Another change occurred in December of 1983, when at the age of 83, due to her failing eyesight, Mrs. Miller sadly gave up her position on the Board of Directors at The Bank of Douglas County. She had been a Director for forty years and had never once missed a monthly meeting![7] But make no doubt about it, just because they had physically left the community, Castle Rock and Douglas County were still "home" in their hearts and Mr. Miller still owned the Bank and went to work one day each week. Some of their biggest philanthropic gestures were yet to come for the Douglas County Library and the Douglas County Fair.

Soon after the Millers left Castle Rock, Mr. Ken Ash purchased and moved the house from the ranch to a location up near Ridge Road on a large piece of property with beautiful views of the mountains and surrounding hills. He subsequently did some extensive remodeling, making it an even more beautiful and elegant place to live.[8] Mrs. Miller was always happy that her house was still out in the country, because as she said, "After all, it was a country home!"[9]

On May 1, 1984, Adam's wife, Dorothy, passed away after a short illness.[10] When Adam had passed away the year before, his body had been cremated and, after his funeral, according to his wishes, the ashes were being held until Dorothy's death. Shortly after she died, their ashes were scattered, together, somewhere on their beloved ranch. In the place where they spent so many years together, they would now finally rest for eternity together. The tall grass swayed and the trees whispered in the summer breeze. Cattle mooed, as if in respect.[11]

In 1985, Mrs. Miller's health made it impossible for her to remain at Tremont any longer. She was totally blind, she suffered from heart problems, and she had even fallen in the apartment, resulting in a few broken bones. She needed more care than either Mr. Miller, the staff at Tremont, or private nurses could give her. In the hardest decision of their lives, they agreed that she should move to Cherry Creek Care Center in Aurora, a beautiful and excellent medical facility close to Tremont, where she had a private, two room suite with twenty-four hour nursing care. This broke Mr. Miller's heart. After 66 years of living together, it was a terrible adjustment when she had to move to the Care Center, where she would spend the remaining years of her life.[12]

Because of his concern for his wife, Mr. Miller spent as much time with her as possible, weather and his own health permitting. Consequently, more responsibilities for the daily operations of the Bank were entrusted to the officers, under the leadership of Willie Buboltz, Executive Vice President. At this time Dona Sherlock and Thomas Waymire were both Vice Presidents. Other officers were Margaret Olson, Teresa Towns-Weatherly, Therold Bateman, and Richard Temple.[13]

On November 2, 1987, one week after the Grand Opening of the new Philip S. Miller Library, Jerry Miller passed away at the age of 87.[14] It seemed almost as if now, with the Miller Library finally completed on what once was the Miller Ranch, she could finally rest.

Mr. Miller was very devastated and what made it even harder was that she died the day before their 68th wedding anniversary. In a very impressive and touching service at Andrews Funeral home in Castle Rock on November 5, 1987, Jerry Miller was honored and remembered as one of the town's and county's most important and influential people. She was buried in Cedar Hill Cemetery west of Castle Rock.[15] Mr. Miller continued to live in his apartment in the Tremont retirement community, but he once said nothing was ever the same again.

Earlier in 1987, Mr. Miller and The Bank of Douglas County were honored with a Tribute from the Colorado State Senate sponsored by Senator Joe Winkler from Douglas County. It read:

COLORADO STATE SENATE TRIBUTE

Senator Joe Winkler requests the following Tribute:

Congratulations to Philip S. Miller, President of The Bank of Douglas County, designated as a "Blue Ribbon Bank."

Philip S. Miller has been with The Bank of Douglas County since its founding and over the years has provided sound leadership and excellent business philosophy, contributing to this coveted honor.

In addition, Philip S. Miller has contributed many years of service to the community and provided support for such things as the library, youth groups and county activities. Douglas County Citizens have benefited greatly from the success of The Bank of Douglas County and Philip S. Miller has certainly been instrumental in that effort.

To extend special honor and distinction for extraordinary service, the Colorado State Senate directs this Tribute be presented on this eleventh day of May 1987.

It was signed by the President and Secretary of the Colorado State Senate, Ted Strickland and Marjorie Nielson.[16]

Mr. Miller received a special copy of this Tribute which hung on the wall in the Bank where it remained until after it was sold. He also had a copy on the wall of his apartment. He was very proud of this honor and it was especially meaningful because it was presented by his longtime friend, then Senator, Joe Winkler.

In December of 1988, my dad, Willie Buboltz, retired as an employee of The Bank of Douglas County after thirty-six years. At that time he resigned his position of Executive Vice President which he had held since January 1973.[17] By now, Mr. Miller didn't come to the Bank anymore and people said, "It won't be the same without Phil and Willie!" But Willie didn't completely leave at that time! He remained as a Director and continued to work at the Bank on a Consultant basis one day a week for five more years, until the end of December 1993. His loyalty ran very deeply toward Mr. Miller and the Bank and he would never completely retire until such time as Mr. Miller retired also. I know for a fact that my dad had a devotion for Mr. Miller equaling that of a son for a father.

On Tuesday, August 29, 1989, The Bank of Douglas County celebrated what would be its most important milestone, The Golden Anniversary, Fifty Years in Business! In honor of the occasion an Open House was held from 9 a.m. to 4 p.m. with refreshments and much reminiscing.[18] Former employees, many customers and family members attended, as well as Bankers from Denver and Colorado Springs. As part of the Golden Anniversary celebration, a drawing was held and sixteen gold coins were given away. Mr. Miller was in attendance for part of the day and was honored as a longtime merchant in Castle Rock who was also the oldest steady businessman in town! As at the 40th Anniversary, The Bank of Douglas County was once again recognized as the longest continuously operating bank in Castle Rock.

In a short speech, Mr. Miller thanked everyone for their loyalty and support over the past 50 years. He said "I couldn't have done it without all of you or Momma (Jerry) and I only wish she were her to celebrate this day with us."[19]

Ken Ash bought Miller's house and moved it to a new location. Here the house is rolling down Wilcox Street as someone lifts up the stop light at 2nd Street!

Local History Collection, Douglas Public Library District, Douglas County, CO.
Courtesy of Ken Ash and Moira Armstrong-Ash.

In an Editorial entitled "A Solid Foundation," The Editor of the Daily News Press wrote:

> "Our hats are off to The Bank of Douglas County which celebrated its 50th Anniversary this week. There are not many businesses that have survived 50 years in this county, and the Bank's Golden Anniversary is a notable event. The Bank, founded by Philip S. Miller, will probably be around in another 50 years.
>
> Apparently, it has found the formula to success in this area. That formula is conservative, honest business practices, community commitment and building friendships.
>
> The Bank consistently is ranked among the top of all banks in Colorado for stability. Simply, it doesn't take many risks. And in this market, that's probably not a bad policy. We've seen many times what happens to institutions that take unnecessary risks and overextend themselves. Two former institutions in Douglas County are no longer around.
>
> Meanwhile, The Bank of Douglas County moves slowly forward, plotting its course very carefully.
>
> Congratulations, Bank of Douglas County. You've been a good neighbor and a good business institution in Douglas County for the past 50 years. We hope the next 50 years will be just as successful."[20]

It must not be overlooked that Mr. Miller always surrounded himself with good employees, people who believed the way he did. Conservative yet visionary, they helped him make the Bank a success as well as usher Castle Rock and Douglas County through the crucial changes that a growing community experiences over the years. The loyalty shown by his employees was evidenced by the mere fact that so many of them remained with him for years and years: Margaret Couch Fry, Frances Winkler Cannon, Helen Longworth, Kathy Anderson, Mary Jane Hart, Margaret Olson, Teresa Towns-Weatherly, Thomas Waymire, Glenda Williams, Ann Diamond, and Nina Weidman.

And then their were the four longtimers: Dona Sherlock, Bob Oliver, Johnnie Osthoff and my dad, Willie Buboltz, who had been there for forty-two years when he finally retired in 1994! Former Mayor Pete Burgess commented in a letter to me that Mr. Miller hired good help in the Bank and that is one of the things that made it a success.[21] I agreed with him, wholeheartedly, since my dad was one of the those good people!

Although these people were trusted employees, there was an element of love and devotion, respect and friendship that went even deeper that just an employee-employer relationship. Mr. Miller was the proud Poppy and these people were his children. They in return looked up to Phil Miller with devotion and respect. This man was more than just a "boss."

In April of 1991, Mr. Miller felt he was to the point that he needed to move to a care center. He wasn't really sick, incredibly, at 94 years old he had just finally slowed down and needed more help than what was available to him at Tremont. He chose the same place in which Mrs. Miller had been, Cherry Creek Care Center in Aurora.[22] He had a very nice, large, private, two room suite, with a living room and a bedroom and twenty-four hour nursing care, if and when it became necessary. The amazing thing about Mr. Miller was that his mind was still sharp, although it wandered every now and then. He could still walk, despite some arthritis. He would go to the dining room for his meals and eat the biggest breakfast of any man there! He would have eaten ten pieces of bacon every morning if the nurses had allowed it! Age had not mellowed his old habit of eating a big ranch breakfast and he still had the appetite of a young man! That is probably one of the reasons he remained as healthy as he did for as long as he did. He liked to eat! It was hard to believe, when watching this ordinary, white haired gentleman, slowly making his way back to his room, that he was one of the wealthiest men in Colorado and was still the President of The Bank of Douglas County!

Mr. Miller was never at a loss for visitors. Loyal former and present employees and friends from the Castle Rock and Denver areas were frequent guests. Jamie LaRue, Library Director of the Douglas Public Library District recalled meeting 94 year old Mr. Miller for the first time at the care center. "He treated me with courtly grace, a selfless majesty. He spoke with great feeling and intelligence about the value of the public library to the community of thirty years ago."[23]

During a trip to Denver from Phoenix, I remember visiting him in the summer of 1991 and he still knew the name of the very first man to make a deposit in the Bank as well as the members of his first Board of Directors! He reminisced about the old days and it was truly amazing the things he recalled about Castle Rock, the people and the Bank. I told him Castle Rock should have been named

"Millerville!" He nixed that idea immediately, saying he already had a street named for him, Miller Boulevard, and "that was enough!"[24]

Even then, his humble and private nature was still very evident. Despite everything he had done for the town, the county and the people, as well as the awards and recognition he had received, he still just considered himself an average citizen! Although he may have been out of sight, he was never out of the minds of the people of Castle Rock and Douglas County. One could not drive by the Bank or the Library or the Fairgrounds without thinking of Mr. Miller and remembering his contributions to the community and his kindness to the people.

In early 1993, Mr. Miller was recognized as a member of the Fifty Year Club by the Colorado Banker's Association at the Annual Convention at the Broadmoor Hotel in Colorado Springs. He was awarded a 50 year pin and a Plaque. He had been a member since 1943 and there were not very many bankers in the state of Colorado who could claim that honor. Due to his health, Mr. Miller was unable to attend so my father accepted these awards for him.[25]

By the middle of 1993, Mr. Miller's health had reached a point where he felt maybe it was time to turn over the reigns of the Bank to someone else. He was not selling it, make no mistake about that, he just felt retirement was inevitable and he would relinquish his positions at the end of 1993. It worked out rather well, actually, because during that same year Dona Sherlock and Johnnie Osthoff were ready to retire and my dad felt he could resign his Directorship at the same time.

Dona Sherlock came to Colorado in 1954 with her husband, Charles, from St. Francis, Kansas, a small farming community in the northwest corner of the state, just twenty-five miles from the Colorado border.[26] For the previous seven years, she had worked as a Teller at a bank in St. Francis. Charles was an auctioneer. They moved to a ranch in Elizabeth where Charles worked as a herdsman for well-known rancher, John Cummings. They also traveled to State Fairs where Charles would show the Cummings' registered Red Shorthorn cattle. It was a long way from her banking career, but she and her husband enjoyed the ranch life and the cattle showing. John Cummings was a good friend of Mr. Miller's. Aware of Dona's banking background, he would tell Mr. Miller, "If she ever applies for a job, you should hire her!"

In 1956, John Cummings sold all his cattle and opened the John Deere store in Franktown. At that time, Dona and Charles moved west of Castle Rock, where Charles worked as a herdsman on a ranch owned by A. W. "Monty" Montgomery, who raised Herefords. In 1957, while living at the Montgomery Ranch, Dona did, in fact, apply for a job at The Bank of Douglas County and Mr. Miller apparently took John Cummings' advice! He hired her as a Teller! She joined a staff of four: Mr. Miller, Willie Buboltz, Bob Oliver and Betty Corey. Not long after that, she and Charles moved to a house in Castle Rock and he worked as an auctioneer.

Dona first became an Officer, Assistant Cashier, in 1971, an office she would hold for eight years. Following the expansion of the Bank in 1972, and after fifteen years as a Teller, she was promoted to the Loan Department where she also handled CD's. In 1979, after holding the office of Assistant Cashier for eight years, she became Assistant Vice President. She held this position until becoming Vice President in 1981. In 1984, the title of Cashier was added to her position as Vice President. Also in 1984, after Bob Oliver retired and Mrs. Miller gave up her Directorship due to her health, Dona became a member of the Board of Directors and remained such until her retirement. In January of 1993, she was named Executive Vice President, a position she also held until her retirement.[27]

Johnnie Osthoff started to work at the Bank in February of 1969.[28] Her husband, Attorney William Osthoff, had recently passed away and she was looking for a job. She laughingly recalled that she didn't even know how to fill out a job application and explained the unusual manner in which she was hired. "Willie called me on the phone and said, 'I hear you're looking for a job. Why don't you come in to the Bank and we'll talk.' I went in and before I left he asked me if I could start work February 1st." One of the advantages to living in Castle Rock in those days was that it was small enough that people cared about each other. Everyone knew what was going on, when neighbors needed help or when someone was looking for work. In this case, my dad knew she wanted a job and contacted her. That is the way it was "back then" in Castle Rock.

She knew very little about the banking business so she started as a clerk, where she worked on a table by the vault, filing checks. She remembered Mr. Miller and Willie were very kind and patient with her. A few years later, when Betty Corey resigned, Johnnie recalled, "Willie came to me and told me I was going to become a Teller!" Eventually she became Head Teller, where she remained until her retirement.[29]

And so it was that on December 31, 1993, Mr. Miller retired as President and Director of The Bank of Douglas County after 54 years; Willis Buboltz resigned his Directorship after 42 years; Dona

Sherlock resigned her Directorship of ten years and her position as Executive Vice President and retired after 37 years; Johnnie Osthoff retired one month short of 25 years, the final ten years in the position as Head Teller.

Although it was a bitterly cold Colorado day, January 7, 1994 saw one of the largest turnouts The Bank of Douglas County had ever experienced at an All Day Open House and a Retirement Party from 4 to 6 p.m. in the evening in honor of Philip Miller, Willis Buboltz, Dona Sherlock and Johnnie Osthoff.[30] Because of Mr. Miller's health, he was unable to attend but he was there in spirit! Everyone could feel his presence. Customers, family members, former employees, Bankers from Denver and Colorado Springs as well as members of the State Banking Commission came to congratulate Willie, Dona, and Johnnie on their retirements and to express gratitude and appreciation for their many years of service and commitment to the community as well as to the banking industry.

My dad received a Certificate of Appreciation from District Judge, Thomas J. Curry. It read,

> "This Certificate of Appreciation is presented to Willis C. Buboltz by the District and County Courts, Douglas County, Colorado in recognition of outstanding service rendered." Signed, Judge Thomas J. Curry.[31]

Frequently during the day and especially during the hours of the party, the lobby was so full, that, even though the snow had started gently to fall, people were waiting outside to get in, an indication of the loyalty they felt for the Bank, Phil, Willie, Dona, and Johnnie. There were tears of happiness and tears of sadness as everyone experienced mixed emotions. These retirements truly indicated the end of an era and a definite changing of the guard. Many people felt nothing would ever be the same again.

On Tuesday, January 3rd, Mr. August Fischer, formerly of Bank of the West in Parker and more recently The First National Bank in Castle Rock, had been named the new President and a Director of The Bank of Douglas County.[32] It is rather interesting to note that in the 54 year history of the Bank, he was only the fourth President. Mr. Louis R. Higby, Sr. was the first President from 1939 until 1943; Mr. Charles L. Mann was the second President from 1944 until 1950; and Mr. Philip S. Miller was the third President from 1951 until 1993.

Two other Directors were announced at that time. One was the popular and well respected local Veterinarian and, former Director of The First National Bank, Dr. Herman Anderson. The other Director was Mr. Lawrence Fain, of Steamboat Springs, Colorado, who was elected Chairman of the Board. These three men comprised the Board of Directors until after Mr. Miller's death and the sale of the Bank.[33]

Other than the change in the Office of President, the other Officers remained the same. Tom Waymire, Vice President and Loan Officer; Richard Temple, Vice President and Senior Lender; Teresa Towns-Weatherly, Assistant Vice President; and Margaret Olson, Assistant Vice President. By the end of 1994, Richard Temple and Teresa Towns-Weatherly had resigned. In 1995, Margaret Olson became Vice President while Shilee S. Neal became Operations Officer and later Cashier. These Officers also remained until after Mr. Miller's death and the sale of the Bank.[34]

On January 18, 1994, Bernice Stewart Benedict passed away at the age of 91.[35] She had outlived her children Shirley and Jim, her husband, Ed, and her sister, Jerry Miller. At the age of 98, Mr. Miller was the only one who had outlived them all.

He turned 99 on October 11, 1994. Dona Sherlock and Johnnie Osthoff took him a cake in honor of the occasion. He received many cards which his nurses hung on the wall. Everyone hoped and planned for a 100th Birthday Celebration for the following year. But it was not to be as Mr. Miller passed away the following summer on June 7, 1995.[36]

Over 250 people attended the funeral of Mr. Philip Simon Miller at the United Methodist Church in Castle Rock on June 10, 1995. This man, the butcher, the banker, the benefactor, was honored by the Masons as well as many bankers from around the state of Colorado, employees, friends and family. He was buried next to his beloved Jerry at Cedar Hill Cemetery west of Castle Rock. Momma and Poppy were finally together, once again.[37]

The Bank of Douglas County the day of Mr. Miller's funeral, June 10, 1995.

Buboltz-Bodle Collection.

ENDNOTES

[1]Obituary, Adam P. Miller, written by his wife, Dorothy, Douglas County News Press, March 23, 1983.

[2]Interview with my parents, Willis and Ellen Buboltz, December 1992.

[3]Conversation between Mrs. Miller and the author at The Bank of Douglas County, June 1983.

[4]Conversation between Mrs. Miller and the author at Tremont, Aurora, CO, November 1983.

[5]Personal recollections after a visit with Mr. and Mrs. Miller at Tremont, Aurora, CO, November 1983.

[6]Death date for Charles Edwin (Ed) Benedict verified by Historical Record of Crown Hill Memorial Park, Denver, CO, October 5, 1983; also headstone Crown Hill Memorial Park, Charles Edwin Benedict, Burial Date, October 7, 1983.

[7]Statements of Condition, The Bank of Douglas County, December 30, 1983 and June 30, 1984.

[8]Interview between Ken Ash and the author at Philip S. Miller Library, Castle Rock, CO, August 1, 1996.

[9]Conversation between Mrs. Miller and the author at Tremont, Denver, CO, November 1983.

[10]Douglas County News Press, Obituary, Dorothy Miller, May 3, 1984.

[11]My own recollection.

[12]Conversation between Mr. Miller and the author, Cherry Creek Care Center, Aurora, CO, August 1991.

[13]Statements of Condition, The Bank of Douglas County, June 30, 1985.

[14]Death Certificate, Jessie Ethel Miller, State of Colorado, November 5, 1987.

[15]Obituary, Jerry Miller, Daily News Press, Castle Rock, CO, November 3, 1987; and Funeral Memorium, Jerry E. Miller, November 5, 1987 from Andrews Funeral Home.

[16]Colorado State Senate Tribute to Philip S. Miller, May 11, 1987. Joe Winkler, Ted Strickland, and Marjorie Nielson.

[17]Statements of Condition, The Bank of Douglas County, January 1973 to December 1988, and June 1989.

[18]Daily News Press, The Bank of Douglas County Golden Anniversary Invitation, August 23, 1989.

[19]Speech, Mr. Miller, Golden Anniversary Open House, The Bank of Douglas County, August 29, 1989.

[20]Daily News Press, Editorial, "A Solid Foundation," August 23, 1989.

[21]Letter from former Mayor, H. G. "Pete" and Hazel Burgess, Castle Rock, CO, November 1996.

[22]Interview with my father, Willis Buboltz, May 1994.

[23]Douglas County News Press, "Library Bindings" by Jamie LaRue, June 14, 1995, p 20a.

[24]Conversation between Mr. Miller and the author at Cherry Creek Care Center, August 1991.

[25]Colorado Bankers Association, Fifty Year Club Plaque, presented to P. S. Miller, 1993. Copy on file at the Local History Collection of the Douglas Public Library District, Castle Rock, CO.

[26]The source of the information and dates regarding Dona and Charles Sherlock comes from telephone conversations and personal interviews with Dona Sherlock, Castle Rock, CO, July 30, 1996, April 16, 1998, and many letters between us during the writing of this book.

[27]The source of the information and dates regarding Dona Sherlock's Officer Titles and Directorship comes from Statements of Condition, The Bank of Douglas County, December 31, 1971 until December 31, 1993.

[28]The source of the information and dates regarding Johnnie Osthoff, Castle Rock, CO, comes from a telephone conversation with her on April 14, 1998.

[29]IBID.

[30]Invitation to the Retirement Party in honor of Willis C. Buboltz, Dona W. Sherlock, Johnnie C. Osthoff, January 7, 1994; also Douglas County News Press article entitled "Saying Thanks For Service," January 12, 1994, p 1.

[31]Certificate of Appreciation presented to Willis Buboltz by Judge Thomas Curry, January 7, 1994.

[32]Douglas County News Press, January 12, 1994.

[33]Douglas County News Press, January 12, 1994, Statements of Condition, The Bank of Douglas County, June 30, 1994 until December 31, 1995.

[34]Statements of Condition, The Bank of Douglas County, June 30, 1994 until December 31, 1995.

[35]Death date for Bernice Catherine Stewart Benedict is verified by Funeral Records of Fairmount Cemetery, Denver, CO, and Interment Records, Crown Hill Memorial Park, Denver, CO, January 28, 1994; and headstone Crown Hill Memorial Park, Burial date, February 1, 1994.

[36]Obituary, Philip S. Miller, Douglas County News Press, June 10, 1995, p 1, 3; and Castle Rock Chronicle, June 15, 1995, p 1, 2, Funeral Memorium, Philip Simon Miller, June 10, 1995, from Andrews, Caldwell, Gibson Funeral Home.

[37]Headstones of Philip S. Miller and Jerry E. Miller, Cedar Hill Cemetery, Castle Rock, CO.

"The Rock" looks down protectively on the 56 year old Bank.

Buboltz-Bodle Collection.

Public invitation to the Retirement Party for Willie Buboltz, Dona Sherlock, Johnnie Osthoff, January 1994.

Dona Sherlock Collection.

Retirement Cake for the three retirees, with The Bank logo across the bottom.

Dona Sherlock Collection.

SEE RETIREMENT IN PHOTO SECTION.

THE SELLING OF THE BANK OF DOUGLAS COUNTY: THE END OF AN ERA

It was with fond memories, sad feelings and a few tears that we, who were customers of The Bank of Douglas County, read the headlines in the News Press on November 25, 1995, "The Bank of Douglas County Sold to FirstBank."[1] Mr. Miller had passed away five months earlier and now "his Bank, our Bank," was being sold. Too many changes, too little time. But as Mr. Miller always said, "You have to move forward. You can't stand still." Even after his death, the Bank would move forward. That is the way he wanted it.

Earlier that week, the trust officers and attorneys administrating Mr. Miller's estate had agreed to allow Lakewood based FirstBank Holding Company of Colorado to purchase The Bank of Douglas County. With assets of $101.3 million and 11,000 customers, the Bank was the largest in Douglas County and one of the strongest in Colorado as well as the nation.[2] Many banks had hoped to acquire it.

FirstBank Holding Company was the parent company of FirstBank of Castle Rock at 221 Wilcox Street which had been in existence since June 18, 1975 when it first opened with Mr. Melvin Sorensen as President.[3] At the time the purchase was announced, FirstBank of Castle Rock reported assets of $55 million.[4] The holding company was planning to consolidate the two banks, and the two names, into FirstBank of Douglas County, N.A. which designates it as National Association.[5]

The acquisition would financially benefit FirstBank of Castle Rock as well as FirstBank Holding Company because the addition of the $100 million assets of The Bank of Douglas County would triple the assets of FirstBank of Castle Rock and increase the assets of the holding company by $100 million. FirstBank of Douglas County, N.A. would then become the largest independent bank in the county, an honor held by Mr. Miller and The Bank of Douglas County for more than 50 years. The transaction was scheduled to be completed in early 1996, and it was reported that Gary Hall, the President of FirstBank of Castle Rock, would become the new President of FirstBank of Douglas County, N.A.[6]

In the interim, the two banks continued to operate separately and independently while the required agencies began the long and arduous process of the approval and official changes. Since The Bank of Douglas County was a privately-owned, independent State Bank, it was under the authority of the Colorado State Banking Commission in Denver. However, FirstBank of Castle Rock was a National Bank and was under the authority of the Federal Regulators at the Comptroller of the Currency in Washington, D.C. Before the sale could be finalized, requirements under both agencies had to be adhered to and approved.

It was also announced in November that when the sale was completed, the two banks would be combined into one location, either the FirstBank facility at Third and Wilcox Streets or The Bank of Douglas County building at Fourth and Wilcox Streets.[7] This immediately set off a rash of speculation as to the fate of The Bank of Douglas County building, which had been constructed in 1922 and is significant to the history of downtown Castle Rock. Additionally, according to Starr and Lionel Oberlin of the Castle Rock Historical Society, the building is eligible for placement on the National Register of Historic Places due to its age and architectural style.[8] It is also on The Castle Rock Inventory of Historic Properties and is eligible for nomination to the Town of Castle Rock Register of Historic Landmarks.[9]

FirstBank, on the other hand, had been built in the mid-70's, and although it was a very nice, modern bank building, it held no real connection to downtown Castle Rock history. It was more remembered for the fact that it was the first bank to bring competition to The Bank of Douglas County after more than thirty years!

The first step in the change-over process took place on January 1, 1996, when the two names became one, FirstBank of Douglas County, N.A., although the actual sale and conversion would not occur until February and March.[10] Slowly but surely, stationery and envelopes, business cards and forms, pens and pencils, and any other items that said "The Bank of Douglas County" were suddenly becoming obsolete.

In the meantime, personnel changes were addressed and it was revealed that although the staff of The Bank of Douglas County would be retained, the Officers and the Board of Directors would be replaced by FirstBank officials when the sale was completed. A few employees who were ready to retire took this opportunity to do so.

On Tuesday, February 20, 1996, the sale of The Bank of Douglas County to FirstBank Holding Company of Colorado was completed.[11] Over the next few weeks preparations for the final conversion began. On the weekend of March 15, all The Bank of

Douglas County computer systems were removed and replaced with FirstBank computer systems. On Monday, March 18, with assurances that the longstanding services and traditions established by Mr. Miller and his employees would continue under the new ownership, the two banks officially became one.[12] That week it was also announced that Mr. Buddy Douglass, who had been Senior Vice President of FirstBank since July 1993, would be in charge of what was formerly The Bank of Douglas County facility.[13] He would hold this position until mid-1998.

A few days later, once again with fond memories, sad feelings and a few tears, residents, employees and downtown business people witnessed the removal of The Bank of Douglas County signs and the two traditional brass plaques, which had hung beside the doors since the Bank's opening. After 57 years, it was the end of an era.

Another important announcement took place during this time but was perhaps eclipsed by all the news surrounding the final conversion. On March 20 it was reported that FirstBank of Douglas County, N.A., had purchased the five-acre piece of property on the corner of Plum Creek Parkway and Wilcox Streets, from Mr. Miller's estate.[14] This transaction immediately renewed speculation as to the fate of the former Bank of Douglas County building.

Finally, in July of 1996, all speculation was put to rest when FirstBank of Douglas County, N.A. announced plans for three locations in the Castle Rock area.[15] Many people were relieved to learn that the former Bank of Douglas County building would remain as the downtown branch, while the FirstBank building on Third and Wilcox Streets would be sold. Additionally, a new 6,500 square foot main branch would be built on the five-acre piece of property previously purchased at Plum Creek Parkway and Wilcox Street. It was also reported that another facility of approximately 4,500 square feet was being planned in the Milestone Center, north of Castle Rock, near King Soopers at Founders Parkway and Front Street.[16] The Milestone Center facility was completed in late 1997. Groundbreaking took place for the main branch on the five-acres at Plum Creek Parkway and Wilcox Street in January 1998, and was completed during the summer of 1998.[17]

According to Sr. Vice President, Buddy Douglass, in March of 1998, FirstBank of Douglas County converted to a State Charter. The correct name for all three branches is still FirstBank of Douglas County but without the N.A. It is now the largest independent State Bank in the county.[18]

In the final analysis, Mr. and Mrs. Miller would have likely been very pleased with the acquisition. FirstBank Holding Company of Colorado is the largest Colorado-owned, independent banking organization and it was very important to them that the Bank be sold to a group with Colorado affiliation, not to some out of state company. The consolidation between The Bank of Douglas County and FirstBank of Castle Rock would have also pleased them, because FirstBank is a local bank, oddly enough, their first competitor, and they had great respect for the Officers and Directors. Yet the thing that may have made them the happiest, throughout this whole transaction, is the fact that FirstBank of Douglas County purchased their five-acres and constructed a bank building on it. Somehow it seems as if it's all still in the family!

Sr. Vice President Buddy Douglas and President Gary Hall in front of the former Bank of Douglas County. July 1996.

Coutesy Castle Rock Chonicle and Amy Brennan.

Gary Hall stands on the five-acres purchased from Mr. Miller's estate.

Coutesy Castle Rock Chonicle and Amy Brennan.

ENDNOTES

[1]Douglas County News Press, November 25, 1995, p 1.

[2]Rocky Mountain News, November 23, 1995, p 77.

[3]Information Buddy Douglass, Senior Vice President, FirstBank of Douglas County, Castle Rock, CO, April 9, 1998.

[4]Douglas County News Press, November 25, 1995, p 1.

[5]IBID.

[6]Douglas County News Press, November 29, 1995, p 1.

[7]Douglas County News Press, November 25, 1995, p 2.

[8]Douglas County News Press, December 9, 1995, p 4, telephone interviews, Lionel Oberlin, April 13, 1998, June 10, 1998.

[9]Letter from Kent Brandebery, March 18, 1998; and telephone interviews, Lionel Oberlin, April 13, 1998, June 10, 1998.

[10]Douglas County News Press, January 6, 1996, p 3.

[11]Douglas County News Press, February 17, 1996, p 1.

[12]IBID; Also Douglas County News Press Salute Section, "The Bank of Douglas County to Merge: Longstanding Traditions Will Go On," February 28, 1996, p 4c.

[13]Douglas County News Press, March 27, 1996, p 7a.

[14]Douglas County News Press, March 20, 1996, p 2a.

[15]Castle Rock Chronicle, July 31, 1996, p A5; and Douglas County News Press, July 17, 1996, p 1a, 3a.

[16]IBID.

[17]Information Buddy Douglass, Senior Vice President, FirstBank of Douglas County, Castle Rock, CO, April 9, 1998.

[18]IBID.

FirstBank of Douglas County was completed on the five-acres in June 1998. Mr. Miller always wanted a bank there!

Buboltz-Bodle Collection.

The Philip S. Miller Bench, dedicated at the Douglas County Fair, August 3, 1996.

Buboltz-Bodle Collection.

Dedication Ceremony. Seated in front: Cecil Whitman, Helen Oliver. Standing with camera: Bob Oliver, behind him Dona Sherlock. Standing at right: Bea and John Lowell, behind them Mr. Miller's Trust Attorney James Nelsen, and Bruff Shea. In far back is Dr. Hal Gannon.

Buboltz-Bodle Collection.

THE LEGACY: THE PHILIP S. MILLER PERPETUAL CHARITABLE TRUST

"Life is measured not only in accomplishments but in the legacy a person leaves behind." Cindy Brick

In the predawn hour of 4 a.m. on June 7, 1995, Philip Simon Miller said to his nurse, "Get me my hat and coat. I am ready to go." These were the first words he had spoken in five days. They were the last words he would speak in his lifetime. A few minutes later he died, in very much the same way he lived—peacefully and quietly.[1] In four months and four days he would have been 100 years old. He left The Bank of Douglas County with over $100 million in assets and a Perpetual Charitable Trust worth over $30 million. His heirs are the people of Castle Rock and Douglas County, Colorado, as well as the children of Denver Children's Hospital and the Shriner's Hospitals for Crippled Children.

His legacy is not only his benevolence and philanthropy to the community but also his many acts of kindness and generosity which will live on in the hearts and memories of people whose lives he touched.

But he wasn't always wealthy.

His life was a series of contrasts. Poor to rich, butcher to banker, broke to millionaire. To quote a friend, "His life was truly a rags to riches story."

It was also a series of challenges.

In 1908 his mother died when he was only thirteen years old. In the early 1920's, as a meat market owner, he was turned down for a loan and lost two of his three markets. During the Depression he shoveled coal for a living. In the late 1930's he helped open a bank which was a risk and a challenge because the townspeople were leery of banks and wanted to keep their money in the mattresses, so to speak. But he never gave up. He worked and slaved and ultimately amassed a fortune.

While he was alive, the people shared in his generosity and reaped the rewards of his labor. He was a generous man with good business sense. The Town of Castle Rock, Douglas County, The Fire Department, The Fair, 4-H, the Libraries, the children, the youth, the schools, all benefited during his lifetime. After his death, it would be no different. His devotion and commitment to these particular entities would continue, forever, thanks to his Trust.

In January of 1980, Mr. and Mrs. Miller established the Trust to manage the Bank and their estate after both of them had passed away. They did this for a couple of important reasons, the first being that they had no children to whom they could pass the Bank and their estate. Second and more importantly, they wanted to make certain that the town, the county and the people would receive monetary benefits, every year. Their commitment would be forever. Not only in life, but in death.

Perpetual and Charitable are important words when describing this type of a Trust. Perpetual means going on forever, year in and year out, from here to eternity, so to speak. Charitable means tax exempt. Mr. Miller, being the wise businessman he was, arranged the Trust in this manner so the beneficiaries would never have to pay any taxes on the money they received.

Although the principal of the Trust, in excess of $30 million, remains the same each year, the money the beneficiaries receive is based on a percentage of the income generated from the Trust for that year. The percentage remains the same, but the amount received by each beneficiary may vary from year to year depending on the total revenues of the Trust, based on such things as interest, dividends and capital gains.

In December 1995, six months after Mr. Miller's death and several weeks after FirstBank Holding Company of Colorado had announced plans to purchase The Bank of Douglas County,[2] the terms of Mr. Miller's Perpetual Charitable Trust were made public.[3]

Douglas County Philip S. Miller Building was completed in October of 1997 at 100 Third Street, diagonally across from Miller's first house at 310 Elbert Street.

Buboltz-Bodle Collection.

Following are the percentage figures and the beneficiaries which will receive money, yearly, from the income of the Trust:[4]

PERCENTAGES AND BENEFICIARIES
Twenty Percent (20%) to Children's Hospital, Denver, Colorado

Twenty Percent (20%) to Shriner's Hospital for Crippled Children, National Headquarters, Tampa Florida

Twenty Percent (20%) to Town of Castle Rock

Twenty Percent (20%) to Douglas County Colorado

Ten Percent (10%) to Douglas County Library

Four Percent (4%) to Douglas County High School located in Castle Rock, Colorado, for Scholarships

Two Percent (2%) to Castle Rock Fire Department

Two Percent (2%) to Douglas County 4-H Council

Two Percent (2%) to Douglas County Fair Association

Beneficiaries and community members alike expressed awe and amazement at Mr. Miller's incredible generosity. However, it was completely characteristic of Mr. and Mrs. Miller to want to continue supporting the entities to which they were so committed during their lives, even after their deaths.

Shortly after the sale of The Bank of Douglas County became final, the first disbursements were made by Colorado National Bank, which, at that time was the Administrator of the Mr. Miller's Trust. (It is currently administered by U.S. Bancorp, Inc. N.A.) Beneficiaries soon began announcing plans for the use of the money.

On April 3, 1996, The Douglas County Board of County Commissioners announced plans for the construction of a new county government office building on the corner of Third and Elbert Streets to be named the Philip S. Miller Building.[5]

Although the land was county owned, three fourths of the building's estimated $6 million costs were to be financed by the bequest to Douglas County from Mr. Miller's Trust.[6] In May, preliminary designs were reported, stating that the building would be 65,000 to 70,000 square feet, four stories high, with ample parking. It would allow for County employees from five different locations in Castle Rock to finally be housed in one building.[7] A projected completion date of late 1997 was met as employees began moving into the Philip S. Miller Building at 100 3rd Street during September and October, 1997.[8]

In August of 1996, in honor of Mr. Miller and his longstanding support and devotion, the 1996 Douglas County Fair Association and Fair Board dedicated the 1996 Fair and Rodeo to him.[9] On the opening day, August 3, the Philip S. Miller Memorial Bench was dedicated just outside the Douglas County Extension Office located on the fairgrounds. The inscription reads, "In Memory of Philip S. Miller, October 11, 1895 to June 7, 1995."[10] Karen Serafini explained that the Board chose this location because with a view of Castle Rock and the fairgrounds, this marble bench represents Mr. Miller's generosity and commitment to every aspect of the Fair and 4-H and his love for the children.[11]

Many friends, family, former employees, present and former Fair Board members and County Commissioners, and 4-H Council members, as well as people from the community were in attendance for the event. I traveled from Phoenix in order to be there. Speeches were given by Karen Serafini, Gill Whitman, John Lowell, and Willie Buboltz as they reminisced about Mr. Miller's life and his accomplishments. Afterward, a reception was held in the Extension Office. That night, in honor of Mr. Miller, free admission was offered to the Rodeo. The final day of the Fair, August 11, was designated as Philip S. Miller Appreciation Day.[12] Additionally, the 1996 Fair and Rodeo Book was dedicated to Mr. Miller, with a series of impressive articles by Wendy Thomas of the Weekly News Chronicle.

The Douglas County Fair Association is a beneficiary receiving yearly income from Mr. Miller's Trust. Although it is run by the Fair Board and encompasses the Douglas County Fair and Rodeo, the Association itself is a county agency and, as such, is governmentally operated under the authority of the Douglas County Commissioners, who determine how the money from Mr. Miller's Trust will be spent.

In early 1997, it was announced that a Douglas County 4-H Foundation Board had been established in late 1996 with a start-up donation from Mr. and Mrs. John Lowell.[13] One of the purposes of this Foundation Board is to act in an advisory capacity to the 4-H Council, which is also a beneficiary receiving yearly income from Mr. Miller's Trust.[14] The 4-H Council is not governmentally run, therefore the members have the authority to be self-governed and to choose the course of action they wish to take in financial matters.

According to former Fair Board President, Karen Serafini, "The Foundation Board and the Council want to make sure that Mr. Miller's money will be used in the way in which he would want, to benefit the kids."[15] In addition to fund raising and awarding college scholarships and grants, the Foundation Board gives 4-H camp scholarships and other continuing education trips. The Foundation Board is made up of former Fair Board members, 4-H Council members, bankers, accountants, lawyers, corporate executives, ranchers and other county residents.[16]

In September of 1997, during a Foundation Board fund raiser at Highlands Ranch, Mr. and Mrs. John Lowell were honored for their monetary contribution and their efforts toward the Foundation and given a Plaque by President, Larry Carnahan. Mr. Miller was also honored at this event for his yearly bequest to the 4-H Council. Additionally, six 4-H members received scholarships and grants from the Foundation. They were: Kelly Clark, Lee Ann Griffin, Melissa Myers, Megan Waide, Chad Williams and Alex Spencer.[17]

In the spring of 1997, the recipients of the Philip S. Miller Scholarship were announced by the Douglas County High School. According to Counselor Kristi Olson, a strict criteria, based on the terms of the Trust, had been formulated by a specific committee of administrators, teachers, a school counselor and a parent. An application was then designed specially for this scholarship with pertinent questions to aid in the decision making process. Finally, a second committee, with the same mix as the criteria committee, selected the recipients based on the results of their applications and interviews for the following scholarships: Two Four-Year Renewable Scholarships; Two Two-Year Renewable Scholarships; Two Vocational Scholarships; Forty-Nine Non-Renewable One-Time Scholarships.[18]

Additionally there are Two Non-Renewable, One-Time Staff Nominated Scholarships awarded, which are determined not by the criteria and application process, but rather by nomination of Douglas County High School Staff Members.

The following is a list of the 1997 Philip S. Miller Scholarship Recipients:

Deven Beeman, Bridget Slevin, Alex McKean, Andrea Adams, Joel Barnes, Sara Bell, Kyle Bradley, Shawn Bratt, Matt Breite, Shannon Bremer, Aaron Brown, Jennifer Buckler, William Cable, Shannon Christ, Gina Cicero, Travis Coleman, David Engfer, Kyle Forney, Susan Fouts, Dinah Frey, Matt Geerdes, Erin Gerkin, Katy Gordon, Emily Gresham, Ryan Hansen, Lindsey Hause, Aaron

Hixson, Brian Homrighausen, Mike Johnston, Heidi Kauffman, Andrew Keller, Kristina Kemper, Jennifer Larson, Jennifer Link, Shannon McCauley, Jeanna McGonegal, Jeremy Miller, Chris Minter, Heather Nelson, Greg Pandolfo, Laura Rankin, Matt Sheflin, Stacey Shelley, Matt Slaby, Suzanne Smerjac, David Spaeth, Vanessa Spencer, Emily Talbot, Brian Thenhaus, Molly Tribble, Amy Turk, Matt Ventura, Kary Wain, Karen Warren, Jeremy Weltman, Cody Wilson, Nick Worley, Jared Kempton, and Tom Stempek.[19]

Altogether, The Philip S. Miller Scholarship recipients of the class of 1997 received $60,500.[20] Counselor, Kristi Olson commented, "Mr. Miller placed an enormous value on youth and confidence in entrusting the future to them. We at Douglas County High School are especially grateful that our students have been included as beneficiaries."[21]

The next year, during the spring of 1998, after adhering to the same strict criteria and following the same previous application process, the recipients for The Philip S. Miller Scholarship were, once again, chosen and announced by the Douglas County High School. As before, available scholarships were: Two Four-Year Renewable Scholarships; Two Two-Year Renewable Scholarships; Two Vocational Scholarships; Forty-Seven Non-Renewable One-Time Scholarships; and Two Non-Renewable One-Time Staff Nominated Scholarships.[22]

The following is a list of the 1998 Philip S. Miller Scholarship Recipients:

Corey Bolton, Sonja Madera, Diana Johnson, Kyle Orr, Joseph Allen, Anthony Bonacquista, Jacklyn Brockmeyer, Shelley Buckwalter, Meaghan Burke, Nathan Camp, Amanda Cavanaugh, Anthony Dalla, Elizabeth Duran, Brooke Fleming, Phoenix French, Marne Gulley, Andrea Hadad, Matt Hartman, Nell Haubert, Heather Headley, Christina Heck, Melissa Kerr, Brent Kinseth, Alaina Labak, Allison Luce, Matt Makens, Gwyneth McClure, Randi Miller, Melissa Meyers, Heidi Olinger, Christopher Ott, Julie Oustecky, Cristin Page, Kristy Papka, Hillary Sauer, Justin Schmitz, Sarah Smith, Rachel Sohren, Meredith Sorenson, Amanda Spaeth, Craig Spring, Jamie Springston, Kathleen St. John, Peter Stoddard, Andrea Tedford, Elizabeth Tyler, Laura Wadsworth, Amanda Wheatley, Regan Wilcox, Sarah Williams, Heather Young, Lindsay Haugland.[23]

Altogether, The Philip S. Miller Scholarship recipients of the class of 1998 received $55,000. According to Kristi Olson, $4,500 will be added to the 1997 renewable recipients, making the 1998 scholarship grand total $59,500.[24] During 1997 and 1998, over $100,000 in scholarships have been awarded to the students of Douglas County High School thanks to Mr. Miller's Trust. Hopefully, in future years, students will apply for the Vocational Scholarships, which to date have never been utilized.

The Douglas Public Library District is another of the beneficiaries and according to Library District Director, Jamie LaRue, during 1996, The Douglas Public Library District received $124,00.00 (which included a January 1997 deposit). In 1997, the District received $157,000 (which included a January 1998 deposit). As of April 1998, $41,300 had been spent exclusively on costs related to improving the stacks lighting at the Philip S. Miller Library in Castle Rock.[25]

Future plans include an expansion of facilities in Castle Rock, possibly a separate structure, to house specific operations and services. In commenting on Mr. Miller's remarkable legacy, LaRue said, "Mr. Miller's bequest, and his focus on capital investment, perfectly suits the needs of a library district in one of the faster growing counties in the United States."[26]

The Town of Castle Rock and the Castle Rock Fire Department are two other beneficiaries. According to Interim Town Manager, Bruff Shea, the new fire and police stations are both being partially funded by disbursements from the Miller Trust.[27]

Although it is not known at this time what the other entities have chosen to do with their bequests, it is obvious from his choices, that Mr. Miller trusted each and every one of them. He knew they would use his money wisely, in a way that would have made him proud. This was his way of giving back to the town, to the county and to the people, including the children, which he loved and held in high regard.

If, in fact, life is measured not only in accomplishments but also in the legacy a person leaves behind, then Philip Miller's life was truly immeasurable.

ENDNOTES

[1]Castle Rock Chronicle, Obituary, Philip Simon Miller, June 15, 1995, p 1, 2; Douglas County News Press, Obituary, Philip Simon Miller, June 10, 1995, p 1a, 3a; Rocky Mountain News, May 10, 1995; and Funeral Memorium, June 10, 1995 from Andrews, Caldwell, Gibson Funeral Home.

[2]Douglas County News Press, November 25, 1995, p 1, 3; and Rocky Mountain News, November 23, 1995, p 77a.

[3]Douglas County News Press, December 20, 1995, p 1, 3; and Rocky Mountain News, Mile High Suburbs Section, December 24, 1995, p 24a, 27a.

[4]Douglas County News Press, December 20, 1995, p 1, 3.

[5]Douglas County News Press, April 3, 1996, p 2a.

[6]IBID.

[7]Douglas County News Press, May 8, 1996, p 2a.

[8]Douglas County News Press, September 10, 1997, September 17, 1997, p 3a.

[9]Douglas County News Press, July 10, 1996, p 1a, 3a; and Douglas County Fair and Rodeo Book, 1996, p 1.

[10]Inscription, Philip S. Miller Bench, Douglas County Extension Office on the Douglas County Fairgrounds, August 3, 1996.

[11]Speech, Karen Serafini, Philip S. Miller Bench Dedication Ceremony, August 3, 1996.

[12]Douglas County News Press, July 10, 1996, p 3a; and Douglas County Fair and Rodeo Book, 1996, p 1.

[13]Interviews between John and Bea Lowell and the author, Castle Rock, CO, February 9, 1996, July 1996, and March 17, 1997; Douglas County News Press, April 30, 1997, p 3a; and Karen Serafini, "A Helping Hand From The 4-H Foundation," Douglas County Fair and Rodeo Book, 1997, p 61.

[14]IBID.

[15]Interview between Karen Serafin and the author, Parker, CO, February 4, 1998.

[16]Karen Serafini, "A Helping Hand From The 4-H Foundation," Douglas County Fair and Rodeo Book, 1997, p 61.

[17]Douglas County News Press, September 17, 1997, p 3a.

[18]Information Kristi Olson, Counselor, Douglas County High School, Castle Rock, CO, October 25, 1997.

[19]1997 List of Philip S. Miller Scholarship Recipients, Douglas County High School, Castle Rock, CO.

[20]Information Kristi Olson, Counselor, Douglas County High School, Castle Rock, CO, October 25, 1997.

[21]IBID, Kristi Olson.

[22]Information Kristi Olson, Counselor Douglas, County High School, May 7, 1998.

[23]1998 List of Philip S. Miller Scholarship Recipients, Douglas County High School, Castle Rock, CO.

[24]Information Kristi Olson, Counselor Douglas County High School, May 7, 1998.

[25]Information Jamie LaRue, Library Director of the Douglas Public Library District, Castle Rock, CO, April 14, 1998.

[26]IBID, Jamie LaRue.

[27]Information Bruff Shea, Interim Town Manager, Castle Rock, CO, June 1998.

WE REMEMBER PHIL

He was the banker with the cowboy hat and the ready smile! He left us with memories which will never be forgotten. Like mini videos in our minds, we will think of him at special times and in special places and we will remember not only the extraordinary feats but the ordinary acts of generosity and kindness he performed each day of his life.

During the years I have been writing this book I have learned many incredible, funny and heartwarming stories about Mr. Miller. As a result, I have decided to devote the final chapter to reminiscing! The story of his life, his many philanthropic gestures and the remarkable legacy he left behind have been documented throughout this book. This chapter simply consists of memories, reflecting his sense of humor and compassion, his devotion to humanity and community, his love of people and life. Furthermore, his frugality and conservatism cannot be overlooked. Without those two traits, he would have never amassed the fortune he did, which ultimately allowed him to leave such an incredible legacy to the people of present and future generations in Castle Rock, Douglas County, or to the children of Shriner's Hospital and Denver Children's Hospital.

There are many memories of Phil Miller. The most familiar image in our minds eye, is probably of him sitting at his desk or standing in the lobby of the Bank visiting with a customer. We will see him lifting a little boy over the mud puddles at the Fair and a couple of weeks later, sweeping snow from a customer's car in front of the Bank. When the 1965 flood washed away Jim Lowell's 4-H steer, Mr. Miller offered him a Shorthorn bull to show at the National Western Stock Show. A few years later we will remember Mr. Miller standing in the pouring rain, bidding on animals at the Douglas County 4-H Livestock Sale in order to help raise money for the kids. The millionaire with muddy boots!

Mildred Brodbeck, who for many years has been a reporter for the Douglas County News Press and has written numerous articles about Mr. Miller, believes that he was, without a doubt, one of the most interesting and enjoyable people she ever interviewed. Because she lives directly across the street from the Cantril Courthouse where the Millers lived when they first moved to Castle Rock, she told me that whenever she sees any kind of a shadow around that building, she thinks fondly of Mr. and Mrs. Miller. We both believe they are here, in spirit!

Some of us, Joe Winkler and me included still have our original savings deposit books! He remembers making his first deposit when Mrs. Miller was a Teller. His deposit book number is thirty-seven and he treasures it as a reminder of Mr. and Mrs. Miller, two very wonderful people and lifelong friends. I still have two coins, one silver, one bronze, which Mr. Miller gave to me in the mid-1960's honoring the Centennial Anniversary of the Colorado Cattlemen's Association. They are two of my most prized possessions.

There were many sides to Mr. Miller's personae and we will fondly remember them all. There was his "good old boy persona," with a little grin and a sparkle in his eye, reflecting his sense of humor and his zest for life. This was best described by his great-niece, Melissa Benedict, "He was a very dignified, respectable gentleman, who had a boyish charm about him when he would laugh or get all caught up in a story he was telling!"

My dad used to travel with Mr. and Mrs. Miller, periodically, and a good example of this "boyish charm" took place shortly after the Millers purchased a new Lincoln Continental in the late 1970's. They were going to Scottsdale for the winter and usually my dad drove the whole trip, regardless of the destination. But this time, just like a typical teenaged boy, Mr. Miller wanted to "drive his new car!"

When they got out on the open road in Northern New Mexico, he took the wheel and really floored that new Lincoln. He got up to about 110 miles per hour and Mrs. Miller finally asked, "Poppy, how fast are you going?" He would grin and say, "Only about 65." A few minutes later she asked, "Willis, how fast is he really going?" To which Willie would reply, "Oh, about a 110." Poppy would slow down, just enough to pacify Momma, but pretty soon he was lead-footing it right back up to 110 and the whole conversation would begin again! This routine, and banter, continued between the three of them for over an hour until Mrs. Miller forcefully said, "Now, Poppy, that's enough! Why don't you let Willis drive?" The amazing thing was that Poppy didn't get a speeding ticket! In fact, they never once even saw a New Mexico State Patrol car!

On the other hand, we will always remember and respect his "distinguished, millionaire persona," depicting a successful businessman who could hold his own with anyone. He fit perfectly into a room full of wealthy bankers! There was never any hidden agenda with Mr. Miller. He was very open and straightforward. His philanthropy and conservatism earned him deep respect throughout the banking community. He was also highly admired because he honestly and diplomatically voiced his opinion, regardless of the fact that it may have been a controversial issue and his opinion may have not been the popular one. Furthermore, he was such a gentleman, he very seldom raised his voice unless he was backed into a corner. Mrs. Miller remembered an incident at the Annual Colorado State Banker's Convention at the Broadmoor Hotel in Colorado Springs during the 1970's when Mr. Miller's diplomacy saved the day, and a lot of money!

He had booked two rooms, one for Miller and one for Buboltz. When they all arrived, there was no reservation for Buboltz! The desk clerk informed them that there were no vacant rooms remaining—except one—the Texas Suite—which my parents could certainly have, at a rate of $200 per night! Mr. Miller very calmly and diplomatically informed the desk clerk that they would be happy to take the Texas Suite, but, they would only pay the same rate as the original room! The desk clerk went into shock and called the manager but Mr. Miller stood his ground and soon my mom and dad were happily settled in the Texas Suite, for the same rate as the original room!

Although Mr. Miller's frugality could be admired it could also be exasperating. On another trip, during the late 1970's, my dad was driving the Millers to Green Valley, Arizona and when the time came to stop for the night, they were in Truth or Consequences, New Mexico. The cheapest motel was $40 and Mr. Miller wasn't going to pay $40 for a motel room! To quote my dad, "I kept driving and driving and finally there was this old, run down, flea bag of a motel, out in the middle of nowhere. But it was only $27.50 a night and that was a price Phil could tolerate. There was no restaurant, so we all went to sleep with no dinner!"

Nonetheless, his extreme generosity usually overshadowed his extreme frugality. His humanity and compassion is reflected in the following memory of one customer, who requested anonymity, but gratefully acknowledged:

"Phil Miller and Willie Buboltz saved my life after my wife suddenly passed away. I had no money for funeral expenses or a burial plot. I was desperate. I sat in the Bank and cried like a baby. Phil told me to make the arrangements and then let Willie know how much money I needed. I truly believe if they had not helped me that day, I probably would have killed myself."

Similarly, Bette Saunders will never forget his kindness to her the day her mother passed away. Mr. Miller helped her sort through everything in the safety deposit box and even gave her his handkerchief when she started to cry!

On a lighter and more humorous note, during a day trip from Arizona to Mexico, while waiting at the border, in a long line of traffic, Mr. Miller gave a quarter to every little kid who banged on the window! Ironically, they were going to Mexico to look for some good deals on gifts to take home and to buy Cutty Sark, which was a dollar cheaper there than it was in the United States! When they drove back across the border that night, the kids recognized the car and came banging on the window again. Of course, Mr. Miller gave them more quarters! When he ran out of quarters, he gave them dimes, when he ran out of dimes, he gave them nickels and when he ran out of nickels he gave them pennies! Needless to say, he gave away more money to those little kids that day than he spent on gifts for his friends or Cutty Sark for himself!

However, his generosity went far deeper than just giving quarters and nickels to little kids. Melissa Benedict related an act of generosity, which changed her life, when she was about to graduate from high school. "Uncle Phil invited my mom and me to lunch and during the meal, he said to me, 'Melissa, would you like to go to college?'" This was a prospect she had never even considered, given their financial situation after her father had passed away. She recalled, "Mom could barely keep me in braces, and here was this extraordinary offer on the table for me to go to college!" She decided to study interior design and enrolled in the Colorado Institute of Art where she graduated with honors and a couple of awards. She worked in the design field for many years and eventually branched in real estate, where her background in interior design is a great asset to her when selling homes. She will always be grateful for her Uncle Phil's generosity and kindness.

Next to his generosity, his "business persona," representing discipline and determination, practicality and prudence, will probably be best remembered. He was a kind and generous man, but when it came to business, he could be as tough as nails. An early employee from 1950 recalled one day at the close of business they came up $500 short when counting the teller drawers. Mr. Miller would not allow anyone to leave until they found that $500. It was midnight before they finally went home!

An elderly business acquaintance, who wishes to remain anonymous, gave me an even earlier illustration of Mr. Miller's business priorities. Apparently, in 1936, for a few hours during one afternoon, there was an unannounced water shut-off in town. Although he was no longer a member, he attended the next Board of Trustees meeting and calmly reported that, on the afternoon of the water shut-off, he had lost $25 worth of business at his meat market. That was a lot of money in 1936 and Mr. Miller felt totally justified in asking for a reimbursement. The Trustees voted to pay him the $25. In researching Town Board records for an unrelated matter, I accidentally discovered the minutes to that meeting. The story is absolutely true!

But there is a flip side to that coin of business priorities: more importantly being the trust he placed in people in whom he believed.

An example of this took place in the early 1940's when two Douglas County men wanted to go into business for themselves. They had to buy special equipment, and after weeks and weeks of searching, they located the equipment in Texas. They made an application for a loan to Mr. Miller, for $3,000, which was a considerable sum of money in those days. But Mr. Miller trusted these men, implicitly, and told them to go get what they needed and sign the note when they came back. Upon arrival in Texas, these two gentlemen discovered the price had increased to $3,200. They called Mr. Miller to ask if they could get an additional $200 on their loan. Mr. Miller, with his great sense of humor, asked them if they were "partying" or if they were "trying to buy the whole State of Texas?" However, over the phone he approved the additional money and told them to, "Get the job done and come on home." These two men became extremely successful in this chosen venture and it is still in existence today, being run by one of the sons. This same scenario was repeated many times, over the years, with customers in whom Mr. Miller totally believed and trusted.

Finally, we will remember his "cowboy persona," as he did ordinary things such as riding his horse out to the Winkler ranch in the early days or doing chores at his own ranch in later days. We see him wearing his favorite straw cowboy hat, happily standing in the midst of his herd of tame and gentle Shorthorn cattle. We can visualize him in front of his house, wiping his brow and looking north toward Castle Rock, the town he loved and helped to develop.

He had inexhaustible drive and energy. He could work on the ranch for four hours in the early dawn and then go to the Bank and work all day for eight hours. He would then go back and work on the ranch until after dark. And he enjoyed every minute of it!

He once gave me a copy of a little write-up he had cut out of the Castle Rock Record Journal in 1921 when they first moved to town, and which he still kept in his wallet. Dog-eared and faded, it was simply entitled "A Prescription." I still have it and this is what it says:

"If you are poor, work. If you are rich, continue to work. If you are burdened with seemingly unfair responsibilities, work. If you are happy, keep right on working. Idleness gives room for doubts and fears. If disappointments come, work. If sorrow overwhelms you and loved ones seem untrue, work. If health is threatened, work. When faith falters and reason fails, just work!"

After I had finished reading it, he said to me, "This is how I live my life." In retrospect, that certainly was the truth!

One interesting but little known fact about Mr. Miller—he was a smoker! However, he had such self-control, that he only smoked five cigarettes a day—for 70 years! The first one would be in the morning after he arrived at work, the second one would be after lunch, the third one would be in late afternoon, the fourth one would be in the evening after dinner, and the fifth one would be shortly before going to sleep. He almost never deviated from this schedule.

During the early years, Joe Winkler remembered frequently going in Mr. Miller's office on business or a social call. "If it was in the morning, Mr. Miller would look at his watch and announce, 'It's 10 a.m. I can have a cigarette!' He would then open his desk drawer and pull out a pack of Winstons or Marlboros and, together, we would enjoy his first cigarette of the day."

My dad recalled that as the years went by, Mr. Miller continued to smoke but enjoyed it less! Every morning after the first cigarette, he would cough and choke and sputter and spit and say, "Gotta quit this damn smoking!" He did finally kick the "five-cigarette-a-day-habit" when they moved to Tremont and he was 88 years old! As Joe Winkler aptly put it, Mr. Miller's discipline and moderation probably contributed to his longevity!

Bank employees have fond memories of this man who was as much a friend as he was an employer. Dona Sherlock remembered Mr. Miller's honesty, his down to earth attitude and his wonderful, dry sense of humor. She recalled how he always knew how to have a good time! He had a little record player at the Bank and he would buy records at Christensen Pharmacy. On Friday afternoons, he would often play records and sometimes even dance!

Johnnie Osthoff's memories of Mr. Miller revolved around his generosity and his kindness to his employees. He often invited them out to the ranch for drinks after work and, as the perfect host, he created an atmosphere which was relaxing and enjoyable for all.

Both Johnnie Osthoff and Margaret Olson specifically remembered one Halloween when all the employees came to work in costumes. Mr. Miller had a great time that day, teasing everyone and laughing about their outfits. At the end of the day, he took everyone, still in costumes, to The Broiler, which was one of the best restaurants in Castle Rock at that time. They had drinks and dinner and he paid for the whole evening! He was very generous that way.

During the late 1970's, Mr. Miller hired a part-time bank security guard, John Colby, a retired gentleman from Castle Rock who everyone liked. He did not dress as a security guard. He just walked around and sat in the front lobby, keeping an eye on people, during the busiest hours of each day and on Saturday mornings. Mr. Colby told me a story when, one hot, summer day, two little boys came in the Bank with bright green plastic squirt guns. He was sitting in a chair by the door and they walked right up to him, squirted him in the face and said, "Give us your money!"

Before he had time to wipe his face, Mr. Miller, who happened to see this mischief, immediately came out of his office. These two tough little kids were suddenly scared out of their wits! However, Mr. Miller, using reverse psychology, said, "That looks so good on a hot day like today, why don't you squirt me, too?" With big eyes, these two little boys looked at Mr. Miller and Mr. Colby, in shock, and amazement, and finally disappointment! One little boy finally said, "Come on, let's get out of here. This is no fun at all!" With that, they dropped the squirt guns on the floor and ran out. Two future bank robbers, reformed and deterred!

I want to close this chapter with three stories which illustrate to us the true essence of Mr. Miller. They come from Melissa Benedict, Ada and Freddie Smith, and Bette Saunders. They are entitled, "Uncle Phil and Mocha!", "Probably Mr. Miller's Last Debt!" and "The Story of the Ants!"

The first story comes from Melissa Benedict and is entitled, "Uncle Phil and Mocha." It is a loving and heartwarming memory about the man who could have anything in this world, but would rather play with a three pound puppy named Mocha!

Shortly after Mrs. Miller went to Cherry Creek Care Center, Melissa and her mom, Shari, adopted a little dachshund-chihuahua mix puppy which they would hide inside a purse, and sneak into Phil's apartment at Tremont! The first time, they didn't tell him about Mocha, they just said, "Peek in the purse!" When he did, his face lit up like a little boy! He gently lifted Mocha out, held him up, cuddled him, petted him and giggled! He was thrilled to hold and play with this amazing little creation! Well, puppies will be puppies and soon Mocha jumped off Phil's lap on to the carpet, ready to "take care of nature!"

While Melissa and Shari watched, in horror, Phil calmly looked down and said, "Oh how cute, I think he is going to poop!"

They continued smuggling Mocha as long as he fit in the purse, after which time Mr. Miller missed the little puppy so much that he started going over to the Benedict house to visit Mocha!

This second story took place more than thirty years ago in Castle Rock and Freddie Smith entitled it, "Probably Mr. Miller's Last Debt!" It demonstrates Mr. Miller's honesty, his integrity and his concern for a little boy. Early one Saturday morning, Ada Smith and her son, Roy, went into the new bakery in Castle Rock. In front of them stood Mr. Miller, picking out some "goodies!" When he got ready to pay, he discovered he was a few cents short and asked the girl behind the counter if he could write a check. She apologized and said she was not allowed to take checks. Mr. Miller replied, with that famous grin, "But I am the President of the Bank!" The girl told him, again, that she was sorry but she couldn't take a check.

Roy, who was four or five at this time, had been listening very carefully to the conversation, and it just so happened that he had a quarter in his pocket! He took it out, walked over to Mr. Miller, reached up and handed it to him! Mr. Miller was quite grateful! He accepted the quarter and paid his bill. He told Ada to come in the Bank on Monday and he would repay the "loan."

Well, according to Ada, "There was no way I was going to walk into the Bank and ask Mr. Miller for a quarter after all the help he had given our family." Consequently, she forgot all about it! A couple of weeks later she was waiting her turn in the teller line, when she felt someone touch her shoulder. She turned around to find Mr. Miller standing there, holding fifty cents in his hand! With a little grin, he said, "Please give this money to Roy and tell him I certainly appreciated that loan!" Embarrassed as she was, she took the money, "for Roy." As she related this story to me she said, "Now, that is what I call doubling your money on a Short Term Loan!"

The final story happened one summer, also over thirty years ago in Castle Rock, and demonstrates that there was no limit to the extent Mr. Miller would go for a friend! It is entitled "The Story of the Ants." Bette Saunders used to do sewing for Jerry. Mr. Miller would drop her off at Bette's house on his way back to work in the afternoon and pick her up on the way home later. During this one particular summer, there was a slope of ground covered with ant hills on the south side of Bette's house. Every time Jerry came to Bette's she had a "fit" about those ants! Finally Jerry said, "I'm gonna tell Phil about them!"

A couple of mornings later, Bette happened to look out her window and there was Mr. Miller, impeccably dressed for work in his suit, tie and cowboy hat, walking up and down the slope, sprinkling white powder all over each and every ant hill! She went out to thank him and laughingly said, "Where else but in a small town could your Exterminator also be your Banker?" And who else could that person possibly be but Phil Miller?

There is no way to end a book such as this because, although Mr. and Mrs. Miller are gone, their legacy will never end. Instead, we can humbly say, "Thank you, both, for your love of life and the memories you gave us, for the people you helped and the lives you changed, for your contributions to the growth and development of Castle Rock and Douglas County, and for the legacy you left us to provide for the future."

In the words of former County Commissioner, Carl Winkler, "Phil Miller was not a typical banker—he was not a power grabbing opportunist. He was a man of great compassion, great humility, great humanity. He did the best he could for his customers and his friends and his actions were always geared toward the community. He wasn't *trying* to be a great man. He just *was* a great man."

Mr. and Mrs. Miller are buried at Cedar Hill Cemetery, west of Castle Rock.

Emil Walz, Jr. Collection.

Portrait of Mr. Miller by Eugene "Red" Everitt hangs in the Philip S. Miller Library.

Local History Collection, Douglas Public Library District, Douglas County, CO.

BIBLIOGRAPHY

OFFICIAL RECORDS

Ballenger and Richards Denver City Directories, published by Ballenger and Richards, 16th & Larimer Streets, Denver, CO, 1907-1917, Volumes 35 to 45, located at the National Archives and Records Administration, Rocky Mountain Region, Lakewood, CO.

Colorado State Bank Commissioner's Records, Colorado Division of Banking, 1560 Broadway, Suite 1175, Denver, CO.

Colorado State Senate: Tribute to Philip S. Miller. By Joe Winkler, Ted Strickland, and Marjorie Nielson. Denver, CO, May 11, 1987.

Douglas County Board of Commissioner's, Proclamation R-82-51, To Mr. and Mrs. Philip Miller. By Carl Winkler, W.G. Duncan, and John Orcutt. Castle Rock, CO, June 21, 1982.

General Indices, Grantee, Douglas County Clerk and Recorder, 301 Wilcox, Castle Rock, CO.

General Indices, Grantor, Douglas County Clerk and Recorder, 301 Wilcox, Castle Rock, CO.

General Indices, Miscellaneous Records, Douglas County Clerk and Recorder, 301 Wilcox, Castle Rock, CO.

Minutes of the Board of Douglas County Commissioner's Meetings, Douglas County Clerk and Recorder, 301 Wilcox, Castle Rock, CO. Various meetings: April 28, 1874; May 26, 1874; June 15, 1874; and May 18, 1880.

Marriage License Division, Denver City and County Clerk, Recorder and Public Trustee, City and County Building, Room 200, Denver, CO.

Peoria County Clerk, Courthouse, Room 101, Peoria, Illinois.

Personnel Records of Military Service, National Personnel Records Center, National Archives and Records Administration Office, St. Louis, MO.

Property Characteristic Reports, Douglas County Assessor's Office, 301 Wilcox, Castle Rock, CO. Castle Rock Police Department Building, 318 Fourth Street; The Bank of Douglas County, 402 Wilcox; Douglas Lodge #153, 300 Wilcox.

Public School Records, Douglas County School Census Records for Consolidated District #37, Parker, CO, 1914-1921.

Public School Records, El Paso County Census Records of Eligible School Age Children, District # 49, Falcon, CO, 1908.

Public School Records for Denver Public Schools; Cumulative Records and Chronology Attendance, Offices of Attendance and Pupil Records. Denver, CO.

Records of Proceedings of the Board of Trustees, Office of the Town Clerk at Town Hall, 680 North Wilcox, Castle Rock, CO. Various meetings from April 3, 1922 to July 8, 1934; also, November 6, 1935; July 1, 1936;

June 7, 1939; June 23, 1939; April 2, 1940, November 1, 1979; and June 21, 1979.

Records of Proceedings, Douglas County Library Board of Trustees, June 17, 1980 and October 6, 1987. Local History Collection, Douglas Public Library District, Douglas County, CO.

United States Department of Commerce, Department of Census, Twelfth Census of the United States, State of Colorado, County of El Paso, Town of Falcon, Precinct # 20, Schedule 1. June 19-23, 1900.

United States Department of Commerce, Department of Census, Fourteenth Census of the United States, State of Colorado, County of Elbert, Town of Elizabeth, Precinct #1, Sheet 1-B, 6-B. January 26, 27, 1920; February 12-14, 1920.

BANK RECORDS

Addendum to the Articles of Incorporation, The Bank of Douglas County, 402 Wilcox, Castle Rock, CO, August 1939.

The Bank of Douglas County, Special Records, Used with permission.

Certificate of Authority, State of Colorado, Office of State Bank Commissioner, Denver, CO. Issued to The Bank of Douglas County, 402 Wilcox, Castle Rock, CO, August 21, 1939.

Federal Deposit Insurance Corporation Certificate, Washington D.C. Issued to the Bank of Douglas County, January 9, 1940.

Statements of Condition, The Bank of Douglas County, 402 Wilcox, Castle Rock, CO, October 2, 1939 to December 31, 1995.

Statements of Condition, Castle Rock State Bank, 402 Wilcox, Castle Rock, CO, various dates from September 11, 1917 to November 1, 1932.

Statements of Capital, Douglas County Bank, (Cantril Courthouse) Castle Rock, CO, Castle Rock Journal, January 1902; June 1902.

Statements of Condition, First National Bank of Douglas County at Castle Rock, 300 Wilcox. Various dates from January 2, 1903 to December 31,1935.

Statements of Condition, State Bank of Castle Rock, Castle Rock, CO. March 6, 1908; November 10, 1909; November 10, 1910.

MAPS

Beeler's Official Map of the City and County of Denver, compiled by E.M.Beeler, Denver Map Company, Denver, CO, 1913.

Castle Rock, Colorado Town Map, The Chamber of Commerce, 420 Jerry Street, Castle Rock, CO published by Four Seasons Publications, Pueblo, CO, 1995.

Denver and Rio Grande Western Railroad Map, #1, Colorado 1C, Denver and Rio Grande Western Railroad, Denver, CO, June 30, 1919.

The Roads of Colorado, available through the Douglas County News Press Office, Castle Rock, CO published by Shearer Publishing, 406 Post Oak Road, Fredericksburg, TX, 1996, p 89-91.

State Map of Illinois, compiled by Donnelley Cartographic Services, Coast to Coast Road Atlas, 1000 16th Street, NW, Washington, D.C., 1990, p 14.

State Map of Wisconsin, compiled by Donnelley Cartographic Services, Coast to Coast Road Atlas, 1000 16th Street, NW, Washington, D.C., 1990, p 39.

CEMETERY RECORDS

Cedar Hill Cemetery, 880 East Wolfensberger Road, Castle Rock, CO.

Crown Hill Memorial Park, 7777 West 29th Avenue, Denver, CO.

Fairmount Cemetery, 430 South Quebec Street, Denver, CO.

Fort Logan National Cemetery, 3698 South Sheridan Boulevard, Denver, CO.

Springdale Cemetery, 3014 North Prospect Road, Peoria, Illinois.

Spring Valley Cemetery, Photograph Album, Compiled by the Douglas County Historic Preservation Board, on file at the Local History Collection, Douglas County Public Library District.

WILLS

Last Will and Testament of Lina Green Kaestler Fischer, May 25, 1910, Peoria, Illinois.

Last Will and Testament of Frank W. Kaestler, December 18, 1947, Peoria, Illinois.

BOOKS

Bare, Jeanette and Cathleen Norman. *Castle Rock Style.* Prepared by the Castle Rock Historic Preservation Board and the Castle Rock Planning Department. Published by the Town of Castle Rock, 1996.

Bremer, Dr. C.D. *American Bank Failures.* New York: Columbia University Press, 1935.

Davis, Kenneth S. *FDR The New Deal Years, 1933-1937, A History.* New York: Random House, 1986.

Ditmars, Mary A. *Who's Who In Colorado.* Boulder: Colorado Press Association, 1938, p 421, 425.

Doti, Lynne Pierson and Larry Schweikart. *Banking in the American West, From the Gold Rush to Deregulation.* Norman: University of Oklahoma Press, 1991.

Feis, Herbert. *1933: Characters in Crisis.* Boston: Little, Brown and Company, 1966.

Fitch, Thomas. *Dictionary of Banking Terms.* New York: Barrons Educational Business Guides, 1993.

Fundamentals of Money and Banking. New York: American Banker's Association, 1963.

Hafen, Leroy. "History of Agriculture." *Colorado and Its People.* Volume 2. New York: Lewis Historical Publishing, Inc., 1948, p 125.

Hafen, Leroy. "Biographical of William Eugene Higby." *Colorado and Its People.* Volume 3. New York: Lewis Historical Publishing, Inc., 1948, p 24-25.

Hutchinson, Harry D. *Money, Banking and the U.S Economy.* Englewood Cliffs: Prentice Hall, 1988.

Jones, James R. (Jim). *Denver and New Orleans, In the Shadow of the Rockies.* Denver: Sundance Publications Limited, 1997, p 143.

Marr, Josephine Lowell and Joan Marr Keiser. *Douglas County, A Historical Journey,* 1983. On file in Reference Section, Philip S. Miller Library, Castle Rock, CO.

McCullough, David G. *Truman.* New York: Simon and Schuster, 1992.

Niehaus, Dr. Fred R. *Development of Banking in Colorado.* Denver: Mountain States Publishing Company, 1942.

Niehaus, Dr. Fred R. *Seventy Years of Progress, History of Banking in Colorado 1876-1946.* Denver: Federal Deposit Insurance Corporation, 1948.

Our Heritage: The People of Douglas County. Castle Rock: Published by The Douglas County Historical Society, 1984.

Public Papers and Addresses of Franklin D. Roosevelt. Volume 2. Item 16. New York: Random House, 1933.

Schulze, Suzanne. *A Century of the Colorado Census.* 1976. Revised on Microfilm Collection by Robert Markham. University of Northern Colorado, Greeley, CO, 1977.

Weiss Research Incorporated. *Bank Safety Directory: A Complete Listing of U.S. Banks and Their Safety Ratings.* Westport: T.J. Holt and Co., 1989. p 18, 252

Yearbook of the State of Colorado, 1919. Denver: State of Colorado Publications, 1919.

NEWSPAPERS

Arapahoe Herald, Littleton, CO.

Castle Rock Chronicle, Castle Rock, CO.

Castle Rock High School Courier, Castle Rock, CO.

Castle Rock Journal, Castle Rock, CO.

Castle Rock Record Journal, Castle Rock, CO.

Daily News Press, Castle Rock, CO.

Denver Post, Denver, CO.

Denver Record Stockman, Denver, CO.

DePere Journal-Democrat, DePere, WI.

Douglas County Express, Castle Rock, CO.

Douglas County News, Castle Rock, CO.

Douglas County News Press, Castle Rock, CO.

Douglas County Trail, Castle Rock, CO.

Impact, Castle Rock, CO.

Littleton Independent, Littleton, CO.

Parker Press, Parker, CO.

Parker Trail, Parker, CO.

Rocky Mountain News, Denver, CO.

Weekly News Chronicle, Parker, CO.

SPECIAL NEWSPAPER SUPPLEMENTS

Pioneer Firms, Douglas County News Press, February 5, 1980.

Pioneer Firms, Douglas County News Press, January 29, 1982.

1988 Pioneer Edition, Douglas County News Press, February 27, 1988.

1993 Pioneer Edition, Douglas County News Press, February 27, 1993.

Twenty Who Made A Difference, Douglas County News Press, January 21, 1995.

This Old New House, Douglas County News Press, October 4, 1995.

Salute to Douglas County Business, Douglas County News Press, February 28, 1996.

Douglas County Fair '96, Douglas County News Press, July 31, 1996.

30 Years of Opening Windows to the World. Douglas Public Library District. Douglas County News Press, August 20, 1997.

SPECIAL NEWSPAPER COLUMNS

For Those Who Like Books, Ellen Buboltz, Douglas County News.

Library Bindings, Jamie LaRue, Douglas County News Press.

The Library Notebook, Alden Briskey, Douglas County News.

Time Traveler, Ruth Miller, Douglas County News Press.

Walk With Our Pioneers, Josephine Marr, Douglas County News.

MAGAZINES

Colorado Real Estate News, November 1904.

Empire Magazine, July 1969.

HISTORICAL ORGANIZATIONS

Castle Rock Historical Society, Box 1572, Castle Rock, CO.

Douglas County Historic Preservation Board, 118 Third Street, Castle Rock, CO.

Preservation Partnership, 1540 Cook Street, Denver, CO.

Local History Collection, Douglas Public Library District, Douglas County, CO.

Western History and Genealogy Collection, Denver Public Library, 10 West 14th Ave. Parkway, Denver, CO.

Genealogy and Family History Library, 41 S. Hobson, Mesa, Arizona.

MISCELLANEOUS WRITTEN RECORDS

Brandebery, Kent. Douglas County Historic Preservation Board. "Douglas County's First Courthouse." March 28, 1995.

Buboltz, Debbie. "The History of Banking in Castle Rock." Prepared for James McKay, American History, Douglas County High School. Castle Rock, CO. March 6, 1967.

"Facts About Dora Moore School." Staff of Moore School, 846 Corona Street, Denver, CO, 1997.

Information letters from Shriner's Hospitals For Children to Trust Attorney, James M. Nelsen. 1515 Arapahoe Street, Denver, CO.

Lyons, Nancy, Preservation Partnership. "History of Ownership of the Keystone Hotel and Chain of Title from 1874-1995."

Oberlin, Starr, Castle Rock Historical Society Newsletter, February, 1996.

Walz, Emil J. Jr. "Anna M. Weishaupl Walz." Walz Family History. Arvada, CO.

SPECIAL SOURCES

Douglas County Fair and Rodeo Books. Advertisements From 1921, 1922, 1923, 1927, 1932, and 1938 on file at the Local History Collection, Douglas Public Library District.

1996 Douglas County Fair and Rodeo Book. "Philip S. Miller Edition." Castle Rock: Douglas County Fair Association and The Weekly News Chronicle, Publisher, Jim Myles. Articles by Wendy Thomas: "A Wealth of Generosity, Philip S. Miller," p 8; "A Community Affair, Douglas County Livestock Sale." p 37; "Douglas County Fair and Rodeo, A Walk Through Time," p 50.

1997 Douglas County Fair and Rodeo Book. "The Best Little Show In The West." Castle Rock: Douglas County Fair Association and The Weekly News Chronicle, Publisher, Jim Myles. Articles by Karen Serafini: "Charlie Will Not Be Forgotten, Charlie Kirk," p 28; "Master Plan," p 40;

"A Helping Hand From the 4-H Foundation," p 61; "More Than Just Pickles!" p 74.

Genealogical Records of Thorwald Christensen Family, Compiled by Ruth Christensen, on file at the Local History Collection, Douglas Public Library District.

Genealogical Records of Kaestler-Miller Families courtesy of Gerd Adam Kaestler, Jr. and Norma Gish, Peoria, Illinois.

Genealogical Records of Stewart-Benedict Families courtesy of Diane Fling, Melissa Benedict, Shari Benedict and Chuck Benedict, Denver CO.

Genealogical Records of Weishaupl-Walz Families courtesy of Emil Walz, Jr., Arvada, CO.

Scholtz Scrapbook, on file at the Local History Collection, Douglas Public Library District. Castle Rock, CO.

Breslow Scrapbook. Originally belonged to Philip S. Miller, now in the possession of Debbie Buboltz-Bodle, Phoenix, AZ.

Blue Prints of 1950 to the Miller Ranch, Courtesy of Ken Ash, Castle Rock, CO.

PHOTO CONTRIBUTORS

Robert Oliver, Willie Buboltz, Emil Walz, Jr., Dona Sherlock, Bette Saunders, John Bodle, Debbie Buboltz-Bodle, Duane and Eleanora Richardson, Kenneth Flansburg, Louise Solberg, Gerd Kaestler, Jr. and Norma Gish, Eugene "Red" Everitt, Photos in the Local History Collection.

FAMILY TREE CONTRIBUTORS

Shari, Melissa and Chuck Benedict

Diane Fling

Norma Jean Gish

Gerd Adam Kaestler, Jr.

Emil J. Walz, Jr.

FAMILY TREE CONCEPT AND DESIGN

Jimmy Olsen, Prescott Valley, Arizona

John Bodle, Phoenix, Arizona

INTERVIEWS AND LETTERS

Josef Winkler in 1967
Charles Bickey Briscoe in 1967
Bette Saunders
Margaret Olson
Helen Daley
Tom Waymire
Starr and Lionel Oberlin
Rosemary Metzler
Kent Brandebery
Velva Bains
Jamie LaRue
Johanna Harden
Ellen and Willie Buboltz
Jane Olsen
Emil and Frances Walz
Gerd Adam Kaestler, Jr.
Jim Folkestad
Norma Jean Gish
Glenda Williams
Mildred Brodbeck
Helen Longworth
Louise Solberg
Frances Cannon
Carroll Hier
Joe Winkler
Gertrude Clarke Kordziel
Bob and Helen Oliver
Pete and Hazel Burgess
Freddie and Ada Smith
Johnnie Osthoff
Gill and Cecil Whitman
Jack Williams
John and Bea Lowell
Don McBreen
Dona Sherlock
Bette VanPelt
Philip Miller
Jerry Miller
Chuck Higby
Dick Higby
Eleanora Richardson
Kathy Reis
Richard Lee
Melissa Benedict
Diane Fling
Shari Benedict
Karen Serafini
Bruff Shea
Bryan Ruth
Kristi Olson

ADDITIONAL PHONE INTERVIEWS

Joan Borowski, Crown Hill Memorial Park, 7777 West 29th Ave., Denver, CO.

Carol Dutenhoeffer, Andrews, Caldwell, Gibson Funeral Home, Castle Rock, CO.

Fred Eyerman, Layman, Saint Elizabeth's Roman Catholic Church, 1060 St. Frances Way, Denver, CO.

Rosemary Fetter, Communications Director, Office of The Executive Vice President for Administration, Auraria Campus, Denver, CO.

John Girten, Parish Coordinator, Saint Elizabeth's Roman Catholic Church, 1060 St. Francis Way, Denver, CO.

Joan Halvercorn, Dora Moore School, 846 Corona Street, Denver, CO.

Gertrude Clarke Kordziel, Historian, Golden, CO.

Ruth Miller, Historian, Parker Historical Society, Parker, CO.

Doug Peden, Director of Human Resources, Falcon School District #49, Falcon, CO.

Kathy Reis, CPA, Fayetteville, AR.

Bryan Ruth, Crum and Forster, San Fransisco, CA.

Louise Solberg, Historian, Falcon, CO.

Laurie Swearengen, Springdale Cemetery, Peoria, IL.

Staff of the Western History and Genealogy Collection, Denver Public Library, 10 West 14th Avenue Parkway, Denver, CO specifically, Bryan, Gwendolyn, and James.

LIBRARIES

Philip S. Miller Library, 961 S. Plum Creek Blvd., Castle Rock, CO.

Parker Library, 10851 S. Crossroads Dr., Parker, CO.

Genealogy Library, 41 S. Hobson Mesa, AZ.

Denver Public Library, 10 West 14th Ave. Parkway, Denver, CO.

APPENDIX

From Miller and Faber to Miller

FRESH MEATS AND POULTRY

MILLER & FABER

MEAT MARKET

Telephone 14-M

Castle Rock, Colo.

Free Delivery Service *Phone Your Orders*

Advertisement before partnership dissolved June 24, 1921.

Castle Rock Record Journal.

ANNOUNCEMENT!

I have purchased the Meat Market from the firm of Miller & Faber, and also the meat business in Castle Rock from the Castle Rock Mercantile and Shellabarger Company. A full line of fresh and smoked meats will always be carried in stock.

I will strive to serve you to your entire satisfaction

P. S. MILLER, Jr.

Mr. Miller's anouncement of his purchase August 19, 1921.

Castle Rock Record Journal.

Look at these prices!

For Saturday and Monday Only, Oct. 22-24

Picnic Hams 17c lb.

Miller's Meat Market

Phone 14-M

CASTLE ROCK, COLORADO

October 21, 1921.

BIG HAM SALE

Tuesday and Wednesday, Oct. 4-5

Swift's Skinned Hams 27c lb.

Miller's Meat Market

CASTLE ROCK, COLORADO

September 30, 1921.

MEATS

Quality Meats at Bargain Prices

LOIN PORK ROAST
11c per Pound

Castle Rock Meat Market

P. S. MILLER, JR., Proprietor

Castle Rock : : Colorado

July 21, 1933.

CHOICE

Castle Rock Meat Market

MEATS

MEAT LOAF
Freshly Ground Pork and Beef
2 Pounds for 25c

P. S. MILLER, JR., Proprietor

Castle Rock : : Colorado

February 16, 1934.

Castle Rock Record Journal.

Cover of a recipe book containing 101 Meat Recipes Mr. Miller gave to his customers in 1926.

Courtesy of Helen Daley, Parker, CO.

Fair Book Advertisements

Mr. Miller's first advertisement, 1921.

Douglas County Fair Books,
Local History Collection,
Douglas Public Library District.

1922

1927

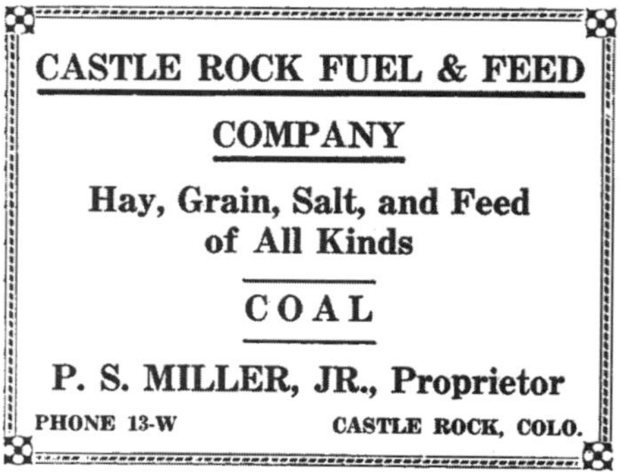

Fuel & Feed advertisement, 1932.

Bank Opening 1939

THE BANK OF DOUGLAS COUNTY WILL OPEN NEXT MONDAY

The announcement that the doors of "The Bank of Douglas County" would open its doors in Castle Rock next Monday morning, August 28th, for a general banking business, is the most important piece of news, as well as the most welcome, that has come to the people of Douglas County for a long time.

A money safe, a posting machine, files and some new furniture is being installed, the necessary supplies will be on hand and everything will be in readiness for the opening of business at the appointed time on Monday morning.

A representative of the First National Bank of Denver will come up to assist in the work of getting the new bank started out in the proper manner.

Mr. H. B. Dopf will be the cashier, and Mr. Philip S. Miller, Jr., as vice president, will be in charge of the bank. Billy Robinson will be employed as bookkeeper.

The Board of Directors will be Messrs. L. R. Higby, H. B. Dopf, P. S. Miller, Jr., H. H. Gandy, Harlan Palm, Josef Winkler, and Norman Smith.

The announcement that this bank would be open for business next Monday morning has been received very enthusiastically in all parts of the county, and this feeling will undoubtedly be shown in a material way as soon as the bank doors are opened for business.

The banking hours will be from 9:00 A. M. to 3:00 P. M.

Individual deposits in this bank will be insured up to $5000.00 the same as any other bank in the country, by the Federal Deposit Insurance Corporation.

The very best wishes of the people of Douglas County is extended to these progressive gentlemen who have invested their money in this financial institution. They are giving the county a service which has been greatly needed for several years.

Greetings to The Bank of Douglas County. May it live long and prosper!

August 25, 1939 article announcing the opening of The Bank of Douglas County on Monday, August 28, 1939.

Castle Rock Record Journal, August 25, 1939, p 1.

The First Week of Business!

RESOURCES 1939	Monday	Tuesday	Wednesday	Thursday	Friday	Saturday
	AUG 28 1939		AUG 30 1939	AUG 31 1939	SEP 1 1939	SEP - 2 193
Loans and Discounts	100 -	100 -	- 0 -	- 0 -		51 00
Overdrafts						6 21
U. S. Bonds				7500 -	7500 00	7500 00
Premiums						
Stocks and Bonds		34 06	34 06	34 06	3034 06	3034 06
Banking House						
Furniture and Fixtures						
Other Real Estate Owned (Reserve agents first)						
First Nat Denv	39063 19	41744 70	40048 02	26618 39	25109 07	27158 65
Expense	15	10 44	11 20	15 22	15 22	16 22
Taxes Paid						
Interest Paid						
Cash and Cash Items	6114 21	6018 30	5864 78	5780 02	5220 96	4368 43
Cash Short					5 00	5 00
	45277 55	47907 50	45958 06	39947 69	40884 31	42139 57
LIABILITIES						
Capital Stock	25000 -	25000 -	25000 -	25000 -	25000 -	25000 -
Surplus	5000 -	5000 -	5000 -	5000 -	5000 -	5000 -
Circulation						
Discount						
Interest	1 -	1 -	1 -	1 -	1 -	2 -
Exchange	60	70	70	70	70	70
Rents						
Undivided Profits						
Individual Deposits	5284 45	7912 30	9456 86	8646 49	9583 11	10777 37
Certificates of Deposit, Demand						
Certificates of Deposit, Time	41 50	41 50	41 50	41 50	41 50	91 50
Certified Checks						
Cashier's Checks	9950 -	9950 -	6450 00	1250 -	1250 00	1750 00
Box Rent		2 -	8 00	8 -	8 00	8 00
Reserved for Taxes						
Rediscounts						
Cash Over						10 00
	45277 55	47907 50	45958 06	39947 69	40884 31	42139 57

Ledger for the first week of business,
The Bank of Douglas County.

W.C. Buboltz, used with permission.

Newspaper Fair Advertisement

WELCOME and Congratulations to STOCKMEN AND FARMERS

* *

Since the opening of the doors of THE BANK OF DOUGLAS COUNTY, August 28, 1939, it has been devoted to the interests of this rich and growing agricultural-livestock region.

A bank is a service institution. It deserves sup port only if it adequately serves its community and the interests of the folks who make up that commun ity. We are proud to have been of service to the progressive rural and urban population and we sha re others' pleasure in this once-a-year exhibition of progress.

- **General Banking Service**
  You will receive courteous, considerate attention in all departments.
- **Commodity Credit Corp. Loans**
  Prompt and efficient handling and competent advice without obligation.
- **U. S. Savings Bonds**
  We are equipped for prompt sale and redemption.
- **Safety Deposit Boxes**
  Don't leave important papers and valuables un-protected.
- **General Agrircultural Loans**
  Experienced, understanding and intelligent service without delay.
- **Automobile Financing**
  Fair treatment assuring reasonable financing and rates.
- **Savings Department**
  Safe, insured, immediately available funds at 2 PER CENT.

The Bank of Douglas County

Each Account Insured Up To $10,000 By The Federal Depos it Insurance Corp.

Mr. Miller's commitment to ranchers, farmers, and the Fair is reflected in this ad.

Douglas County News September 9, 1953, used with permission.
Also in Breslow scrapbook.

CHRISTMAS GREETINGS

December 10, 1953.

Douglas County News,
used with permission.
Also in Breslow scrapbook.

December 24, 1954.

1954 Bank Advertisement

TO GET ACQUAINTED
WITH OUR

Friendly Bank Services

BANK BY MAIL

Deposits by Mail Efficiently and Quickly Processed. Duplicate Receipts Mailed To Customers The Same Day Deposits Are Received —

● **General Banking Service**

You will receive courteous, considerate attention in all departments.

● **Television Financing**

Prompt and efficient handling and reasonable terms.

● **U. S. Savings Bonds**

We are equipped for prompt sale and redemption.

● **Safety Deposit Boxes**

Don't leave important papers and valuables un-protected.

● **General Agrircultural Loans**

Experienced, understanding and intelligent service without delay.

● **Automobile Financing**

Fair treatment assuring reasonable financing and rates.

● **Savings Department**

Safe, insured, immediately available funds at 2 PER CENT. Compounded semi-annually.

The Bank of Douglas County

Castle Rock **Phone 119**

Deposits Insured up to $10,000 by Federal Deposit Insurance Corp.

November 5, 1954.

Douglas County News, used with permission. Also in Breslow scrapbook.

Stationery Letterheads Over the Years

J. H. VREELAND
MANAGER
J. H. McCORMICK
SECRETARY

W. R. HILLS
T. R. FLETCHER
K. M. VREELAND
R. M. UNDERWOOD
ASSISTANT SECRETARIES

SCOTTISH UNION & NATIONAL INSURANCE COMPANY

P. S. MILLER, Jr.
CASTLE ROCK, COLO.

HARTFORD, CONNECTICUT.

Scottish Union Insurance.

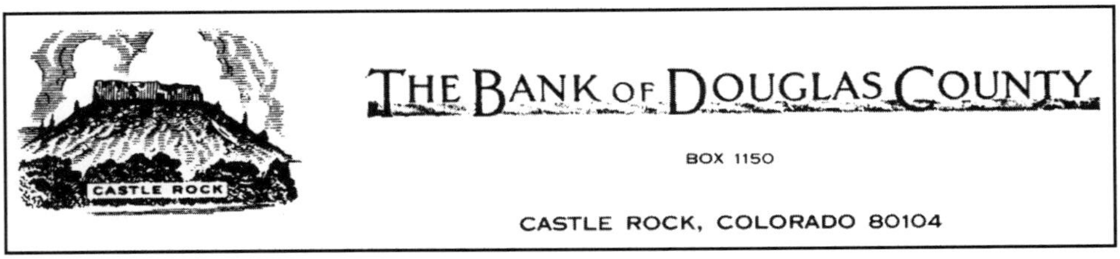

THE BANK OF DOUGLAS COUNTY

BOX 1150

CASTLE ROCK, COLORADO 80104

The Bank of Douglas County.

THE BANK OF DOUGLAS COUNTY

402 Wilcox Castle Rock, CO 80104

P.O. Box 1150 (303)688-3113

The Bank of Douglas County.

PRESIDENT
THE BANK OF DOUGLAS COUNTY

P. S. MILLER
CASTLE ROCK, COLORADO

REGISTERED
SHORTHORN CATTLE

Mr. Miller's personal letterhead.

Buboltz-Bodle Collection.

Deposit and Withdrawal Slips Over the Years

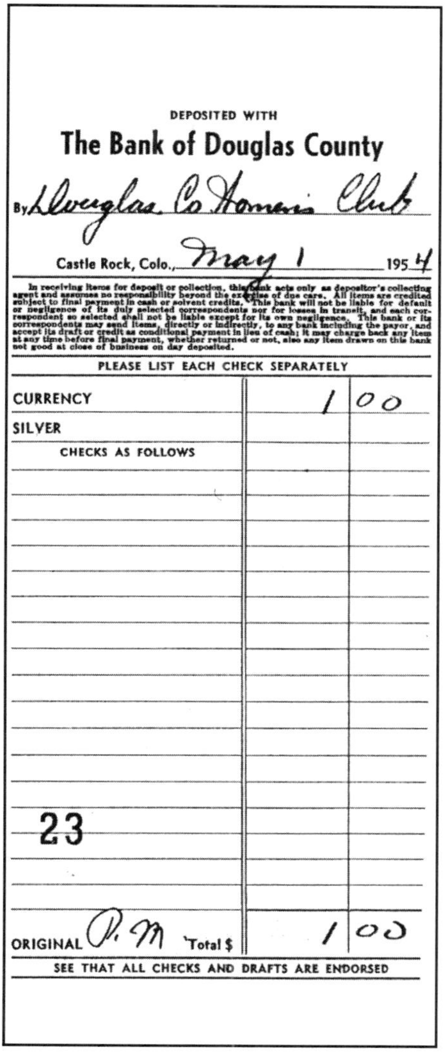
DEPOSITED WITH

The Bank of Douglas County

By Douglas Co. Woman's Club

Castle Rock, Colo., May 1 1954

In receiving items for deposit or collection, this bank acts only as depositor's collecting agent and assumes no responsibility beyond the exercise of due care. All items are credited subject to final payment in cash or solvent credits. This bank will not be liable for default or negligence of its duly selected correspondents nor for losses in transit, and each correspondent so selected shall not be liable except for its own negligence. This bank or its correspondents may send items, directly or indirectly, to any bank including the payor, and accept its draft or credit as conditional payment in lieu of cash; it may charge back any item at any time before final payment, whether returned or not, also any item drawn on this bank not good at close of business on day deposited.

PLEASE LIST EACH CHECK SEPARATELY

CURRENCY	1	00
SILVER		
CHECKS AS FOLLOWS		
23		
ORIGINAL P. M Total $	1	00

SEE THAT ALL CHECKS AND DRAFTS ARE ENDORSED

Deposit slip from 1954 with Mr. Miller's initials.

Local History Collection, Douglas Public Library District.

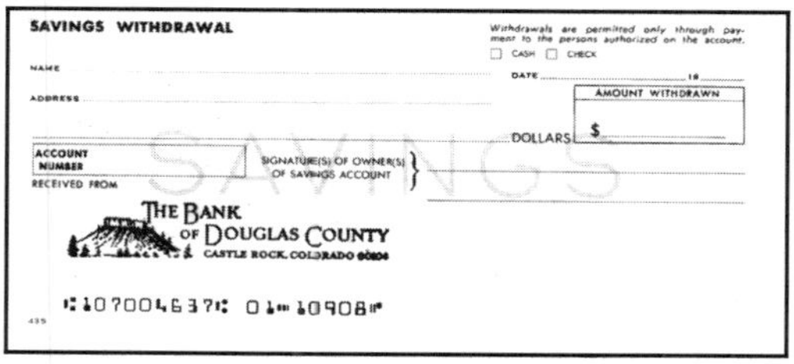
SAVINGS WITHDRAWAL

Withdrawals are permitted only through payment to the persons authorized on the account.

CASH CHECK

NAME

ADDRESS

DATE 19

AMOUNT WITHDRAWN

DOLLARS $

ACCOUNT NUMBER

RECEIVED FROM

SIGNATURE(S) OF OWNER(S) OF SAVINGS ACCOUNT

SAVINGS

THE BANK OF DOUGLAS COUNTY

CASTLE ROCK, COLORADO

107004637 01 10908

Savings withdrawal.

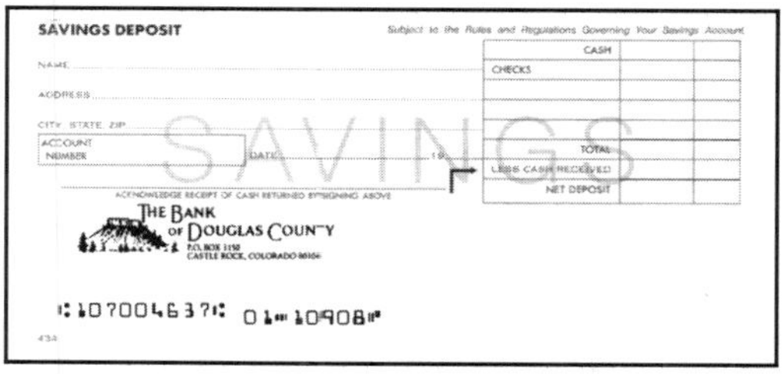
SAVINGS DEPOSIT

Subject to the Rules and Regulations Governing Your Savings Account

NAME

ADDRESS

CITY STATE ZIP

ACCOUNT NUMBER

DATE 19

ACKNOWLEDGE RECEIPT OF CASH RETURNED BY SIGNING ABOVE

CASH		
CHECKS		
TOTAL		
LESS CASH RECEIVED		
NET DEPOSIT		

SAVINGS

THE BANK OF DOUGLAS COUNTY

P.O. BOX 1150

CASTLE ROCK, COLORADO 80104

107004637 01 10908

Savings deposit.

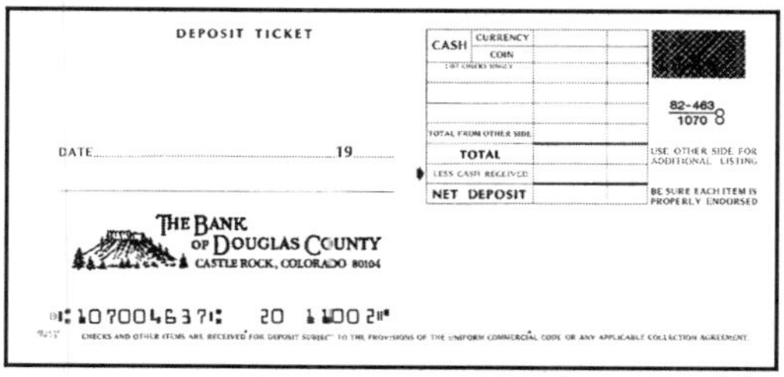
DEPOSIT TICKET

DATE 19

CASH	CURRENCY		
	COIN		
TOTAL FROM OTHER SIDE			
TOTAL			
LESS CASH RECEIVED			
NET DEPOSIT			

[redacted]

82-463 / 1070 8

USE OTHER SIDE FOR ADDITIONAL LISTING

BE SURE EACH ITEM IS PROPERLY ENDORSED

THE BANK OF DOUGLAS COUNTY

CASTLE ROCK, COLORADO 80104

107004637 20 11002

CHECKS AND OTHER ITEMS ARE RECEIVED FOR DEPOSIT SUBJECT TO THE PROVISIONS OF THE UNIFORM COMMERCIAL CODE OR ANY APPLICABLE COLLECTION AGREEMENT.

Checking deposit.

Buboltz-Bodle Collection.

Bank Checks Over the Years

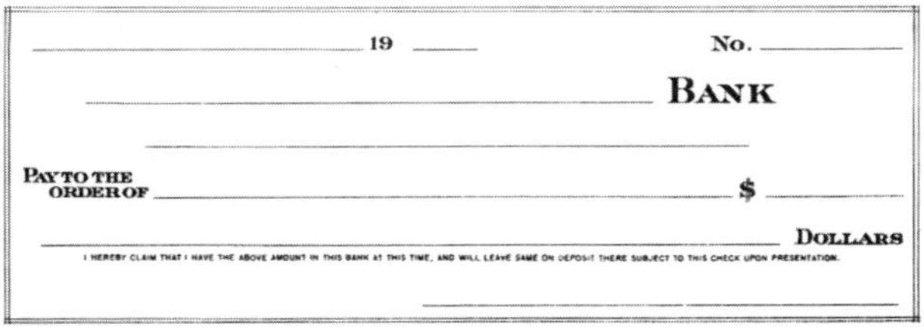

19 No.

BANK

PAY TO THE ORDER OF $

DOLLARS

I HEREBY CLAIM THAT I HAVE THE ABOVE AMOUNT IN THIS BANK AT THIS TIME, AND WILL LEAVE SAME ON DEPOSIT THERE SUBJECT TO THIS CHECK UPON PRESENTATION.

Early check. Year unknown.

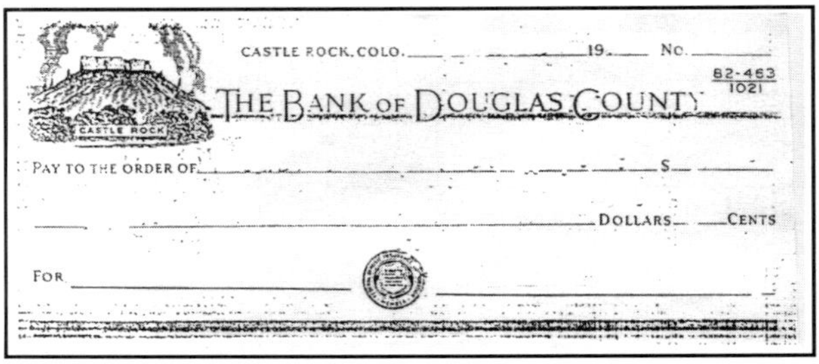

CASTLE ROCK, COLO. 19 No.

82-463
1021

CASTLE ROCK

THE BANK OF DOUGLAS COUNTY

PAY TO THE ORDER OF $

DOLLARS CENTS

FOR

Check from 1954. Note: no number in left lower corner, FDIC logo in center.

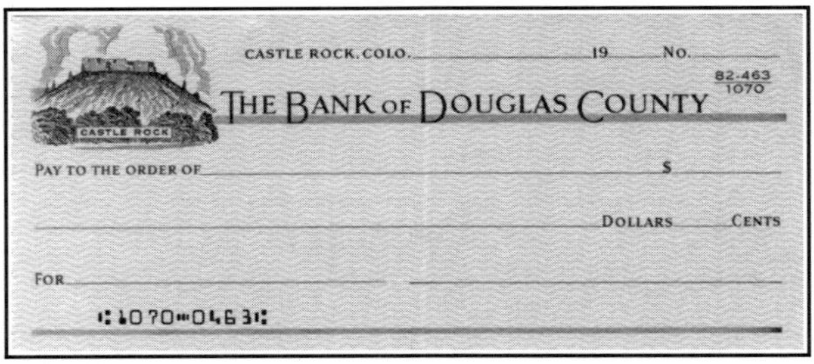

CASTLE ROCK, COLO. 19 No.

82-463
1070

CASTLE ROCK

THE BANK OF DOUGLAS COUNTY

PAY TO THE ORDER OF $

DOLLARS CENTS

FOR

⑆1070⑉0463⑆

Check after computer conversion December 28, 1979. Note: number in left corner, FDIC logo gone.

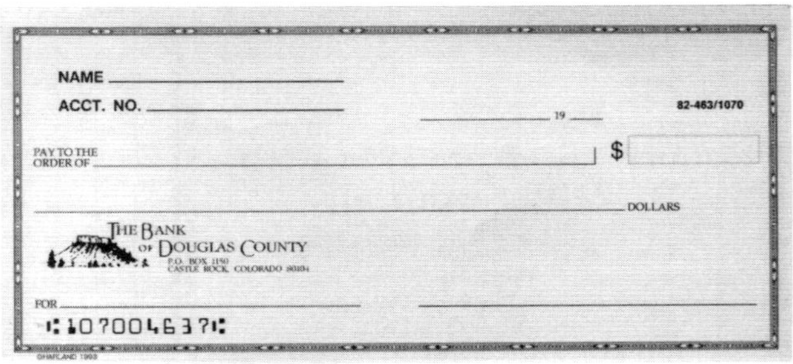

NAME

ACCT. NO.

19

82-463/1070

PAY TO THE ORDER OF $

DOLLARS

THE BANK OF DOUGLAS COUNTY

FOR

⑆107004637⑆

Check from the 1990's.

Buboltz-Bodle Collection.

Bank Statement Insert
1975-1976

NO SERVICE CHARGE ON ANY CHECKING ACCOUNT
With minimum balance of $300.00

AUTOMATED TELLER MACHINE 24 HOUR BANKING
Cash withdrawals with your Visa Bank Card. Cash advances with Visa Card and Master Charge.

SAVINGS PLANS	INTEREST
Passbook	5¼%
90 Day Notice Pass Book	5½%
1 Year Certificate	6%
30 Month Certificate	6½%
4 Year Certificate	7¼%
6 Year Certificate	7½%
8 Year Certificate	7¾%
Money Market Certificate $10,000 Min Deposit	rates chg. wkly
Individual Retirement Account	8%

HIGHER RATES OF INTEREST AVAILABLE FOR TIME CERTIFICATES OF DEPOSIT OF $100,000 OR OVER

• • • •

Federal law prohibits the payment of a time deposit without substantial penalty.

✓ **BANK LOBBY FULL SERVICE**
9 a.m. to 4 p.m.
Monday thru Friday

✓ **MASTER CHARGE AVAILABLE**

✓ **VISA AVAILABLE**

✓ **DRIVE UP SERVICE**
8 a.m. to 5 p.m. Mon. thru Thurs.
8 a.m. to 6 p.m. Friday
8 a.m. to 12 Noon Saturday

✓ **NIGHT DEPOSITORY**
7 DAYS — 24 HOURS
Use our night depository located on the 4th Street side of the Bank Building 'round the clock - all week

402 WILCOX **688-3113**
established 1939

Dependable Banking Service for Dependable People

The BANK of DOUGLAS COUNTY
Member of the Federal Deposit Insurance Corp.
Castle Rock, Colo.

FDIC
Each Depositor Insured to $40,000

Buboltz-Bodle Collection.

40th Anniversary!

The Express

DOUGLAS COUNTY

Vol. II, No. 5
Aug. 29, 1979
Castle Rock, Colo. 80104

A JOURNAL OF OPINION SERVING THIS FINE COUNTY

THE BANK OF DOUGLAS COUNTY

1939 to 1979

Front page of Douglas County Express on 40th Anniversary of The Bank of Douglas County.

August 29, 1979, used with permission.

Prospering in the 1980's

The Bank of Douglas County tops list of safest institutions

While some banks may be collapsing thanks to the pressures of bad loans, The Bank of Douglas County is not only surviving, it's thriving.

The Castle Rock-based bank came out at the top of a survey of more than 14,000 commercial banks in a "blue bank" test. The survey, by Veribanc, Inc., a bank research firm, identified 21 banks in the states of Colorado, Utah, Nevada and New Mexico with strong capital positions, the ability to meet short-term obligations and profitability.

The Bank of Douglas County ranked first in the state and second in the region in equity-to-assets ratio on that gold-plated list.

That bank has benefited from the explosive growth in this area, and its conservative philosophy hasn't hurt it either. Growth in assets has more than doubled from $24 million in 1978 to $52 million in 1985, Richard Temple, assistant cashier, said. The bank earned $1 million last year, boasting one of the highest capital ratios in the Rocky Mountain region at 15 percent.

The bank also has a loans to deposit ratio of only 35 percent. It invests the remainder of the money it gathers from deposits in high-grade U.S. government bonds and municipal bonds.

STRONGEST BANKS IN THE ROCKIES

Commercial Bank Name	Location	Profitability Ratio (%)	Equity/Assets Ratio (%)	Liquity Ratio (%)	Average Assets (000s)	Average Equity (000s)	Annualized Net Income (000s)
Barnes Banking Co	Kaysville, Utah	3.40	15.17	60.28	$55.372	$8.401	$1.884
Omnibank Southeast	Denver	2.23	9.46	53.51	56.371	5.333	1.258
Nevada State Bank	Las Vegas Nev	2.12	13.17	53.12	206.891	27.250	4.386
The Bank of Douglas County	Castle Rock	1.99	15.01	86.38	51.883	7.790	1.030
First Nat'l Bank of Canon City	Canon City	1.94	8.20	50.83	58.918	4.829	1.144
First Nat'l Bank in Loveland	Loveland	1.59	9.83	48.46	105.533	10.377	1.682
First Nat'l Bank of Farmington	Farmington N M	1.58	9.84	61.09	202.000	19.879	3.194
First Nat'l Bank in Alamogordo	Alamogordo N M	1.48	7.96	46.45	103.567	8.243	1.530
American National of Silver City	Silver City N M	1.45	9.46	58.67	63.906	6.047	924
United Bank of Monoco	Denver	1.43	7.72	56.74	52.032	4.017	746
Southwest Nat'l Bank	Albuquerque	1.43	7.69	52.32	55.566	4.270	794
IntraWest Bank of Bear Valley	Denver	1.41	8.56	50.22	98.211	8.402	1.384
Bank of American Fork	American Fork, Utah	1.30	10.65	52.89	65.333	6.955	848
Carlsbad National Bank	Carlsbad, N M	1.22	9.11	57.25	113.767	10.362	1.392
IntraWest Bank of Southglenn	Arapahoe Co Colo	1.12	8.04	58.80	90.949	7.310	1.018
Security Bank & Trust	Alamogordo N M	1.01	7.96	53.51	58.676	4.674	594
Sunwest Bank of Raton	Raton N M	0.93	8.31	52.76	75.556	6.281	702
Minnequa Bank	Pueblo	0.80	8.14	51.91	105.281	8.567	844
First Nat'l Bank of Longmont	Longmont	0.79	9.84	52.78	110.549	10.876	870
Arapahoe Bank & Trust	Arapahoe Co Colo	0.52	7.70	55.82	63.191	4.867	330
Colorado Nat'l Bank Pueblo	Pueblo	0.20	8.05	55.39	178.572	14.369	358

This table is based on the Federal Reserve Board Reports of Condition and Reports of Income for the bank reporting period ending Dec. 31, 1985 and earlier periods. The most recent data was released by the Federal Reserve Board on April 10, 1986. Wyoming banks were not included in this survey.

Source: Veribanc Inc., Wakefield, Mass.

Douglas County Daily News Press,
August 20, 1986,
used with permission.

Golden Anniversary

GOLDEN ANNIVERSARY

You are Invited to our Open House

Tuesday, August 29 - 9 a.m. to 4 p.m.

Please join us during our open house so that we can express to you our sincere appreciation for your loyalty through the years.

As part of our anniversary, we are holding a drawing for 16 gold coins. Come in soon to enter. The drawing will be held at 3:00 p.m.

50th Anniversary Invitation from The Bank of Douglas County, August 29, 1989.

Douglas County News Press, used with permission.

Statements of Condition

December 31, 1970

STATEMENT OF CONDITION

THE BANK OF DOUGLAS COUNTY

CASTLE ROCK, COLORADO

December 31, 1970

RESOURCES		LIABILITIES	
Loans & Discounts	$ 2,513,082.05	Capital	$ 100,000.00
U. S. Government Bonds	2,531,600.93	Surplus	200,000.00
Municipal Bonds	1,182,042.26	Undivided Profits	525,976.22
Furniture & Fixtures	1.00	Reserves	45,059.46
Banking Premises	1.00	Deposits	6,600,951.95
Other Real Estate	1.00		
Cash Due From Banks	1,243,141.84		
Accrued Interest Purchased	2,117.55		
	$ 7,471,987.63		$ 7,471,987.63

OFFICERS and DIRECTORS

P. S. Miller, President

W. C. Buboltz, Vice President and Cashier

R. G. Oliver, Assistant Cashier

J. E. Miller

Member Federal Deposit Insurance Corporation

Bank of Douglas County Records 1970-1995.

December 31, 1975

STATEMENT OF CONDITION

THE BANK OF DOUGLAS COUNTY

CASTLE ROCK, COLORADO

December 31, 1975

RESOURCES		LIABILITIES	
Loans & Discounts	$ 5,725,499.33	Capital	$ 200,000.00
U. S. Government Bonds	3,227,400.00	Surplus	300,000.00
Municipal Bonds	3,258,605.73	Undivided Profits	900,401.62
Funds Sold	400,000.00	Reserves	100,927.02
Furniture & Fixtures	1.00	Deferred Income	107,605.38
Banking Premises	1.00	Deposits	12,092,673.41
Cash & Due From Banks	1,087,965.59		
Accrued Interest Purchased	2,134.78		
	$13,701,607.43		$13,701,607.43

OFFICERS

P. S. Miller, President
W. C. Buboltz, Exec. Vice President and Cashier
R. G. Oliver, Vice President
Betty Corey, Assistant Cashier
Dona Sherlock, Assistant Cashier
C. S. Slife, Jr., Auditor

DIRECTORS

P. S. Miller J. E. Miller W. C. Buboltz

Member Federal Deposit Insurance Corporation

Bank of Douglas County Records 1970-1995.

December 31, 1980

STATEMENT OF CONDITION

THE BANK OF DOUGLAS COUNTY

CASTLE ROCK, COLORADO

December 31, 1980

ASSETS		LIABILITIES	
Loans & Discounts	$11,473,680.07	Capital	$ 200,000.00
U. S. Government Bonds	7,590,717.80	Surplus	800,000.00
Municipal Bonds	6,541,226.35	Undivided Profits	2,577,449.44
Furniture & Fixtures	43,051.25	Reserves	134,891.98
Banking Premises	158,203.24	Deferred Income	200,469.28
Cash & Due From Banks	2,605,523.15	Other Liabilities	244,218.42
Other Assets	442,665.81	Deposits	24,698,038.55
	$28,855,067.67		$28,855,067.67

OFFICERS

P. S. Miller, President
W. C. Buboltz, Exec. Vice President
R. G. Oliver, Vice President and Cashier
Dona Sherlock, Ass't. Vice President
Thomas Waymire, Ass't. Cashier

DIRECTORS

P. S. Miller J. E. Miller W. C. Buboltz R. G. Oliver

Member Federal Deposit Insurance Corporation

Bank of Douglas County Records 1970-1995.

December 31, 1985

STATEMENT OF CONDITION

THE BANK OF DOUGLAS COUNTY

CASTLE ROCK, COLORADO

December 31, 1985

ASSETS		LIABILITIES	
Loans & Discounts	$13,287,881.36	Capital	$ 1,000,000.00
U.S. Government Bonds	19,984,901.83	Surplus	1,000,000.00
Municipal Bonds	12,074,812.35	Undivided Profits	5,899,179.33
Furniture & Fixtures	43,360.96	Reserves	134,891.98
Banking Premises	137,276.43	Other Liabilities	377,896.78
Cash & Due From Banks	4,522,139.88	Deposits	43,543,917.91
Funds Sold	1,000,000.00		
Other Assets	905,513.19		
	$51,955,886.00		$51,955,886.00

OFFICERS

P.S. Miller, President
W.C. Buboltz, Executive Vice President
Dona W. Sherlock, Vice President & Cashier
Thomas Waymire, Vice President
Margaret Olson, Assistant Vice President
Therold M. Bateman, Assistant Cashier
Teresa Jenik, Assistant Cashier
Richard E. Temple, Assistant Cashier

DIRECTORS

P.S. Miller W.C. Buboltz Dona W. Sherlock

Member Federal Deposit Insurance Corporation

Bank of Douglas County Records 1970-1995.

December 31, 1990

STATEMENT OF CONDITION

THE BANK OF DOUGLAS COUNTY

CASTLE ROCK, COLORADO

December 31,1990

ASSETS		LIABILITIES	
Loans & Discounts	$ 11,919,488.31	Capital	$ 2,000,000.00
U.S. Government Bonds	43,396,533.87	Surplus	3,000,000.00
Municipal Bonds	3,421,662.30	Undivided Profits	6,942,867.31
Furniture & Fixtures	8,120.00	Reserves	311,460.48
Banking Premises	87,546.00	Other Liabilities	339,559.14
Cash & Due From Banks	3,903,702.26	Deposits	54,210,294.62
Funds Sold	3,000,000.00		
Other Assets	1,067,128.81		
	$66,804,181.55		$66,804,181.55

OFFICERS

P.S. Miller, President
Dona W. Sherlock, Vice President & Cashier
Richard E. Temple, Vice President
Thomas D. Waymire, Vice President
Therold M. Bateman, Assistant Vice President
Margaret A. Olson, Assistant Vice President
Teresa L. Towns, Assistant Vice President

DIRECTORS

P.S. Miller W.C. Buboltz Dona W. Sherlock

Member Federal Deposit Insurance Corporation

Bank of Douglas County Records 1970-1995.

December 31, 1995

STATEMENT OF CONDITION

THE BANK OF DOUGLAS COUNTY

CASTLE ROCK, COLORADO

December 31, 1995

ASSETS		LIABILITIES	
Loans & Discounts	$ 8,349,780.51	Capital	$ 2,000,000.00
U.S. Government Bonds	74,793,934.97	Surplus	4,000,000.00
Municipal Bonds	2,867,042.61	Undivided Profits	13,104,406.79
Furniture & Fixtures	61,397.79	Other Liabilities	412,458.29
Banking Premises	63,814.47	Deposits	81,324,367.50
Cash & Due From Banks	4,486,431.76		
Funds Sold	8,300,000.00		
Other Assets	1,918,830.47		
	$ 100,841,232.58		$ 100,841,232.58

OFFICERS

August J. Fischer, President
Thomas D. Waymire, Vice President
Margaret A. Olson, Vice President
Shilee S. Neal, Cashier

DIRECTORS

August J. Fischer   Herman Anderson   Lawrence Fain

Member Federal Deposit Insurance Corporation

Bank of Douglas County Records 1970-1995.

Early Years

344 St. Paul Street in Denver, Colorado where the Miller family lived from 1907-1910. Lena Kaestler Miller died in this house in 1908.

Buboltz-Bodle Collection.

Corona School, now known as Moore School, at 846 Corona Street where Philip and Adam attended.

Buboltz-Bodle Collection.

The corner of Third Avenue and Detroit Streets, location of the first Miller Meat Market, is now part of the Pendleton Store in upscale Cherry Creek North.

Buboltz-Bodle Collection.

Apartment at 1035 Tenth Avenue where Philip, Sr., Adam and Philip, Jr. moved in 1910.

Buboltz-Bodle Collection.

House at 88 West Cedar Avenue,
where the three Miller men moved in 1912.

Buboltz-Bodle Collection.

They tore down Sandersons to put up a parking lot!

Buboltz-Bodle Collection.

The first photo in Anna Weishaupl's album of Philip Miller standing by the Miller Meat Market Wagon, circa 1914-1915.

Local History Collection, Douglas Public Library District, Douglas County, CO.

Philip Miller and Anna Weishaupl, a very attractive couple, circa 1916.

Local History Collection, Douglas Public Library District, Douglas County, CO.

Adam and Phil at Bill Weishaupl's farm in Littleton, CO, circa 1916.

left to right: Adam, Phil

Local History Collection, Douglas Public Library District, Douglas County, CO.

Phil and Adam in Denver, CO, circa 1916.

left to right: Phil, Adam

Local History Collection, Douglas Public Library District, Douglas County, CO.

Augusta Miller.

Courtesy of Emil Walz Jr.

Augusta Miller with Caroline Aldinger, Hazel Shoemaker's mother.

Courtesy of Glenda Williams.

Phil in Elizabeth, CO, raising Spotted Poland China Hogs, Circa 1917.

Local History Collection, Douglas Public Library District, Douglas County, CO.

Adam in Elizabeth, CO, milking a cow, circa 1917.

Local History Collection, Douglas Public Library District, Douglas County, CO.

Adam and Grandmother Augusta, Elizabeth, CO, circa 1917.

Local History Collection,
Douglas Public Library District,
Douglas County, CO.

The house where Phil and Jerry Miller lived from 1919-1921 at 384 West Kiowa Avenue in Elizabeth, CO, is now a Re-Max Realty Office.

Buboltz-Bodle Collection.

Above the now famous Duffy's Restaurant are rooms which were once a Gentlemen's Residence Quarters where Adam Miller lived in 1916 and 1917 before enlisting in the Navy.

Buboltz-Bodle Collection.

U. S. S. HARRISBURG.

U.S.S. Harrisburg, the Navy ship on which Adam served in World War I.

Emil Walz, Jr. Collection.

St. Elizabeth's Roman Catholic Church on the Auraria Campus, stands just one block north of where the second Miller Meat Market and the two residences on Champa Street were once located.

Buboltz-Bodle Collection.

Elbert Street in 1925. Phil and Jerry Miller lived in the tree-nestled white house.

Local History Collection, Douglas Public Library District, Douglas County, CO.

Present day 310 Elbert Street. Millers lived here from 1925 until 1950.

Buboltz-Bodle Collection.

Douglas County Public Library

Library Groundbreaking Ceremony at 300 Gilbert Street, August 10, 1968. Mr. Miller happily turns the first shovel full of dirt!

left to right: Contractor, Chuck Prescott, County Commissioner, Hank Kimbrough, Board of Trustee President, Nicky Mead, Benefactor Philip Miller, Mayor Pete Burgess, Librarian Alden Briskey.

Local History Collection, Douglas Public Library District, Douglas County, CO.

Laying the foundation for the Library, August 1968.

Local History Collection, Douglas Public Library District, Douglas County, CO.

Laying the brick for the Library building, August 1968.

Local History Collection, Douglas Public Library District, Douglas County, CO.

Installing the Library roof, September 1968.

Local History Collection, Douglas Public Library District, Douglas County, CO.

118

LIBRARY BENEFIT

Book Review & Tea

D.C.H.S. Auditorium & Library

Tuesday, April 9th — 2:00 - 4:00 p.m.

$1.00 per person

No 078

LIBRARY BENEFIT

Book Review and Tea

Wednesday, April 28th — 2:00 - 4:00 p.m.

D.C.H.S. Auditorium & Library

$1.00 per person

LIBRARY BENEFIT

Book Review and Tea

Wednesday, April 29th — 2:00 - 4:00 p.m.

D.C.H.S. Auditorium & Library

$1.00 per person

135

Three years of tickets to the annual Library Benefit Book Review and Tea which raised money for new books.

Buboltz-Bodle collection.

Members of Douglas Lodge #153 and the Most Worshipful Grand Lodge of Colorado. A.M. & F.M. lay the cornerstone at the Library, September 28, 1968.

Local History Collection, Douglas Public Library District, Douglas County, CO.

Dedication of the Douglas County Library, 300 Gilbert Street, April 26, 1969.

left to right: Russell Higginson, Pete Burgess, Willie Buboltz, Hank Kimbrough, Ellen Buboltz, Helen Serrell, Jerry Miller, Philip Miller, Herbert Shauer, Nicky Mead, James McKay, Alden Briskey, and Betty Prince.

Local History Collection, Douglas Public Library District, Douglas County, CO.

Ellen Buboltz with the award-winning "Birth of the Library" Album at the April 26, 1969 Dedication Ceremony.

Local History Collection, Douglas Public Library District, Douglas County, CO.

Photographer Eugene "Red" Everitt and Nicky Mead with the portrait of Mr. Miller which was donated at the Dedication Ceremony.

Local History Collection, Douglas Public Library District, Douglas County, CO.

James McKay, President of the Library Board of Trustees accepts a check from the Second Annual Friends of the Library Douglas County on Parade Home Tour, September 1969.

Members of the committee left to right: Lou Gannon, Ann McConnell, Ellen Buboltz, and Nancy Kimbrough.

Local History Collection, Douglas Public Library District, Douglas County, CO.

Ceremony to dedicate the Library at 300 Gilbert Street to Mr. Miller and to officially change the name to the Miller Branch was on August 19, 1980.

Douglas County News Press, August 12, 1980, used with permission.

The current Philip S. Miller Library at 961 South Plum Creek Boulevard was dedicated on October 24, 1987 and stands on land that was once part of the Miller Ranch. Mr. and Mrs. Miller made an original donation of $130,000 toward its construction. In 1988, Mr. Miller donated $510,000 to retire the debt on the Library.

Buboltz-Bodle Collection.

1972 Bank Grand Opening

Mr. Josef Winkler, Mr. Art Bridgewater, former Vice President of Central Bank and Trust, and Mr. Miller at Grand Opening.

Dona Sherlock Collection.

Mrs. Miller and Mrs Bridgewater at Grand Opening.

Dona Sherlock Collection.

Bob Oliver and Dona Sherlock at the Grand Opening May 13, 1972.

Dona Sherlock Collection.

Mr. and Mrs. Miller at the Grand Opening.

Douglas County News May 18, 1972, used with permission.

Mr. Josef Winkler, Mr. Miller and Mrs. Miller at Grand Opening.

Dona Sherlock Collection.

Willie Buboltz at his desk during Grand Opening.

Dona Sherlock Collection.

Mr. Miller at his desk during Grand Opening.

Dona Sherlock Collection.

Retirement

Willie, Dona and Johnnie on Retirement Day, January 7, 1994!

Dona Sherlock Collection.

Ellen Buboltz with Bob and Bette VanPelt.
left to right: Ellen, Bob, Bette.

Dona Sherlock Collection.

Johnnie Osthoff with Beulah Peters and Bette Saunders.
left to right: Johnnie, Beulah, Bette.

Dona Sherlock Collection.

Linda Shepherd, Dona Sherlock and Lella Shepherd.
left to right: Linda, Dona, Lella.

Dona Sherlock Collection.

Crowd shot of the lobby, still filled with people at 5 pm!

Dona Sherlock Collection.

Dona, Louise Christensen, former County Commissioner Warren Christensen, and Willie.

left to right: Dona, Louise, Warren, Willie.

Dona Sherlock Collection.

Hazel Burgess, Willie, and former Mayor "Pete" Burgess.
left to right: Hazel, Willie, Pete.

Dona Sherlock Collection.

Joe Root of Travelers Insurance, former Bank Director, Bob and Helen Oliver.
left to right: Joe, Bob, Helen.

Dona Sherlock Collection.

Willie with Don Hoffman, former President of Central Bank and Trust.

Dona Sherlock Collection.

Gill Whitman and Johnnie.

Dona Sherlock Collection.

Teresa Towns-Weatherly, Vice President.

Dona Sherlock Collection.

Tom Waymire, Vice President and Loan Officer, Richard Temple, Vice President and Senior Lender.

left to right: Tom, Richard.

Dona Sherlock Collection.

Nina Weidman.

Dona Sherlock Collection.

Kathy Anderson, Margaret Olson Assistant Vice President, Carrie Copeland, Pat Carnahan, Glenda Williams and Helen Longworth.

left to right: Kathy, Margaret, Carrie, Pat, Glenda, Helen.

Dona Sherlock Collection.

Debbie Warren, Debbie Warren (YES there were two!), Wendy Dalla, and Mary Jane Hart.

left to right: Debbie, Debbie, Wendy, Mary Jane.

Dona Sherlock Collection.

Connie Johanns, Kelly Valdez, Irene Wardrip, Diana Bramer, and Ann Diamond.

left to right: Connie, Kelly, Irene, Diana, Ann.

Dona Sherlock Collection.

My favorite photo of Adam and Dorothy Miller in front of their ranch home in Parker. It hangs in the Adam and Dorothy Miller Community Room in the Parker Library.

Local History Collection, Douglas Public Library District, Douglas County, CO.

The ranch house at 9100 East Parker Road in Parker, CO, where Adam and Dorothy Miller lived from 1937 until their deaths in the 1980's.

Buboltz-Bodle Collection.

My favorite photo of Mr. and Mrs. Miller in front of their ranch home south of Castle Rock.

Douglas County News Press, August 30, 1979, used with permission.

Philip S. Miller

Every so often God gives us a man who stands out. Someone who can put a smile on a frowning face, who can find encouragement in the bleakest of times, who would help a stranger in need and ask for nothing in return. Philip S. Miller was such a man. From selling all his cattle and most belongings to start a bank in 1939; to donating thousands of dollars. He even gave loans with nothing more than a trusting handshake.

This friend of all will truly be missed.

Tim Fleming

Tribute to Mr. Miller, June 15, 1995.

Courtesy of Castle Rock Chronicle and Tim Fleming..

ACKNOWLEDGEMENTS: WITH GRATITUDE

A project of this magnitude, compiled over a six-year period of time, encompassing nearly 100 years of history, cannot be undertaken or accomplished alone. Hundreds of people contributed to this book and I like to think of it as a combined effort on the part of every person involved. Some were family members, some were close friends, some were new friends, some were old friends and some were friendly voices over the phone with whom I spoke frequently, always remembering their names, but never knowing their faces. There are not enough words to express my gratitude to all the many people who have helped make this book a reality.

I must first thank my family. My mom and dad, Ellen and Willie Buboltz, became researchers, photographers, interviewers, interviewees, statisticians, editors, and historians. My husband, John, is a computer genius and along with supporting me for the past six years, he has pulled me out of some horrendous computer glitches that my MacIntosh and I have created! His patience has been a testimonial to his belief in this project. My sister, Shelley, my brother-in-law, Wes, and my niece and nephew, Stephanie and Stephen, have kept me balanced and connected to reality with phone calls and e-mail regarding Star Wars, Leann Rimes and the two new dogs!

Bette Saunders became my chief researcher when it had to do with facts regarding early Castle Rock history, people and places. Some of the best things in this book came from her and I will always be grateful for her support, her dedication, and her friendship. Johanna Harden at the Local History Collection of the Douglas Public Library District became my own personal gold mine, with treasures galore, in her rooms at the Philip S. Miller Library. Anything I asked for, she miraculously discovered and much of this book is due to her help and effort. Mr. and Mrs. Emil Walz, Jr. of Arvada became involved in this project because Mr. Miller's first girlfriend was Mr. Walz's mother! Without even being asked, they researched and uncovered a ten year gap during Mr. Miller's life that I always called the "Missing Years" and discovered the identity of the "mystery lady." They also gave me a map from 1913, which became one of the most valuable assets to this book.

I want to especially thank Mr. Gerd Adam Kaestler, Jr. and Mrs. Norma Jean Gish who live in Peoria, Illinois and are Mr. Miller's second cousins. Because of them, I have a deeper understanding of

Mr. Miller's life. Although I was a total stranger, they were willing to lend me photographs, documents, wills and family information, answering questions about Mr. Miller's childhood in Illinois and the death and burial of his mother, Lena, which had become my biggest mystery, my most frustrating challenge! Another valuable asset to this book was the Kaestler Family Tree, which Mr. Kaestler compiled for me.

I also owe a special thanks to Mrs. Miller's family: her niece, Shari Benedict, great-nieces, Diane Fling and Melissa Benedict and great-nephews, Chuck and James Benedict. Diane compiled for me, over the phone, the whole Benedict Family Tree, from memory! Shari answered specific questions about Mrs. Miller's early years. Melissa wrote me a heartwarming, eight-page letter full of memories about Uncle Phil and Aunt Jerry.

Next, I want to thank the following people for their never-ending support and encouragement, both professionally and personally. Most of these people are my friends, and for that I am additionally thankful:

Dona Sherlock, Johnnie Osthoff, Bob Oliver, Glenda Williams, Margaret Olson, Frances Cannon, Helen Longworth, Dr. Herman Anderson, and Tom Waymire of the former Bank of Douglas County. Also Buddy Douglass, Senior Vice President of FirstBank of Douglas County.

John and Bea Lowell, Gill and Cecil Whitman, Bruff Shea, and Karen Serafini of the Douglas County Fair Board and 4-H Foundation Board.

James LaRue, Cindy Murphy, Moira Armstrong-Ash, Suzanne Riches, Elaine Weaver, Penny Perkins, and Holly Deni of the Douglas Public Library District.

Starr and Lionel Oberlin of the Castle Rock Historical Society and Kent Brandebery and Bob Lowenberg of the Douglas County Historic Preservation Board, and Nancy Lyons of Preservation Partnership.

Kristi Olson, Counselor at the Douglas County High School and member of the Philip S. Miller Scholarship Committee.

Former Mayors, Carroll Hier, H. G. "Pete" Burgess and his wife Hazel; Freddie Smith and his wife Ada, and Attorney Jim Folkestad.

Ken Ash, Dr. Hal Gannon, Lou Gannon, Bette VanPelt, Helen Daley, Ruth Miller, Velva Bains, Jack Williams, Helen Oliver, Bryan Ruth, Chuck Higby, Dick Higby, Richard Lee, Joe Winkler, Jim McKay, Rosemary Metzler and Don McBreen.

Historians, Louise Solberg, from Falcon, Colorado and Gertrude Clarke Kordziel from Golden, Colorado. Also Jackson Webb from Allenspark, Colorado, President of the Rocky Mountain Writer's Association, Max Brooks, former President of Central Bank and Trust, and James Nelsen, Trust Attorney for Mr. Miller.

Additionally I want to thank the staff at the Douglas County Clerk and Recorder's Office, the staff of the Douglas County Assessor's Office and the staff of the Castle Rock Town Clerk's Office for all their help in locating official records and documents.

Next I need to thank Richard Bangs and Matthew Vuletich of the Douglas County News Press, Jim Myles and Tim Fleming of the Daily News Chronicle and the Castle Rock Chronicle, and all the local journalists who wrote about Mr. Miller over the years: Specifically Mildred Brodbeck, Virginia Grantier, Jim Duffy, Jamie LaRue, Cindy Murphy, Wendy Thomas, Susan Casey, Dianna Gordon, Penny Perkins, and Sharon Almirall.

There are not enough words to thank my Editors, Floyd and Chris Allen, and Janet Lusher. Floyd's suggestions were inspired! Bruce Fischer, my Publisher, has provided me with invaluable guidance and assistance, which has enabled me to finally complete this project. I owe them all a tremendous debt of gratitude.

Finally I have to thank my closest friend, Kathy Reis, who has encouraged me for six years, and has pulled me through some very dark moments. Also my other close friends, Jane and Jim Olsen, Juanita Bower, Jacque Chastain, Debbie Mitchell, Jeanne Kusterer, Bryan Ruth, Sue DeSimone, Ken Case, Ken Wilson, Renee Rafacz, Glenna and Rex Stone, Martha and Dave Janda, Miles and Eleanor Miner, Naomi and Russ Lloyd, Cindy Kolber, Dianne Skaff, Renee Merlino, Virginia Gilman and Dorothy Hull. Also, Jack Siebert for taking over my teaching job so I could finish this book! A special thanks goes the Wednesday night "Little People," who have kept me sane through these final months: Jerry and Trudy Skelton, Ed and Dee O'Connor, Jack and Jeanine Greene, Mel and Vicki Burke, Bill and Estelle Taylor, Russ and Sharon Diaz, Barb and Dean Edmondson. Lots of Yellow Rocks to you guys!

IN MEMORIUM: WITH GRATITUDE

Many of the people in this book who were associated in one way or another with Mr. Miller, The Bank of Douglas County, The Douglas Public Library District, The Douglas County Fair, The Town of Castle Rock and The County of Douglas are no longer with us. Some passed away prior to and others during the writing of this book. Regardless of the dates, these are our losses.

Jim Folkestad once said to me there were specific people who, by their personality and reputation, gave character and distinction to Castle Rock. He also, sadly, lamented that many of them are not with us any more. This is a list of some of those people and to them we also owe a huge debt of gratitude.

Philip and Jerry Miller
Adam and Dorothy Miller
Charles "Bickey" Briscoe
Duane and Eleanora Richardson
Clyde Richardson
Carl Winkler
Josef Winkler
Glen and Ollie Ramsour
Arlie Gordon, Sr.
Robert VanPelt
Genevieve "Nicky" Mead
Margaret Couch Fry
Charles Sherlock
Ben Saunders
Jim Oltmans
Lou Higby, Sr.
J. B. Godley
John Lowell, Jr.
Josephine Lowell Marr
John Paulk
John Colby
Glenn and Hazel Shoemaker
Genevieve "Jean" Riesselman
H. G. "Pete" Burgess
and Bandit

MEET THE AUTHOR

Debbie Buboltz-Bodle was a longtime Castle Rock resident and friend of Philip S. Miller. Born in Denver, Colorado in 1950, she moved to Castle Rock in 1952 when her father, Willie Buboltz, accepted a position with Mr. Miller at the bank, continuing to work with him there for the next forty-two years. Her mother, Ellen Buboltz, was Douglas County Librarian, and was one of those instrumental in the development of the Douglas County Library.

Debbie attended school in Castle Rock from first grade until she graduated from high school. Following high school, she attended beauty school in Denver and then became owner of The Powder Box Beauty Salon in Castle Rock during the early and mid-70's. It was during this time, as Mrs. Miller's beautician, that she began her informal research for a book she did not yet know she would be writing!

After selling her salon, Debbie taught at Beauty Schools in Denver, Englewood and Greeley, CO. This was followed by her first experience in the realm of Journalism, which began at the Rapp Street Journal in the mid-80's in Littleton, CO. She began as a staff writer, then progressed to news editor, assistant editor, and finally was appointed editor.

Debbie continued her education by getting a Bachelors Degree in English and Education, graduating from Ottawa University *magna cum laude*. She then utilized this degree to teach GED at the Arizona Institute of Business and Technology in Phoenix, Arizona, where she currently lives with her husband, John, who is a Design Engineer for Honeywell. Debbie is a member of the Rocky Mountain Writers Association.

This biography of Mr. Miller is her first published book-length work. She felt compelled to write this book, not only because Mr. Miller's life was so fascinating, but also because she felt that he needed to be both honored, and "saved for the ages." This work allowed her to make sure both of these goals were accomplished.

Additionally, Mr. Miller's birthday will always be special in her family because on October 11, 1990, her sister, Shelley, gave birth to a baby boy, Stephen Sugino. Mr. Miller was always very pleased that Willie's grandson was born on his birthday!

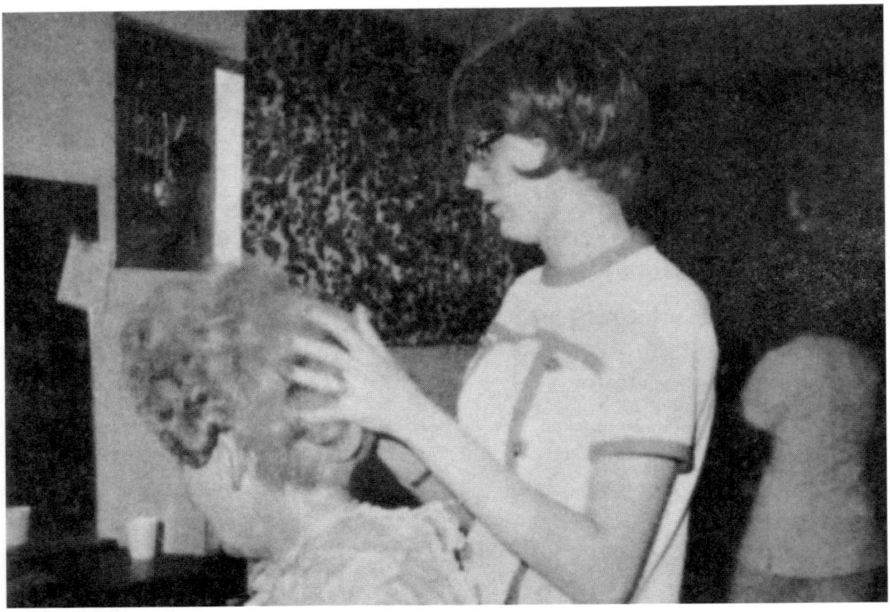

Debbie doing Mrs. Miller's hair at Powder Box Beauty Salon, August 1973.

Douglas County News, August 8, 1973, used with permission.

Willie and Debbie diligently working on this book, January 1997.

Buboltz-Bodle Collection.

INDEX

D

E

F

G

H

I

J

K

L

M

N

O

P

Q

R

S

T

U

V

W

Y

ORDER FORM

To order additional copies of *Philip Simon Miller Butcher, Banker and Benefactor,* please complete and mail the following:

I would like to order ________________ copies @ $19.95.

My check is enclosed for ________________ (include $4.00 S/H per book).

☐ Please advise of future books on Castle Rock, CO.

Name ____________________________ Telephone No.______________

Address____

City__________________________ State________ AZ______________

Mail order form to: Debbie Buboltz-Bodle
P.O. Box 43432
Phoenix, AZ 85080

Phone: 602-843-4858
Fax: 602-843-4091